Orientalist Lives

Orientalist Lives

Western Artists in the Middle East
1830–1920

James Parry

The American University in Cairo Press
Cairo New York

This edition published in 2018 by
The American University in Cairo Press
113 Sharia Kasr el Aini, Cairo, Egypt
420 Fifth Avenue, New York, NY 10018
www.aucpress.com

Published by arrangement with M. Shafik Gabr

Exclusive distribution outside Egypt and North America by I.B.Tauris & Co Ltd., 6 Salem Road, London, W4 2BU

Dar el Kutub No. 23482/16
ISBN 978 977 416 835 2

Dar el Kutub Cataloging-in-Publication Data

Parry, James
Orientalist Lives: Western Artists in the Middle East, 1830–1920 / James Parry.—Cairo: The American University in Cairo Press, 2018.
p. cm.
ISBN 978 977 416 835 2
1. Orientalist
2. European Arts
709.034

1 2 3 4 5 22 21 20 19 18

Designed by Fatiha Bouzidi
Printed in China

Contents

Acknowledgments

My greatest debt of gratitude is to Mr. Shafik Gabr for proposing what has proved to be one of the most stimulating and revealing book projects on which I have yet worked. Tirelessly supportive throughout, he remembered a conversation we had in Cairo several years ago about how the voice of the Orientalists was so little heard nowadays, and then allowed me the privilege of exploring their world and helping ensure that they are listened to once more. My heartfelt thanks go also to Emily Weeks and Briony Llewellyn, whose advice, experience, encouragement, and friendship helped me work my way through what was at times a complex landscape to navigate, as well as to Caroline Williams, who generously shared her knowledge and insights into the complexities of how the Orientalists portrayed architecture in particular. I am grateful also to all of the following for their contributions and assistance: the late Gerald Ackerman, Max Bendixen, Roger Benjamin, Özalp Birol and Barış Kıbrıs of the Pera Museum, Marisa Bourgoin of the Archives of American Art, the Smithsonian Institution, Judith Bronkhurst, Katherine Chabla and Lisa Thornell of the Yale Center for British Art, Waltraud Chapman, Neil Cooke, Kathryn Croxford of the National Trust at Lyme Park, Susan Day, Lorenzo Di Campo, Edhem Eldem, Joe Florentino, Mary Healy, Charles and Clare Howard-Vyse, Andrew Humphreys, Ken Jacobson, Jeremy Maas, Deb Manley, Krystyna Matyjaszkiewicz, Gina McDermot, Duncan McLintock, Alex McMorrow of Christie's London, Aleksandra Medic, Dina Nasser-Khedivi, the staff at the National Art Library, V&A, Charles Newton, Claude Piening and Lord Mark Poltimore of Sotheby's London, Frances Rankine and Miranda McLaughlan at the V&A, Angela Reid, Sir Samuel Roberts, Bt, Polly Sartori, Meg Steer, and Margaret Strode of Sotheby's New York, Anthony Sattin, John Scott, Janet Starkey, Robin Start, Jason Thompson, Frances Topp for picture research, Peter Trippi, Zeynep Uzuner, Nicholas Warner, Kent Weeks, Tiffany Weaire, Sue and Malcolm Whittley, Barbara Wright and Herbert Zemen. My gratitude also goes to Nigel Fletcher-Jones, Neil Hewison, Nadine El-Hadi, and Kevin Dean at the American University in Cairo Press. Finally, thank you to my partner, Andrés Hernández-Salazar, for his patience and support on this particular Orientalist journey.

Foreword

It is with pleasure that I write the foreword to this book, and I am pleased that its research and production were funded by the Shafik Gabr Foundation. *Orientalist Lives* is a testimony to a remarkable set of artists, explorers, and, above all, communicators between the East and the West.

It is somewhat difficult for us, as twenty-first-century global citizens, to truly understand how or what Orientalist painter–travelers must have experienced as they embarked on their journeys. Certainly some of us are adventurers and like to explore faraway lands, but given current technology, and the speed and comfort of modern travel, even the most distant lands are only a click or a flight away.

Travelling to the Orient, as the Middle East was termed in the nineteenth century, required meticulous planning, time, and courage. Routes were long and slow, and often hazardous. Before their travels, the artists educated themselves by reading books and talking to people who went before them. There was advice to be heard that ranged from topics such as accommodation and the best routes to take, to how to behave, speak, and dress. After all, these were uncharted waters, full of particular customs and languages that Western ears were not accustomed to. Whether the motivation to travel was a romanticized escape, a sense of curiosity and adventure, or career advancement, some artists started their journeys with open minds, others with prejudices, great or small.

Once there, all took their time to completely immerse themselves in what they found, and consequently this experience made its way into their paintings and drawings. They strove to make these as detailed and as accurate as possible, even if this was at times little different from the straightforward copying of a particular building or scene that they had witnessed. What some call 'fantasies' of the Orientalist painters in some cases may have simply been their wish to express a complete experience, to articulate a synesthesia of colors, smells, sounds, faces, and places rather than just some part of it. In a sense, is not this way of painting actually more true to life than simple, objective, and completely detached copying? Rather than a harsh divide between realism and fantasy, it is a reality augmented by a lived experience and intense feeling.

Whether a completely accurate rendering of a scene or a combination of them, every single painting tells a story of the Orient experienced, truly lived in, by these artist–travelers. What for me is truly fascinating is the effort they made to understand the life, the people, and the culture of the countries they visited. Many became part of the community, even if temporarily. They shared the locals' culture, their climate, their food, and their lodgings, and much of their traditions. Some of the painter–travelers lived in cities and communities for years, like John Frederick Lewis in Egypt or Émile Deckers in Algeria, and others made repeated visits. They experienced beauty and they experienced fear. They saw the good, the bad, and the ugly. They had their prejudices put to the test and completely, or at least partially, overturned. They may have made a few enemies along the way, but they established even closer friendships. Many mastered the language, and some even ended up spending the rest of their lives in the region, marrying and taking the faith of Islam, like Étienne Dinet in Algeria.

They were two-fold ambassadors. Once in the Orient, they were ambassadors of the West, bringing their own customs and having to earn the trust of the locals. After weeks, months, or even years, they would travel back home, and become ambassadors of the East. Doubtlessly they would tell all they experienced. Some would also publish letters, memoirs, and books, such as Arthur Bridgman's *Winters in Algeria*, but most vividly their experience would remain alive in their paintings. At a time when news traveled slowly and people even more so, the paintings and sketches of the Orientalist artist–travelers represented the early newsreels. Those first newsreels, shown in the Paris Salon or London's Royal Academy of Arts, brought much more than simply a street scene in a faraway city. Each painting told a story, and even an everyday scene evokes an effort on the part of the painter to catch at least a glimpse of the essence of the culture. Fantasy is replaced by fact, which is in turn justified by experience and a deep understanding, which did not make it any less interesting. On the contrary, as often in life, reality proved to be even more insightful and rewarding than imagination.

In this day and age we are engulfed by technology, constantly only a touch away from anywhere or anyone in the world. However, this does not imply that we have learned, understood, or appreciated the commonality and diversity that exists among us on this planet. We have not become effective listeners but relentless speakers who make knee-jerk reactions based on superficial information rather than judgments based on deep comprehension. Today, our understanding and appreciation of different cultures is undermined in the cold and uninformed digital world. Never has there been such a deep need to learn from the Orientalist painter–travelers the importance of building bridges of understanding via face-to-face interactions.

There is an urgent and desperately critical need to regain this sense of understanding and collaboration between the East and the West. So, at least for a moment, let us turn to Ludwig Deutsch and to Jean-Léon Gérôme, to John Frederick Lewis and to Théodore Frère, rather than to sensationalist newspapers and warmongering politics. Let this book take you on a journey with the early global artist–travelers that really knew not only how to look and to talk but how to observe and to listen.

M. Shafik Gabr

Cairo, London, Washington D.C.

2018

Prologue

Great names are made only in the Orient.
—Napoléon Bonaparte

The second of May 1839. After an arduous journey of several weeks, conducted on foot and horseback over precipitous terrain and with the last stage endured in persistent heavy rain, the artist David Roberts and his party arrived at the town of Baalbek in the east of present-day Lebanon. Exhausted, drenched to the skin, and suffering from acute fever, Roberts felt able to make only a cursory visit to the town's Roman ruins before taking to his sickbed. When returning two days later, and by now recovered, he immediately understood the epic significance of the massive ancient temple before him. "The beauty of its form, the exquisite richness of its ornament, and the vast magnitude of its dimensions, are altogether unparalleled,"[1] he marveled, as he began work on sketches that were to help make his name as one of the greatest Orientalist painters of all time.

The history of overseas artists like Roberts engaging with the sights, sounds, and cultures of what they knew as the Orient, but which we now call the Middle East and North Africa, goes back several centuries. Over that time much has been said and written about their interest in that region, but the romanticized image described above is typical of the way in which Orientalist artists portrayed their subject to what were overwelmingly Western audiences. Such was the appeal of this type of imagery during the nineteenth century, when exotic scenes inspired by the mysterious East were *de rigueur* in the galleries and salons of London and Paris, that many European painters of the time, as well as a smaller group of Americans, could be said to have enjoyed an Orientalist moment or two.

Some artists expressed their personal vision of the Orient in the comfort and security of their own studios, these furnished—albeit temporarily, in some cases—with props and *objets* brought home by traveler friends and with bookshelves laden with travelogues and albums of engravings depicting often whimsical and inaccurate views of foreign lands and

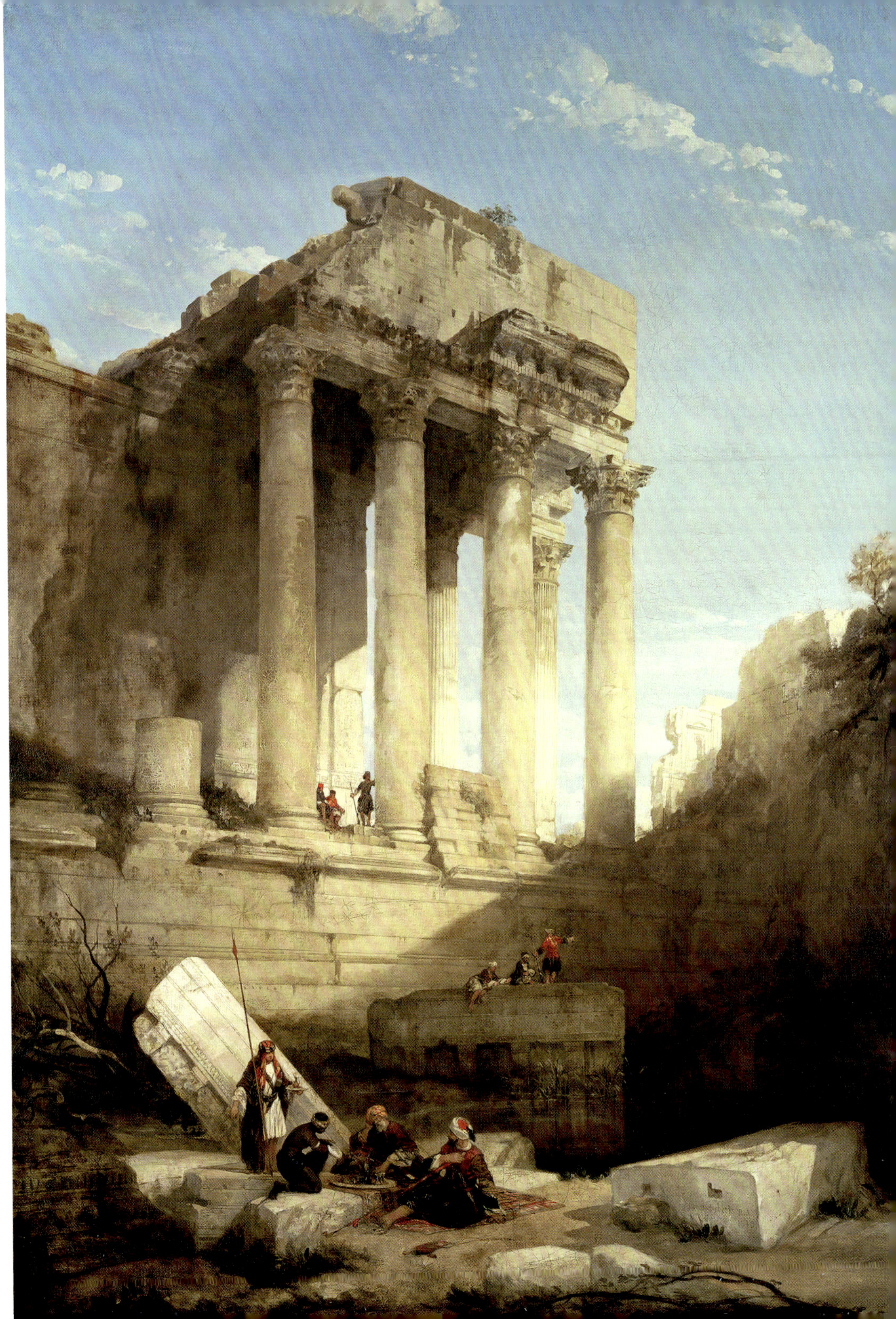

1. David Roberts, *Baalbec—Ruins of the Temple of Bacchus* (1840). Oil on canvas, 182.2 x 132 cm. After spending several days at Baalbek sketching the temple, Roberts had intended to travel to Damascus, but was prevented from doing so by "the unsettled state of the country." Instead he went to Beirut, which he described as "one of the prettiest towns in Syria."

their peoples. From such sources it was possible for these artists to produce 'Orientalized' studio works without the time and bother of having to travel and experience the Orient at firsthand. This lack of direct knowledge did not, however, preclude their works from helping define Western expectations and interpretations of the Orient, which as late as the early 1800s remained a largely artificial construct driven more by fantasy and imagination than by reality.

It fell to another group of artists to try and redress this imbalance. A mixture of the adventurous, intrepid, resourceful, and perhaps just plain foolhardy, they chose to pack their paintboxes and canvases and head off on what were often grueling and lengthy journeys to destinations such as Egypt, Morocco, Palestine, or Turkey. Most did so in a quest to experience on a personal level what it was that had so electrified earlier visitors to these strange and distant lands, and to then attempt to communicate their discoveries to audiences back home. Some of these artist–travelers only went once. In a handful of cases they failed to return home, having become the victims of disease. Others made repeated expeditions, and in some cases chose to spend years of their lives in the Orient. What they found there, and what it inspired them to say through their art, still resonates with us today.

Our understanding of who these artists were, and why they traveled to the East, has been shaped largely through analysis and discussion of their paintings, both on an individual basis and as an overall expression. Art historians and scholars have usually focused on the end product and on the techniques, practices, and impact of the paintings that captivated nineteenth-century audiences across Europe and North America. Yet while artworks can serve as a useful cipher for analyzing the character and motivations of the man or woman behind the brush or palette knife, they will only yield part of the human story involved. We remain largely unsighted on a surprising number of the major Orientalists, with frustrating gaps in our knowledge of where and when they traveled, what they did while there, and with whom and why. Several famous names still await serious monographs and *catalogues raisonnés*, and although a few individual artists have bequeathed a wealth of fascinating and revealing material in the form of diaries, travel journals, letters, and memoirs, others left little or nothing.

The literature on how the Orientalists as a group traveled, worked, and developed their profession is similarly scant and incomplete. This book sets out to present a wide-ranging yet coherent picture of this aspect of their history, using original documents and a range of published sources to examine and explain their lives and careers as artist–travelers. It describes what inspired them to set off on what were, in many cases, the most important journeys they would ever undertake; their reactions, artistic and otherwise, to what they encountered while overseas; how they dealt with living and working in such difficult yet stimulating conditions; the nature of their relationships with each other, their peers, and—most critically—the local people; how they set about interpreting the Orient and telling its stories; the impact of photography and other changes in taste and fashion; and the ways in which major reputations and careers were built once back home, only for some of these to crash dramatically as Orientalism fell from favor. Finally, the book assesses the legacy of the Orientalists from a contemporary perspective, beyond the skewed political agenda of some late twentieth-century commentators and focused on discerning what the Orientalists and their experiences might contribute to ongoing work aimed at building and sustaining dialogue between East and West.

Definitions and Outlooks

The term 'Orientalism' first appeared in the eighteenth century and initially had a strictly academic definition. It was used to describe the study of the languages, religions, and cultures of the Orient, a term which is immediately problematic for a modern-day audience. Historically expansive and imprecise, today it prompts responses mostly connected with that part of the world more usually known as the Far East. Yet throughout much of history the Orient—derived from the Latin *oriens*, meaning 'east' (from *orior*, to rise, denoting dawn)—meant somewhere entirely different. The Romans used it to encompass the Balkans and the territories beyond that fell within the Roman sphere of influence, such as present-day Turkey, Syria, and the wider Levant. It was a definition that was to hold good for over a thousand years.

By 1550, as European knowledge of the rest of the world was expanding in an age of exploration and discovery, so the continent's spatial landscape was changing fast. In the wake of the achievements of seafarers such as Vasco da Gama and Ferdinand Magellan, European horizons were extending as far east as India and China, yet the term 'Orient' steadfastly lagged behind. It remained rooted much closer to the European homeland, to the regions around the eastern end of the Mediterranean basin. At the same time, the geographical interpretation of what constituted the Orient had assumed a cultural attribution that classed—one might even say confined—all Arabs and Muslims as Orientals. Egypt and the other lands of the North African littoral were thereby encompassed in European minds into the wider Orient, despite not being geographically 'east' of Europe.

The perceived gateways to the Orient proper were often surprisingly far west and included both Greece—until 1832 under Ottoman rule and seen by early nineteenth-century Romantics as the last frontier of civilization before the barbarism of the East—and Spain, whose southernmost province of Andalusia not only offered an accessible geographical and cultural bridge to the Orient as manifested in North Africa but was itself so steeped in Arab influence that it provided an early impetus to the Orientalist careers of artists such as David Wilkie (1785–1841), David Roberts (1796–1864), and John Frederick Lewis (1804–76).

While common understanding remained relatively constant in terms of where the Orient might be, by 1800 wider cultural attention was being paid to what Orientalism might actually entail. The term was increasingly used to cover many aspects of Western interest in the region, including art. The power, energy, and commercial appeal of the broader Orientalist idea—artistically, it was more of a concept than a genre or school, and expressed itself across the whole cultural spectrum, from architecture to opera—was such that it became one of the most popular themes in the galleries and artistic venues of London, Paris, and other European capitals. From the specific point of view of pictorial representation, Orientalism took the traditional categories of Western art—portraiture, landscape, and genre painting—and gave them a particular treatment, fashioning them in a way that was

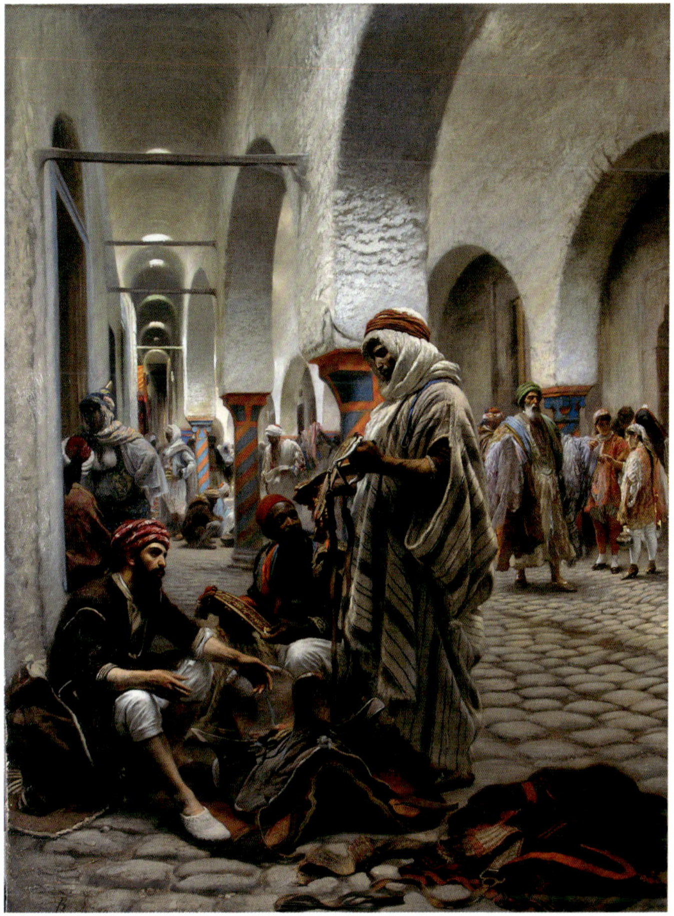

2. Anton Leinweber, *The Souk el Koumach, Tunis* (1889). Oil on canvas, 179.7 x 128.2 cm. Depictions of markets and traders were standard fare for most Orientalist artists and part of a continuing mercantile dimension to the relationship between East and West.

inevitably dictated and determined by Western perceptions of the Orient and its inhabitants.

As the nineteenth century unfolded, further revisions and refinements in nomenclature were prompted by the growing influence of the European colonial powers. New political realities meant that the days of the Orient in Europe's backyard were soon numbered, with the term increasingly displaced by appellations—enduringly Eurocentric—such as the "Near East." Whether by fashion or design, this label soon lost ground to the "Middle East," particularly in the wake of World War I and the recast political mapping that was unfurled across the region following the Treaty of Versailles. By the mid-twentieth century, in an age of socio-political science and amid the first stirrings of political correctness, the term Orient—as applied to the Middle East and Arab world—was virtually airbrushed from view. Orientalism became an equally outmoded and anachronistic notion, tarred with a neo-colonialist brush and with its protagonists at risk of being seen as "half-blind witnesses to imperialist domination."[2] The publication in 1978 of Edward Said's *Orientalism* struck what many saw at the time as a defining nail in the Orientalist's coffin and offered an indictment of an international relationship that had lasted more than 1,500 years.

Early Overtures from the East

In Europe the formalized study of the Orient can be traced back to 1312, when Pope Clement V established chairs at the universities of Bologna, Oxford, Paris, Rome, and Salamanca for the teaching of "the Oriental languages"—namely Arabic, Chaldee, and Hebrew—"so to facilitate the conversion of the heathen." The traumatic legacy of the Crusades notwithstanding, during the Middle Ages and Renaissance the single most obvious opportunity around which East and West could have coalesced artistically was Palestine, the Holy Land, familiar as a name and imagined landscape to millions of people across Europe via Christian teaching and the Bible.

Yet it was not until the late eighteenth and early nineteenth centuries that European artists such as Luigi Mayer* (and, later, most notably David Roberts) began to capture the religious monuments of the Holy Land on canvas and paper in a direct and organized manner. Until that time, artistic connections between Europe and the Middle East were made not so much via religious conduits as on the back of trade routes and associated diplomatic links. For millennia, the ports of the Mediterranean—primarily Venice—had maintained trading links with important mercantile centers further east. Foremost among these was Constantinople (present-day Istanbul), the political and commercial capital of the vast and diverse Ottoman Empire.

Interestingly, the first major catalyst for Western artists to venture eastward came not from any European initiative but via an invitation from the East itself. During the 1460s the Ottoman sultan Mehmed II extended requests to the rulers of Naples, Rimini, and Venice to send talented artists and medalists to Constantinople. It was an act that was to be echoed nearly four centuries later by the Egyptian ruler Muhammad Ali, who in the 1830s encouraged Western experts, including artists, to visit his country as part of a policy of modernization and reform. As with Sultan Mehmed II, foremost among Muhammad Ali's priorities for visiting artists was the production of Western-style portraits of himself—in his case, David Roberts, David Wilkie, and John Frederick Lewis, among others, were all to oblige.

The first Italian artist known to have paid an extended visit to the Ottoman capital was Costanzo da Ferrara (*c.*1450–after 1524), who spent several years in Constantinople during the 1470s and produced a fine series of bronze portrait medals of Sultan Mehmed II. His achievements were reinforced by the arrival in the city in 1479 of Gentile Bellini (*c.*1429–1507), marking the advent of a new chapter in European artistic interest in the Orient. Bellini's credentials were already well established in Venice, where he was a noted portrait painter, and during his two years in Constantinople he produced a variety of sketches, medals, and oil paintings.

Bellini returned to Venice inspired by what he had seen and, in the same way as later Orientalist artists, invested elements of his direct experience into subsequent works. Among these is *St Mark Preaching in Alexandria* (1504–07) (Figure 3), in which he incorporated a range of Oriental motifs, from a backdrop of minarets to the group of veiled

* Mayer (1755–1803) was a German-born watercolorist and draftsman who was engaged by Sir Robert Ainslie, British ambassador in Constantinople, to produce drawings of the Ottoman lands. As part of this commission Mayer traveled to Egypt and Palestine, with the results published in London in three volumes (1801–1803).

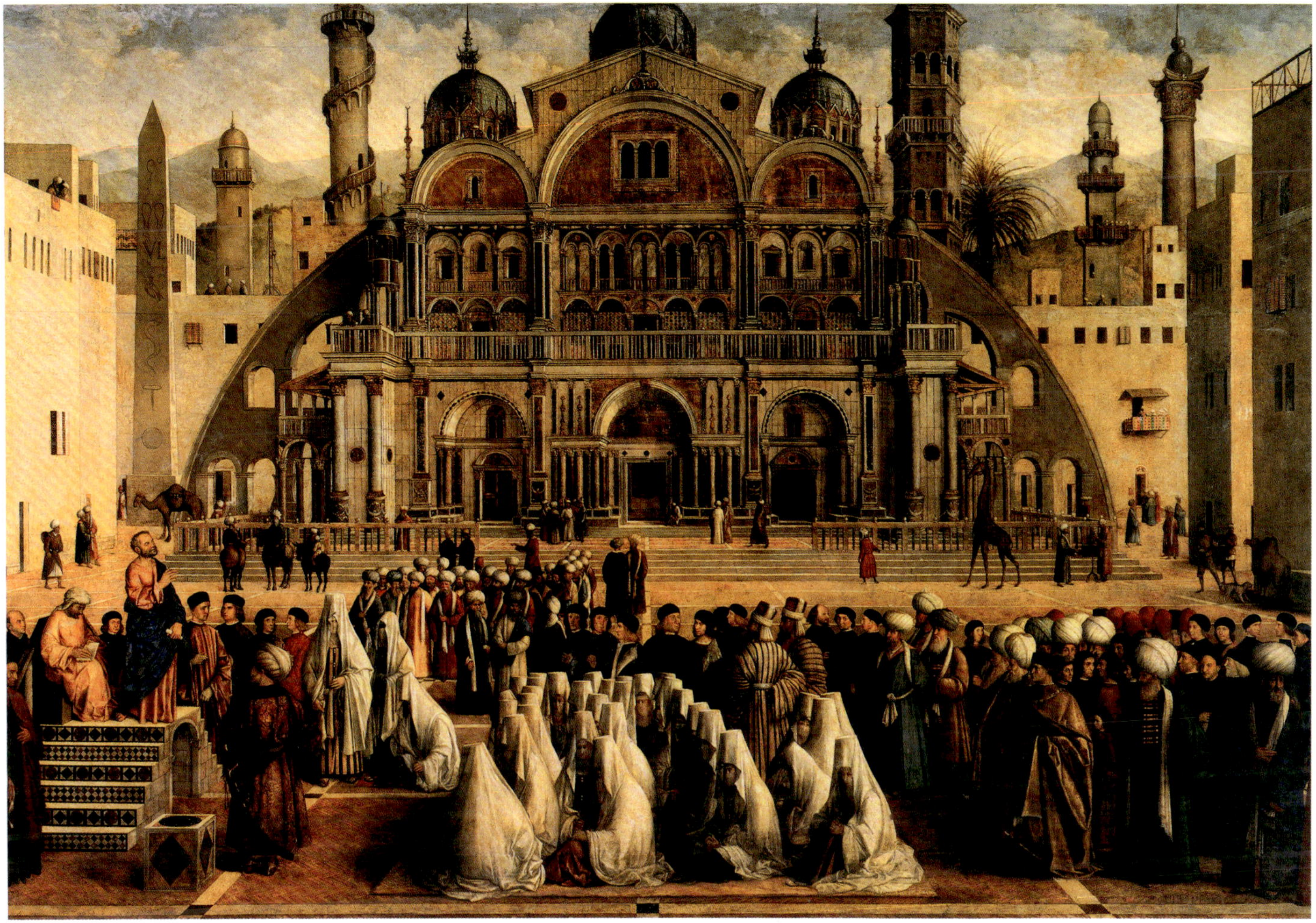

3. Gentile Bellini and Giovanni Bellini, *St Mark Preaching in Alexandria* (1504–07). Oil on canvas, 347 x 770 cm. The painting was started by Gentile in July 1504 and is believed to have been largely complete when he died in February 1507. It was finished by his brother Giovanni, under the terms of Gentile's will.

women that occupies the center foreground of the painting. While Bellini had firsthand knowledge of Constantinople, the diversity of Eastern-themed symbols in this work suggests that he almost certainly supplemented his own resources with ideas gleaned from contemporary travel accounts and pattern books. It was an approach that was to be emulated by many of the later Orientalists, reflecting the *capriccio* manner that was to characterize—if not plague, in its more random manifestations—aspects of Orientalist art through the centuries. For some artists, it was more important to imbue their works with an exotic or fashionable dimension than to create a realistic portrayal of life in the Orient. Authenticity in their works is often therefore elusive, sacrificed on the altar of imagination and effect.

Venice enjoyed special trading privileges with the Ottomans and the presence of Turkish and other Eastern merchants and representatives in the city was well established. Venetians would have been familiar with the different dress and habits of these foreigners in their midst, and so the appearance of "Eastern figures" in works by Vittore Carpaccio (*c.*1465–1525/26) comes as no surprise. In addition to completing several portraits, from life, of Eastern sailors and merchants who were either visiting or resident in the city, Carpaccio also painted *The Miracle of the Relics of the Cross* (1494), which features two characters in Oriental dress, complete with long beards and turbans, as part of the crowds gathered alongside the Grand Canal. This scene presages the reverse scenario five centuries later of Europeans depicted in Oriental cities, as in *A Street Scene, Damascus* (*c.*1887) (Figure 36) by Gustav Bauernfeind and *The Persian Carpet Seller* (1888) (Figure 4) by Osman Hamdi.

A Second Wave

As had been the case in the 1400s, during the seventeenth century it was a series of overtures from the East that served as the catalyst for new episodes in Western artistic contact with the region. One such event was the arrival in 1600 of the Moroccan ambassador at the court of Queen Elizabeth I of England. Sent by the Moroccan sultan Ahmad al-Mansur, 'Abd al-Wahid bin Mas'ud bin Muhammad al-Annuri was the subject of the earliest known portrait of an Eastern envoy to the English court and sparked a rush of interest in North Africa and in Moorish dress, artifacts, and architecture. The portrait (Figure 5), by an unknown artist, is considered to have been one of the inspirations for the character of Othello in Shakespeare's eponymous play, published a few years after 'Abd al-Wahid bin Mas'ud's visit to London.

North Africa was a particular source of fascination to Peter Paul Rubens (1577–1640). In *c.*1609 he painted a portrait of Mulay Ahmad, the Berber king of Tunis, copied from a now lost work by Jan Vermeyen (*c.*1500–59), which Rubens may have owned personally. Vermeyen had served as court painter to Margaret of Austria, Duchess of Savoy, and was with her nephew, the Hapsburg emperor Charles V, at his victory over the Ottomans in the 1535 Battle of Tunis. Vermeyen subsequently produced a series of paintings and tapestries entitled *The Conquest of Tunisia*, based on his experiences in the Maghreb and which Rubens used as source prototypes for his Moorish figures in such paintings as *The Tiger Hunt* (*c.*1616).

The East also loomed large in the works of Rembrandt van Rijn (1606–1669) in the form of the opulent and theatrical compositions he created to depict scenes from the Bible.

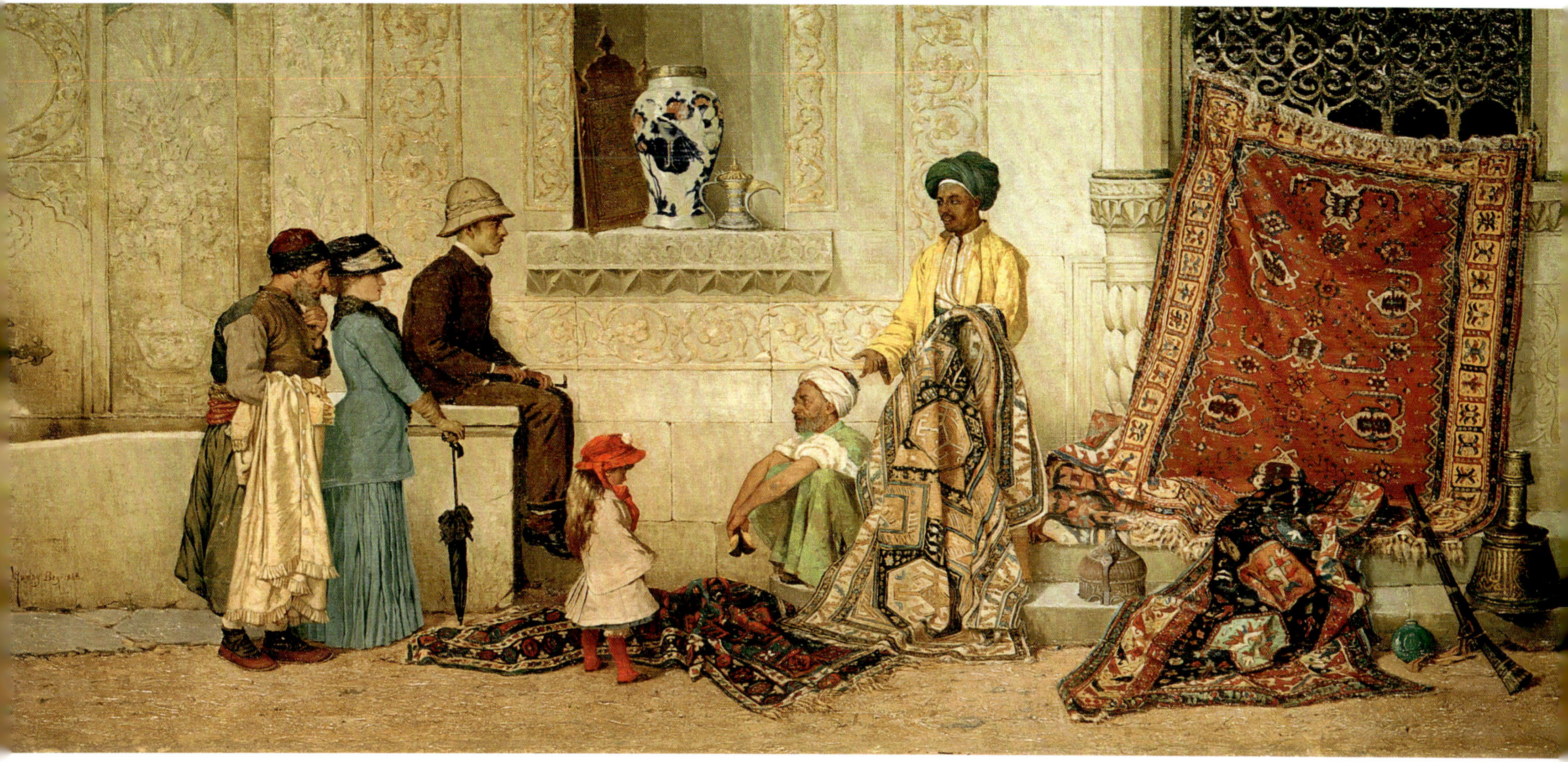

4. Osman Hamdi, *The Persian Carpet Seller* (1888). Oil on canvas, 60 x 122 cm. The depiction of Europeans in everyday Oriental settings (other than of artists in self-portraits), such as this scene in a Turkish shop, is surprisingly unusual.

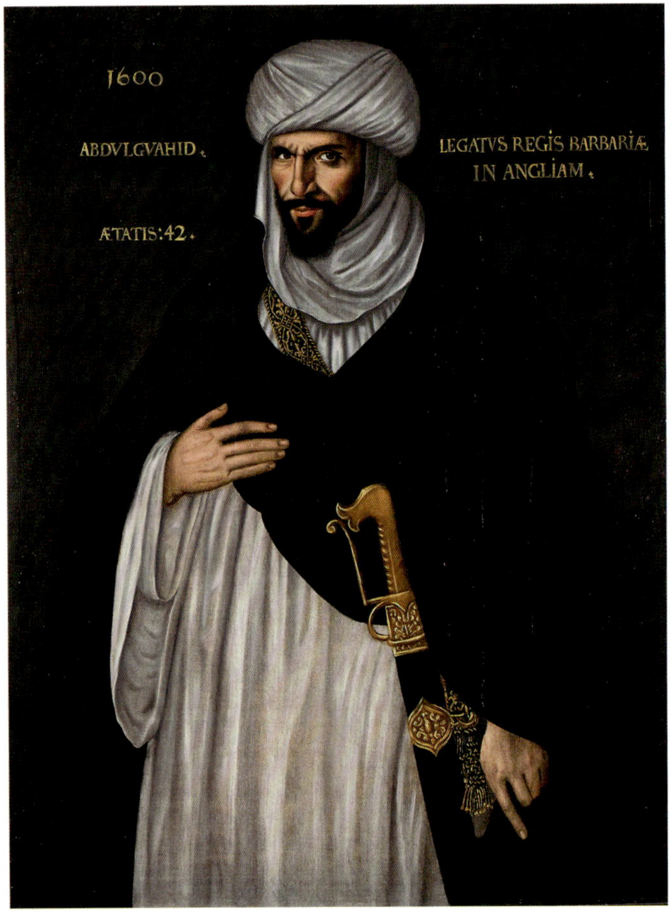

5. Unknown artist, British school, *'Abd al-Wahid bin Mas'ud bin Muhammad al-Annuri, Moorish Ambassador* (1600). Oil on wood, 114.5 x 79 cm. 'Abd al-Wahid bin Mas'ud came to England to propose an Anglo–Moroccan alliance against Spain.

Rembrandt never traveled outside the Netherlands, but what has been described as "the luxuriant character of his imaginary Orient"[3] allowed him to indulge in the contemporary vogue for the exotic while simultaneously presenting works that sat firmly at the heart of the conservative religious values prevailing in his own country.

The growing levels of diplomatic exchange that characterized the seventeenth century saw a stream of Western envoys heading east. At the same time, increasing numbers of European merchants and adventurers were taking up residence in the major cities of the Orient, the processes of social and cultural exchange between East and West becoming ever more diverse. Some Europeans secured powerful positions for themselves, among them the Englishman Sir Robert Shirley, who between 1608 and 1624 undertook two protracted diplomatic tours of Europe as a roving ambassador for Abbas I, Shah of Persia. Dressed in extravagant Persian costume, Sir Robert made return visits to London that caused a tremendous stir and aroused unprecedented levels of interest in Persia, the wider Orient, and in the wearing of Oriental clothes. He was painted in full regalia by Anthony van Dyck (1599–1641), as well as by the unknown artist responsible for the famous portraits of him and his Circassian wife, Lady Teresia.

Although he was certainly not the first European to don Oriental clothes, Sir Robert's appearance in London is notable in terms of its context. The vogue for Orient-inspired dress and decorative motifs—often derived from Ottoman sources and generally known by the French term *turquerie*—had started in Italy during the sixteenth century and soon spread to France and England. The fashion for the Turkish style spanned a wide range of expressions, including architecture and furniture, but in terms of costume was confined largely to leisure and pleasure activities—fancy dress parties and masked balls or masquerades. Yet here was Sir Robert in what was effectively his official working attire. His dramatic form of dress not only served to establish his credentials as the emissary of the Persian ruler and someone with a genuine understanding of the Orient but it also enhanced the exotic reputational mythology of Persia and the East among a Western audience. Affirming authenticity through such a sartorial declaration was an early incarnation of the approach adopted by some nineteenth-century Orientalist artists. One of the main motivations of their being depicted in Oriental dress—whether pictorially or photographically, as several were to be—was to emphasize their credibility as commentators on the Orient. In a competitive market, this could help give an artist the vital edge over his peers.

Among the relatively few seventeenth-century artists who were able to bring firsthand experience of Oriental dress and customs to bear in their paintings were Franz Hermann, Hans Gemminger, and Valentin Müller, who were all members of the delegation led to Constantinople by Hans Ludwig von Küfstein as the Holy Roman Empire's ambassador to the Ottoman court during 1628–29. The oil painting *A Scene from a Turkish Harem* (1654) (Figure 6) appears to have been created much later in Vienna, based on a series of gouaches made in the Ottoman capital a quarter of a century earlier.[4] It depicts a group of harem ladies variously greeting visitors or dancing while four musicians play at one end of the room. The ladies' apparel, the carpets, and musical instruments are all meticulously painted and would have served as a valuable resource, not simply for those contemplating their own expeditions to the Orient but also for the growing numbers of non-travelers fascinated by the perceived exoticism of the region.

One of the leading protagonists in the eighteenth-century English craze for *turquerie* was Lady Mary Wortley Montagu (1689–1762), the erudite and sagacious wife of the British ambassador in Constantinople. She lived there with her husband in 1717–18 and her fascinating observations, mostly recorded in epistolary form, were later published in her *Turkish Embassy Letters*. The extent to which Lady Mary engaged in Oriental life provides an interesting comparison with the experiences of later Western travelers and Orientalist artists, for whom her writings became essential reading (see pages 21–24).

European interest in Turkey generally, and in the ethnic and cultural diversity of the Ottoman Empire particularly, was also awakened by the works of Jean Baptiste Vanmour (1671–1737). Initially invited to Constantinople by the French ambassador, Charles de Ferriol, the Marquis d'Argental, Vanmour was to stay in Constantinople for more than thirty years. He soon developed an extensive and lucrative network of courtly and ambassadorial contacts, and specialized in the depiction of audiences with the sultan. Reception imagery of this sort was already well established in the Western art tradition, as was costume portraiture, a genre at which Vanmour also excelled. In 1707 the marquis commissioned him to paint a hundred single-figure studies of different nationalities from across the Levant, as well as representatives of the Ottoman court and different religious communities and professions. Although primarily studies of dress, these paintings are also heavily ethnographical and feature Armenians, Georgians, Greeks, Jews, Persians, Turks, and others,

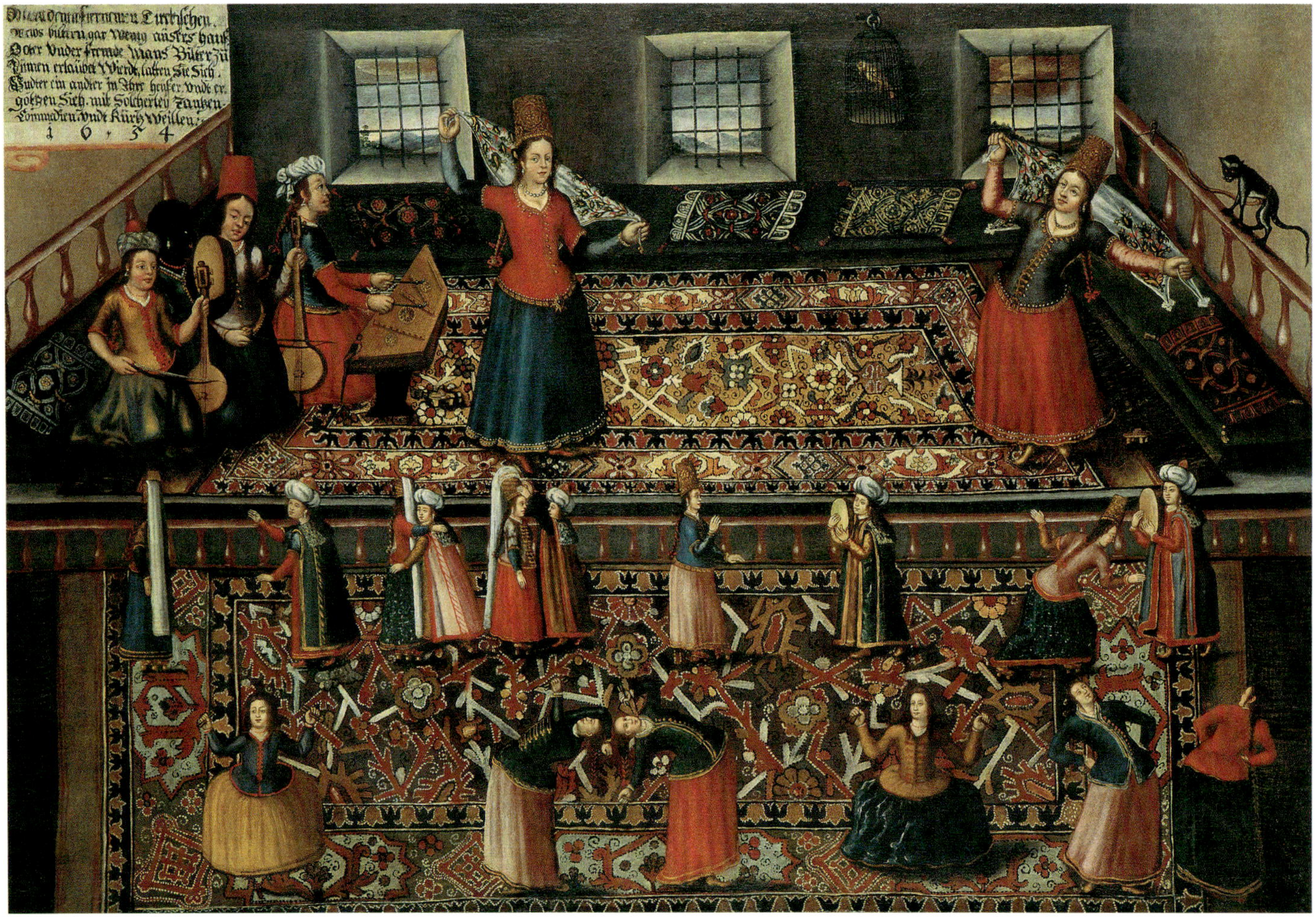

6. Franz Hermann, Hans Gemminger, and Valentin Mueller, *A Scene from a Turkish Harem* (1654). Oil on canvas, 130 x 193.5 cm. The inscription above the painting reads: "Because it is not the custom for distinguished Turkish ladies to leave the house or to meet foreigners, they invite each other to their houses and entertain themselves with dance, comedy, and other such entertainment."

with carefully crafted details depicting the differences between cultural groups, religious sects, and economic classes.

The documentary value of these portraits was maximized through their publication as engravings, which provided a wider European audience with their first accurate and comprehensive visual snapshot of the diverse multicultural character of Constantinople and wider Ottoman society. Vanmour's Oriental personalities and his portraits of European residents in local dress—he painted Lady Mary Wortley Montagu and her son Edward (Figure 9), among others—were mirrored by works from the hand of Jean-Étienne Liotard (1702–1789), who lived in Constantinople for five years. Both artists reaffirmed the Ottoman capital as the principal lens through which contemporary Europe viewed the Orient.

A Change of Direction

This situation changed dramatically with Napoléon Bonaparte's invasion of Egypt in July 1798. Although ultimately a failure in terms of its military and political objectives, the French emperor's foray into Africa proved to be a landmark event in the evolution of Western understanding and appreciation of the Orient. Not only was European political attention focused on Egypt for the first time since the Romans but the French incursion prompted an awakening of intense cultural interest in the country, its ancient history, and heritage. The 25,000 French troops that arrived in Egypt that summer were accompanied by several hundred civilians, which included the *savants*, a team of architects, engineers, historians, and geographers charged with the recording and documentation of the country. Their endeavors were to transform Western understanding of Egypt, generate new levels of fascination and excitement about the Orient generally, and set in train the events that were to see Orientalism and its art reach their peak during the second half of the nineteenth century.

Among the civilian team that arrived with the military cohorts was Dominique Vivant Denon (1747–1825), a skilled draftsman and former diplomat who was later to become the first director-general of the Louvre Museum in Paris. Denon was to play a key role in the development of Egyptology and Orientalism generally, due in no small part to the impressive number of drawings he produced while in Egypt and the publications he orchestrated in the wake of the French campaign. Foremost among these was the multi-volume *Description de l'Égypte*,* published between 1809 and 1829 and which in its entirety contained over nine hundred engravings and four thousand drawings of a vast range of subjects, supported by text descriptions and other narratives.

Not only was the *Description* groundbreaking in terms of its scope and content but it also had a profound and far-reaching impact. It became an instant and essential source of reference material for artists and scholars interested in Egypt, as well as sparking wider interest in Egyptian history and heritage and in the Orient generally. This extended beyond a fascination with the ancient Egyptians and their hieroglyphs (with the Rosetta Stone famously decoded by Jean-François Champollion in 1822) to interest in the epic architecture of the pharaohs, illustrated so dramatically by

* The publication's full title was *Description de l'Égypte, ou Recueil des observations et des recherches qui ont été faites en Égypte pendant l'expédition de l'armée française*. (Description of Egypt, or the collection of observations and research which were made in Egypt during the expedition of the French Army).

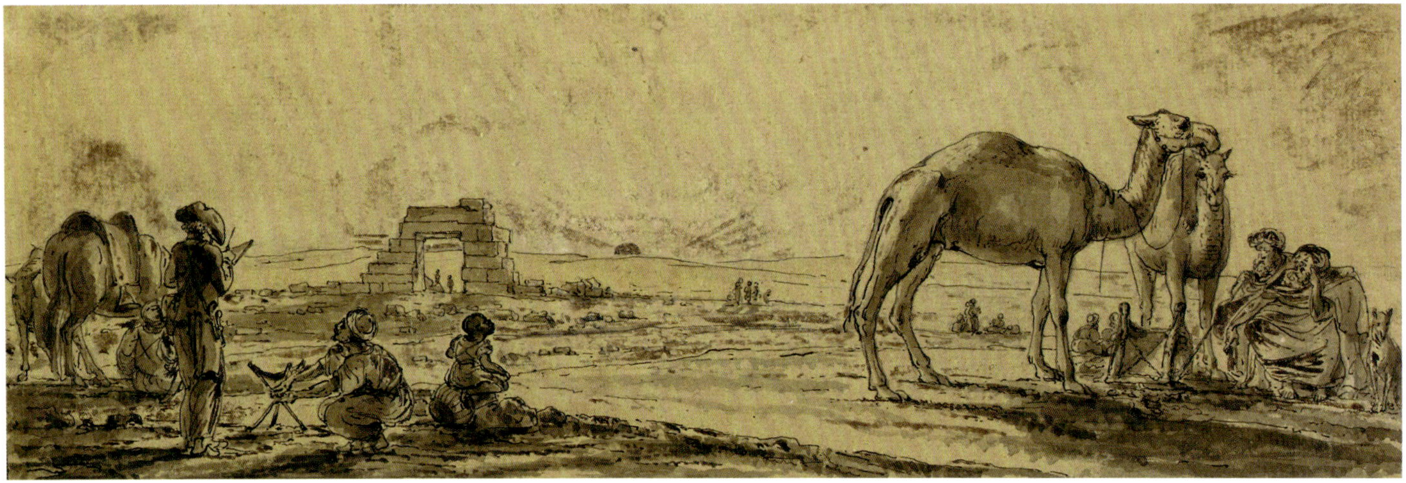

7. Dominique Vivant Denon, *Ruines d'Hieracon-polis* [sic], (*c*.1802). Pen and gray ink, brown and gray wash, on tracing paper, 11.5 x 32.9 cm. The artist (second figure from left) has depicted himself standing while sketching.

Denon and compared favorably by Western audiences with the achievements of ancient Greece and Rome. A cult of "Egyptomania" swept Britain in particular during the first decades of the nineteenth century, prompting a rash of Egyptian-inspired works of art and a blaze of pharaonic motifs in buildings that ranged from otherwise prosaic town halls to ornate cemetery tombs adorned with pyramids and with their doors guarded by carved serpents. Not for a hundred years, since the days of *turquerie* and Lady Mary Wortley Montagu, had Western interest in the Orient been so intense.

As a result, European travelers began to flock to Egypt in unprecedented numbers. No longer was Constantinople Europe's principal "eye on the East." It was to fashionable Egypt that the cognoscenti now turned, to a land that offered everything an artist in particular might need in order to experience the Orient and then satisfy the public clamor for exotic imagery. The opportunities were immense: ancient monuments set in epic desert landscapes; picturesque and vibrant markets, Bedouin encampments and merchant caravans laden with luxury commodities; domestic and religious architecture exquisite in its form and decoration; curious customs and traditions seemingly unchanged for centuries; plus a dazzling array of exotically costumed characters with which to populate street scenes and feature in portraits.

It was an irresistible cocktail and one that proved to have lasting allure. Quite how enduring its effect would be was brought home to me personally in 1994, in the unlikely surroundings of a cave in Saudi Arabia. I was visiting the ruined Nabatean city of Mada'in Saleh and then, as now, there were few if any foreign tourists in the country. My companion and I had the ruins to ourselves. It was May, and fiercely hot, so after viewing the main monuments we retreated to the shade of a nearby cave. Seemingly from nowhere, a young man appeared with a document wallet tucked under his arm. After the customary greetings, he opened the wallet and pulled out a sheaf of dog-eared color prints, fanning them out on the ground in front of us. Peering down, I recognized them as faded reproductions of David Roberts's iconic views of the "other" Nabatean city, Petra.

It struck me as remarkable that the results of Roberts's artistic endeavors on his only trip to the Orient were available for purchase in a cave, in a remote corner of Arabia, more than 150 years later. Roberts never saw Mada'in Saleh, in his day unknown to outsiders and not visited by a Westerner (Charles Doughty) for another fifty years. His images of Petra have clearly proved their durability as an emblem of Western artistic appreciation of the East, but what do they say about Roberts the man? Art is often surprisingly silent on such terms. For me, the real story of Orientalism lies behind the façade of the canvas, beyond the debate over its alleged political agenda and legacy, and is rooted instead in an understanding of the lives and experiences of individual artists who, like Roberts, traveled to the Orient to see great things and ply their trade. This book sets out to tell their story.

1. Departure

The first wave of what was to become the heyday generation of Orientalist artists grew up in the early 1800s, at a time when the world was fast becoming a smaller place, both intellectually and physically. European knowledge of what lay beyond that continent's eastern and southern boundaries had expanded hugely during the 1700s, with improved techniques in navigation, surveying, and cartography combining to help fill what had hitherto been virtual blanks on the geographical canvas as far as Western Europe was concerned. Increased levels of topographical knowledge brought a greater sense of security and confidence on the part of those offering routes by which travel overseas was possible. Demand for access was also growing, prompting improvements in transport infrastructure and methods of travel, as well as the emergence of recognized itineraries. For a European artist preparing to venture abroad, the options had never been greater.

The Grand Tour had been well established since the late seventeenth century as a rite of social, geographical, and cultural passage for wealthy young men and, to a lesser extent, women; but times were changing. Many of the tour's potential participants were no longer satisfied with following in the well-trodden footsteps of their parents or grandparents to the classical sites of Italy or even Greece, still then regarded as the eastern limit of the "civilized world." New destinations were required. The lexicographer Samuel Johnson (1709–84) had famously once remarked, "A man who has not been in Italy, is always conscious of an inferiority, from his not having seen what it is expected a man should see."[1] Yet by 1830 his words were decidedly out of date. In the wake of the disruption caused by Napoléon's invasion of Italy in 1796, Constantinople, and, increasingly, Egypt had replaced Italy as the greatest prizes in any young nobleman's "gap year," a fashionable foray along the Bosphorus or to the Pyramids easily trumping a traditional tour of the Coliseum. The classical comparisons to be made with the Orient were especially attractive to the gilded youth of the English aristocracy and French bourgeoisie, reared on an educational diet of Homer, Seneca, and their peers. The potency of such imagery is defined in works such as Gavin Hamilton's *James*

Dawkins and Robert Wood Discovering the Ruins of Palmyra (1758) (Figure 8), which depicts the two travelers dressed in classical togas as they approach the ruined city.

Eugène Delacroix (1798–1863), one of the earliest artists to visit North Africa,* proclaimed what he saw as a latter-day manifestation of the classical world in the newly unveiled Orient. Struck by what he saw as the dignity of the Arabs and the simplicity of their dress, which he likened to the traditional garb of the ancient Greeks and Romans, he announced, "Rome is no longer in Rome . . . . Imagine, my friend, what it is to see figures from the Age of the Consuls, Catos, Brutuses, seated in the sun, walking in the streets . . . . The Antique has nothing lovelier."

Advances in governance and technology were meanwhile opening up large swathes of the world's land and sea surfaces to new and improved forms of access. Not only was it becoming possible to visit countries and regions that had previously been off-limits to any but the most intrepid outsiders but journey times at home and abroad were also being reduced dramatically. Improved roads in Britain and France meant that the process of physically getting to a port to catch a ship was easier, quicker, and more comfortable. Early nineteenth-century horse-drawn coaches were capable of reaching speeds of up to 12 mph (19 kmph) on the main routes out of London and Paris, with roads to ports such as Dover and Calais generally kept in good condition, at least in dry weather. Journey times were slashed accordingly. In 1640 it took two days to travel by coach from Cambridge to London, but by 1820 this had been reduced to just seven hours.

New and better forms of marine transportation were also making a crucial difference, particularly for travel to the Middle East and North Africa across the Mediterranean Sea. Foremost among these improvements was the advent in the 1830s of screw-propeller ocean-going steamships. These helped reduce sea journey times by "packet boats"—so-called because they often transported mail—by up to one half and offered much greater reliability, if not necessarily comfort. Passenger accommodation was often added as an afterthought (the earlier boats being designed solely for carrying cargo, although this changed as passenger demand grew), and, on some shorter routes at least, passengers were compelled to travel on deck with little shelter. Nonetheless, passenger services proliferated, among them regular steamship connections from Marseille and Toulon to North African cities such as Algiers, Oran, and Tunis. In 1847 a steamship took just sixty-three hours to reach Oran from Toulon, setting a new record. There were also regular services from London to Constantinople, with a choice of four routes through the Mediterranean and one via the Danube and Black Sea.

8. Gavin Hamilton, *James Dawkins and Robert Wood Discovering the Ruins of Palmyra* (1758). Oil on canvas, 309.9 x 388.6 cm. Wealthy scholars Dawkins and Wood visited both Palmyra and Baalbek as part of an extended Grand Tour, making detailed measurements and drawings of the sites they visited. Hamilton's painting was commissioned by Dawkins's brother Henry to commemorate their achievements, a year after James had died.

* Delacroix traveled to Morocco and Algeria in 1832 on an official French government mission. It was to be his only visit to the Orient.

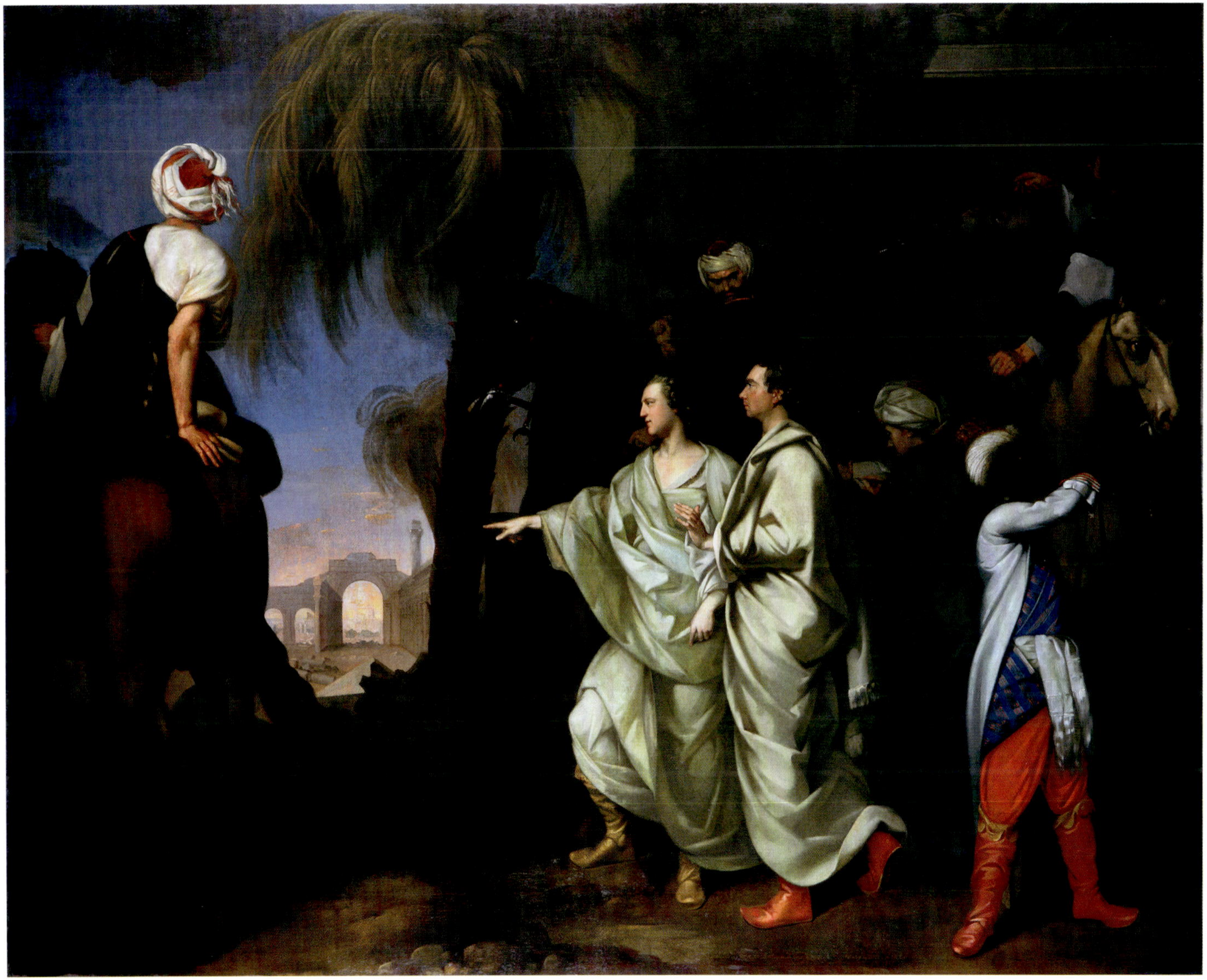

Particularly significant was the expansion in services to Egypt. As early as 1839 there were "eighteen regular opportunities to and fro every month from Alexandria to Europe by steam,"[2] with one of the most popular services among British and French travelers leaving from Marseille. Usually calling at Malta en route, this service opened up Egypt to thousands of travelers, including many artists, and was a critical stage on the most popular route from Europe to India. Another crucial development in attracting increasing numbers of foreign visitors to Egypt had been the efforts of Thomas Waghorn in the late 1830s to create and secure 'The Overland Route' for the transportation of mail, goods, and passengers between Britain and India. Rather than sailing around the Cape of Good Hope, Waghorn's much faster alternative took eastbound travelers via the Mediterranean and into Alexandria by steamship; thence along the Mahmoudieh Canal (completed in 1820) to the Nile, up to Cairo, and then across the desert by carriage—staying en route in well-organized rest houses—to Suez, where they would embark on a steamer for India. Waghorn's system cut journey times between Britain and ports like Calcutta by more than half and revolutionized contact between Europe, India, and the Far East.

Alexandria offered steamship connections to other destinations in the Middle East, such as Beirut and Jaffa, which were also connected to Piraeus and Trieste, as well as to Constantinople. As a result of the increased passenger traffic, the regional shipping business boomed and even more so after the opening of the Suez Canal in 1869—the same year in which Thomas Cook escorted his first party to Egypt and Palestine, marking the start of what was to become the world's first great tourism enterprise.

Another seminal piece in the traveling jigsaw came mid-century with the advent and rapid proliferation of a railway network across much of Europe. Direct lines were opened between London and Dover in 1861, connecting with the steamboat ferry to Calais and railway from there to Paris, with the line from the French capital to Marseille having opened by 1856 (coincidentally the same year that the final section in the rail link between Alexandria and Cairo was completed). By using this route—which was quicker than the direct twice-monthly steamboat service from Southampton to Alexandria via Gibraltar and Malta, for example—it became possible to travel from London to Egypt in less than two weeks, an incredible achievement to contemporary minds. The result was an unprecedented number of people now traveling to, from, and within the region.

Learning the Ropes

Such rapid rates of innovation and change had implications for those, like artists, who made their living from the depiction and sale of ideas and situations. From the arrival in Europe of the earliest travel accounts and woodcut prints, the public had demonstrated its thirst for information about the great new world that was opening up, and artists were under pressure to deliver. For many, their journeys to the Orient started in the drawing rooms and salons of London or Paris. It was here that the artistic set and chattering classes of the British and French capitals gathered to discuss topical issues and events. It is tempting to conclude that such forums amounted to little more than opportunities for idle gossip and fatuous banter over what was in fashion and what was not, and long hours were doubtlessly whiled away in such conversations. However, along with the cafés, restaurants, and tea- and coffeehouses which were proliferating in cities across Europe, these venues also served as vital points of information exchange on a wide range of topics, from social reform and politics through to art, culture, education, and travel.

London's first coffeehouse—more of a shack, by all accounts—had a clear link to the Orient, being opened in 1652 by a Greek émigré from Smyrna (present-day Izmir) named Pasqua Rosée. It was soon swarming with curious Londoners, eager to taste the novel Turkish brew and learn more about the exotic land from which it, and Rosée himself, had come. Anyone interested in traveling to Turkey would very likely have called in there to gather information and advice. The coffee craze took off—Rosée was soon selling over six hundred dishes of coffee per day, despite its being called the "bitter Mohammedan gruel" by *The London Spy* in 1701—and early eighteenth-century London supported more coffeehouses than any other city in the world save Constantinople. They were hugely busy throughout the day and night, with the largest able to accommodate up to ninety customers and individual coffeehouses developing reputations for the quality and content of the debate and discussions that took place within their walls.

Coffeehouses were unique in cutting across Britain's traditionally rigid social and political hierarchy to attract customers from all walks of life. The Swiss nobleman César de Saussure, who visited London in 1726, remarked how "workmen habitually begin the day by going to coffee-rooms to read the latest news."[3] This democratization of access to news and opinions saw, in theory at least, scholars and artists sharing tables with chimneysweeps and abattoir workers, helping break down the tradition of political debate being the preserve of the social elite. It also served to disseminate international news and share information about the topography, peoples, and cultures of foreign lands, hitherto largely the stuff of myth and legend. Coffeehouses were therefore very fertile territory for artists seeking new ideas and horizons, especially those interested in the Orient.

The privileged few at or near the top of the social ladder could also seek advice at the dining tables of fashionable society hostesses, for it was here that pioneers on the earliest significant voyages to the Orient were often invited on their return home. None more so perhaps than Lady Mary Wortley Montagu, one of the most well-connected women of her generation. In May 1717 Lady Mary left England with her husband, Sir Edward Wortley Montagu, on his ambassadorial mission to the Ottoman court. Sir Edward was contracted to spend at least five years in post in Constantinople, but in the event he stayed only until July 1718, his mission cut short by Austrian military victories over the Turks (British allies) in the Balkans and by wider political uncertainty.

Despite spending less than a year in the Ottoman capital itself, Lady Mary lost no opportunity to immerse herself in local life. She learned to speak Turkish fluently, regularly wore Ottoman dress, and took a keen and active interest in local affairs, ranging from art and architecture to Turkish dialects, smallpox inoculation, and the rights of Muslim women. Most notably, her gender gave her unparalleled access to the holy grail of male Orientalists and one of the defining motifs of Orientalist art: the harem. Lady Mary's account of what lay behind the seraglio screens is one of the earliest firsthand descriptions by a non-Muslim, and offered contemporary

European eyes a new reality of a world largely hidden to outsiders. Such insight was a major social coup, and ensured that on her return to London she was fêted by the literary and cultured circle in which she mixed (which included the celebrated poets John Gay and Alexander Pope), helping further fuel the prevailing fashion in London for all things Turkish.

Lady Mary's accounts of her time in Constantinople appeared as her *Turkish Embassy Letters* in 1763, the year after she died. She had carefully edited and marshaled her material and had made special arrangements for its publication after her death. For Western audiences, and artists in particular, this book remained the main source of reference on Turkey for over a century and, in the absence of similarly credible reports from elsewhere, served as a general guide to the manners, customs, and culture of the wider Orient. Full of accurate and revealing commentary, it provided essential and inspirational pre-departure briefing for artists and others interested in learning something of the distant and exotic lands they were preparing to visit. It was also an absorbing read for less adventurous armchair travelers.

Published travel accounts were becoming both more common and popular by this time, but Lady Mary had a confident view of the distinct advantage her status and gender gave her in terms of access to different levels of Ottoman society and thereby of the contribution she could bring to Western understanding of life in Constantinople. She was scornful of the accounts of some earlier travelers, targeting their frequent misapprehensions and misinformation about the Orient. In a letter dated 17 June 1717 to an unnamed correspondent, Lady Mary wrote: "Your whole letter is full of mistakes from one end to the other. I see you have taken your ideas of Turkey from that worthy author Dumont,* who has writ with equal ignorance and confidence. 'Tis a particular pleasure to me here to read the voyages to the Levant, which are generally so far removed from truth and so full of absurdities I am very well diverted from them. They never fail to give you an account of the women, which 'tis certain they never saw, and talking very wisely of the genius of men, into whose company they are never admitted, and very often describe mosques which they dare not peep into. The Turks are very proud and will not converse with a stranger they are not assured is considerable in his own country. I speak of the men of distinction, for as to the ordinary fellows, you may imagine what ideas their conversation can give of the general genius of the people."[4]

Lady Mary understood the unique value of her descriptions of life in Turkey, and perhaps never more so than when describing life in the harem—a hidden fantasy world for European men. One of her greatest contributions to the debate about the Orient was her controversial affirmation that the women in the harem were actually more free than

9. Jean Baptiste Vanmour (attributed), *Lady Mary Wortley Montagu with her son, Edward Wortley Montagu, and attendants* (*c*.1717). Oil on canvas, 69.3 x 90.9 cm. Lady Mary was a great celebrity in her day and positioned herself skillfully as an expert commentator on the Orient.

* Jean Dumont (1667–1727) was a French traveler and historiographer who published, among other titles, *Nouveau voyage du Levant* (1694) and *Voyages en France, en Italie, en Allemagne, à Malte, et en Turquie* (1699).

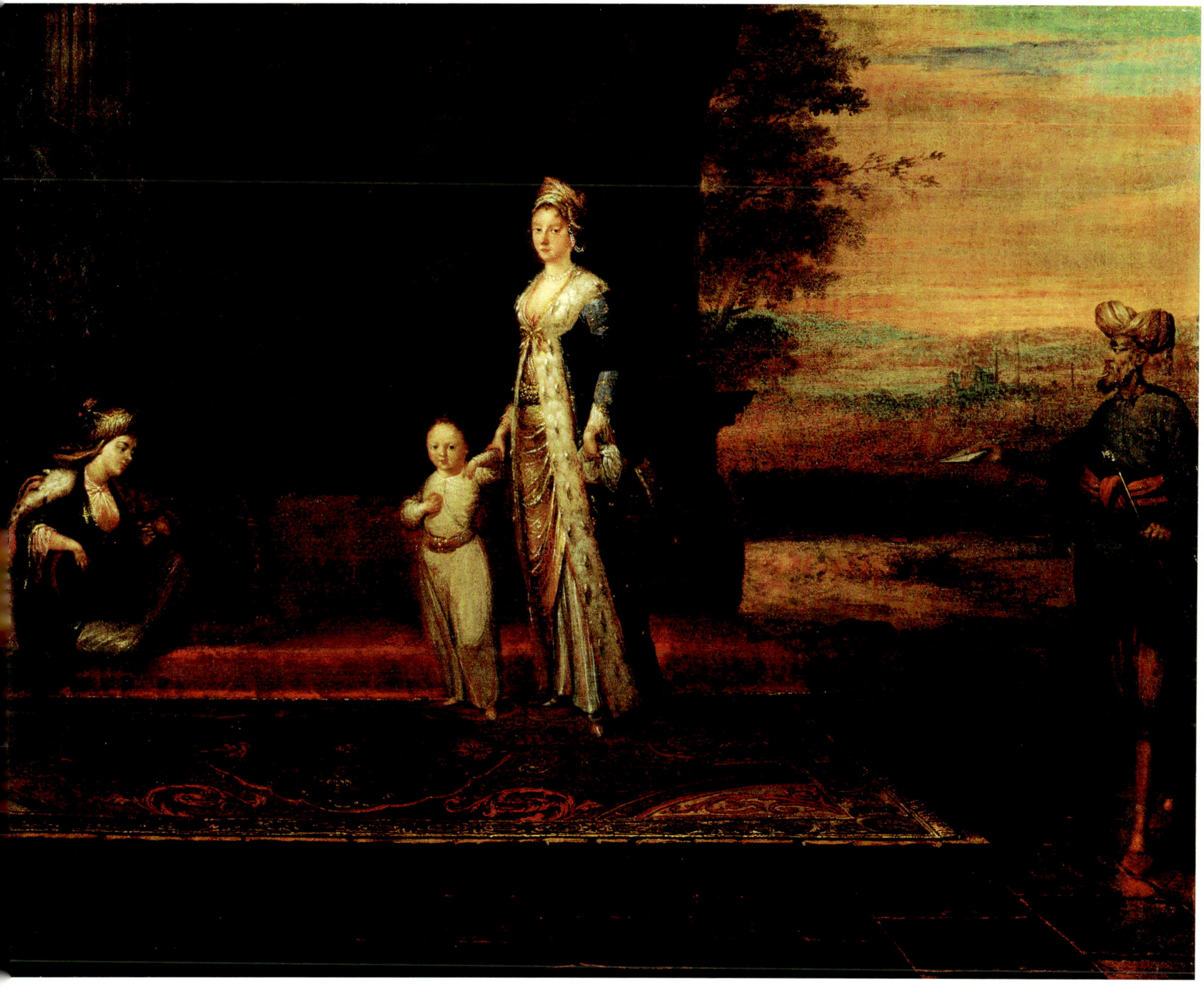

their European sisters. While not losing the opportunity to create an opulent and engaging image of the scenes she had witnessed, she used a predominantly factual narrative to divest the situation of any lewd sexual context and provide a unique insight for those to whom harem access was logistically impossible or expressly forbidden: "The first sofas were covered with cushions and rich carpets, on which sat the ladies, and on the second their slaves behind them, but without any distinction of rank by their dress, all being in the state of nature, that is, in plain English, stark naked, without any beauty or defect concealed. Yet there was not the least wanton smile or immodest gesture amongst them. They walked and moved with the same majestic grace which Milton describes of our general mother. There were many amongst them as exactly proportioned as ever any goddess was drawn by the pencil of Guido or Titian, and most of their skins shiningly white, only adorned by their beautiful hair divided into many tresses, hanging on their shoulders, braided either with pearl or ribbon, perfectly representing the figures of the Graces . . . . In short, 'tis the women's coffee house, where all the news of the town is told, scandal invented, etc."[5]

There was even a mischievous comment about the special value her harem observations had for artists: "To tell you the truth, I had wickedness enough to wish secretly that Mr Gervase* could have been there invisible," Lady Mary wrote. "I fancy it would have very much improved his art to see so many fine women naked, in different postures, some in conversation, some working, others drinking coffee or sherbet, and many negligently lying on their Cushions while their slaves . . . were employed in braiding their hair in several pretty manners."[6] Such direct firsthand experience made Lady Mary an obvious source to which Orientalist artists and other travelers gravitated. Lord Byron read the *Turkish Embassy Letters* and became fascinated by her, even carrying out his own research into her life and correspondence.

Lady Mary's entertaining but factual description of what she found in Constantinople revealed a sophisticated and advanced culture that embodied many of the values that the Enlightenment purported to extol and advance, and which many artists—Orientalists and otherwise—were seeking to express and explore. Yet popular Western clichés focused on Oriental despotism and lascivious sensuality ensured that the vision of the harem as a place of enslaved women and depraved cruelty continued to triumph over the reality that Lady Mary strove to present, her audience still largely preoccupied with fantasy rather than fact. It was another hundred years and more before the handful of nineteenth-century female Orientalists began to explore the harem and the role of women generally in the Orient and to confirm much of what Lady Mary had ventured to suggest.

A New Approach

The cultural army that accompanied Napoléon's fighting force to Egypt in 1798 provided an empirical and documentary focus that was to inspire a new generation of artists and help reposition Orientalist interest away from Turkey. Driven from Egypt by the British three years later, the French returned home with a vast bank of material. Some of this

* The artist Charles Jervas (*c.*1675–1739) had painted Lady Mary's portrait in 1716, before she left England for Constantinople.

was distilled into Dominique Vivant Denon's *Voyage dans la Basse et la Haute Égypte* (*Travels in Lower and Upper Egypt*) of 1802, which was an immediate success and acclaimed for providing "the public with the facts and images of a living universe, encountered face to face, described vividly, without any scholarly apparatus, without the sacred respect of ancient discourse."[7] It was, however, just a taste of greater things to come, namely the *Description de l'Égypte*, the first volumes of which appeared in 1809. Although views varied on how accurate the information was as reproduced—David Roberts later making it clear that he regarded "the drawings of the French Commission in Egypt as very incorrect"*—the *Description* remained one of the most important publications of its type for the remainder of the nineteenth century. Of particular interest to artists were the sections on *Arts et Métiers*, depicting crafts and agricultural activities; *Costumes et Portraits*, which showed a variety of 'typical' local figures; and *Vases, Meubles et Instruments*, an eclectic gazetteer of various objects including pots, musical instruments, decorative carvings, tents, weapons, and garments.

The *Description* fell short, however, in terms of satisfying the curiosity of the growing band of Western Egyptophiles for more about the character of contemporary life in the country and in particular the habits and culture of its people. Relief came in 1836 with the publication of Edward William Lane's *An Account of the Manners and Customs of the Modern Egyptians*. Lane had first visited Egypt in September 1825, later recalling how "as I approached the shore [in Alexandria], I felt like an Eastern bridegroom, about to lift the veil of his bride, and to see, for the first time, the features which were to charm, or disappoint, or disgust him."[8] A decade later, it was clear that Lane had become more than charmed by what he had found in Egypt. By then he was deeply immersed in Egyptian culture and set upon a career that was to see him confirmed as the outstanding Arabist of his generation. Not only was he the author of a bestselling book—his *Manners and Customs*—but he had also compiled an Arabic–English dictionary, which would also stand as the most important reference of its type, and translated *The Arabian Nights*, one of the icons of Arabic literature and which was, through Lane, made available to English readers worldwide.

Lane's credentials were such that *Manners and Customs* became a bible for those seeking information about Egypt and its people (and remains in print today). "I have associated, almost exclusively, with Muslims, of various ranks in society," he explained in the preface; "I have lived as they lived, conforming to their general habits." Lane always wore local dress when in Egypt, was a highly proficient Arabic speaker, and went by the name of Mansur Effendi. He was more integrated into Egyptian society than most, if not all, of his contemporaries, prompting one modern commentator to remark that, "Lane loved Egypt, unreservedly loved almost everything about it. From his arrival, his entire life and the work he undertook would be an act of devotion and service to this country and culture that he so much loved and in which he felt, almost from the start, more at home than he did in his own land."[9]

* Roberts had doubts about the veracity of the *Description* even before visiting the sites concerned for himself in 1838–39. He made his views clear in the notice that prefaced his *The Holy Land, Syria, Idumea, Arabia, Egypt and Nubia* of 1842–49.

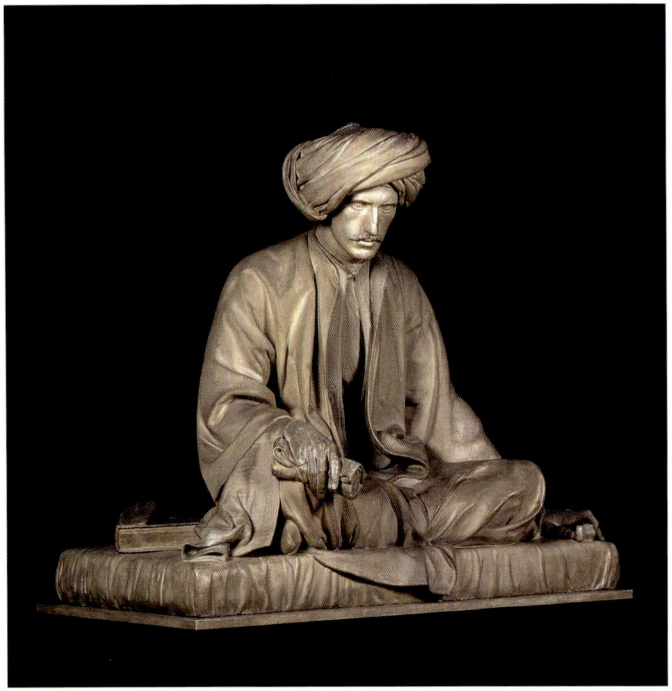

10. Richard James Lane, *Edward William Lane* (1829). Plaster statue, 95.3 cm high. Richard was the elder brother of Edward and a skilled and prolific artist, appointed lithographer to Queen Victoria in 1837.

The material presented in *Manners and Customs* had begun life as part of a much more ambitious tome. Lane's great project was his comprehensive *Description of Egypt*, which he had taken to the London publisher John Murray but which had fallen foul of the 1831–32 British political crisis and been put on hold. Murray had insisted in any case that the *Manners and Customs* section be dropped, and so when it became clear that publication of the *Description* had stalled, Lane took the removed section to a different London publisher: The Society for the Diffusion of Useful Knowledge. Having secured their backing for its stand-alone publication, he returned to Egypt to carry out further research and recast his text. A year later he had completed his manuscript and the ensuing book proved an immediate and enduring success. Ironically—and to Lane's great disappointment—his *Description of Egypt* never made it into print during his lifetime.

Lane marshaled his material in *Manners and Customs* with consummate skill, using his black-and-white drawings to great effect and successfully conveying the dynamism, diversity, and richness of Egyptian life during the Ottoman period. No other publication of the time offered foreign visitors (and, indeed, expatriate residents) such expert insights and informed advice on subjects as diverse as government and administration, class distinction, religious practices, domestic life, education, superstitions and magic, dancing, music, storytelling, and weights and measures. While primarily an early sociological study, perhaps the first of its type in the modern sense, *Manners and Customs* also comprised a travel guide of unusual breadth and quality. Lane was well aware of his book's potential value to artists in particular. In a section on the ornaments worn by Egyptian women, he suggested, "If the subject be not interesting to general readers, it may at least be of some use to artists, who are often left almost entirely to their own imagination in representing Arabian costumes and ornaments." The same could be said for many of the other aspects of Egyptian life depicted and described by Lane; a lack of firsthand experience and accurate second-hand information, combined with overly vivid imaginations, had led many artists into dangerous creative

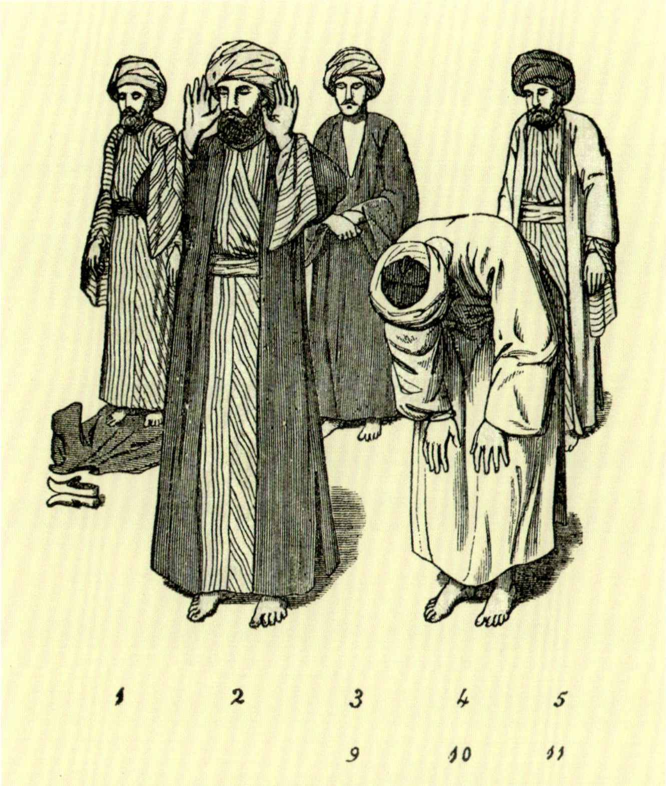

Postures of Prayer. (Part I.)

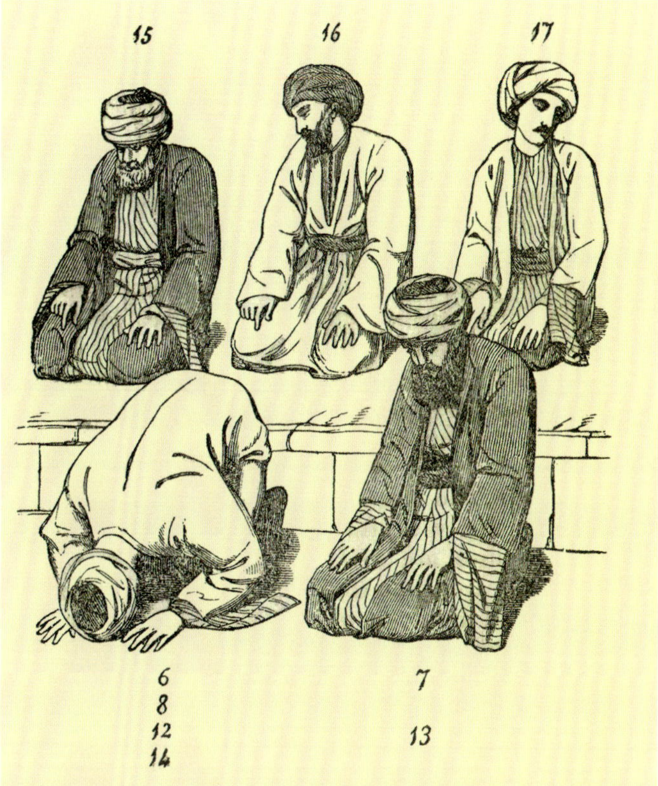

Postures of Prayer. (Part II.)

11. Edward William Lane, "Postures of Prayer Parts I and II" from *Manners and Customs*, Vol. 1 (1836). These figures proved to be an invaluable and enduring reference for artists when compiling mosque scenes.

territory. *Manners and Customs* helped rescue the situation, with artists regularly using Lane's drawings as the basis for figures and scenes in their own works and regarding his narrative as the most reliable source of accurate information. Among his admirers was Edward Lear (1812–88) who, on his first visit to Egypt in 1849, wrote to the Earl of Derby: "This strange place [Cairo] is so remarkable that I cannot describe it,—& Lane's works give a better account of it than I can."[10]

Lane's book was complemented by the publication the following year (1837) of *Manners and Customs of the Ancient Egyptians*, written by another outstanding authority on the Orient and long-term Cairo resident, John Gardner Wilkinson (1797–1875). David Roberts is known to have owned and regularly consulted a copy of Wilkinson's tome, as doubtless did other artists. Lane's and Wilkinson's publications together provided overseas visitors with unprecedentedly comprehensive information about Egyptian social history and culture.

A further popular source of information and guidance for those preparing to visit Egypt, and especially for Francophones, were the publications of Émile Prisse d'Avennes (1807–79). This remarkable polymath lived and journeyed extensively in the Orient for over four decades, variously as an archaeologist, architect, engineer, ethnographer, teacher, and writer. Often traveling in local dress, he eventually converted to Islam and lived under the name Edris Effendi. A prolific writer of scholarly articles, mostly in French, in 1848 Prisse published in London his most significant English book: *Oriental Album—Characters, Costumes, and Modes of Life, in the Valley of the Nile*, a collection of chromolithographs depicting the people and costumes of the Nile Valley.[11]

In 1869–77 Prisse produced in Paris the four-volume *L'Art arabe d'après les monuments du Kaire depuis le VIIe siècle jusqu'à la fin du XVIIIe (Arab Art as seen through the Monuments of Cairo: From the Seventh Century to the End of the Eighteenth)*. This unparalleled survey of predominantly Egyptian art and architecture was based on the hundreds of drawings, sketches, photographs, and plans that he had gathered during his travels. As with the *Oriental Album*, it became an essential source book for artists interested in studying or depicting the Orient and Prisse was well aware of its potential value to them. "We shall discuss all the arts, all the industries cultivated by Orientals with so much taste, brilliance, and fantasy," he explained. "We will present splendid reproductions of the monuments, objects of art and luxury, which provide evidence of an advanced civilization, the influence of which has been felt even in Europe." Through these two books, Prisse positioned himself as the artist's ally, a source of information, ideas, and, most importantly, access.[12]

The Picture Elsewhere

Mid-nineteenth-century artists preparing to visit Egypt were exceptionally well served by figures such as Lane and Prisse, but for other parts of the Orient—including Turkey—there were not always such equivalently authoritative written sources on which to draw. Lady Mary Wortley Montagu's account of early eighteenth-century Constantinople remained the standard source of information on the city for many decades thereafter, with the paintings of artists such as Vanmour and Liotard enabling outsiders to build a more visual picture of the Ottoman capital's court life and its inhabitants. More helpful from the point of view of conveying the appearance of Constantinople at large were the works of Antoine Melling (1763–1831), who lived there for eighteen years. He served as imperial architect to two sultans during that time, a position that gave him exceptionally privileged access. His *Voyage pittoresque de Constantinople et des rives du Bosphore* (1819) was illustrated with engravings based on his keenly observed drawings and offered artists a wealth of material, especially for backgrounds in genre scenes (Figure 12).

A further essential point of reference for those considering traveling to Constantinople was *The Beauties of the Bosphorus* (1838), a collaboration between artist William Henry Bartlett (1809–54) and poet and writer Julia Pardoe (1806–62). Engravings of Bartlett's original works were supported by extensive and detailed descriptions by Pardoe of the main monuments and sites of the Ottoman capital. Her elegant and compelling prose served as a barely concealed incitement to artists to head eastward. "The great charm of Constantinople to an European eye exists in the extreme novelty, which is in itself a spell; for not only the whole locality, but all its accessories, are so unlike what the traveller has left behind him in the West, that every group is a study and every incident a lesson."[13]

Pardoe first arrived in Turkey with her military father in 1836, living there for two years and acquiring an intimate knowledge of the great city and the lives of its inhabitants. Her book *The City of the Sultan* gives a detailed account of local customs and demonstrates a rare insight and sensitivity about cross-cultural relationships in particular. "That the Turks as a people, and particularly the Turkish females, are shy of making the acquaintance of strangers, is most true," Pardoe wrote; "their habits and feelings do not lend themselves readily to a familiar intercourse with Europeans; nor are they induced to make any extraordinary effort to overcome the prejudice with which they ever look upon a Frank, when they remember how absurdly and even cruelly they have been misrepresented by many a passing traveller, possessed neither of the time nor the opportunity to form a more efficient judgment."[14]

Reliable accounts about life and conditions in the wider Levant were few and far between. Among the most useful—and a typical example of the contemporary European tradition of eclectic reportage—was Dr. Alexander Russell's *The Natural History of Aleppo and Parts Adjacent* (1756), which offered information and advice for potential visitors to Syria. Originally conceived as an account of the diseases—notably plague—that periodically ravaged the country, Russell expanded it into a more general compendium that included descriptions of the city's layout and architecture, the internal arrangements of the houses and of public facilities such as hammams, as well as information about the local climate, agriculture, flora, and fauna. Edward William Lane praised Russell in the preface to his own *Manners and Customs*, while not losing the opportunity to make the point that Russell's publication "is, upon the whole, rather an account of *Turkish* than of *Arab* manners," and that neither the author nor his half-brother Patrick (who revised and expanded the book into a new edition after Alexander's death) were "sufficiently acquainted with the Arabic language to scrutinize some of the most interesting subjects of inquiry which the plan of the work required them to treat."[15]

Nonetheless, as a physician and keen naturalist Russell made some useful observations about the local population. In particular he noted that "the people in general are of a

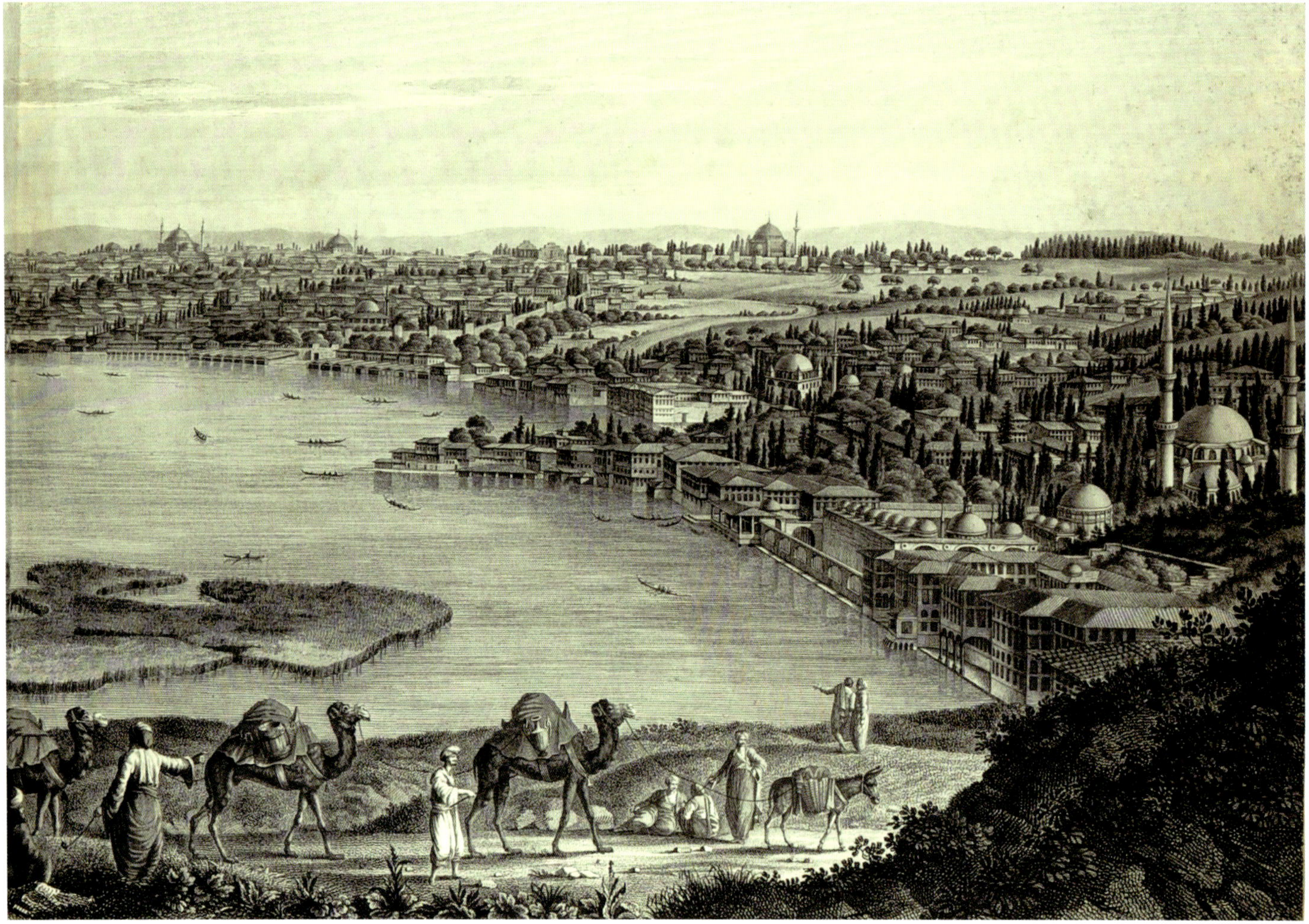

12. Antoine Melling, a view of Constantinople from *Voyage pittoresque de Constantinople et des rives du Bosphore* (1819). Melling studied architecture in his native Germany before traveling to Egypt and then Turkey, where he was engaged first by Hatice Sultan, the sister of Sultan Selim III. His close relationship with the princess helped further advance his position at the Ottoman court.

middle stature, rather lean than fat, indifferently well made, but not either vigorous or active. Those of the city are of a fair complexion; but the peasants, and such as are obliged to be much abroad in the sun, are swarthy . . . . Both sexes are tolerably handsome when young; but the beard soon disfigures the men; and the women, as they come early to maturity, fade also as soon, and in general look old by the time they reach thirty." He also felt moved to comment, somewhat disapprovingly, about a subject that was an enduring source of interest for foreign visitors and one particularly associated in the European public mind with artists and others of a creative disposition: opium. "Opium is not of so high esteem with the inhabitants of Aleppo as at Constantinople, and some other places," Russell noted, "nor could I ever find the taking [of] it so general a practice in Turky as is commonly apprehended, being chiefly practised only by debauchees. . . . The consequences of a long use of it are, that they soon look old and besotted, like such as in Europe have ruined their constitutions by hard drinking."[16]

The Impact of Guidebooks

Dr. Russell's warnings notwithstanding, the first stirrings of what was to later become "tourism" led to a huge expansion in the market for travel literature. Publishers responded accordingly with new and tailormade offerings, ranging from those in the heavily illustrated 'picturesque travel' genre to more prosaic and text-led publications designed to inform and guide those visiting particular destinations. The foremost English-language titles in the latter category were Murray's *Handbooks for Travellers*, a series of travel guides which first appeared in the 1830s. The word "handbook" may very well have been coined by John Murray[17] and his new product was an immediate success, with twenty different titles available by 1857. For those heading to the Orient, the most relevant were *A Hand-book for Travellers in the Ionian Islands, Greece, Turkey, Asia Minor, and Constantinople*, published in 1840; the *Hand-book for Travellers in Egypt*, which first appeared in 1847 and was a condensed and recast version of *Modern Egypt and Thebes*, an earlier (1843–44) book by John Gardner Wilkinson; *A Handbook for Travellers in Syria and Palestine*, which followed in 1858; and *A Handbook for Travellers in Algeria* (1873), which was revised and expanded in 1878 to include Tunis. In a review of the Algeria guide, *The Spectator* of 15 November 1873 reported that, "The plan of these volumes is so well known and their reputation for trustworthiness so well established, that we need not do more than commend the volume to our readers."

Murray's *Handbooks* offered a wealth of practical and often very detailed information, including "Maxims and Hints for Travellers in the East" and ranging from historical and geographical accounts and useful expressions in the local language to assessments of the character of the local people and tips on how best to avoid disease. Suggested excursions, routes to take, and sights to visit were also included, as well as maps and plans and guidance on prices for a vast range of services and products. The total cost of traveling from London to Alexandria, for example, was estimated in the *Hand-book for Travellers in Egypt* at £41 (approximately £2,300 at current prices)—a considerable sum and an indication of how travel to the Orient was the preserve of the wealthy.

Guidebooks were also published for French- and German-speaking travelers. The latter were most notably served through the series published by Karl Baedeker, who

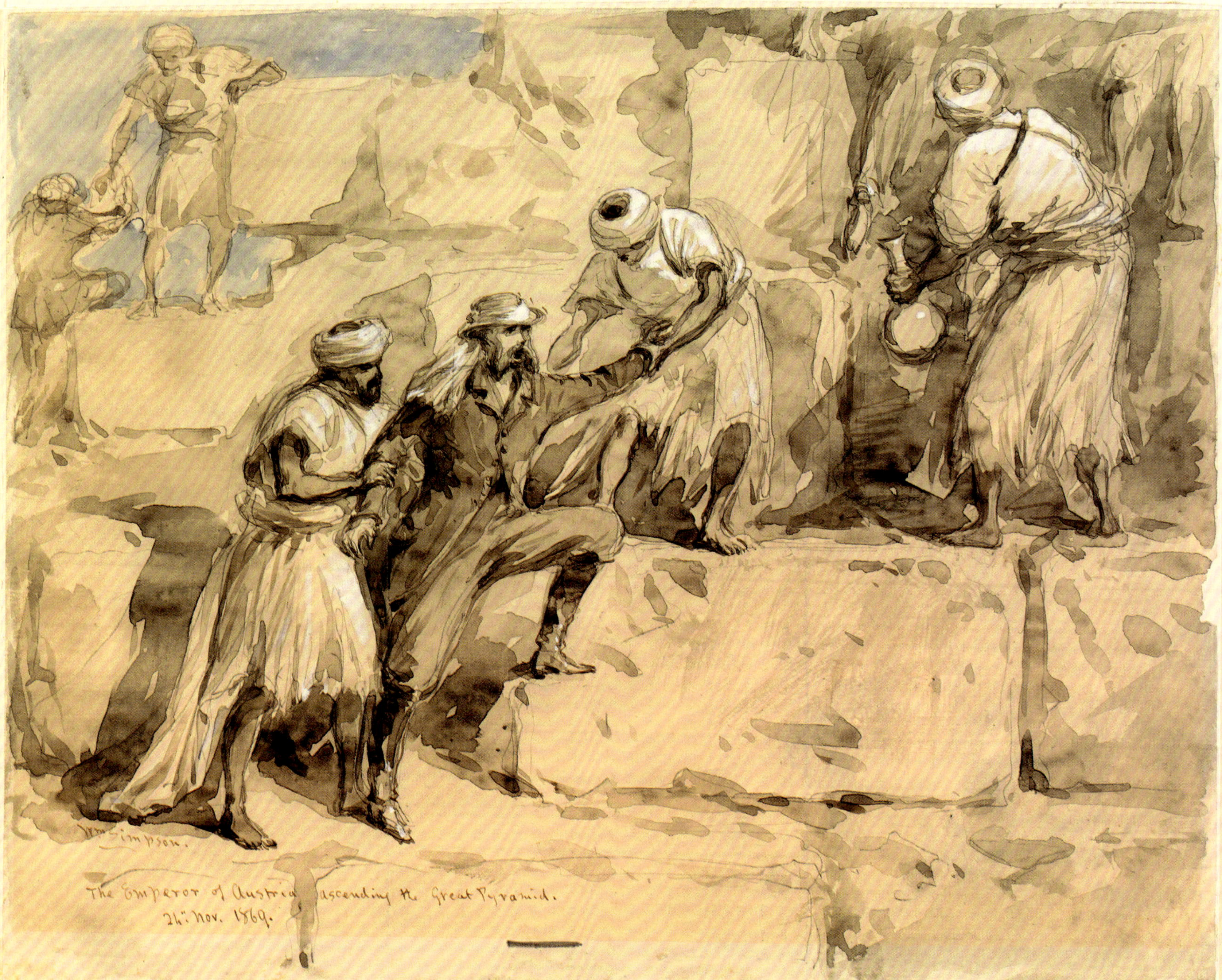
Wm Simpson.
The Emperor of Austria ascending the Great Pyramid.
24th Nov. 1869.

was publishing travel guides to Europe earlier than Murray and with whom he initially collaborated closely. The Baedeker publishing house produced German translations of Murray handbooks before starting their own English language series in 1861. Meanwhile, European bookstores such as Galignani in Paris, which opened in 1801, catered for the growing trade in travel literature by offering the latest guides in English as well as French. The range of travel-related titles was matched only by the diversity of people penning them: poets, soldiers, civil servants, commercial travelers, professional travel writers, missionaries, and, indeed, some artists all turned their hand to the new genre. For some artists the plethora of travel literature was a spur to go abroad themselves to improve their own craft and create a more accurate picture than that presented in the travel guides. In 1855 William Holman Hunt (1827–1910) wrote to William Michael Rossetti from Jerusalem: "I am not satisfied with the thousand books of travel that come out every year, but even these in all their trivialities and superficialities are a keen reproof for painters. I have a notion that painters should go out, two by two, like merchants of nature, and bring back precious merchandise in faithful pictures of scenes interesting from historical consideration or from the strangeness of the subject itself."[18]

13. William Simpson, *The Emperor of Austria Ascending the Great Pyramid* (1869). Pencil and watercolor heightened with white, stuck down on card, 22.1 x 28 cm. Tourists in Egypt often found themselves hauled around the sites by enthusiastic local helpers eager for baksheesh. Simpson described in his biography how one day he had witnessed the Austrian emperor "lugged to the top of the Great Pyramid by two Arabs as if he had been only an overland passenger."

The wealth of travel-related literature reflected wider public and governmental interest in foreign places and their cultures. The Great Exhibition held in London in 1851 was the first of a series of world fairs which, during the second half of the nineteenth century, brought the cultures, art, and architecture of the Orient into the heart of Europe and North America and into the minds of artists and their potential audiences. Exhibitions on Algeria, Egypt, Morocco, Tunisia, and Turkey regularly featured at such events, showcasing Oriental handicrafts, architecture, and other cultural aspects such as music and dance. The much-acclaimed Egyptian pavilion at the Vienna World's Fair of 1873 was an obvious potential source of inspiration for artists based in that city, including Ludwig Deutsch (1855–1935), Rudolf Ernst (1854–1932), and Leopold Carl Müller (1835–92), all of whom traveled repeatedly to Egypt in the years that followed.

The Rigors of Travel

Would-be travelers were faced with a range of potential dilemmas for which there was no shortage of advice. One aspect that preoccupied many—and especially those artists in search of a particularly 'authentic' experience—was whether or not to adopt local dress. John Gardner Wilkinson gave quite unequivocal guidance in his handbook for Egypt: "If the traveller inquires if the Oriental dress be necessary, I answer, it is by no means so; and a person wearing it, who is ignorant of the language, becomes ridiculous. One remark, however, I must be allowed to make on dress in that country—that a person is never respected who is badly dressed, of whatever kind the costume may be, and nowhere is exterior appearance so much thought of as in the East."[19] Opinions

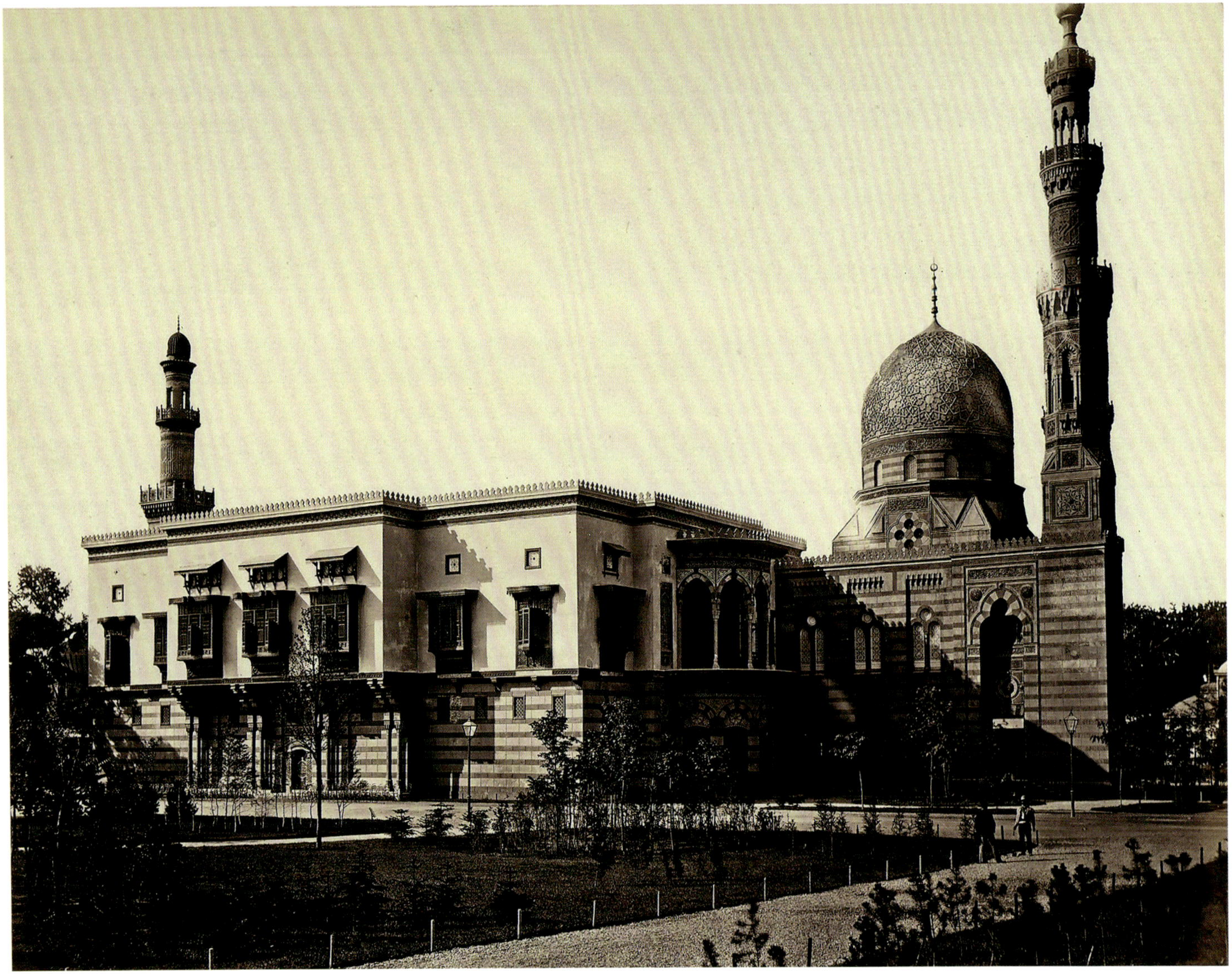

14. The Egyptian Pavilion at the 1873 Vienna World's Fair proved an enduring source of interest and inspiration for artists and others intrigued by the Orient. Photographed by Oscar Kramer.

on the wisdom or otherwise of dressing *à la turque* continued to exercise travelers and expatriate residents alike for the rest of the nineteenth century.

The issue of servants was a further area of concern. The concept of looking after oneself was inconceivable to most nineteenth-century travelers, with the wealthier among them sometimes preferring to journey overseas accompanied by a servant—often their valet or ladies' maid—brought from home. For over twenty-five years Edward Lear was accompanied on his travels by his personal valet, Giorgio (George) Kokali, for example. However, the transition from domestic service at home to adventuring abroad was not necessarily straightforward, as the introduction to *A Hand-book for Travellers in the Ionian Islands* (1840) makes clear: "It is very difficult to find a servant in England capable of acting as an interpreter in Eastern countries, though a few such may be found; one, named Misseri,* has been found a most invaluable servant to travelers in the East. Guides and interpreters must be taken in each country, if the traveller be unprovided with a servant who can supply their place. English servants are in general rather incumbrances than otherwise, as they are usually but little disposed to adapt themselves to new customs, have no facility in acquiring foreign languages, and are in general more annoyed by hardships than their masters."[20] Local servants, guides, and a dragoman—the term used across the Middle East for a senior guide–translator–interpreter—were essential, particularly for artists wanting access to unusual locations or wishing to recruit models. Although relatively easy to obtain locally in most locations, concerns over the standards, reliability, and rates of pay of such "fixers" were an endless source of vexation to those seeking to hire them (see pages 65–66, 99).

Murray's *Handbooks* also offered suggestions on what supplies to carry out from home and what sort of clothing to pack. Advice on such matters was not in short supply from other quarters, either. E.A. Wallis Budge, Keeper of Egyptian and Assyrian Antiquities at the British Museum 1894–1924, offered the following sartorial guidance to those planning to visit Egypt: "It is always desirable when travelling to dispense with unnecessary luggage, at the same time, if the traveller intends to journey for months, he must be well supplied with clothing. Gentlemen should take with them an evening suit, thick and thin light-coloured tweed suits, a suit of some dark-coloured material for wearing upon special occasions, a flannel suit or two, riding breeches and gaiters, thick and thin pairs of shoes both in black and brown leather. A pair of thick-soled shoes, or boots, will be found invaluable in exploring ruins. Woollen socks, flannel and linen shirts, slippers, straw and felt hats, cloth caps, white umbrella lined with green, cork sun helmet, and an Ulster [a type of double-breasted overcoat], make a fairly complete outfit."[21]

Budge did, however, make a concession to the usefulness of local garments: "A *keffiyeh*, or turban cloth, to be tied round the hat or helmet in such a way that a good portion of it falls over the neck and sides of the face, should not be forgotten." His advice to ladies on what to wear was less

* Misseri was a Greek guide and dragoman who traveled with writer, historian, and (later) Member of Parliament, Alexander Kinglake (1809–91). Their travels took them to Greece, Cyprus, Palestine, Egypt, and Syria, and were described by Kinglake in *Eothen; or Traces of travel brought home from the East* (1844). *Eothen* is Greek for "Oriental." Misseri was later to run a hotel in Constantinople that catered particularly for British travelers (see page 61).

complete, perhaps reflecting his lack of experience in such matters. "They will find very useful thick and thin brown shoes or boots," he wrote, "and short blue serge skirts, white or coloured cotton and linen shirts, dresses of thicker material for cold days and evenings, wrappers and cloaks, etc. If shoes are worn in exploring ruins, gaiters will be found most useful for keeping out the sand and for protection against the bites of insects."

The availability of art supplies was a constant concern for artists. In the mid-nineteenth century specialist art equipment was not generally obtainable in the Orient and either had to be ordered specially from Europe, a costly and lengthy process (see pages 87–88), or carried out from home in adequate quantities to last a whole trip. Understandably, most artists kept their art materials with them and under a close eye, although, curiously, in 1858 Frederick Goodall (1822–1904) chose to send his out to Egypt by a different route from the one he took himself.* Working in the Islamic world also brought particular restrictions on what equipment could be used. When David Roberts was given permission to paint inside the mosques of Cairo, "a privilege never before given to a Christian," it was subject to the requirement that "he was not to desecrate the mosque by the introduction and use of brushes made of *hog's bristles*"[22]—pigs being deemed unclean by Muslims. While no 'packing list for artists' has yet come to light from any of the likely sources, helpful advice on what to include or to leave out was doubtlessly passed on an informal basis between friends and acquaintances.

National Preferences

By the 1850s artists were heading to the Orient in unprecedented numbers. Who were the people forming this exodus? At first glance they appear to be a decidedly homogenous group, overwhelmingly male, largely of a comfortable middle-class background or even aristocrats in a few cases, often with a private income. Closer analysis reveals a far more diverse group of individuals, their varying motivations and destinations reflecting their eclectic nature. From the deeply conservative and religiously minded to the socially aspirational and free-spirited, from the hugely wealthy to the financially desperate, and with some notable women among their ranks, the Orientalists were a representative cross-section of the dynamic and complex Western societies that had emerged in the wake of the Enlightenment and Industrial Revolution.

The geographical destinations favored by individual artists varied, but national preferences are easy to detect. Most British artists headed for Egypt, which from the early nineteenth century onward was increasingly within the national sphere of influence as the British government sought to secure the route to its colonial jewel of India. German and Austrian artists also appear to have favored Egypt with the majority of their visits, while Constantinople was also a popular venue with the British, as was the Holy Land. For French artists North Africa was the obvious choice, especially after their country's annexation of Algeria in 1830 and subsequent consolidation of colonial ambitions across the whole of the Maghreb. However, such a crude and generalized analysis

* Goodall, *Reminiscences*, 63. Goodall does not explain why he chose to send his equipment separately, but it was a risky strategy. See page 215 for what happened on the return journey.

precludes the many exceptions, individuals who bucked the usual national trends, such as Charles Robertson (1844–91), a British artist who began his experiences of the Orient in Algeria, and the German Gustav Bauernfeind (1848–1904), who specialized in depicting the Levant and Palestine. There were also Orientalists for whom the Orient was much closer to home: as a native of the Ottoman Empire, Osman Hamdi (1842–1910) was interpreting his own country for an audience made up of foreigners and his fellow Westernized Turks, while for Russians such as Vasily Vereshchagin (1842–1904), the Orient started at the southern frontiers of their own country, in the Crimea, the Caucasus, Turkestan, and Uzbekistan.

Establishing the precise reasons why particular individuals chose to head for the Orient on an artistic foray is often less than straightforward. Diaries, letters, and travel journals—where they exist, which is only in the minority of cases—can shed some light, but in most instances they focus primarily on the actual processes of travel rather than the motivation for it. Much therefore remains speculative, but some common factors can be identified behind the decision to buy a steamer ticket to Alexandria, Algiers, or Constantinople.

Speculation on motives was as rife then as now. In his biography on Sir David Wilkie, Allan Cunningham speculated on the reasons why Wilkie set off for Constantinople "suddenly" in the autumn of 1840: "It was said that he went charged with royal commissions from home to paint for the palace galleries portraits of the young ruler of Turkey and the old ruler of Egypt. This was in turn contradicted, by the assurance that this great painter was regarded coldly in the high places of the land, and was, on court authority, held deficient in that grace of style which captivates the high

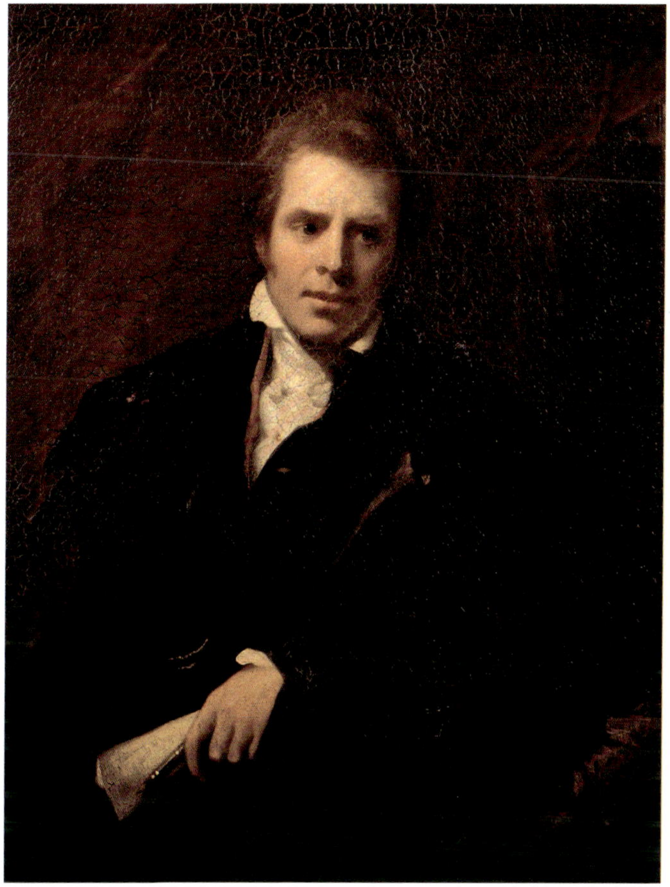

15. Thomas Phillips, *Sir David Wilkie, R.A.* (1829). Oil on canvas, 99.7 x 76.2 cm. Wilkie's only trip to the Orient took him to Constantinople, Smyrna, Jerusalem, and Alexandria, with the Ottoman Sultan Abdul Mejid and the Egyptian ruler Muhammad Ali both sitting for him. Wilkie tragically died on his voyage home and was buried at sea off Gibraltar.

bred and polished. This gave way to a third rumour, that he longed for 'fresh fields and pastures new,' and desired to merit the applause of the multitude by pictures of remote scenes and strange manners and employments. The devout had a rumour of their own, that Wilkie was on a visit to the Holy Land, to realize those visions present to his mind, when he first opened the Bible in the village of Cults, and behold Jerusalem as it came in glory from the hand of Solomon, or sunk in sorrow under the sword of Titus. While a fifth party, who were intimate with the state of his health, whispered that he went on a tour to the warmer regions of the East in the hope that their sunnier shores and more odorous vales would do for him what they had done for some who less deserved the mercy of health. That truth claimed a share in these rumours it would be idle to deny: we may say with certainty that he went with enlarging notions of his art; that he was not encumbered with royal commissions, and hoped amendment to his health by a visit to a land endeared to his heart by a thousand associations, and all of them devout."*

Cunningham's review of the reasons why Wilkie may have decided to travel east serves as a convenient running list against which any Orientalist artist might be assessed. Certainly, there were some who went overseas for health reasons. Gustave Boulanger (1824–88) first traveled to Algeria in 1845 on the instruction of his uncle, who was concerned for the young man's delicate physical condition; Leopold Müller (1835–92) was fearful that he had inherited weak lungs and so fled regularly to Egypt in winter, visiting the country nine times in total and deliberately painting alfresco so the sun could warm his body and ease his respiration. The climate was a definite attraction to some: the art critic Clarence Cook noted of Théodore Frère that "[he] does not tell us just what moved him, it is like enough that he was attracted by some pictures of Oriental scenery in the Salon that contained his picture; but, however that may have been, he says only that he was strongly drawn by the sun, and that in the search for it he went to Algeria."[23]

Other artists were drawn by the lure of the Holy Land and its role in the birth and evolution of Christianity. Western audiences viewed the Orient primarily through the prism of the Bible and therefore as the context for biblical events and characters, with religious revivalism during the nineteenth century prompting a spike in demand for art inspired by biblical scenes. Popular and commercially successful works such as the Finden brothers' *Landscape Illustrations of the Bible* (1836) and John Carne's *Syria, The Holy Land, Asia Minor, &c* (1836–38)** generated a rash of visits by artists seeking to match religious myth with reality in their own works. Both Frederick Goodall and William Holman Hunt made journeys to Palestine in order to refine their skills and specialism, "intent on remaking religious art for a modern Protestant audience."[24] James Tissot (1836–1902) visited the Holy Land three times, in 1886–87, 1889, and 1896, making sketches and taking photographs that he used to create works for illustrated editions of the

* Cunningham, *The Life of Sir David Wilkie*, 284–85. Ironically, Wilkie was to die on his journey home from the Orient, probably from drinking contaminated iced lemonade when in Malta.

** Carne's book was illustrated with works by topographical artists Thomas Allom and William Bartlett, who visited the region specially to compile on-the-spot sketches.

Bible, while John Singer Sargent (1856–1925) traveled to the Orient during the 1890s as a result of a commission from the Boston Public Library to paint a series of murals depicting the development of religious thought.

For French artists in particular, traveling to the region on official government commissions was a realistic option. Delacroix journeyed to Morocco and Algeria in 1832 as part of a diplomatic mission (although he had to pay his own way) and Horace Vernet (1789–1863) first visited Algeria in 1833 to document the French annexation of that country. Serendipity must have played a part in the decision by Étienne Dinet (1861–1929) to accompany an artist friend and his beetle-collecting brother on a trip to Algeria in 1884—Dinet fell in love with the country, later converted to Islam, and lived the rest of his life there (see pages 110–111). For others, it was a sheer enthusiasm to explore new horizons that drew them abroad. Such spirit of adventure was surely foremost in Charles Robertson's mind when he set off for Algeria in 1862 at the age of eighteen on the first of a series of trips over the next twenty-seven years that saw him travel regularly to the Orient, visiting Turkey, Egypt, Morocco, Palestine, and Syria, in some cases more than once.

Commercial Imperatives

Joie de vivre and the desire to see new things notwithstanding, it is also clear that the vast majority of artists were drawn to the Orient because of the potential of its subject matter to bring them fame and fortune. Indeed, as the popularity of Orientalist paintings grew in the galleries and showrooms of London and Paris, so did the number of artists seeking to take financial advantage. For many, "the voyage to the Orient was a transitory experience intended to bear fruit long after the return home,"[25] a way of acquiring material and experiences that could be stored and recycled later. The potential financial rewards of painting the Orient were not lost on the novelist and satirist William Makepeace Thackeray, when he visited Egypt in 1844 (meeting John Frederick Lewis while he was there, see page 73). "There is a fortune to be made for painters in Cairo," he remarked, "and materials for a whole Academy of them. I never saw such a variety of architecture, of life, of picturesqueness, of brilliant colour, of light and shade. There is a picture in every street, and at every bazaar stall."[26]

Some artists were fortunate enough to travel in the advance knowledge that their costs would be covered and their works destined, in principle at least, for ready acceptance and acquisition by a particular client. Among these "hired hands" was Antonio (Anton) Schranz (1801–65), of German origin but based in Malta from 1818. Schranz worked as a professional draftsman and between 1823 and 1847 made at least ten expeditions to the eastern Mediterranean and Egypt, accompanying various wealthy British patrons on their travels. These included Viscount Castlereagh, whose subsequent book was illustrated with engravings after drawings made by Schranz on location.[27] The artist later took up photography and opened the first professional photographic studio in Cairo (see page 156).

Another artist hired by a wealthy patron as a traveling companion was Charles Gleyre (1806–74), who had studied in Rome with Horace Vernet. Gleyre was encouraged by Vernet to accompany American businessman and philanthropist John Lowell, Jr. on his extended travels through Greece, Turkey, and Egypt from the spring of 1834 onward.

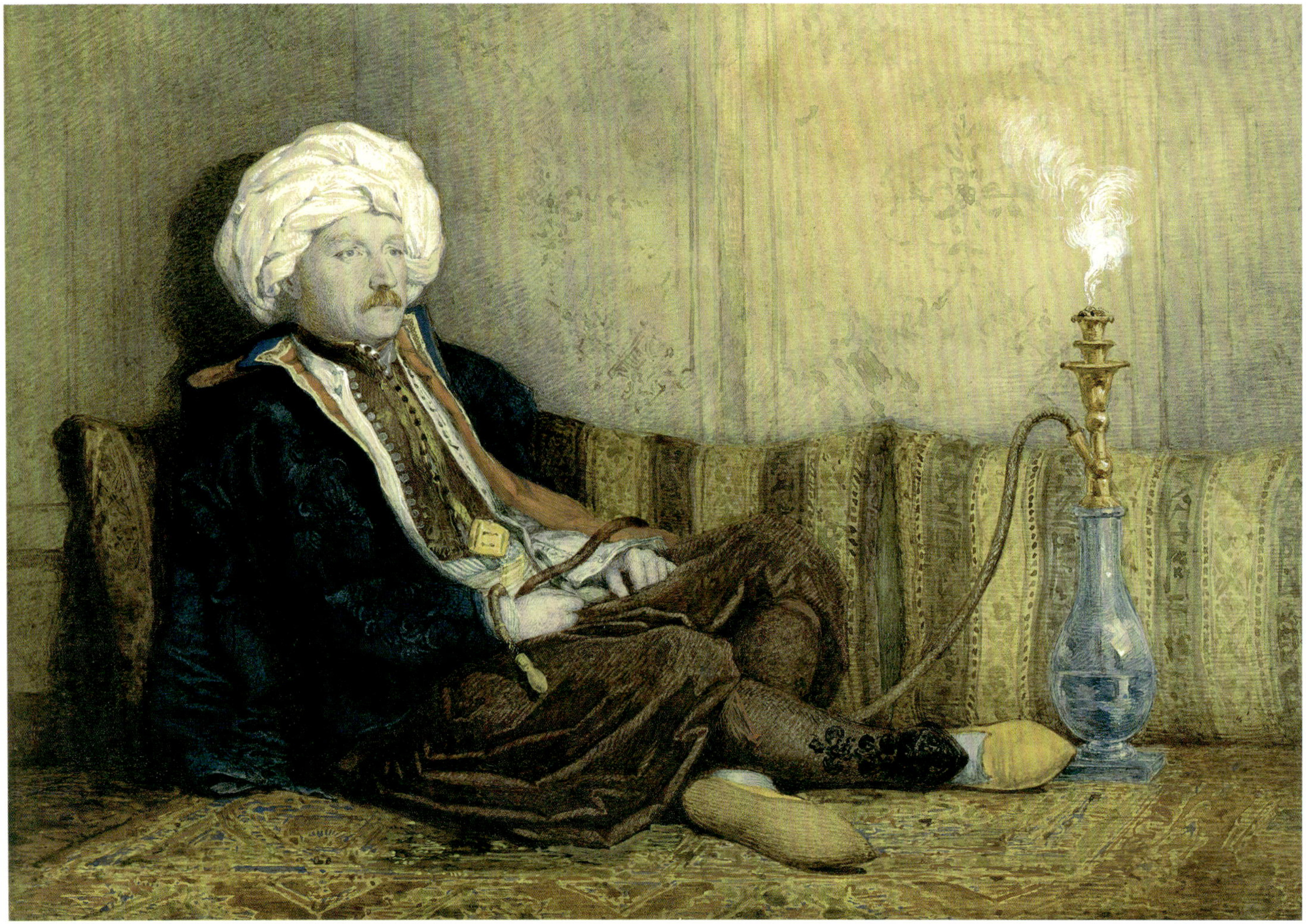

16. Richard Dadd, *Portrait of Sir Thomas Phillips in Eastern Costume, Reclining with a Hookah* (1842–43). Watercolor heightened with white on paper, 17.8 x 25.4 cm. Dadd painted two portraits of Phillips; this one, showing his employer in Turkish dress, was probably done in Constantinople. The other shows Phillips in Arab clothing.

Gleyre completed a fine series of watercolor studies during the trip, not returning to Paris—ill and almost blind—until 1838. He was later to teach Jean-Léon Gérôme (1824–1904), among others, in the Paris atelier that he took over from Paul Delaroche. Lowell, however, did not survive the expedition. He became ill in Egypt, where he is said to have written a codicil to his will while sitting in the temple at Luxor, detailing his intentions for what was to become the Lowell Institute in Boston. He died in March 1836, shortly after arriving in Bombay.

A few years later, during the winter of 1842–43, the wealthy art patron Sir Thomas Phillips arrived in Cairo accompanied by the artist Richard Dadd (1817–86). The two had followed a similar route to Lowell and Gleyre, traveling through Greece and Turkey to Damascus, Jerusalem, and Jaffa, from where they caught a boat to Alexandria. In Cairo they met John Frederick Lewis and it was while in Egypt that Dadd began to suffer from the madness—probably paranoid schizophrenia—that was to see him end his days in a London psychiatric institution over forty years later.* While incarcerated he continued to produce works based on his sketches and memories from his Middle Eastern travels with Phillips.

Commissioned expeditions like those enjoyed by Schranz, Gleyre, and Dadd were increasingly unusual after about 1850. Most artists had no such security and, in the early stages of their careers at least, were likely to be setting off overseas speculatively. Many headed for Constantinople or Egypt, encouraged by the growing enthusiasm for Western art—and especially portraiture—among the Ottoman elite and particularly Muhammad Ali, the Egyptian ruler. Traveling European artists were often successful in obtaining audiences with him and in landing one or two commissions. Even so, there were no guarantees that they would ultimately be able to repay their costs through these or via speculative works sold later.

Some artists were clearly blessed with a better commercial eye than others, and few more so than David Roberts. He spent the first few months of 1832 preparing to travel abroad, his original intention being to make his way to Italy. However, in a letter to his friend David Ramsay Hay, dated 28 June that year, he revealed a change of plan: "I think of altering my route from Italy to Spain, as nothing has been done that gives any idea of the magnificent remains of the Moorish architecture which are there."[28]

The Lure of Spain

Roberts had spotted a niche in the market and was well placed to exploit it, having trained in interior decoration and in the painting of theatrical scenery. Not only was Spain's architectural heritage little known to a British audience at that time but the country's wider cultural and topographical attractions were much less publicized and appreciated than those of Italy, which had been a firm fixture on the Grand Tour for over a century. Roberts was convinced—quite rightly, as subsequent events would demonstrate—that there would be a market back home for the drawings and

* Dadd became obsessed with ancient Egyptian religion and convinced he was an instrument of the will of Osiris. He was committed to a psychiatric institution after murdering his father, only a few months after returning to England from Egypt.

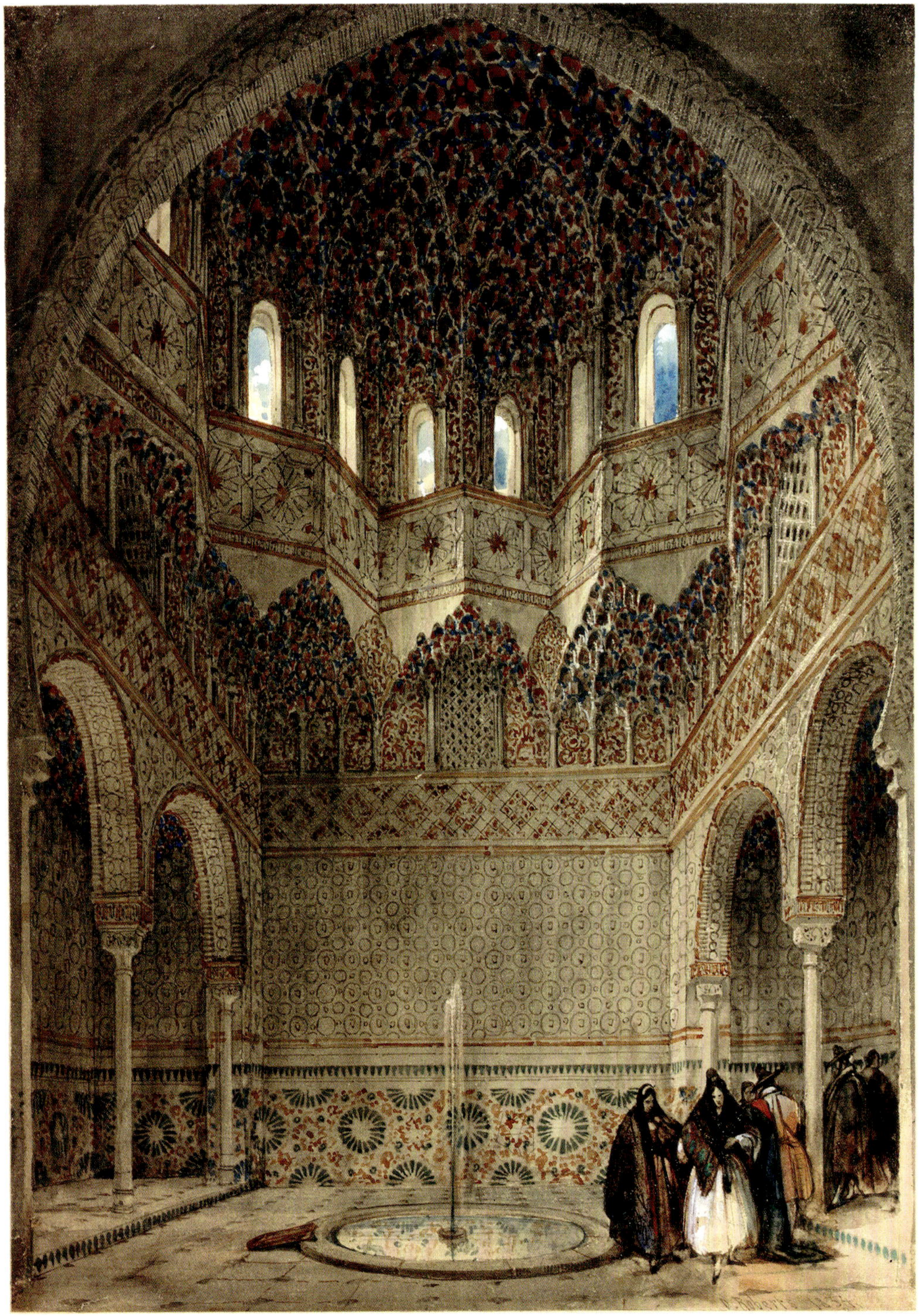

paintings he intended to compile on his Spanish travels, and so he changed his destination accordingly.

The reasons why the time was right for Roberts and his Spanish trip were largely to do with the invention of new printing processes (see chapter 4). Drawings and watercolors could now be reproduced in formats suitable for reproduction on paper, making good-quality illustrated books much cheaper to produce. This led to a boom in publishing and the expansion in the publication of travel books in particular meant that there was a great demand for topographical artists, who were kept busy producing views of scenery, towns, and buildings. Newspapers and magazines were also increasingly interested in carrying illustrations of foreign destinations in their pages, with opportunities for artists specializing in this sort of work never greater.

A diligent planner, Roberts prepared well for his departure overseas, as confirmed in another letter to Hay, dated 24 September 1832: "I hope to leave in a fortnight from this date. I owe no man in England a shilling. I have sufficient means to sustain me for twelve months. I am burning to retrieve the time I have lost, and am determined either to 'mak' a spoon or spoil a horn.'"[29] The latter expression, meaning to make a determined effort to achieve something (from the traditional practice of fashioning spoons from cow or sheep horn), is confirmation of Roberts's sense of purpose and vision for his expedition. He carefully researched and planned his itinerary, listing the towns he intended to visit in that same letter to Hay and highlighting in particular his desire to see the Alhambra in Granada.

The iconic Moorish palace had attained almost quasi-mythical status among Roberts and his peers, who were intrigued by its history, architecture, decoration, and artistic potential.* It served not only as a symbol of the dramatic built heritage of southern Spain but also as a tantalizing first encounter with Islamic architecture and with what lay across the water in Arab North Africa and further east. Roberts was encouraged in his mission to visit and depict the Alhambra by his friend David Wilkie, who had visited Spain himself in 1827–28 and inspired Roberts and also John Frederick Lewis to make their own journeys there. Wilkie had identified Spain as being of potential interest to a British audience and a subject especially well-suited to Roberts's artistic skills in particular. He wrote to him, when Roberts was already in Spain, in supportive terms: "The Alhambra, if at all paintable, will excite from your hand the highest expectations. After all we have heard and read, it remains for your art to give us an idea of the visible appearance of that romantic fortress."[30]

Artists often relied on the support and advice of their peers when planning travels overseas and deciding where and

17. David Roberts, *In the Alhambra Palace, Granada*, (1834). Bodycolor, pencil, and watercolor on wove paper, 23.2 x 32.7 cm. Andalusia was regarded by Roberts (and other artists, notably Wilkie and Lewis) as the ideal introduction to the sights, sounds, and culture of the Orient proper.

* Contemporary interest in the Alhambra was fueled by the works of writer and historian Washington Irving, who reintroduced the subject to a Western audience through his 1832 collection of essays *The Alhambra: a series of tales and sketches of the Moors and Spaniards*. He later (1842–46) served as United States ambassador to Spain.

when to go. Roberts was not alone in his quest to see the Alhambra, and prior to his departure had been in contact with John Frederick Lewis. The two men knew each other well, their mutual friends including not only Wilkie but also John Sell Cotman (1782–1842).[31] Roberts and Lewis were to end up traveling separately through Spain at the same time, even visiting the same towns, but somehow always just failing to meet up with each other. Although they were as much artistic rivals as good friends, there is no evidence to support the speculation that Lewis deliberately avoided Roberts while in Spain. Communications at the time were poor, and coordinating a rendezvous when on the move would have been less than straightforward.

Although Roberts set off for Spain with a clear sense of what he wanted to achieve, it appears that he left home with no definite commissions. He quickly appreciated the value of what he found abroad, however. "The fact is, that nothing is known of Spain; those who could have appreciated the richness of its architecture have generally gone to Italy or Greece," he wrote from Córdoba in January 1833. "My portfolio is getting rich, the subjects are not only good, but of a very novel character."[32] Lewis, meanwhile, departed England with specific requests to fulfill and was seeking to gather enough material to form "a sort of picturesque tour of Spain, having orders for young ladies' albums and from divers booksellers, who are illustrating Lord Byron."[33] In the event, both Roberts and Lewis made successes of their trips, each publishing acclaimed albums of lithographs based on their works. Lewis did so well with these, and with the watercolors he exhibited, that he secured a reputation for himself as "Spanish Lewis."

For both artists Spain was to prove a creative and professional departure along the road to even greater achievements in the 'real' Orient.* Roberts's expedition to Egypt and the Holy Land in 1838–39—his one and only to the region—was arguably the single most important trip of its type in the history of Orientalist painting. His experience as a transient visitor was markedly different from that of Lewis, who lived in Cairo for ten years. Yet in both cases their time in the East—albeit one much longer in duration than the other and arguably less immediately focused on longer-term objectives—proved ultimately to be equally key elements in the artistic and reputational self-advancement of the two individuals involved.

Rivalry and Support

The competitive atmosphere among artists was nowhere more apparent than in Paris, the center of the Orientalist art world during the second half of the nineteenth century and to where artists of all nationalities were drawn.** There they gathered around the celebrated figures of the day, the ateliers and studios thronged with would-be artist–travelers enthusiastically picking the brains of the experts and discussing possible overseas trips with their instructors and each other. Of particular significance was Charles Gleyre, "whose enthusiasm for the Near East may have had the greatest influence of all upon Jean-Léon Gérôme, stimulating in him

* Other artists also found Spain the natural entrée to the wider Orient, including Rudolf Ernst, who started his Orientalist career by sketching the Moorish buildings of Granada and Toledo.

** The Société Orientale was established in Paris as early as 1843.

an interest that would later lead him to the Orient and—so to speak—to his destiny."[34] Twenty years later, Gérôme was in turn to inspire and encourage the more capable and adventurous of his own students and others at the École des Beaux-Arts to make the same journey, not least the Americans Frederick Arthur Bridgman (1846–1928) and Edwin Lord Weeks (1849–1903).

Yet the support and encouragement of one's tutors, peers, and social circle prior to departure overseas could not be taken as granted. Some artists found their friends actively attempting to dissuade them from traveling overseas at all. Any expedition would necessitate several weeks if not months of absence from home, longer in some cases, away also from the studios, galleries, salerooms, and clients around which artistic careers were constructed. Disappearing from public view at home and dropping out of the all-important network of patronage and contacts was, in the minds of some, potentially ruinous and too risky a prospect to entertain.

William Holman Hunt related how "my good friend Egg urged me carefully to reconsider the resolution to go abroad; he insisted that it was only after a continuously bitter struggle that I had succeeded in getting recognition; that now there was an excellent prospect before me . . . . He knew of cases where men, changing their subjects, and being away for a time, had had to begin the battle all over again."[35] Even more powerful—if largely spurious—reasons for staying at home came from other directions: "Friends with a simple personal feeling pressed me to remember the fate of Wilkie,* and hesitate before taking a course which would probably end, if not in leaving my bones in the desert, at least in implanting in my blood Syrian fever, that would leave me a miserable invalid for the rest of my days."[36]

Choosing to ignore the advice of Mr. Egg and other harbingers of doom, in February 1854 Hunt set off for the Middle East. He was quite clear why he was going, but the journey appears to have had a lengthy gestation period. "My project of going to Syria had originated when I was a boy at school when lessons from the New Testament were read," he recalled. "Although the revelations of science, and more transiently the conclusions drawn from these by theorists and commentators, had often compelled me to reconsider my earlier understanding of the story, yet the doings of that Divine Master in Syria never ceased to claim my homage."[37]

Hunt had also been encouraged by his friendship with fellow artist Edward Lear, fifteen years his senior. The two men had earlier discussed the potential trials, tribulations, and rewards of an artist venturing overseas, with Lear losing little opportunity to extol its benefits to the traveling novice. "Certainly fate could not have sent me a more agreeable or profitable companion to prepare me for my settled purpose of painting in Egypt and Syria," recalled Hunt. "He had not then been to either of these countries, but he had travelled throughout Calabria, Albania, and Greece, and he had hundreds of drawings of the sacred spots in these places, which he brought forth from portfolios each evening to make permanent the pencil outlines, describing the localities and their relation to one another. While we were at work out of doors he would tell stories of the incidents of his many wanderings, and surprised me by showing that he

* David Wilkie died while returning from his only trip to the Orient; see page 37.

was uncombative as a tender girl, while at the same time the most indomitable being in encountering danger and hardship. Nothing daunted him, and yet no one could be more fearful than he of certain difficulties he had to face as the fixed conditions of travelling."*

The support Lear had shown to Hunt in the latter's travel preparations was repaid later when Lear was struggling to master painting in oils; it was Hunt who encouraged him to persevere. Despite a perhaps inevitable subtext of professional rivalry, supportive relationships emerged regularly among the Orientalists, the result perhaps of the particular rigors of traveling and working in what were often very demanding conditions—a case of friendships being forged in the face of adversity. Among those artists who traveled together, some were related (for example, Leopold Müller and Rudolf Swoboda, who were uncle and nephew); others were tutor and pupil (Jean-Léon Gérôme and Paul Lenoir) or friends and acquaintances (Gérôme and Gustave Boulanger, William Holman Hunt and Thomas Seddon, Frederick Goodall and Carl Haag, Ludwig Deutsch and Arthur von Ferraris, Étienne Dinet and Paul Leroy), who joined forces for part or all of an expedition; some artists journeyed alone but were in regular correspondence with one another (David Roberts and David Wilkie, William Holman Hunt and Edward Lear). Even when traveling solo, there was always the likelihood of running into a fellow artist by chance, as Wilkie discovered in Constantinople in October 1840. "We have encountered John Lewis—from Greece and Smyrna," wrote Wilkie to his brother Thomas. "He is making numbers of drawings. I said I was sure he would cast up in our route."[38]

When pieced together through analysis of correspondence and references in diaries and travel journals, this interconnecting web between individual artists sheds much-needed and revealing light on the lives and working practices of the Orientalists generally. Even with those artists who are not known to have traveled abroad together but who certainly enjoyed close friendships at home—Ludwig Deutsch and Rudolf Ernst, for example—there was a commonality of interest and mutual respect for each other's work that helped underpin the sharing of individual experiences.

Opportunities Overseas

In some cases an artist was prompted to try his or her hand abroad after struggling to secure reputational or commercial success at home. Gustav Bauernfeind trained initially as an architect before moving into painting but struggled to sell

18. Willem de Famars Testas, *L'Expédition en Orient* (1868). Ink, graphite, and watercolor on paper, 12.9 x 20.2 cm. In January 1868 Jean-Léon Gérome set off on his third trip to the Orient, accompanied by two of his students (Paul Lenoir and Richard Goubie), three fellow artists (Léon Bonnat, Ernest Journault, and Willem de Famars Testas), and his brother-in-law Albert Goupil, who was the expedition photographer. De Testas made this sketch of the group in Aqaba on 19 March of that year, by which time they had been joined by Wilfrid de Barthélémy. Also in the sketch is the group's dragoman, Joseph Moussali (fourth from the right).

* Hunt, *Pre-Raphaelitism and the Pre-Raphaelite Brotherhood*, vol. 1, 331–32. Hunt's reference to Lear not yet having visited Egypt or Syria is curious, as Lear had made his first trip to Egypt in 1849, five years before Hunt set foot there.

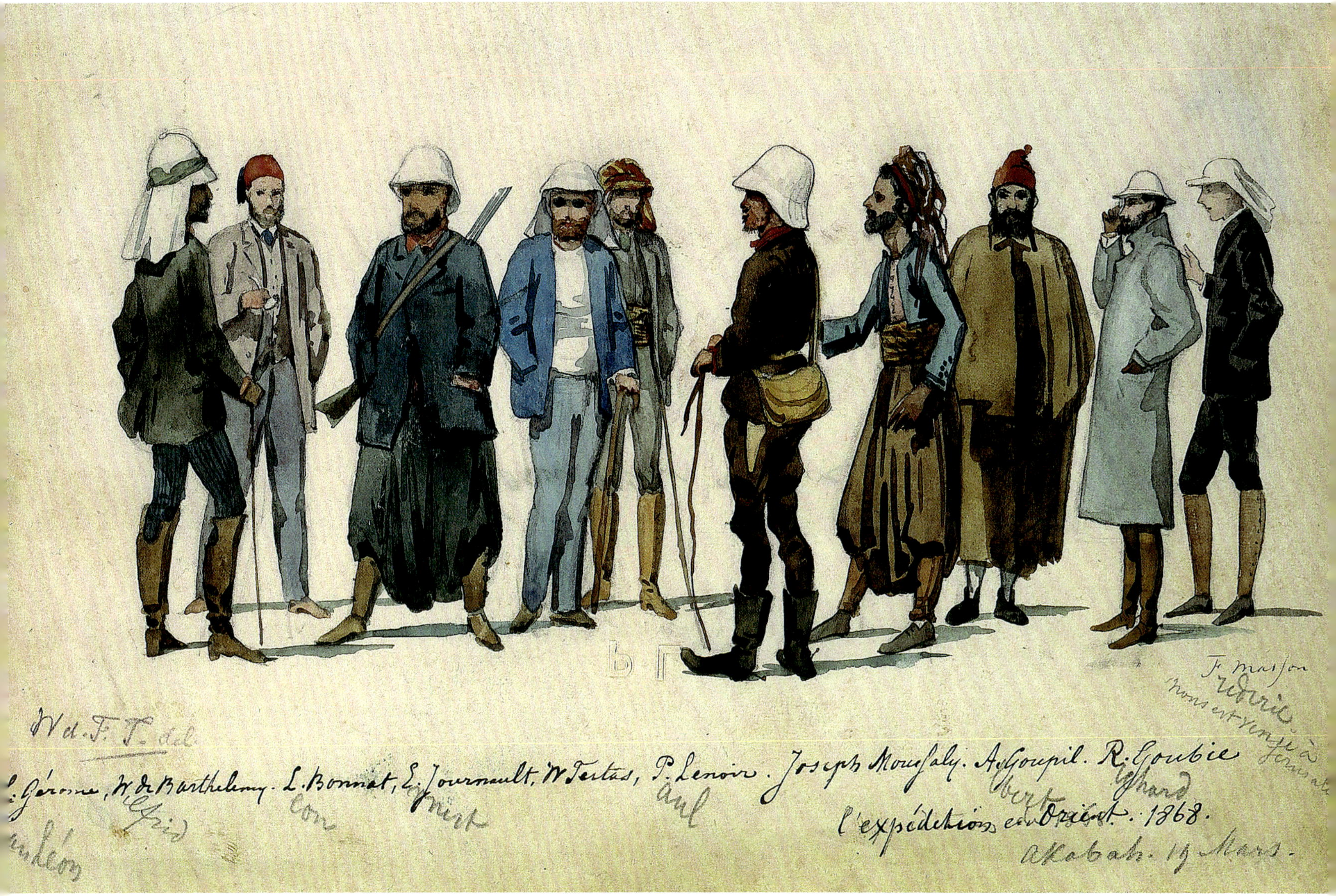
L. Gérome. W. de Barthelemy. L. Bonnat, E. Journault. W. Tertas, P. Lenoir. Joseph Moussaly. A. Goupil. R. Goubie
l'expédition en Orient. 1868.
Akabah. 19 Mars.
F. Masson

enough of the village and town scenes in which he specialized to make a decent living. An apparent break came when King Ludwig II of Bavaria commissioned him to paint a large watercolor of the interior of the old opera house in Bayreuth, but rather than building on such a potentially lucrative connection at home, Bauernfeind instead used the fee to fund his first trip to the Orient in 1880. His sister and brother-in-law were at that time living in Beirut as missionaries and had encouraged him to join them there: "Everything which is in our power to do to make the Orient pleasant and interesting shall be done. Of course, I must tell you beforehand, you will find Syria to be no Italy. No such abundance of architectural art treasures are to be expected here; all the same, I should think that in spite of this, an artist could find a worthwhile field for his studies here, and would not regret his journey."[39] Meanwhile, one of Bauernfeind's friends and peers in Germany had impressed upon him the wisdom of turning his hand to suit the contemporary vogue for Orientalist paintings. He took their advice, and was to make three trips to the Middle East over the next few years, as a result of which he produced what are now regarded as some of the most accomplished Orientalist works.

Elisabeth Jerichau-Baumann (1819–81) is one of few professional female Orientalist artists to have achieved widespread recognition. Her early paintings had prompted only a lukewarm response in her adopted home of Denmark (she was born into a German family living in Poland, but married a Dane), their bold colors being deemed "un-Danish" and "saccharine."[40] She did, however, strike up what proved to be a crucial friendship with the Danish princess Alexandra, who was to become the wife of the British Prince of Wales, the future King Edward VII. Alexandra introduced Jerichau-Baumann to the British court circle and London society, which took to her works much more enthusiastically than the Danes. Buoyed by this reception, and seeing the opportunities presented by the popularity among British audiences of Orientalist paintings, Jerichau-Baumann began to work in that style and in October 1869 set off on the first of her three trips to the Orient. Traveling alone, she journeyed by steamship and overland from Copenhagen to Varna and then by ship again to Constantinople, where she spent several weeks. From there she continued to Athens and Piraeus, subsequently taking a steamship to Alexandria in February 1870.[41]

Having a future queen as a friend was always likely to open doors for an artist. Jerichau-Baumann set off from home armed with letters of introduction from Alexandra, which helped facilitate access to a range of potential and influential clients at each of her ports of call. Contemporary etiquette required such formalities, and any artist intending to travel overseas would have been expected to carry such confirmation of their social and professional credentials. Before leaving for the Orient, William Holman Hunt, for example, had met with Sir Austen Henry Layard, politician, diplomat, and archaeologist (he excavated at Nimrud), who "gave me advice, and furnished me with letters to several officials of high standing in my probable line of route."[42] David Roberts ensured that he was equally well provided for by contacting William Mark, who had been the British consul in Málaga when Roberts visited Spain in 1833. "I am glad that you are satisfied with the letter of introduction I procured you from the Foreign Office," wrote Mark in a letter to Roberts shortly before the artist left for London for Egypt on 31

August 1838. "I so managed it that it will not only serve to make you known to Captain Campbell at Alexandria, but to any other British functionary in your way. You must indeed have plenty to do before adopting so long a march. Take your talent-box with you, and a fig for everything else."[43]

It was advice that all artists setting off overseas at that time would have done well to heed. Despite the camaraderie often found among them, the world of the Orientalists was an increasingly competitive one and it was important to get ahead of the game if one wanted to be in with a chance of achieving commercial and critical success back home. A productive working trip to countries such as Algeria, Egypt, and Palestine required flexibility, resilience, endless resources of patience, and no small amount of luck. Planning in advance by reading the available literature and seeking the advice of seasoned travelers could help pave the way. Yet no amount of preparation was ever likely to make the arrival of newcomers to the Orient of the mid- to late nineteenth century anything less than overwhelming, exciting, and rich with new experiences. For many artists, it marked the beginning of a new chapter in their lives, both professionally and personally.

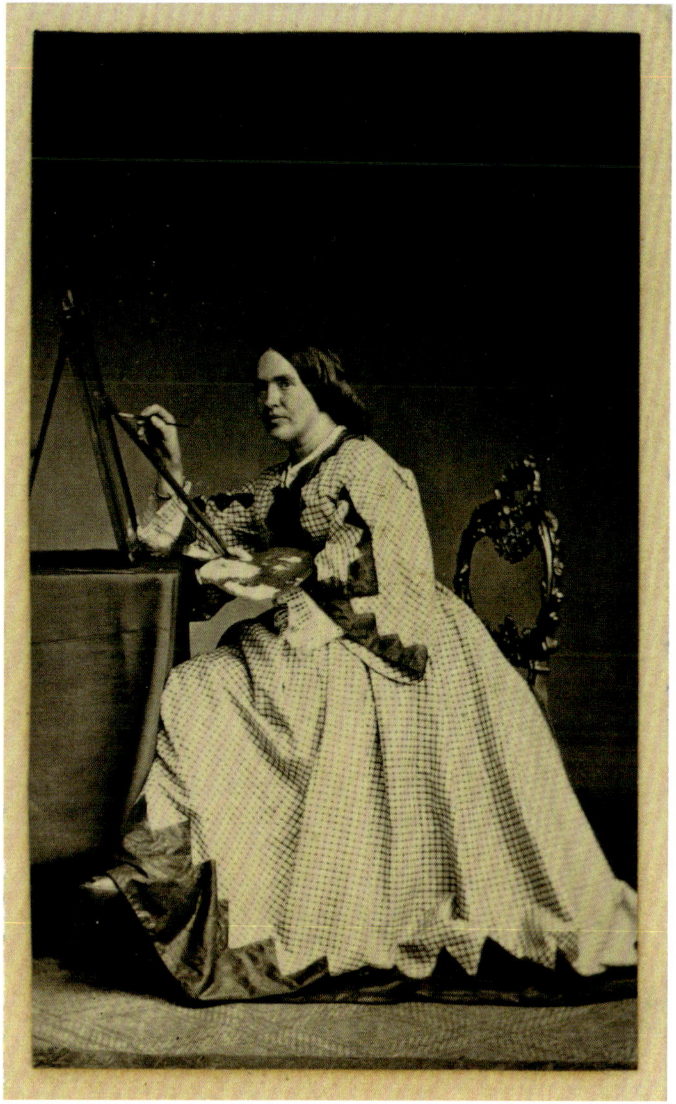

19. Rudolph Striegler, photographic portrait of Elisabeth Jerichau-Baumann (1861–62).

2. Arrival

Traveling to the Middle East in the mid-nineteenth century remained an often arduous affair, despite dramatic improvements in terms of conveyance, routes, and journey times. For most travelers it involved crossing the Mediterranean Sea, which even during the summer months is prone to sudden storms. "The Mediterranean is what it is," wrote Eugène Fromentin (1820–76). "You can say all possible good or evil about it but it's still the most beautiful, the bluest, and perhaps the most treacherous of all the world's seas."[1] Rough conditions could mean not only days of delay for the packet boats and other craft that plied their way to and fro but also a distinctly unpleasant experience for those on board. Conditions were often cramped and primitive, even for the wealthiest passengers, and few regarded the sea leg of their journey to the Orient as anything more than a means to an end. Reaching one's final destination usually came as a welcome relief, even if the act of arrival itself presented yet more challenges.

One of the most striking first impressions of an initiation into the hurly-burly of the Orient comes from the pen of a writer rather than an artist. Gustave Flaubert traveled to Egypt with his friend Maxime du Camp and du Camp's manservant, a Corsican ex-dragoon named Sassetti, by a steam packet which, according to Flaubert, "rolled like a drunken man and made but little headway," from Marseille via Malta. They had their first taste of Egypt in autumn 1849 as they steamed into Alexandria and a bewildering barrage of sights, sounds, and—doubtlessly—smells. "Landing took place amid the most deafening uproar imaginable," Flaubert wrote to his mother on 17 November, "negroes, negresses, camels, turbans, cudgelings to right and left, and ear-splitting guttural cries. I gulped down a whole bellyful of colours, like a donkey filling himself with hay."[2]

David Roberts had met with a similar assault on the senses when he arrived at the same city in 1838. He described in a letter to his daughter Christine: "Our ship was surrounded by the most picturesque boatmen in the world, pulling, hauling, and bawling—each fighting for which should have the passengers. On landing from the boats the scene was still more exciting: such scrambling among the poor black porters to get hold of the luggage, that it was with difficulty you could keep it under your eye; and they submitted to be kicked and buffeted, all for the sake of a few halfpence."[3]

For Richard Dadd, writing from a steamer off Jaffa in 1842, what had confronted him ashore was little short of overwhelming. "At times the excitement of these scenes has been enough to turn the brain of an ordinary weak-minded person like myself," he explained, continuing—in an ominous portent of his later fate (see page 41)—how "often I have lain down at night with my imagination so full of wild vagaries that I have really and truly doubted of my own sanity. . . . could you but glance on the princely beggary of these imperial ragamuffins, you would beat your breast and gnash your teeth until they came through your lower jaw!"[4]

Such scenes may well have constituted a baptism of fire for European *ingénus*, but it was usually possible for an artistic eye to see through the maelstrom and find aspects of beauty, as well as food for creative thought. David Wilkie immediately understood the significance and artistic value of Constantinople on his first sight of the city in October 1840: "On the evening of Sunday, the 4th, we entered the Bosphorus, and cast anchor opposite the palace of the Sultan, and next morning saw Constantinople by daylight, in all her glory. . . . Of course everything we saw was a wonder—the streets, houses, and roads, dilapidated, yet crowded with people; nothing clean or tidy, all bustle, hurry, and business; yet no appearance of wealth, all living as if hand to mouth, with dresses splendid and dwellings wretched, still recalling, in all their doings, a race and a time from which civilization had sprung."[5]

Given the impact of such powerful first impressions, and that for most Orientalist artists their first physical encounter with the East will have been at a port, it is no surprise to find port scenes featuring in their paintings. Many artists are known to have sketched onboard ships as they traveled to and from the East, including Elisabeth Jerichau-Baumann (see page 116) and Jean-Léon Gérôme, who worked until dark every night when sailing back to Europe from the Orient.[6] Coastal views of Constantinople and the Bosphorus in

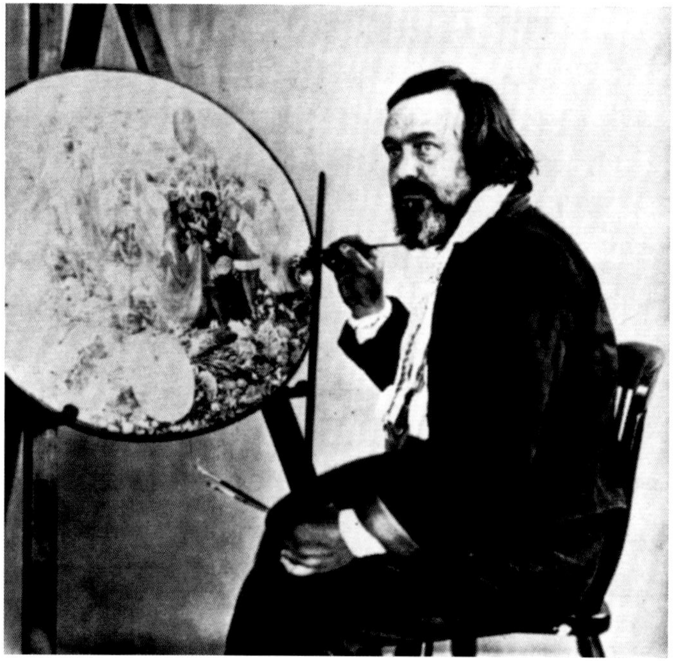

20. Henry Hering, photographic portrait of Richard Dadd painting *Contradiction: Oberon and Titania* (*c.*1856). Dadd was hired by Sir Thomas Phillips as companion–draftsman on an expedition from July 1842 to May 1843 to Italy, Greece, Turkey, Syria, Palestine, and Egypt. The trip had a profound impact on Dadd and influenced his work for the rest of his life.

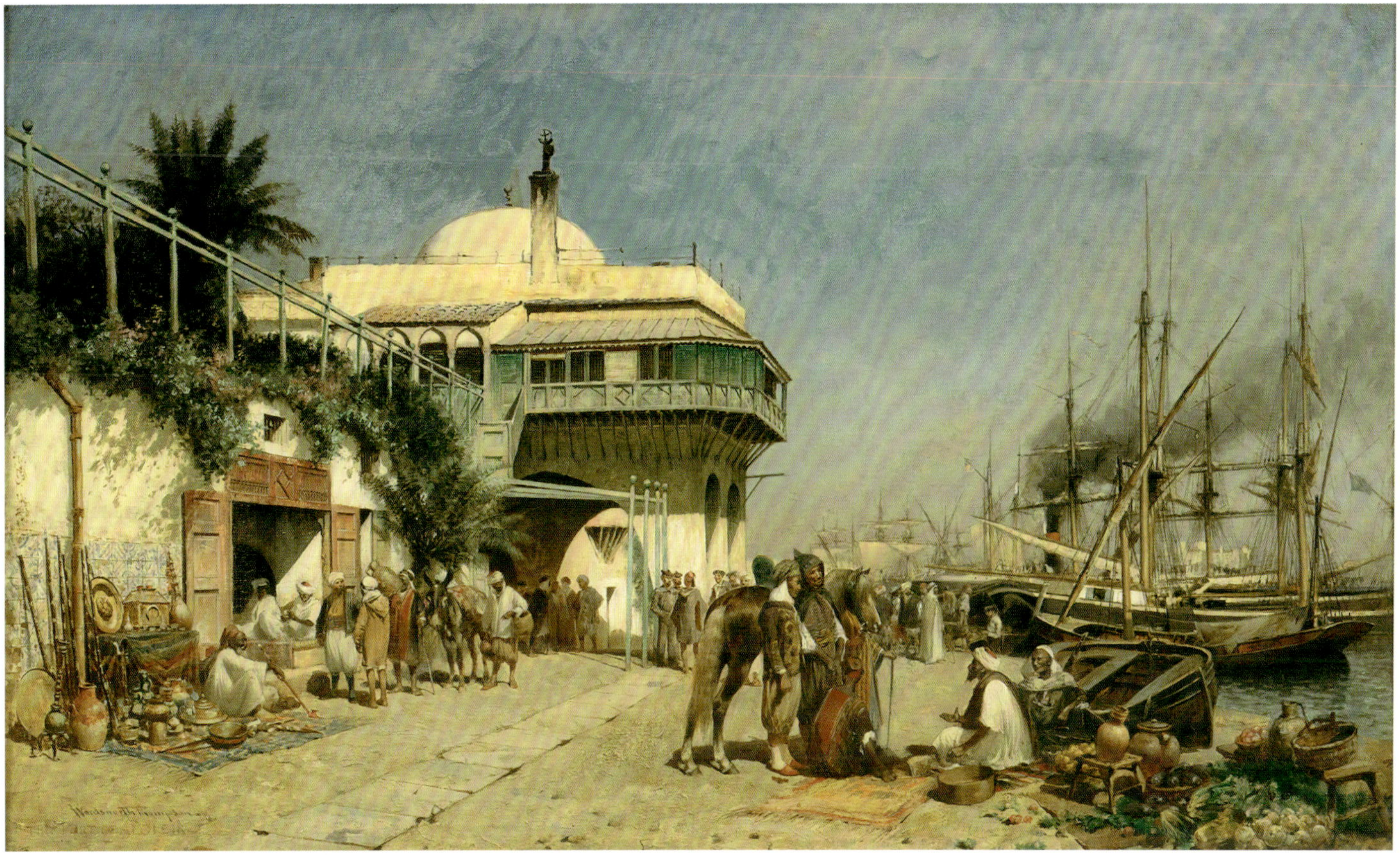

21. Alfred Wordsworth Thompson, *The Port of Algiers* (1883). Oil on canvas, 55.2 x 92.1 cm. American artist Thompson studied with Charles Gleyre in Paris and visited North Africa with his wife Mary in the winter of 1882–83. This view of Algiers was one of many Orientalist works he exhibited in the years that followed.

particular were commonplace by 1800, and more detailed studies of other ports across the region were to follow as the traffic in artist–travelers grew.

A particular favorite was the harbor at Algiers, for three centuries the impregnable stronghold of the fabled Barbary corsairs (until the French annexation of 1830), and therefore rich in iconography and glamor. It was painted by William Wyld in 1833 and again by Alfred Wordsworth Thompson exactly half a century later. Thompson's *The Port of Algiers* (Figure 21) depicts a busy scene of ships moored, tidy harbor buildings, and merchants engaged in business transactions. Other artists favored a more romantic interpretation, with Frederick Arthur Bridgman conjuring a nostalgic image in his book, *Winters in Algeria*. He describes wistfully how, four decades earlier, before the construction of a modern quay and boulevard in Algiers, "the Arab town came down to the water's edge, and boats were moored to rings in the very walls of the houses. What a picture!"[7]

The timeless quality of the location clearly struck a chord, as Bridgman went on to say how many of the traditional fishing smacks were still there at the time he was writing (the late 1880s), "their coloured sails thrown over the boom to shelter sailors making their *bouillabaisse*, the blue smoke curling up through the rigging." He produced various studies of the port in Algiers, one featuring as an illustration in *Winters in Algeria* and at least three of which were part of his major exhibition at the Art Institute of Chicago in May 1890. The traditional corner of the port, away from the modernized section built by the French colonial authorities, was also a focus for Albert Besnard (1849–1934), who in 1893–94 produced the romantically charged work, *The Port of Algiers at Dusk*.

Elsewhere, David Roberts depicted the ports at Suez and Tyre, views that were to form part of his bestselling lithography series with Louis Haghe (see pages 203–205), and in 1872 Edwin Lord Weeks painted the harbor at Tangier, the earliest known of his works in the Orientalist style.[8] Gustav Bauernfeind's *Jaffa, Recruiting of Turkish Soldiers in Palestine* (1888) (Figure 22) is notable for its depiction of a port not as a scenic subject but as the location for a particularly dramatic event: the enforced conscription of soldiers taken away by boat and the reaction of their distressed families on the shore.

First Footfall

Once passengers were disembarked, there were usually customs checks to be undertaken. This was an often random exercise, as Edwin Lord Weeks discovered on arrival at Trebizond (Trabzon) in Turkey, in July 1892: "An ancient Turk, who has been detailed to burrow into our bags and boxes, mercifully ignores the fire-arms and cartridges, but pounces at once on Murray's hand-books for Bengal and the Punjaub [Weeks's ultimate destination was India], and Adams's Cable Codex, which he scrutinizes severely. The printed page in an unknown language is considered by the Ottoman official to be fraught with peril to the peace of all true believers. These suspicious volumes are detained for the examination of the censor, but were kindly returned to us on the following day, duly indorsed on their fly-leaves, to the effect that nothing detrimental to the religion of Mohammed had been found."[9]

Having successfully negotiated customs and any other bureaucratic obstacles, travelers—by now usually accompanied by a retinue of (often uninvited) helpers and hangers-on—headed off to find accommodation. In many cases this was prearranged, the result of recommendations from home. Many artists arrived with letters of introduction from well-placed friends and acquaintances and, armed with such credentials, would take an early opportunity to seek out the most highly placed local officials or national representatives. Frederick Goodall arrived in Egypt in 1858 with letters of endorsement in his bag written by none other than David Roberts, whom he described as "my dear old friend."[10] Murray's *Handbooks* stressed what an essential part of pre-departure planning such documents were but equally conceded that all was not lost if one arrived without any: "Should the traveller be unprovided with letters, he will do well nevertheless, to call on those holding official situations. From them he will obtain correct information as to the state of the countries in which they reside, and how far travelling is practicable; any advice so given should be strictly adhered to."

In the early years of European travel to the Orient providing such advice to visitors was unlikely to prove too much of an imposition on "those holding official situations." The number of travelers was relatively small and for European officials posted abroad the new arrivals offered the prospect of welcome relief from the long weeks, if not months, of enforced social monotony in remote locations. However, as tourism expanded and the trickle of visitors grew into a steady stream, providing the level of service and support that had been feasible previously must have become increasingly irksome, if not impossible, for consuls and other foreign representatives. This was particularly the case in well-visited countries such as Egypt, where European diplomatic representatives had traditionally offered hospitality to visitors at their own residences. The British consul-generals in Egypt, Henry Salt (in post from 1815 to 1827) and John Barker (1827 to 1833), were often inundated with requests for accommodation and during the popular winter months rarely had the consular residence to themselves. Not only were consuls and other officials called upon to host passing travelers but they were also expected to provide advice and assistance on a myriad of different matters ranging from the hiring of servants to protective measures against malaria.

So it was that, soon after his arrival in Alexandria in 1838, David Roberts was being entertained at the dining table of the consul, Alexander Thorburn, and meeting with the consul-general, Patrick Campbell. The latter was "indefatigable in his endeavours to serve me," wrote Roberts, "and has given me letters of introduction to Mehemet Ali [the Egyptian ruler]."[11] Not all consuls were quite so quick off the mark. Edwin Lord Weeks, when visiting Rabat in Morocco in 1877, went to pay a call on the Spanish consul, who had previously extended a most enthusiastic invitation to visit the city and do him the honor of staying at his residence. "I found him in bed," recalled Weeks, "but having realized that his arduous duties of host and cicerone had fairly begun, he was soon ready to return with me to the custom-house and exert his official authority."[12]

Following pages: 22. Gustav Bauernfeind, *Jaffa, Recruiting of Turkish Soldiers in Palestine* (1888). Oil on canvas, 148 x 280.4 cm. This work is based on a real incident witnessed by Bauernfeind at Jaffa in 1885. In a letter to his mother and sister, he described a scene "where aged fathers wanted to embrace their sons for their last time, and were beaten off with cudgels by the rough soldiery. . . . Still, enough of this cruel spectacle!"

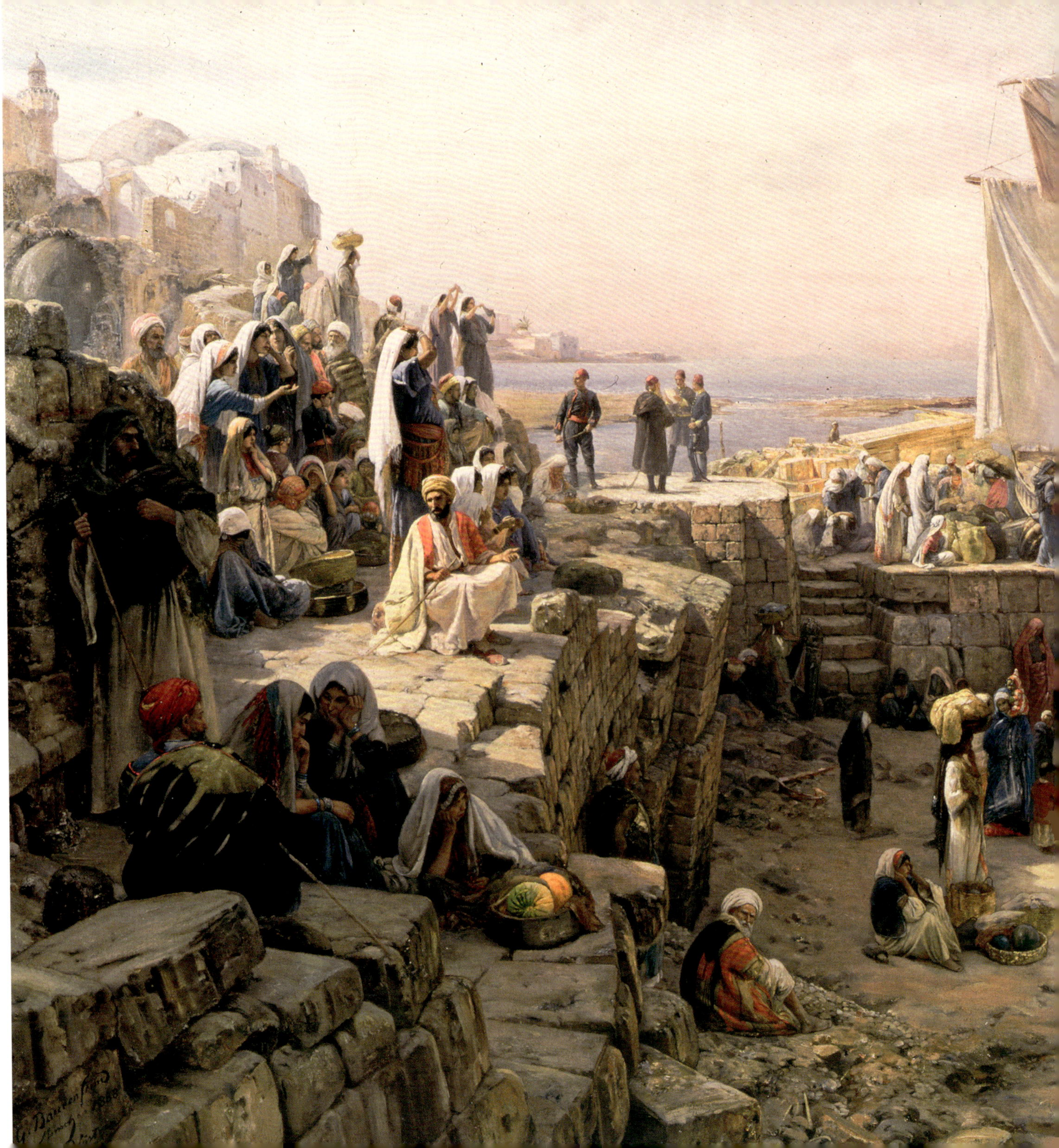

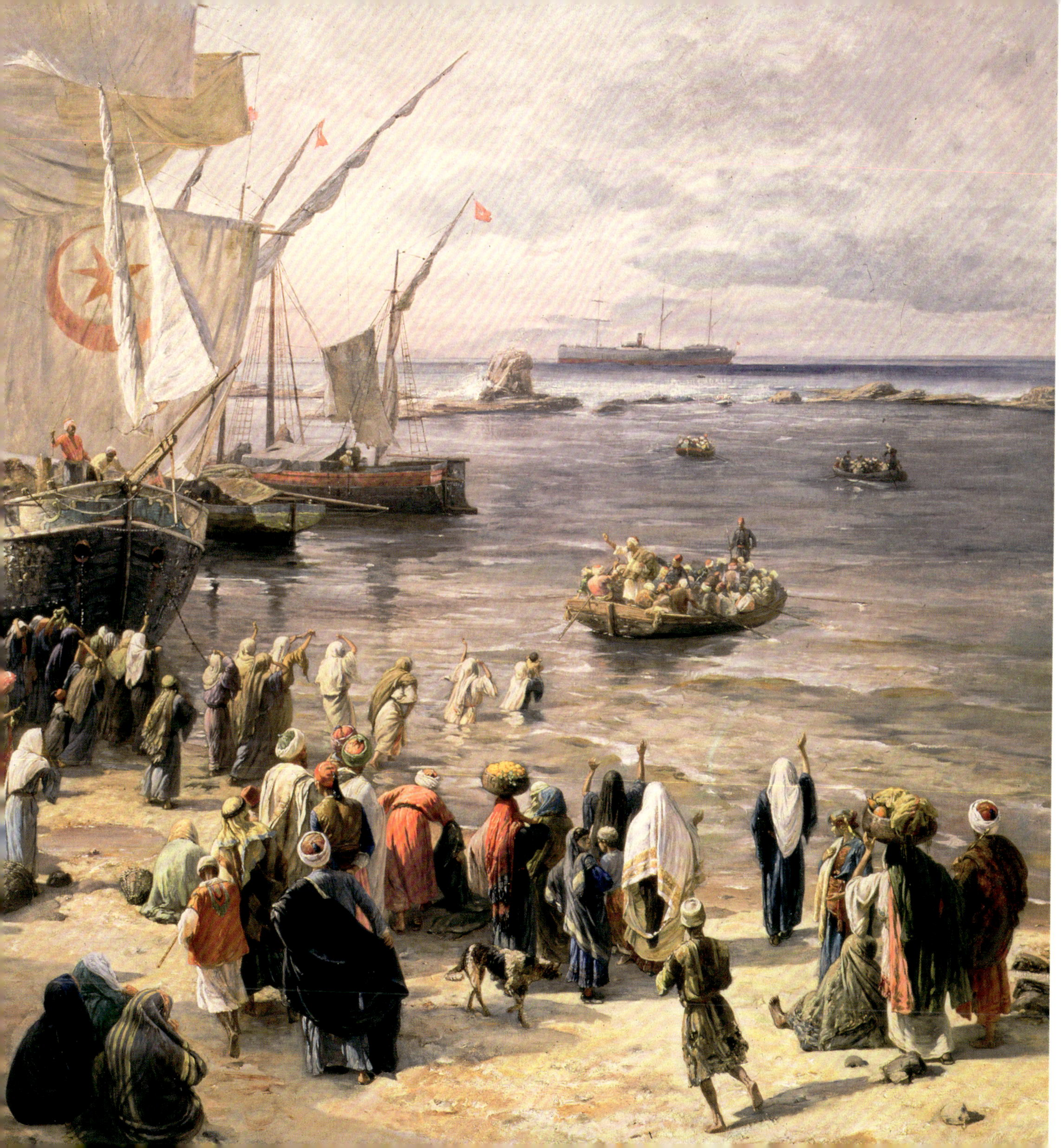

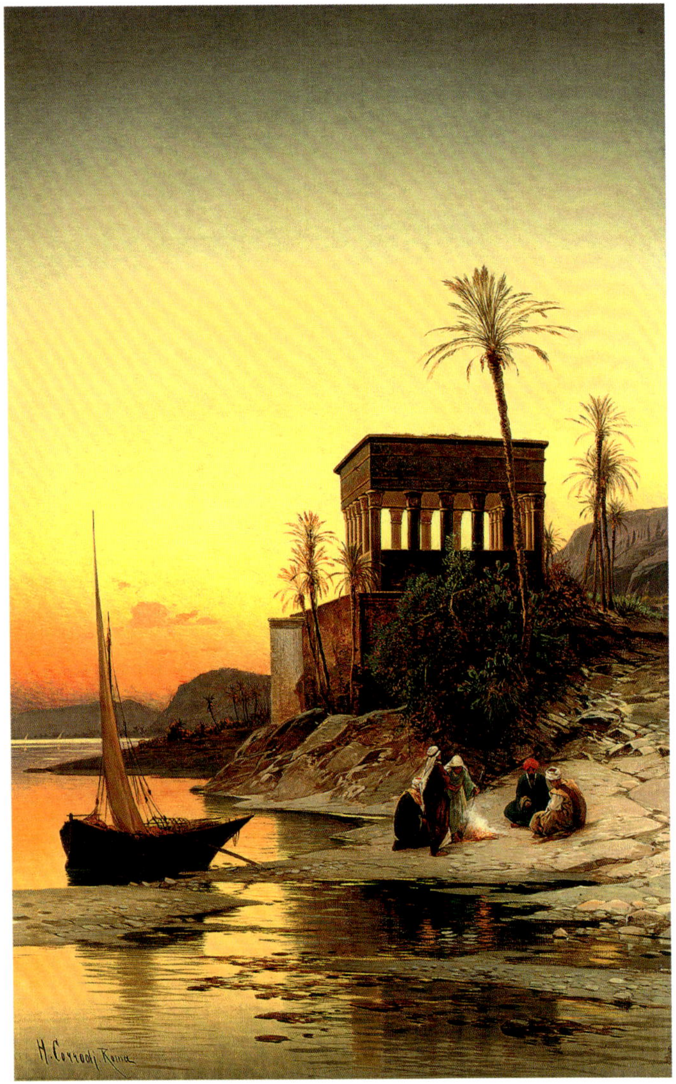

23. Hermann Corrodi, *Kiosk of Trajan, Philae on the Nile* (date unknown). Oil on canvas, 100.3 x 64.2 cm. Although Corrodi traveled to Turkey, North Africa, Egypt, and Syria, most of his works—including this one—were painted in his Rome studio.

The fact that Weeks, an American, should have forged a connection with a Spanish consul was not at all unusual. Fellow compatriots were usually the first port of call, but in their absence—or failure to oblige—artists would approach any person of influence, regardless of nationality. In any case, European or American interests in remoter locations were often represented by a local national or other expatriate, as Thomas Seddon (1821–56) discovered in Jaffa (see facing page). For artists particularly, the objective in seeking out these people was one of self-advancement and the procurement of special favors and access, including to possible clients; namely, the same principles as they would have applied at home, the demands of commerce being nothing if not universal.

Some artists were able to attract very senior clients indeed. Hermann Corrodi (1844–1905) spent the winter of 1876–77 in Egypt making studies for several pictures ordered by the country's ruler, Ismail Pasha.[13] It appears to have been the artist's first ever trip to the Orient and occurred at a time when the rulers of both Turkey and Egypt were actively commissioning works from European artists. Even so, few painters were able to land such a prize without having excellent connections, although it is not clear what these were in Corrodi's case, at least initially. The visit to Egypt was to change the direction of his career, for after returning to Rome to complete his paintings for Ismail Pasha he began to specialize in Orientalist works and later traveled to Syria and Palestine on commissions for Kaiser Wilhelm I, his reputation by that time clearly secured.

A similar level of patronage was enjoyed by Stanisław Chlebowski (1835–84), who studied in St. Petersburg, Munich, and then in Paris, where he was tutored by Gérôme (and with whom he began a long friendship).* Chlebowski's paintings came to the attention of the Ottoman sultan Abdülaziz, who in 1864 invited the artist to Constantinople, possibly as a result of the intervention of Chlebowski's compatriot Władysław Kościelski (known as Sefer Pasha), the sultan's *aide-de-camp*.[14] Chlebowski was appointed court painter and given a studio in the Dolmabahçe Palace, remaining in Constantinople until the overthrow of Sultan Abdülaziz in 1876. During that period he painted a large number of works, including portraits of the sultan, genre scenes of Constantinople street life, and an extensive series depicting Ottoman military triumphs through the centuries.

Local contacts, even when of less exalted status than the ruling monarch, were always valuable from the point of view of facilitating access to potential sitters, as Thomas Seddon discovered when he visited Jaffa in 1854: "We called on the consul, M. Assaed Kayat, who is a Syrian, but has been for some time in England, and has learned to appreciate us; so that, to our astonishment, we found a piano and an English governess in the house. The consul is very polite, and offers, if we stop, to introduce us to native families who would sit for painting."[15]

Securing the patronage and protection of a local ruler or potentate could also afford protection from the unwelcome attention of crowds and of petty officials on the cadge for a bribe. In an interview in 1898, Carl Haag (1820–1915) explained how essential such support could be. "I had to be protected against outbursts of fanaticism," he revealed, "and as I was under the wing of the Sultan [the Ottoman, Abdülmecid], so to speak, the Pasha, who was responsible for my well-being, had to make all sorts of arrangements before he could satisfy himself that there was no danger of my being molested."[16] Haag's connections were such that when in Jerusalem in 1859 he had—in a highly exceptional gesture—been given permission to paint the al-Aqsa Mosque, thanks to a *firman* (letter of consent) granted by the sultan at the specific request of Queen Victoria.

The impeccably well-connected British artist William Simpson (1823–99) had similar success in the same city a decade after Haag. He had traveled to Jerusalem from Egypt, where he had been given a personal tour of the almost completed Suez Canal by Ferdinand de Lesseps, its creator and mastermind. Simpson had a specific request to make of the British representative in Jerusalem, Noel Temple Moore, who was able to oblige. "I wished to make sketches of the Sacred Rock, under the Dome of the Rock, and Mr. Moore, our consul, made arrangements for me," Simpson wrote. "He gave orders that I was to be allowed to do as I pleased, and my pleasure was to get the place all to myself that morning. This desire I practically realised. A man attended upon me, but while I sketched he fell sound asleep . . . . On this morning, as I sat sketching, there was a perfect silence. Only a clock could be heard ticking, and a cat could be seen at times."[17] For an artist to enjoy such privileged access and be able to sketch in peace and at leisure was a rare treat.

* Gérôme stayed with Chlebowski when visiting Constantinople in 1875 and the two artists worked together, both in the city (at Rustem Pasha Mosque, for example) and further afield, on trips to Bursa and Adrianople. See Wójcik, "Jean-Léon Gérôme and Stanisław Chlebowski: The Story of a Friendship." See also page 165.

Places to Stay

In the early 1800s hardly anywhere in the Orient could boast hotels of the sort in which European travelers felt confident enough to stay. In cities such as Jerusalem and elsewhere in the Holy Land one option was to stay in local religious establishments such as monasteries and mission houses, but with a few exceptions the hotels were best avoided. In 1832 a British visitor to Algiers had condemned the four main establishments in the city as "execrable," but within a decade the situation had changed dramatically across much of the region. Increases in the number of overseas visitors prompted a proliferation of hotels and guesthouses, with ambitious modernization schemes transforming cities such as Alexandria.

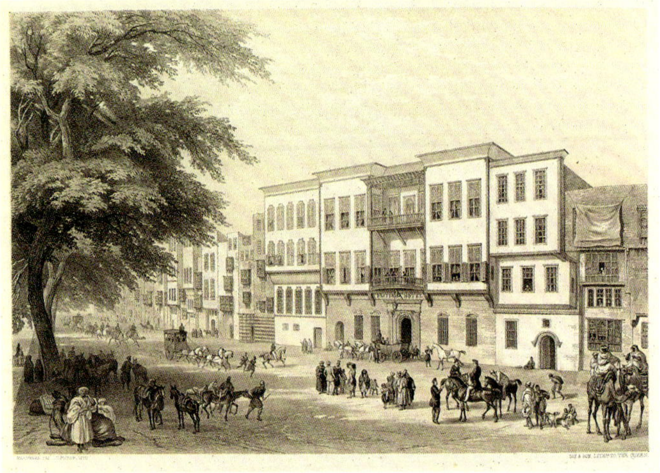

24. Shepheard's Hotel, Cairo, *c.*1849. Lithograph by Thomas Picken, after a drawing by Machereau. Originally known as the Hotel des Anglais and the British Hotel, Shepheard's remained popular with British visitors to Cairo until its destruction by fire during anti-British riots in January 1952.

Egypt's second city had undergone a dramatic facelift since the visit of British traveler Eliza Fay, who arrived there with her husband on 23 July 1779 en route for Calcutta and dismissed it as "little more than a heap of ruins."[18] In the intervening years Alexandria had been rejuvenated, becoming home to a prosperous and expanding European community and with an increasingly cosmopolitan atmosphere. As early as 1834, one expatriate resident remarked, "Everyone has building mania and there are several houses which would be magnificent even in Paris."[19] The potentially ironic comparison to France was one that would not have been lost on the large number of French or Paris-based artists who were traveling to Egypt at this time, despite its being increasingly within the British sphere of political influence and with the memories of Napoléon's invasion becoming ever more distant.

By the 1850s, hotels established primarily for foreigners had proliferated in all the main Oriental cities, especially Cairo.* An early standard was set by the Hôtel du Nil, which opened in 1836 and was favored by French visitors in particular—Flaubert stayed there in 1849. The Hôtel d'Orient and Shepheard's Hotel came slightly later, but both were to become institutions in their own right and the latter became the preferred choice among British travelers. As meeting-places for artists the Cairo hotels were second to none—David Roberts writes of having gone to "to Hill's Hotel to hear the news of England"[20]—and while for some visitors patriotism doubtlessly influenced their choice of

---

* Even so, some travelers preferred to rent houses rather than lodge in hotels. See pages 71–75 for examples.

where to stay, there was a decidedly international atmosphere in most of the establishments. William Thackeray had experienced this when he visited the city in 1844, staying at the Hôtel d'Orient, and musing on how it was "finding England here in a French hotel kept by an Italian, at the city of Grand Cairo, in Africa."[21] A quarter of a century later the advent of mainstream foreign tourism into Egypt, a phenomenon largely engineered by Thomas Cook, saw that company later build hotels for its guests in both Luxor (The Luxor Hotel, opened in 1877) and Aswan (The Cataract, 1900). Both were stayed in regularly by artists, as was the Winter Palace in Luxor, which opened to guests in 1907.

Similar quality hotels were also opened in the other great cities of the Orient, notably Constantinople, where artists regularly gathered at the Hôtel d'Angleterre—more often known as Misseri's and run by the eponymous ex-dragoman (see page 35)*—and at the Pera Palace, which opened to guests in 1895. Earlier in the century many travelers and artists had headed for Madame Josephine's, a boarding house sometimes known as the Hotel Constantinople, described as "excellent of its kind"[22] and run by the eponymous lady, who in October 1840 sat for David Wilkie in Turkish dress.** Damascus was traditionally less well served than either Cairo or Constantinople, but the modest Dimitri's Hotel on the Street Called Straight was a popular focal point for visiting foreigners from the 1840s to the 1860s and was frequented by the likes of Lady Jane Digby and Richard Burton.[23] Beirut boasted Bassoul's, another establishment aimed at Western visitors and run by a former dragoman.

The busiest period for hotels in the Orient was from October through to April when, like the vast majority of overseas visitors to the region, most artists chose to travel. Oppressive humidity, sandstorms, and poor visibility could combine to make high summer unbearable, especially in Egypt, the Maghreb, and lowland Levant. The cooler weather and—usually, at least—clearer light and atmosphere of the winter months was far more conducive to sightseeing and to sketching or painting outdoors, even if the throngs of fellow visitors could be irksome at times.

Geographical Preferences

Certain artists only made one expedition to the Orient—Eugène Delacroix and David Roberts being two of the most famous examples—but others developed a much more long-term relationship with the region and indeed with particular countries within it. Some traveled there repeatedly over many years, one of the most far-ranging being Théodore Frère (1814–88). After an initial visit to Algeria in 1836, Frère traveled widely and regularly to many parts of the broader region for the next three decades and more, his last trip being to Egypt when he accompanied the Empress Eugénie of France to the opening of the Suez Canal in 1869 (an event at which many other artists were also present). It was a fitting finale to an extraordinary and episodic odyssey that took Frère from Constantine and Constantinople to

* Thackeray stayed at the hotel in 1844 and remarked: "Misseri, the faithful and chivalrous Tartar, is transformed into the most quiet and gentlemanlike of landlords, a great deal more gentlemanlike in manner and appearance than most of us." See *Notes of a Journey from Cornhill to Grand Cairo*, 103–104.
** The resulting portrait, *Madame Josephine the Landlady of the Hotel Constantinople in a Turkish Dress* (Figure 25), featured in Wilkie's *Oriental Sketches*.

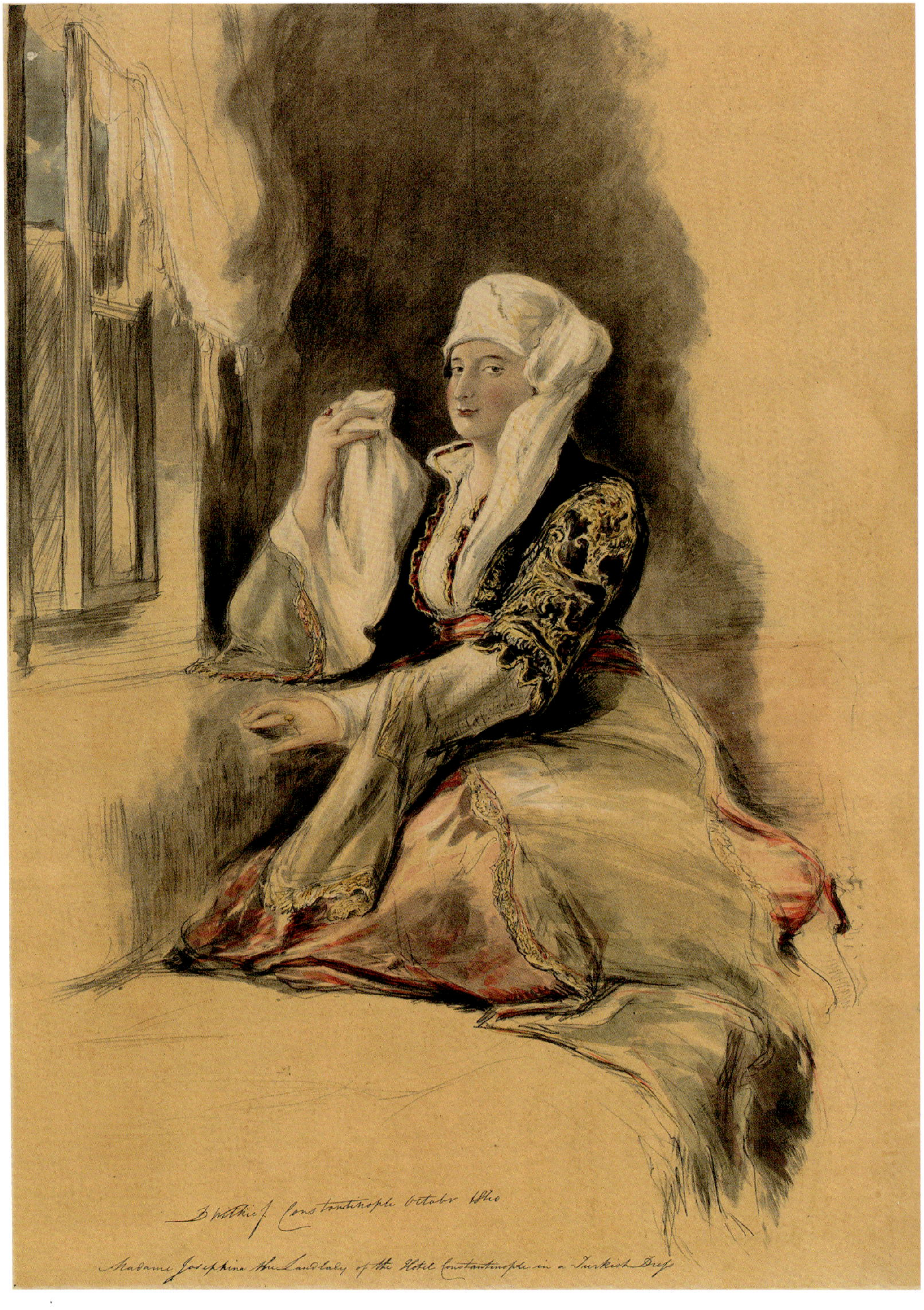

25. David Wilkie, *Madame Josephine the Landlady of the Hotel Constantinople in a Turkish Dress* (1840), from Wilkie's *Sketches in Turkey, Syria & Egypt, 1840 & 1841*. Hand-colored lithograph, 45 x 32.8 cm.

Smyrna, Cairo to Nubia, and Beirut to Palmyra, and which made him one of the few French artists to have ever painted Jerusalem and Damascus.

Although many of the Orientalists traveled widely, if not quite as extensively as Frère, the single most visited country was undoubtedly Egypt. Figures such as Ludwig Deutsch, Rudolf Ernst, John Frederick Lewis, and Leopold Müller derived much (and, in some cases, all) of their firsthand experience of the Orient from their visits there. Other artists, including Frederick Goodall, Carl Haag, William Holman Hunt, Edward Lear, David Roberts, and Thomas Seddon, all spent time in Egypt but also traveled extensively in the Levant, with Constantinople also regarded by many artists as somewhere they needed to visit at least once on their peregrinations. For the majority of French artists, and the Paris-based Americans Frederick Arthur Bridgman and (to a lesser extent) Edwin Lord Weeks, their focus was primarily on North Africa.

While there was no insuperable formal division between artists who concentrated on the Maghreb and those who favored Egypt and the Levant, a sense of two parallel worlds emerged in the Orientalist psyche. An insight into these two geographical camps can be gleaned from examining the experience of Étienne Dinet, whose long relationship with Algeria is one of the most fascinating stories of any Orientalist artist. Dinet was not the first Orientalist artist to explore Algeria—Eugène Delacroix, Eugène Fromentin, and Gustave Guillaumet (1840–87), among others, had all been there before him—but it was Dinet's name that became inextricably linked to that country and particularly in connection with the tribal communities of the desert fringe. From his very first visit in 1884, Dinet was captivated by Algeria's landscapes, its people, and their culture. He eventually settled in the picturesque oasis town of Bou-Saâda, where he had fallen in love with the southern light,[24] and later converted to Islam, taking the name Nasreddine.

Less well known is Dinet's 1897 visit to Egypt. His lukewarm response to what he found there flags up the artistic and emotional gulf that divided some artists—geographically, at least—from their peers. "Visitors to this country should view it from the standpoint of either tourists or scholars," Dinet wrote dismissively in a letter to Léonce Bénédite, the president of the Société des Peintres Orientalistes Français in Paris.[25] Dinet nonetheless produced some interesting works as a result of his Egyptian sojourn, including two panoramic views of Old Cairo (one of which is reproduced as Figure 26), and his reaction was not necessarily typical of the "maghrébophiles."

Eugène Fromentin had also been a specialist in Algerian scenes until he visited Egypt in 1869, a journey that prompted a new and highly successful chapter in his work. Meanwhile, the geographical favoritism demonstrated by the French in the Maghreb and the British in Egypt cut both ways; when discussing the relative ease and safety he enjoyed while sketching on the streets of Alexandria, Frederick Goodall observed, "Had it been in the north-western corner of Africa [which was French-controlled], I might have had considerable difficulty in being permitted to draw at all, and had I penetrated toward the interior I should have had to provide myself with a tiny army."[26]

Those artists visiting the Middle East regularly would typically spend some or all of the winter there, returning home in time for the spring exhibitions at the Paris Salon or London's Royal Academy. This was a pattern followed almost

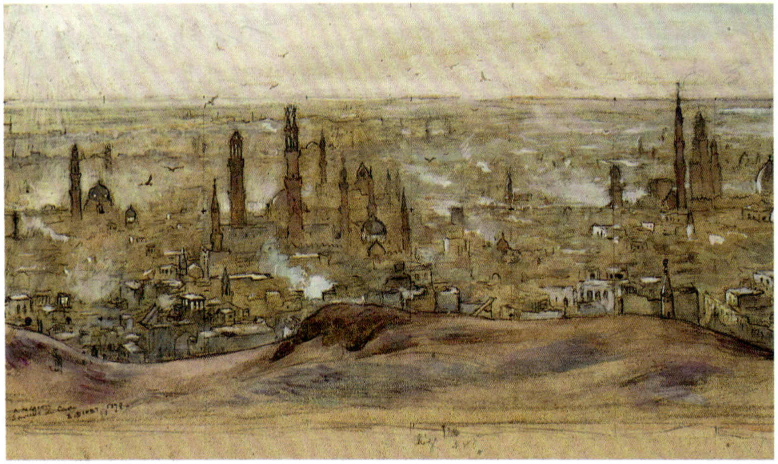

26. Étienne Dinet, *Le Caire: brumes, poussières et fumées du matin* (Cairo: haze, dust, and morning smoke) (1897). Watercolor, gouache, charcoal, and pencil on paper, 27.7 x 47.7 cm.

religiously by Jean-Léon Gérôme in particular. He made repeated and prolonged visits to Egypt, as well as shorter trips to Turkey, Palestine, and Algeria, but was always anxious to maintain his presence, reputation, and professional responsibilities back in Paris. Frederick Arthur Bridgman favored a similar seasonal pattern. The link to home and to one's clients and the market was an important one, not least for securing and promoting sales. Even Dinet, so settled in Algeria, returned regularly to France in order to finish the pictures he was preparing to show at the Salon or for his Parisian dealer.

These were journeys that in just a few decades had, for the rich and privileged at least, passed from being intrepid expeditions to something that, while not exactly akin to hopping on a city omnibus, was something of a routine: "Visits for the winter to Tunis or Algiers were so easy and frequent that they are often not even recorded in the biographies of the painters who made them, and are almost unmentioned in their diaries and letters."[27] This can make the piecing together of the precise dates and frequency of visits by individual artists, let alone the content of specific itineraries, particularly problematic. What is much clearer is that whether an artist made only one journey to the Orient or several, at the end of each trip there was a need to return home, open up the studio, and start the job of turning the sketches, notes, and photographs into paintings and cash (see chapter 4).

Most artists visiting Egypt arrived first at Alexandria, described by Paul Lenoir as "the inevitable antechamber of Cairo, as, in a badly planned apartment, one is forced to pass through the kitchen in order to reach the drawing-room."[28] Few of them stayed there for long, however. The city had only a handful of sights, notably Cleopatra's Needle (buried in sand, and then removed to London in 1877), Pompey's Pillar, and the local bazaar, a short list of attractions to which could be added the ghoulish voyeurism of the infamous slave market. Both David Roberts and Thomas Seddon paid a visit to the latter, with Seddon describing it as "a most painful scene"[29] and Roberts finding it "a sickening sight, and I left it proud that I belonged to a nation who had abolished slavery."[30] Such reactions provide an interesting counterpoint to the frequently stylized depiction of slaves and slavery in Orientalist works, exemplified in *The Slave Market, Constantinople* by William Allen (1782–1850). The artist manipulated the horror of the real situation in favor of a sanitized version that was more appealing to his audience. Equally tailored portrayals (if rather more accurate in terms of content) were offered by William James Müller (1812–45) in his 1841 work, *The Slave Market at Cairo, Egypt*, and by Jean-Léon Gérôme, who was to use the slave market as a vehicle for his presentation of naked white women. These were usually off-limits as an appropriate subject for painting, but masqueraded in these situations as "Circassian slaves" and were therefore acceptable.*

The main Egyptian destination for artists was Cairo, accessible from Alexandria by water via the Mahmoudieh Canal and the Nile, or by rail after the mid-1850s. What awaited them there was little short of a revelation. Carl Haag, who first visited the city in the autumn of 1858, wrote in a letter to the secretary of the Old Water-Colour Society, "Tell those that are in search of new ground of subjects for their pencil that there is but one Cairo, and artists ought to see it."[31] William Holman Hunt had been similarly impressed four years earlier. In a February 1854 letter to his patron, Thomas Combe, he waxed lyrical: "Last night was the most brilliant and calmest moonlight night I ever saw—after dinner we all went into the garden and sat for an hour and more smoking our hookahs and admiring the beauty of the scene. In truth I believe this country would suit me much better than any other in the world and I think if I could have a few friends with me I should stop in the East altogether."[32] He rekindled his initial reaction to Cairo in his book *Pre-Raphaelitism and the Pre-Raphaelite Brotherhood*, describing how "the noise of life was like the ringing bells of a festa and it was impossible to turn one's eyes from the open window, where each minute brought forward a new scene, each scene being one of the perennial dramas of the East, heard of, imagined often, but hitherto cut off from me by the intervening leagues of sea."[33]

* Relevant works by Gérôme include *The Slave Market* (1866), *For Sale* (*The Slave Market*) (1871), *For Sale* (*The Slave Market*) (1873), and *Slave Sale at Rome* (1884).

Dragomans

An early priority for many arriving foreigners was the hiring of a dragoman. Modern parlance has them as 'cultural mediators,' but nineteenth-century dragomans were seen at the time as translators, interpreters, guides, and fixers—the English word dragoman being derived from *tercuman*, a term of ancient Semitic origin which later entered Arabic and then Turkish to mean 'interpreter.' The earliest references to dragomans date back to at least the early sixteenth century and in the Ottoman realm particularly they were an essential element in the worlds of trade and diplomacy, a professional cadre of skilled men who played an important role with visiting merchants and foreign delegations, helping shape commercial and political relations. It was an esteemed and influential position, with dragomans appearing regularly in paintings of the Ottoman court alongside sultans, viziers, and ambassadors. Some were significant and wealthy enough to appear in their own portraits, among them the dragoman for the French ambassador in Constantinople, who was painted by the artist Fenerci Mehmet Efendi in 1811.[34]

Dragoman skills were readily extended to include providing services to other types of more casual visitor and the nineteenth century saw a huge increase in their number, especially in Egypt with that country's growing popularity among foreign visitors. However, this expansion coincided paradoxically with a downgrading of the seniority and strategic role that dragomans had enjoyed previously. Increased diplomatic representation across the Middle East and North Africa saw many of the responsibilities previously discharged by dragomans, particularly in the fields of interpreting and translating, increasingly handled direct by professional foreign diplomats trained in Arabic or Turkish, or by expatriates of longstanding who had become fluent in one or both of these languages. As a group, dragomans were to find themselves demoted, fulfilling a role primarily concerned with servicing tourists.

Nineteenth-century handbooks such as Murray's recommended dragomans as an asset to any visit, giving advice on how to hire them as well as details on appropriate rates of pay and the services that could be expected. Yet the same sources also paint a generally poor picture of these supposed "assets," betraying a deeply rooted assumption that, unless proven otherwise, they were unreliable and thieving scoundrels who had to be watched at every turn. Contemporary handbooks are full of warnings and tips on how to avoid being fleeced or misled by one's dragoman, and even as late as 1916 the new edition of *Macmillan's Guide to Egypt and the Sûdân* stressed the importance of keeping them in their place: "Travellers must remember that the dragoman, whether Egyptian or Syrian, dressed in European, Turkish, or Arab dress, is merely a servant, and should always ride on the box and not *in* the carriage. They are quick to take advantage of the slightest familiarity."

Despite such potential tribulations, dragomans were an essential part of a traveler's time in countries such as Egypt. As general factotum, a dragoman was responsible for almost every aspect of a visit, usually dealing with his clients on at least a daily basis when in Cairo, Constantinople, or Jerusalem and accompanying them around the clock when on excursions further afield. Indeed, those visitors—including many artists—who wanted to explore beyond the main sights of these cities could often only do so through the auspices of a dragoman. The services of those based in Cairo, for example, included not only the arrangement of boat trips up the Nile but also more ambitious expeditions to Sinai and beyond, into Palestine and Syria. It was on such extended trips that artists were particularly dependent upon their dragoman and his team, sometimes establishing very positive and rewarding relationships. Efficient and reliable dragomans were understandably much in demand and often recommended between travelers (see chapter 3).

Sartorial Concerns

Once settled in Cairo, and with a dragoman hired, the minds of many new arrivals turned toward the thorny issue of whether to invest in local apparel. The wearing by Westerners of Oriental dress—or "cross-cultural dressing," as twenty-first-century parlance might have it—had fascinated outsiders to the region for centuries and particularly since the appearance in their midst of cosmopolitan, trans-cultural figures like Sir Robert Shirley and Lady Mary Wortley Montagu and the accompanying fad for masquerades and costume parties (see pages 10–11). However, dressing *à la turque* in a London ballroom was one thing; to do so while actually in the Orient was a different matter entirely.

In the early decades of the nineteenth century the wearing of local dress was the norm for European visitors and it was considered "not merely inconvenient but often dangerous to travel there as a European."* By the 1830s the situation in the cities at least was changing, largely as a result of the increase in diplomatic representation and improved protection afforded to foreign visitors by their consulates. By wearing "Turkish dress" the potential risk of blending in—visually, at least, because the game was usually up the second anyone opened their mouth—was such that Henry Salt, the British consul-general in Egypt 1815–27, felt moved to warn visiting British ladies against the wearing of local dress "as being a species of disguise which rendered it impossible for him to be responsible for the safety of those who wore it."[35] By mid-century—when senior Ottoman officials and military personnel were themselves increasingly adopting Western dress as part of the Tanzimât reforms**—for a first-time visiting European in the increasingly cosmopolitan cities of Cairo or Constantinople to don the traditional robes and headgear of the local people and then wander the streets was regarded as at best an affectation and at worst an incitement.

Different practicalities applied outside the major cities. For visitors such as artists, often intent on going off the beaten track, there were obvious practical advantages in passing successfully as a local. Access to mosques and other Islamic holy sites was denied to non-Muslims and in January 1839 David Roberts had been informed by the British consul that the only way of visiting them safely was to go in disguise. "I must assume the Turkish dress," he noted in his journal, "and tomorrow must have my whiskers shaved off. This is too bad; but having taken such a long journey, I must not stick at trifles; and having been the first artist who has made drawings here, I hope for a successful result."[36]

Donning local dress also allowed artists to move around less conspicuously in busy situations such as markets and thereby avoid the sort of negative attention and hassle which for many was a major obstacle to sketching, painting, photographing—or even observing—in public. There was also a practical value to wearing local clothes, which were usually more suitable to the prevailing climate and conditions than traditional European outfits.

Whatever misgivings might have existed about new arrivals in the Orient sporting local attire, there is ample evidence of Orientalist artists doing so, both newcomers and old hands, and especially when "on the road": Gérôme, Goodall, Haag, Roberts, and Seddon are all recorded as doing so, and many others doubtless did likewise. In *Diary of a Journey to Damascus* (1847), Lord Castlereagh describes his own visit to an outfitter in the Cairo bazaar, and the frustrations he expressed over the protracted nature of the process were doubtless echoed by many of the artists who did likewise. "The merchant goes through the form of pipes, coffee, and rigmarole with you," Castlereagh explained, "but then you must wait, while he proceeds to another stall, where he gets a pipe, and more rigamarole; and if he returns

* Thompson, "Osman Effendi: A Scottish Convert to Islam," 88. The wearing of European dress, even by visiting Europeans, had been banned by successive Ottoman sultans and in 1777 Alexandria was the only town in Egypt where it was considered possible to do so safely; see also Rodenbeck, "Dressing Native."

** The Tanzimât was a series of centralizing Ottoman reforms, heavily influenced by European notions of government and justice and introduced between 1839 and 1876 during the reigns of Sultan Abdülmecid and Sultan Abdülaziz.

again to you, the same farce is repeated, so that the whole affair of cloth, silk, buttons, lining, lace, measuring, fixing, time, and fashion, may occupy half a day, and yet the work may be unfinished."*

Once finally acquired, the new costume usually produced the required transformation. In a letter home from Cairo early in 1854 Thomas Seddon described the effect of his outfit, even adding a sketched self-portrait (Figure 83): "You will wonder what that horrible brigand on the first page of this letter means. It is an attempt to portray myself as I walk about in the sun, a kufeeya wrapped around my head, with a crimson-and-gold striped handkerchief, and innumerable small tassels dangling from it. To avoid annoyance from the boys, I have locked up my wide-awake [a European-style hat with a low crown and wide brim], and donned a tarbouch; and having now a very respectable beard, I pass current for an average Mussulman."[37] Seddon sketched a second self-portrait of himself in local dress a few weeks later when at the Pyramids and traveling with William Holman Hunt. This sketch shows him "in my painting costume, consisting of wide-awake hat, with my kufeeya round it as a turban, and a long white Arab shirt and shawl! This has many conveniences, which I cannot make Hunt appreciate. All above the girdle forms a huge pocket, into which anything and everything may be stuffed."[38] Hunt was indeed unconvinced by what he considered an unnecessary "adoption of the costume," and initially refused to wear any local apparel. He was also less than flattering about Seddon's appearance, describing it in a letter to Dante Gabriel Rossetti (Figure 27) as "simply amusing" and including a semi-caricature in his own hand of Seddon in full Arab regalia, shown billowing in the wind with the Pyramids behind and complete with curly-toed slippers.[39] Despite his early objections, Hunt was later to find it expedient to adopt certain items of local clothing, including the keffiyeh.

Beyond practicalities, there was another, more symbolic, advantage to dressing like a local. For those foreigners who chose to reside in the Orient for longer periods, such as Edward William Lane, John Gardner Wilkinson, Émile Prisse d'Avennes, and John Frederick Lewis, the wearing of local clothes was an absolute given. These men mixed in Arab, Muslim society—Lane, Wilkinson, and Prisse more so than Lewis—and as such were outside the sartorial code that applied to other expatriate visitors. Lewis in particular was very successful in building around himself a cult of the "expert gentleman abroad." More transient foreign residents sought to enhance their legitimacy by adopting similar habits and in so doing establish the idea that special rules applied to them. Foremost among these was the wearing of Arab dress, a privilege reserved for those foreigners who, it was inferred, spoke Arabic, understood the local culture, and knew the country and its people almost as well as their own. This was rarely if ever true, but it helped a select band of

27. William Holman Hunt, caricature of Thomas Seddon in local dress. Ink on paper, 8.3 x 11 cm. Drawn by Hunt at the Pyramids at Giza and incorporated into a letter to Dante Gabriel Rossetti dated 29 March 1854.

* Castlereagh, *A Journey to Damascus*, vol. 1, 186. Castlereagh was depicted in Arab dress by John Frederick Lewis in *A Frank Encampment* (Figure 41).

is at the Pyramids – painting a landscape with the three blocks as principal objective – I never knew such
an extraordinary combination of ability &c and absurdity &c as he is – his devout admiration of the arabs is
perfectly exasperating – they are the meanest sneaks in the world and yet he never tires in praising them. his
adoption of the costume is simply amusing in the result for somehow the wind and other little circumstances disturb
the arrangement with a familiarity never assumed towards a native if this indeed were
all however I should merely regard him with that amiable consideration
which we should ever extend towards our fellow creatures who
exhibit the weaknesses of cockney nature but to my shame,
a few weeks ago he sat down gravely before a Snake charmer
with the landlord of our hotel present, and went through
the incantation to render him venom proof with
as much solemnity and evident faith as any church
ceremony could have received I am certain he
will get into some frightful danger from this
stupid degrading act for he professes a belief with more
seriousness than I have seen him assume in any other matter
since I arrived that he could handle serpents and scorpions
with impunity and indeed two or three days ago when he was here he
assured me that he had had several of these reptiles in his
hands and he attributed his escape to the virtue of the charm
I have done all I can – if he will be foolish despite every
argument of mine nothing but good fortune can save him – He makes considerable progress with
the language and thus in business arrangements is a useful companion – If you or others write to me
after receiving this observe that you are to address it immediately Poste restante Jerusalem – or if after
a week or two to Beyrout – I go to the Holy city within a week or two but I fear that it will be impossible
for me to stay very long – I dreamt the other night that I met old Woolner in the other hotel – tell me how
he is – Remember to all William especially and your Mother and sisters especially also Yours W Holman.

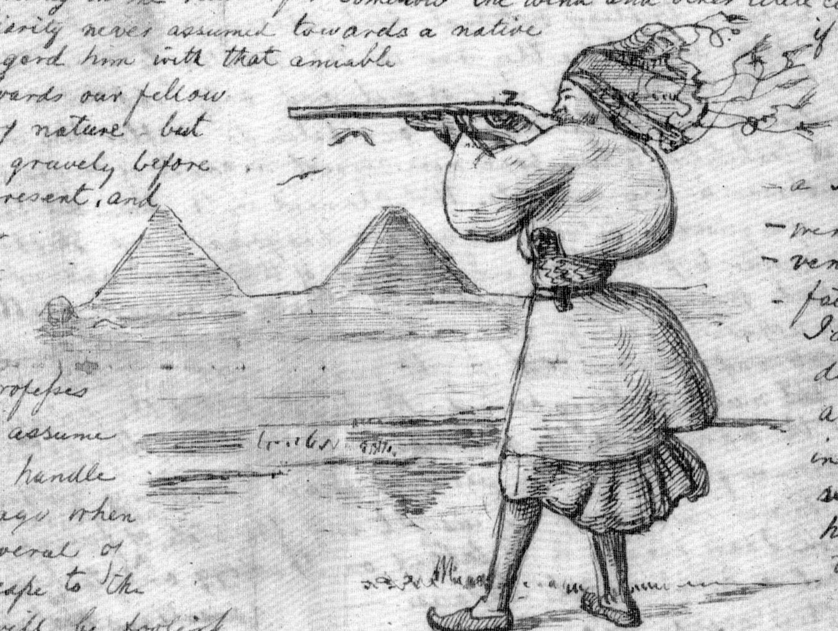

106

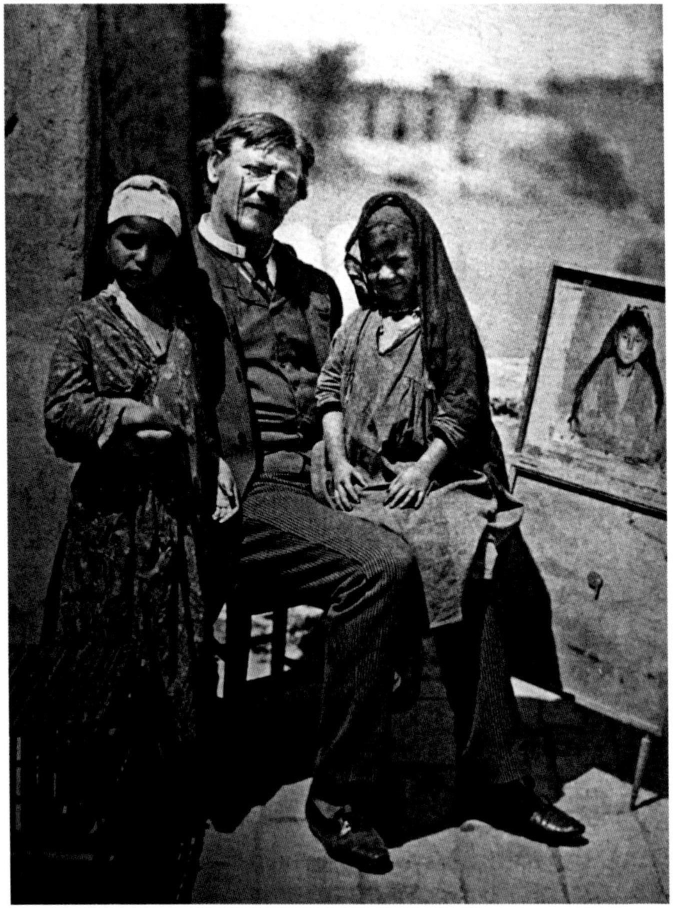

28. Leopold Müller, photographed on the terrace of his studio in Cairo, with two girl models. Photographer unknown, date probably late 1870s–early 1880s. Unlike some of his Orientalist peers, Müller eschewed the wearing of local dress when visiting the region.

artist–travelers to establish clear water between themselves and the increasing numbers of more casual tourists, a contemporary equivalent perhaps of the distinction made today by those favoring local homestays over mass tourism hotels.

Meanwhile, other artists found themselves in a state of sartorial limbo. Some, among them Leopold Müller, refused to make any concession to local conditions—he was photographed painting outdoors in the heat, incongruously wearing a starched collar and tie as if he were at home in Vienna. This is all the more surprising given that Müller is known to have visited Egypt on no fewer than nine occasions between 1873 and 1886, often staying for several months at a time. Gustav Bauernfeind appears to have adopted a hybrid style, combining European and Oriental apparel, and was amused by the reaction of local people to his idiosyncratic appearance. "Some are quite amazed that I should have a parasol on my Tarboosh (the red hat they wear)," he wrote, "others called me Father of the Casserole (Abu Aanshereh) because my hat looked like I'd clapped a pot on my head."[40] This last piece of apparel may well have been the pith helmet or topee—the clichéd icon of the nineteenth-century European abroad—that Bauernfeind chose to depict himself wearing in a busy Damascus street (see page 92). In similar vein, Edward Lear attracted attention for an extraordinary hat with a brim "as large as a cart-wheel," designed to give protection from the sun and which earned him the nickname from the locals of "the father of the white turban like a table."[41]

Times were changing however, and some later artists felt less inclined to wear items of local dress. During the second half of the nineteenth century those foreigners who did so in everyday situations increasingly risked the disparaging accusation from their compatriots of having "gone native." This was partly a response to the fallout of the Indian Mutiny of 1857, which had irreparably fractured the relationship between the British colonial overlords and their subjects across India. As a result, fraternization and intermarriage—quite commonplace earlier in the century—were very much discouraged and there was increasing professional and social segregation between races. This revision to the social code seeped insidiously but rapidly into most corners of the British Empire and was particularly relevant in Egypt, the main staging-post between Britain and India and which acted as a "decompression chamber" for India-based British military officers, civil servants, and their families when on leave. At the same time, the increasing numbers of Europeans who were traveling in the Orient had an impact on the dress-code situation—the sheer weight of their numbers bred both a confidence on their part and increasing familiarity among local people of Western dress and ways, thereby helping erase any last remnants of the visitors' sense that they needed to "blend in."

Yet the quasi-theatrical dimension that underscored the wearing by European artists of local clothes when living and traveling in the Orient was far from redundant. Its role in establishing their credentials and credibility as expert authorities on the Orient remained potent as a reputational device once back home. It also conferred a romantic and exotic quality, always an asset when it comes to self-promotion and something that several artists were able to use very effectively to help define their public and professional personae (see chapter 4).

Taking Up Residence

One option for those artists seeking a more authentic Oriental experience (and a greater degree of privacy), potentially at least, was to rent a house. This had the added advantage of being cheaper (usually) than staying in a hotel and made even greater sense if the intention was to stay in one place for some time. When Frederick Goodall arrived in Cairo in 1858 he set about securing a house almost immediately. It was, inevitably, a process in which useful contacts played their part. "Most of the first fortnight was spent in taking a house—to get settled for work—in the Copt quarter," Goodall wrote. "I was helped in this business by a German photographer, who was acquainted with the Copt Patriarch. The matter would have been prolonged indefinitely had it not been for my newly found friend; he arranged to have everything carried through without delay. The final negotiations were conducted at twilight in the court-yard, by the light of a lantern, by three priests in their great black turbans. The scene was perfect in its chiaroscuro, and Rembrandt would have loved to paint it." Goodall goes on to describe the less romantic aspects of his new accommodation, not least its infestation with flies, the eggs of which could be destroyed by "a strong decoction of juice of capsicum." He was advised to limewash the interior, partly in white and partly in color, and then set about buying necessary household goods such as cooking utensils and commissioning an upholsterer to make cushions and mattresses, which was achieved "luxuriously for a few pounds."[42]

The day after the house was ready for occupancy, Goodall had a chance meeting in the street with his friend Carl Haag. Haag had traveled to Egypt from England via Germany, Trieste, and Athens, and when he ran into Goodall he was preparing

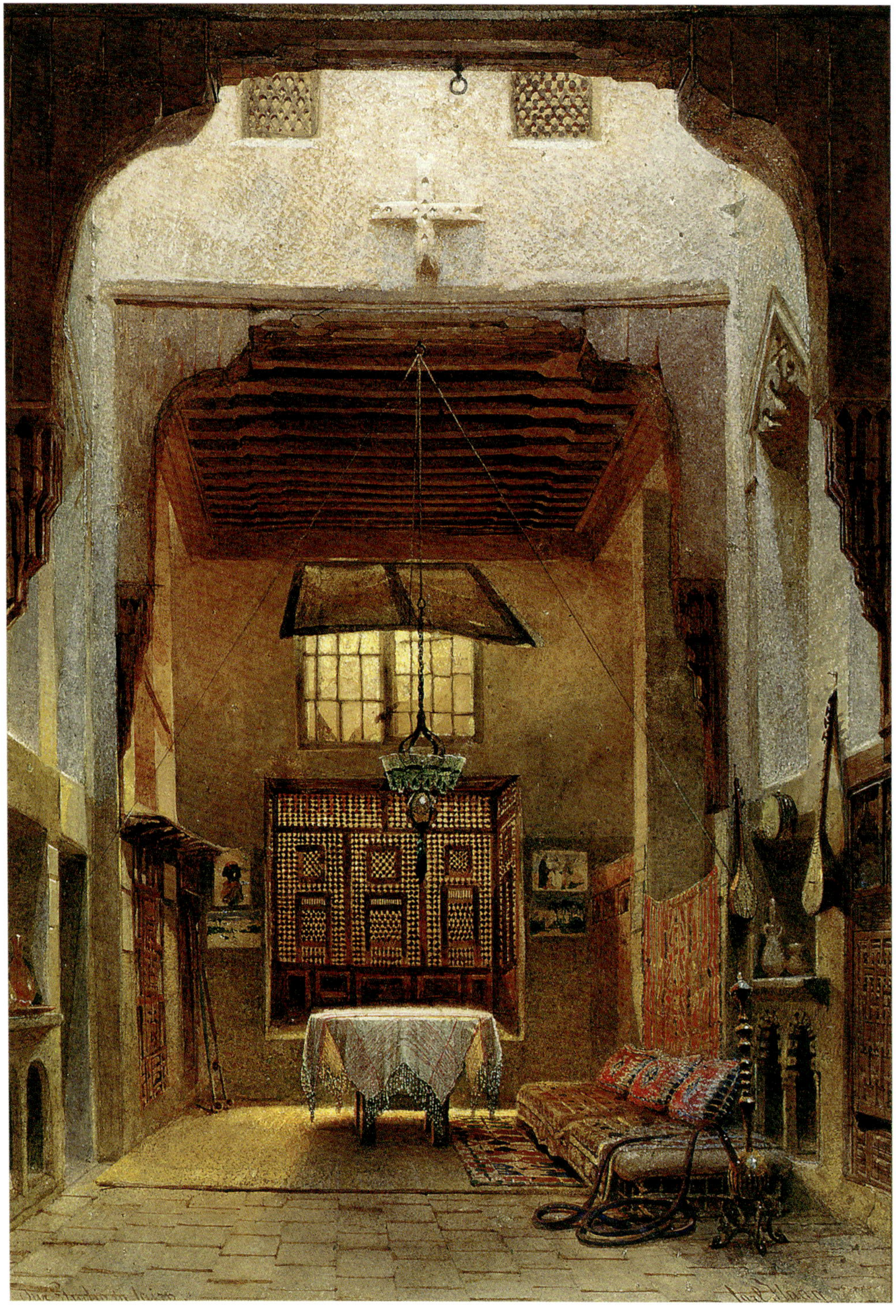

to continue to Jerusalem. Goodall however invited Haag to lodge with him, and the two spent the next few months sharing Goodall's new house and traveling and sketching together, both in and around Cairo as well as further afield. A daily routine emerged, with Goodall relating in his *Reminiscences* how the two men would always take a pre-breakfast ride along the Shubra Road and use "every hour of daylight for our work. In the court-yard we frequently had camels to paint from, and sometimes a group of musicians." Goodall and Haag's residence became something of an attraction for European visitors, particularly in the wake of a "wonderful" Christmas plum pudding made by Goodall with ingredients ordered specially from England.[43] The two men shared a studio space in the house, of which Haag made a painting (Figure 29)—their works can be seen hanging on either side of a central *mashrabiya* screen.

Although the evidence suggests that life in the Goodall house remained largely European in character, some other expatriate artists in Cairo stayed in the city long enough to enjoy a more significant encounter with the local culture and atmosphere. The most famous of these was John Frederick Lewis, who arrived in Egypt in 1841 and stayed for almost ten years. A mythology has developed around Lewis's time and life in Cairo, largely a result of the way in which his situation was presented by William Thackeray in *Notes of a Journey from Cornhill to Grand Cairo* (1846). Thackeray's detailed and well-publicized description of Lewis, his house, and his life there, based on Thackeray's visit in 1844 (the two men knew each other from England and were already good friends), created images about Lewis that have stuck steadfastly ever since. The most powerful of these is that of Lewis as an exotic artist-cum-Oriental nobleman, dressed in extravagant clothing, living in decadent pampered luxury, "a languid Lotus-eater—a dreamy, hazy, lazy, tobaccofied life." It was a seductive picture, as Thackeray doubtless intended, but not an entirely accurate one.

Lewis's residence was in the general area of Azbakiya, a district in Cairo especially favored by expatriates, but the precise location of the house remains a mystery. In all likelihood the building no longer exists, but it is nonetheless reasonably well documented in terms of its general appearance. In addition to Thackeray's description, there is a series of plans and drawings of the house made by James Wild (1814–92), a British architect who spent several years in Egypt. Most vivid of all from the point of view of appreciating the beauty and scale of the Lewis residence are the artist's own paintings, several of which include views of the house, either named as such or unnamed but in all probability inspired by its interiors and decoration. In addition, two detailed drawings by Lewis of parts of his house also survive. Unfortunately, a combination of all this material is still not sufficient to make possible a meaningful three-dimensional reconstruction of Lewis's Cairene house, the detail of much of which remains speculative.[44]

The nature of Lewis's lifestyle in Cairo is similarly open to conjecture, but the evidence suggests that it was not quite as Oriental as Thackeray would have his readers believe. Lewis maintained regular British habits (such as drinking beer, as

29. Carl Haag, *Our Studio in Cairo* (1859). Watercolor with gum Arabic, 49.5 x 35 cm. Haag and Goodall were visited in their Cairo house on one occasion by Prince Alfred, Queen Victoria's second son, who came to Egypt while serving in the Royal Navy.

Thackeray reveals) and mixed easily with the city's expatriate British community, inviting them regularly to his house. He may well also have received senior Egyptians there, but his contact with this stratum of local society was certainly not as developed as that of Edward Lane—with whom he appears to have been acquainted, if not exactly friends—and who was far more engaged with Egyptian society. Lewis spent most of his time in Cairo, but made trips to Suez and Sinai and in 1850 he sailed up the Nile to Philae, a trip on which he met Florence Nightingale and her party (see page 114). His credentials as an Orientalist *par excellence* were very strong, but there is no doubt that in the eyes of the British audience they were enhanced by Thackeray's account—something that suited Lewis well and would hold him in good stead when he returned to England.

Other artists took houses in Cairo, but little or nothing is now known about them. In 1838 David Roberts rented a house there formerly owned by the Scots dragoman, Osman Effendi (see pages 104–105); in 1853 Théodore Frère had a studio in Cairo, but no details have survived; letters by Thomas Seddon indicate that he was seeking to rent a house there on his second visit to the city in 1856, but he died of dysentery before his plans came to fruition.[45] Jean-Léon Gérôme rented a house in Cairo for several months on at least one occasion, which presumably would also have served as a temporary studio; in 1861 Frank Dillon (1823–1909) rented a traditional house at Giza, which he shared with fellow artists George Price Boyce and Egron Lundgren; some twenty years later, Leopold Müller is known to have maintained a studio in Cairo (see Figure 28); and in 1891 John Singer Sargent worked in a studio in Cairo, researching and painting Old Testament subjects for his mural commission from the Boston Public Library.

In Constantinople, among the many artists who visited the city one particularly stands out in terms of length of stay and immersion in the local culture: Amadeo, 5th Count Preziosi (1816–82). After first arriving there in the autumn of 1842 from his native island of Malta, Preziosi was to spend much of the next forty years living among the cosmopolitan inhabitants of the Turkish capital. He established a studio in Pera, at that time the most European part of Constantinople, and was visited by local people, expatriate residents, and travelers alike. The latter included in their number Empress Eugénie of France, as well as the future King Edward VII of England, who, as the Prince of Wales, called upon the artist in 1869 and bought paintings from him. Preziosi specialized in the depiction of local people (see page 110), but was also celebrated for his classic city scenes. "For an excellent rendering in watercolours of the life, which is visible on the [Galata] bridge, no one who visits Constantinople should fail to see Mr. Preziosi's studio," extolled British visitor Hubert Jerningham in 1873.[46]

While North Africa had no focal equivalent to Cairo or Constantinople around which artists coalesced to quite the same extent, many gravitated toward Algiers. Frederick Arthur Bridgman took a studio there on his first visit to the city in 1872–73, writing about "a whole villa at Mustapha [a well-heeled suburb] which with its extensive grounds and gardens, had been placed at our entire disposal." On a subsequent trip he installed himself in the house of an Algerian widow, an episode in his travels that helped create his travelogue *Winters in Algeria*. However, by Bridgman's day Algiers was already heavily Europeanized and regarded by many artists as an increasingly unrewarding place in which to search for interesting subject material. A much more attractive proposition were the still largely unspoilt settlements of the desert fringe, among them Biskra, frequented by many artists and where Bridgman himself once rented a studio in a poor neighborhood. He used this as a base from which to explore local villages and visit the encampments of nomads, encouraging local people—often in vain—to come and sit for him in his studio (see page 117).

The Algerian oasis town of Bou-Saâda also became a popular destination, frequented by figures such as Gustave Guillaumet, Eugène Girardet (1853–1907), and, most significantly, Étienne Dinet, who made his base there from 1904. Bou-Saâda offered access to the pristine desert landscapes of the Sahara and became increasingly valued as one of the last refuges of Algeria's indigenous tribes and therefore of ethnographic authenticity. The town's popularity among artists continued well into the mid-twentieth century, thanks largely to Édouard Verschaffelt (1874–1955), who settled there, married a local woman, and lived and worked in the town until his death (see page 141).

Jerusalem was an essential destination for those artists interested in exploring Palestine's biblical heritage in their works. William Holman Hunt first visited the city in 1854–55, and although it had a profound impact on him, he did not return for another fourteen years, until August 1869. He was to stay three years on that occasion and, having a keen interest in architecture, assisted the British consuls there with a survey of the city's historic buildings. It was during this period that he began looking for a suitable house in the city to rent and use as a studio, eventually taking a three-year lease on a house in the Muslim quarter. He ordered various alterations so that he could create well-lit spaces in which to work, relating in his memoirs how he arranged for "two wooden houses constructed on the roof, to ride on rollers, one open to the horizontal beams of the sun, so as to get the correct light and shade on my model; this was wheeled into place in the afternoon, to catch the glow of the setting sun. The other hut was to shade myself and my picture, and this also was movable."[47]

Hunt left Jerusalem again in July 1872. On his return three and a half years later he found that the landlord of his house had carried out no maintenance and the building was now uninhabitable and virtually derelict. "Having suffered from want of space and light while painting previous pictures," he wrote, "I bought a piece of ground to build a house thereon with a large studio."[48] Hunt took occupancy of his new residence in 1876 and, although still not ideal—the roof leaked and he had to protect his canvases with tarpaulins—the house, built in local limestone and in typical Ottoman style, served as his home and studio for the next two years. He locked it up again when he returned to England in 1878, returning to Jerusalem again only for three months in 1892. The house still stands, retaining many of its original features but now divided into apartments. A contemporary record of its appearance during Hunt's time survives in the form of a painting by his wife, Edith.

Gustav Bauernfeind had also explored the possibility of building a house in Palestine, at the time of his impending marriage in the summer of 1887. He asked both for a suitable building site in the German colony in Jerusalem and for a German building contractor to prepare costs for the construction of a purpose-built house in Jaffa, but neither scheme appears to have come to fruition.[49]

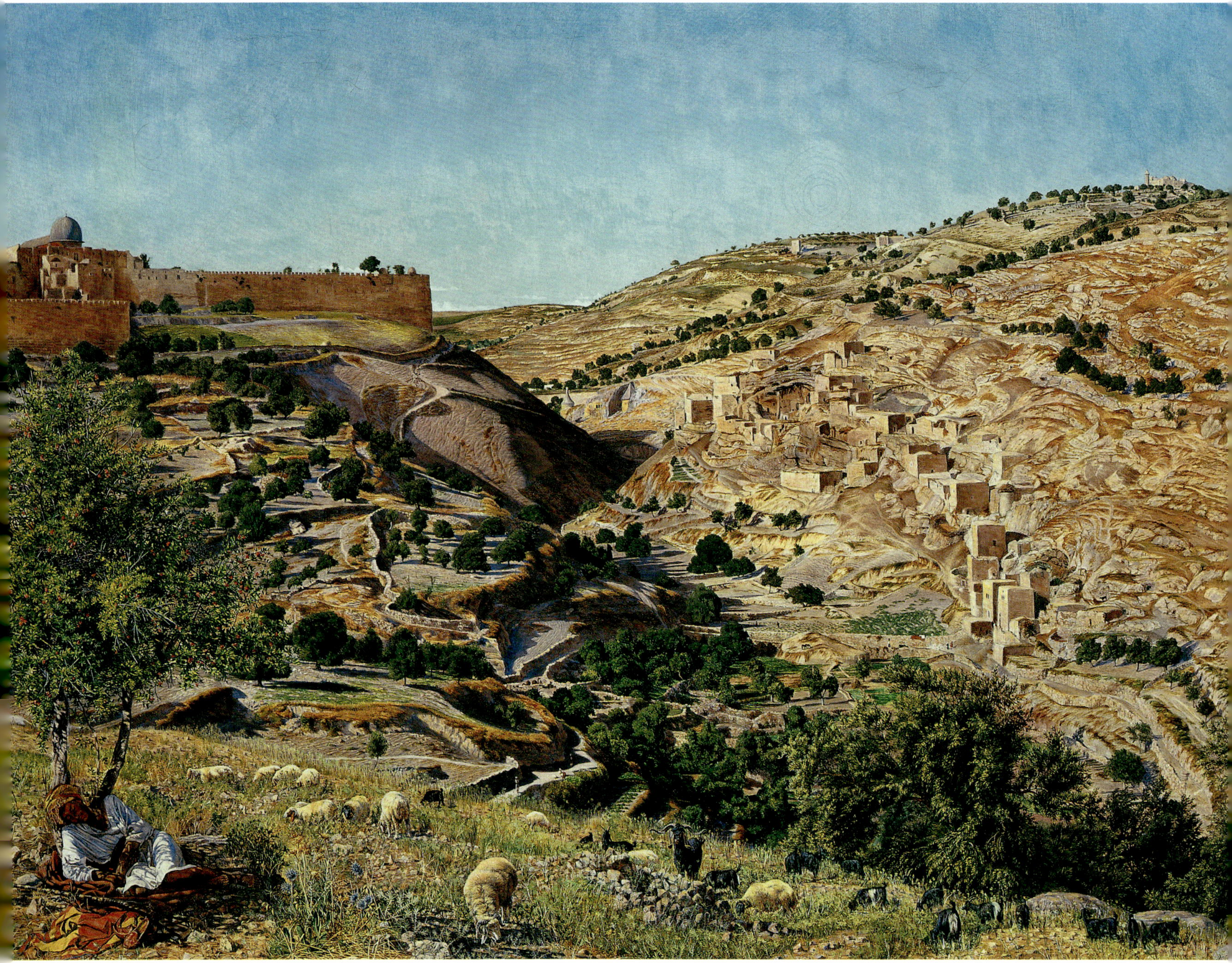

Out and About

Once settled, it was time to explore. With so much to attract an artist's eye, those on a tight schedule tended to head for the main sights—a well-trodden route that in Cairo led to the monuments of the old city and its markets. The latter were the most diverse and fascinating in the entire Orient, with the possible exception of Constantinople, and it was in their narrow streets and alleyways that many artists spent long hours observing the scenes of daily life that were to form the basis of their paintings. Not only were they observing, sketching, and, in some cases, photographing, but they were also often negotiating to buy artifacts, the vital props which they used to populate their works and confer the degree of realism and authenticity that was expected by their audiences back in Europe and North America. Artists such as Bridgman, Deutsch, Frère, Gérôme, Goodall, and Haag, among others, amassed vast collections of objects of wide-ranging materials and functions, shipping them home to their studios and continuing to draw on this resource for their paintings through many years to come (see page 146).

30. Thomas Seddon, *Jerusalem and the Valley of Jehoshaphat from the Hill of Evil Counsel* (1854–55). Oil on canvas, 87 x 103 cm. Seddon saw Jerusalem for the first time on 3 June 1854 and, in a letter a week later, he described how, after visiting "every part of the city and surrounding country, to determine what I would do, I have encamped upon the hill to the south, looking up the Valley of Jehoshaphat; I have sketched the view which I see from the opening of my tent." This painting is based on that sketch and photographs by James Graham (see pages 154–156).

Goodall had a particularly large selection of Oriental garments. On at least one occasion he instructed his dragoman to buy old clothes off the backs of passers-by in the Cairo streets, because these "had been worn and exposed to the sun, which makes the colour, to the artist's eye, so much more beautiful."[50]

Visiting cities like Cairo entailed a busy routine for any artist intent on seeing as much as possible. The daily pattern was to head out in the cooler hours of the morning into the maelstrom of the old city to look, record, and absorb, returning to the hotel during the heat of midday, before another foray in the late afternoon and then dinner back at the hotel, usually with a mêlée of fellow Western visitors. Securing the best material for a potential painting often meant placing oneself in incongruous situations, as Jean-Léon Gérôme discovered when visiting the Sinan baths in Bursa. "As the temperature was exceedingly high, I did not hesitate to make myself . . . completely naked;" he recalled, admitting that "seated on my campstool, my colour box on my knees, my palette in my hand, I was a little grotesque."[51]

For many artists it became increasingly imperative to get away from the hordes of other foreign travelers. By the mid-nineteenth century the more popular sites, such as the Pyramids, had become so well visited as to be unbearably crowded in the opinion of some. In his *Cairo Notes*, a three-page typed account in quasi-note form of a visit to the Pyramids and the Sphinx, Edwin Lord Weeks described what he called "the pyramid business." The date of visit is unrecorded but was possibly during 1872, the year of Weeks's first trip to Egypt, as his peevish comments read very much like unfavorable first impressions (spelling,

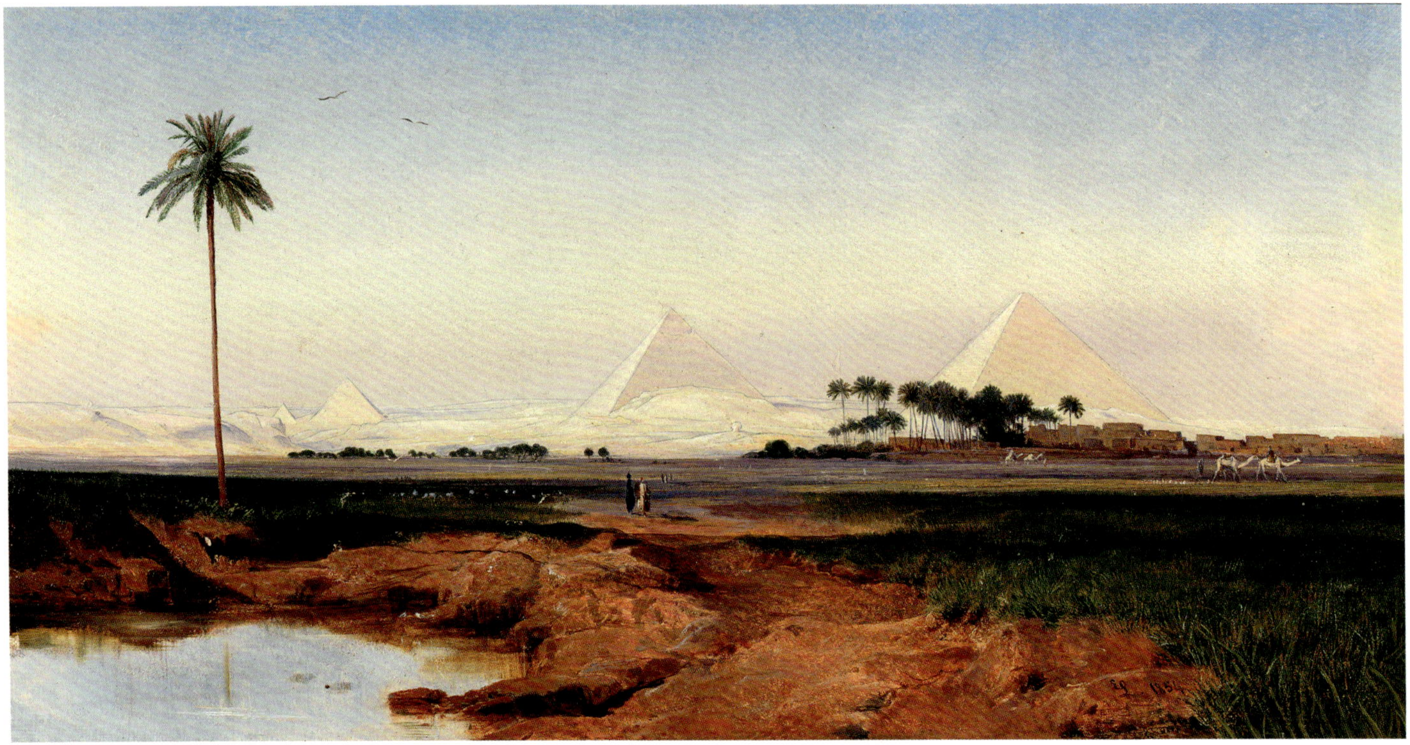

31. Edward Lear, *The Pyramids at Giza, Early Morning* (1854). Oil on canvas, 25 x 46 cm. Lear had mixed feelings about Egypt, often complaining about the rigors and frustrations of traveling there, but he was very mindful of the commercial appeal of depictions of major sites such as the Pyramids, to which he returned several times.

syntax, and punctuation are as per the original text): "Reach the pyramids. Crowd of importunate grinning Arabs. All speak English all want to help us up pyramids, look yellow. Dragomen arranges with the sheik. Arabs seize us and we are hustled up. Talk about buckshish all the way up. Brazillian Gentleman (fat one) quite used up. Top of pyramid covered with names. They take us up over the biggest steps; see that it is quite possible to go up an easier way. Humbug. Come down again. Buckshish. My deaf friend puts his hand in his pocket from time to time draws forth buckshish. Arabs want more. Bores at the bottom want us to buy coins, images, trinkets. Go inside. Slide through inclined passage dust clothing. Arabs drag us part way. Chant all the way: about buckshish. Flourish torches; look wild. Don't experience any emotion. Get into chamber horrible echoes. More names. John Smith glad to get out; buckshish. Go to see sphinx. Arabs run in front to show the way. Sit down on a stone; draw breath and contemplate sphinx. Small boy with jar of water squats on one side begs piteously for buchshish, carried the water up the top and down inside for me to drink didn't drink any. Won't pay him. Idiotic old grizzley old beggar on the side, buchshish. Gets between me and sphinx, poke him out of the way with a stick. Brazillian comes to contemplate sphinx. Completely blown, is borne aloft on the shoulders of a dozen Arabs, all clamor for buchshish, ridiculous sight. Arabs produce more coins. Having contemplated sphinx retire, bodyguard twenty Arabs. While we are on top one of 'em ran down and up the other one didn't do it in ten minutes, humbug. Get into carriages. Sheik alongside wants more buchshish but at him with whip. Small boy runs along other side with jar of water, no buchshish. Goodbye, give him cut with the whip. Small trots alongside holds up his water jar whines piteously for buchshish, give him a cut. Goodbye."

Nonetheless, few artists could afford to ignore the Pyramids, as they remained popular with the buying public. However, it became ever more important for artists to find new subjects to paint, as well as different perspectives of what were increasingly familiar scenes. William Holman Hunt famously achieved this with his painting of the Sphinx (*The Sphinx, Gizeh, looking towards the Pyramids of Sakhara*, 1854), viewed from behind and thereby stripped of its obvious iconography. David Roberts had depicted the Colossi of Memnon from a similarly unconventional angle over a decade earlier. In terms of where else to go, for foreign travelers to Egypt a trip up the Nile was standard fare and already a mainstream activity by the mid-nineteenth century. While the sites and landscapes of the Nile Valley were on a scale to absorb the winter crowds and of a grandeur to satisfy most artists, those in search of more adventurous settings tended to head east across the desert, to Sinai, and ultimately into Palestine and Syria.

In some cases, initially positive impressions of a place quickly gave way to frustrations and a desire to move on. Just a few weeks after he had enthusiastically extolled the joys of Cairo and of Egypt generally, Hunt was lamenting the lack of satisfactory subject matter for a creative eye. "There are palm trees about, which attract my passing admiration, but for all else one might as well sketch in Hackney Marsh," he grumbled in a letter to John Everett Millais in March 1854. "The country offers nothing to me but landscapes and buildings of antiquarian interest; you know I want figures."[52]

Expeditions further afield, beyond the immediate environs of cities such as Cairo, had to be largely self-sufficient and so took much planning, time, and money. Their organization was usually entrusted into the hands of a dragoman, but packing lists and handy hints for more ambitious trips were offered by a variety of returned travelers, both seasoned and otherwise. Some of the most interesting suggestions were supplied by Lady Francis Egerton in her *Journal of a Tour in the Holy Land*, published in 1841. Lady Egerton not only listed those items that she considered useful when 'on the road' but also gave advice on where they could be obtained. "For the benefit of future travellers," she wrote, "it may be well to enumerate as many of the necessary articles as I can remember, which it is desirable to take into Syria:

Tents according to the number of travellers—those with walls preferable to others;
A canteen, containing knives, forks, spoons, dishes, plates, cups and saucers, tea-pot, teakettle, salt-cellar;
Leathern bottles for carrying water, to be got at Alexandria, and most eastern towns;
Corks for bottles—very necessary—and stout corkscrews;
Candlesticks, and a provision of wax candles—those to be had in the East being peculiarly bad, and almost useless;
Turkish lanterns to hang up in the tent—these are absolutely necessary, and to be had in Jerusalem;
A kitchen apparatus, large coffee-pot, etc.;
A Dover arm-chair is a great comfort, when one comes in tired from the day's ride;
Spades, to level the ground for the tents, with hooks, to cut away weeds &c.;
An umbrella, covered with white calico, the best preservative from the sun;
Green or blue spectacles, as the glare of the white rocks is injurious to the eyes;[53]

To Lady Egerton's list could be added a retinue of servants, all ostensibly under the supervision of the dragoman, as well as camels and packhorses or donkeys for the transportation of luggage and supplies. As far as the latter were concerned, she advised taking portable soup, sea biscuit, pasta, "cheese from England," and "plenty of tea," but also served a warning that locally available provisions are "very scanty indeed; tough fowls and rice being almost the only things one can get, and, now and then, a sheep. No vegetables scarcely—no butter to be got."

Expeditions up the Nile naturally required the appropriate transport. Cairo's port of Boulak was the usual point of departure for those traveling upstream to the monuments of the Nile Valley and Upper Egypt, but it presented a grim aspect to European *ingénus* seeking to charter a boat. The writer and artist Amelia Edwards (1831–92) was bewildered by the choice of up to three hundred very similar-looking craft she encountered on her first visit to Boulak ("a desolate place by the river") in 1873. "Now, most persons know something of the miseries of house-hunting," she wrote, "but only those who have experienced them know how much keener are the miseries of dahabeeyah-hunting."[54] A Nile *dahabiya* was usually the boat of choice for foreign visitors to Egypt, being generally the largest type of passenger craft on the river and offering a degree of space and comfort that had traditionally made it popular among the Egyptian elite. A *dahabiya* was nominally under the command of a *rais* or captain, who would aggressively tout his craft and services to potential clients, making the business of trying to decide which boat was most suitable even more fraught and stressful.

During the first half of the nineteenth century at least, many of the vessels on offer at Boulak were of dubious quality and often infested with vermin. Standards improved in later years, but in those earlier decades it was common practice for a boat to be periodically and temporarily sunk or submerged to ensure the departure of any unsavory creatures lurking therein. David Roberts remarked how, before setting sail up the Nile, he had ordered his boat to be sunk overnight for this very purpose.[55] The consequences could be serious when such care and attention was not paid, as William Bartlett discovered on his first trip up the Nile in 1845. As darkness fell soon after setting sail from Boulak, "from every chink and crevice in the old planks hundreds [of bugs] came forth, scenting the blood of an Englishman; books, matting, and clothing were all in a swarm with the disgusting vermin, from the swollen old patriarch to the youngest of his descendant fry. We threw the mats overboard to begin with, removed all the furniture, and by dint of sundry pails of water, furious scrubbing, ferreting out the nests with an iron pike, stuffing the chinks with camphor, and then subjecting every separate article to a rigid investigation, we routed the main body the first day, and by a watchful look-out till the second evening, and cutting off stragglers, had fairly gained the victory."[56]

Winter was the most popular season for Nile cruising, not simply on account of the more agreeable temperatures but because the prevailing northerly winds at that time of year aided a speedy passage upstream. With Abu Simbel almost eight hundred miles upriver from Cairo, most travelers faced a voyage of between four and six weeks to get there, a fair wind and favorable water levels permitting. It was not uncommon for boats to run aground, or for the crew to resort to rowing or even towing their craft on occasion. "It is the rule of the Nile to hurry up the river as fast as possible," observed Amelia Edwards, "leaving the ruins to be seen as the boat comes back with the current; but this, like many another canon, is by no means of universal application. The traveler who starts late in the season has, indeed, no other course open to him. He must press on with speed to the end of his journey, if he would get back again at low Nile without being irretrievably stuck on a sand-bank till the next inundation floats him off again."[57] Despite such mishaps, standards of safety and comfort on Nile boats generally improved during the nineteenth century, to the point that a cruise to Luxor and beyond became standard fare for foreigners visiting Egypt.

The Road Less Traveled

Expeditions into the desert offered artists the chance to break away from the more usual locations and subjects, find new material of their own, and enjoy the sense of liberation that such a landscape afforded. William Thackeray had identified the appeal of the desert to John Frederick Lewis, when he visited him in Cairo in 1844. "And even this life at Cairo was too civilized for him," Thackeray wrote. "Englishmen passed through; old acquaintances would call; the great pleasure of pleasures was life in the desert,—under the tents, with still *more* nothing to do than in Cairo; now smoking, now cantering on Arabs, and no crowd to jostle you; solemn contemplations of the stars at night, as the camels were picketed, and the fires and the pipes were lighted."[58]

Desert life was not always quite as bucolic as Thackeray claimed. In 1858 Frederick Goodall and Carl Haag traveled from Cairo across the desert to Suez, Goodall remarking on the complete absence of any fresh water for most of the route, which was marked by the scattered bones of camels that had expired while attempting the journey. Goodall and Haag took shelter at night in the wooden sheds that a few years earlier had housed British troops involved in the Crimean War. Days were spent sketching, sightseeing, and gathering a wealth of material and experiences for later use in paintings. Goodall specifically related how his work *The Sword of the Faithful* was based on studies he had made of an incident witnessed at first hand in the bazaar in Suez during this trip.[59]

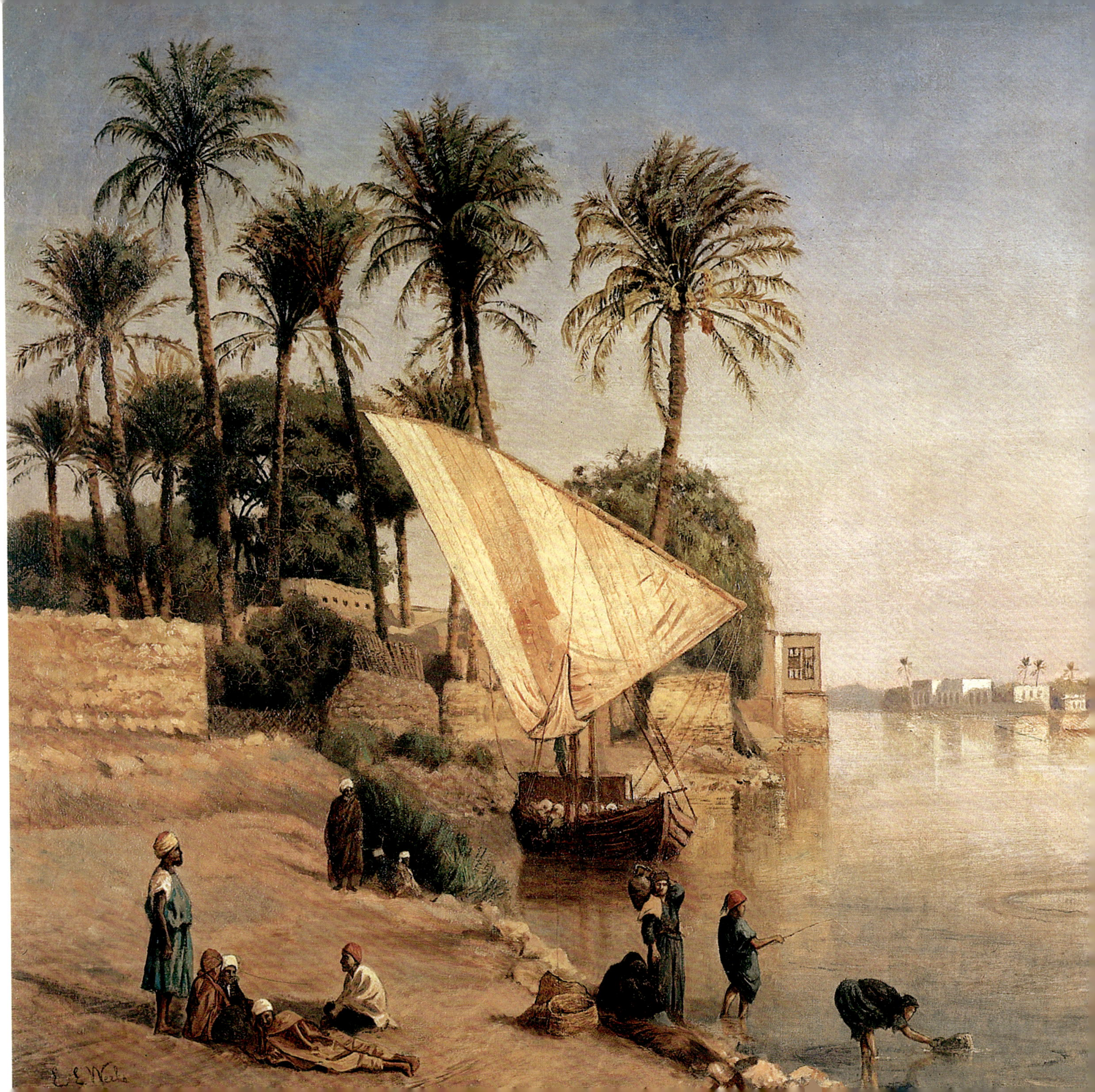

Jean-Léon Gérôme's first expedition into the desert proper took place in early 1862, leaving from Cairo for Damascus. "It took seventeen days to cross the Desert of Syria," he recalled, "we had supplied ourselves carefully with everything necessary to our material existence, above all with Nile water, a precaution all the more important since we took with us four horses, and we were obliged to load the water these animals were to consume, on the back of the camels."[60] Gérôme's caravan progressed through Gaza and into Judea, past the Dead Sea and Lake Tiberias before reaching Jerusalem, from where it headed north to its final destination. "Arrival at Damascus after a two days' march [from Jerusalem]," Gérôme wrote. "It was the crown and end of our journey, as Cairo had been the beginning. Damascus! Cairo! The most remarkable cities of the Orient; those which have remained longest untainted by the impure breath of Europe."

The heady, liberating qualities of desert trips and the romance of life on the open road were eagerly embraced by most artists. "Nothing could be more agreeable, more poetic, than our encampments in this solitude, with its added charm of novelty and the unknown," continued Gérôme. "Although fatigued by long marches in the full blaze of the sun, I began my work with ardour as soon as the halting-place was reached; but alas! How many things I was forced to leave behind, only a bare memory of what I could take away." For some, the

32. Edwin Lord Weeks, *A View on the Nile near Cairo* (1874). Oil on canvas, 81.9 x 129.5 cm. The Nile was an inescapable focus for all visitors to Egypt, although the logistics of travel along its length were often formidable.

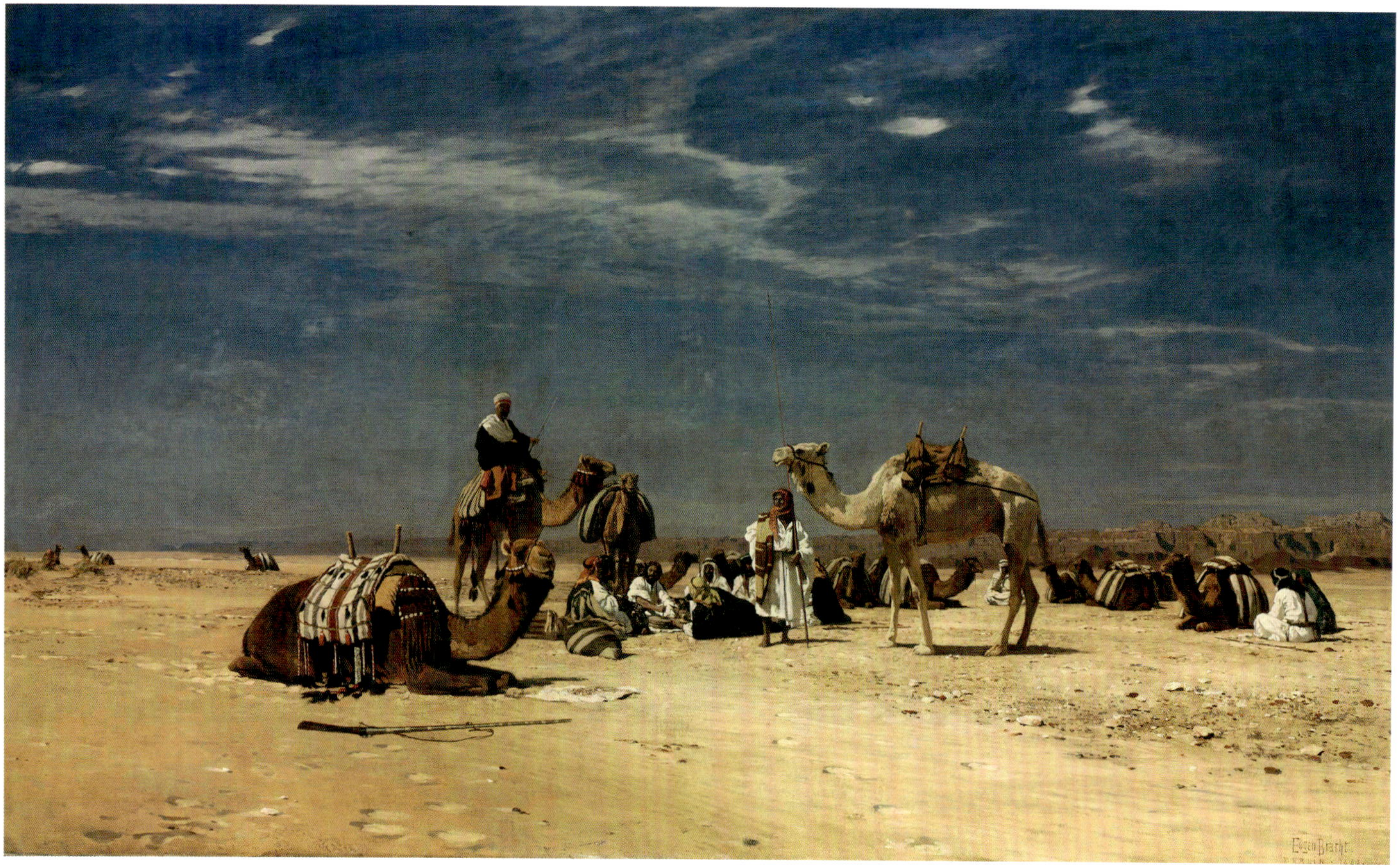

33. Eugen Bracht, *Rast in der Araba* (Rest in the Desert) (1883). Oil on canvas, 118 x 200 cm. The majestic scale of desert landscapes and skies, and the exotic appeal of the Bedouin and camels who lived there, made them popular subjects for the Orientalists. Swiss-born Bracht traveled to Syria, Palestine, and Egypt in 1880–81.

experience of desert travel proved life-changing, Carl Haag recalling how "I rode nearly all the way from Cairo to Jerusalem on the back of a camel, and I never experienced anything more exhilarating."[61]

While an essential component of desert life, camels were not loved by all of those who traveled on or with them. They could be notoriously cantankerous, as Edward Lear discovered when traveling in a caravan with a particularly uncooperative individual in Palestine in the spring of 1858: "The pleasant progress of the morning was frequently delayed by the wicked camel utterly refusing to go on; for whenever one of the cocks in the cage, from a cheerful sympathy with nature in general, or a wish to make an audible comment on his own particular elevation, gave way to crowing,—that moment the huge beast abandoned himself to extreme spasms of terror, shaking, screaming, and kicking till all the roba, including the guilty fowls, was on the ground."[62]

Such difficulties aside—or perhaps because of them—most artists developed a routine during their time in the desert. David Roberts described the scene in his diary entry for 14 February 1839: "As usual, start at daybreak, take a cup of coffee, walk two hours, spread our carpets on the sand. The remnants of our yesterday's dinner in our leather wallet, and a drink of water from our leather bottle, is our breakfast, relished with a gusto I have not experienced since boyhood."[63] Thomas Seddon maintained a similar daily pattern: "I get up at five, or soon after—breakfast—paint from soon after six till ten or eleven—come in, sleep under my tree, and dine and read for half-an-hour, till two—and then paint as long as I can after."[64] Seddon was remarkably industrious, constantly sketching and painting. He particularly relished life outdoors and coped well with the often spartan conditions, relating how he was "quite hardened now," able to sleep soundly on rough ground and use a stone as a pillow.

Edward Lear was equally enthusiastic about the freedom of desert trips, walking for miles while constantly scanning the landscape with his binoculars in search of interesting subjects to sketch. He was a successful artist before turning his hand to Orientalist scenes and so often traveled to the region with various commissions already secured. He would write regularly to his clients while on his travels, assuring them of his diligence and efforts to secure exactly what it was they wanted. In a letter to Lady Waldegrave, one of his most important patrons, Lear wrote from Damascus in 1858, "My stay in Jerusalem or rather opposite the City,—for I pitched my tents on the Mount of Olives when I had ascertained the point I thought you would like best for your picture, was the most complete portion of my tour."[65]

One artist particularly anxious to find "the road less traveled" was Edwin Lord Weeks. He first visited the Middle East in 1872–73, traveling to Morocco, Egypt, the Holy Land, and Syria, and was accompanied by his friend A.P. Close, an illustrator. The two men explored the mountains of Lebanon, visiting the fabled cedars and with Weeks describing the attention that they attracted when camping overnight near the village of Hasroun. "No sooner were the mules unloaded and Abdullah['s] cooking utensils out than we were surrounded by a curious throng of villagers who squatted about the tent," wrote Weeks. "I have the impression that some of the villagers who displayed such an interest in the menagerie of living wonders which our dragmen [sic] had brought to show them, remained on the spot all the time we were there.

They were squatting around the fire the last thing at night and when the tent door was opened at sunrise, there they were squatting in front wating [sic] patiently to see what the Howadjins* were going to do next."[66]

Tragically, Close was to die of a fever in Beirut during their expedition, Weeks subsequently returning to his native United States of America with a large number of drawings and sketches and a passion for North Africa in particular. He returned to Egypt in the spring of 1875, having meanwhile established his Orientalist credentials with a highly successful exhibition in his hometown of Boston and enrolment at the École des Beaux-Arts in Paris under Léon Bonnat (1833–1922).

The following winter saw Weeks back in Morocco. It was probably on this trip that he met with the British artist Robert Gavin (1827–83), who was then living in Tangier, and discussed a future trip to the remoter parts of the country away from the north, which was by then firmly on the tourist trail. Gavin knew Morocco well and would have been perfectly placed to advise Weeks on how to avoid the growing numbers of European and American visitors and experience something altogether more authentic and unspoilt.

So it was that in the autumn of 1877 Weeks returned to Tangier (this time accompanied by his wife, Fanny) and set out with Gavin for the city of Rabat, at that time a remote part of the country to which outsiders very rarely ventured. Such was the volume of luggage they had with them, much of it comprising supplies and household utensils in anticipation of there being no hotels in Rabat, that they decided to go by coastal steamer rather than overland. They arrived successfully but the next few months proved very testing. Local crop failures were to plunge the region into an acute famine and the visitors soon found themselves dispensing food to the needy. Weeks was still able to sketch and paint, however, visiting local towns and sites of interest never previously visited by an artist and thereby gathering a mass of unique material that was to form the basis of several future paintings.

The very day the party attempted to leave Rabat in February 1878, the Weekses were struck down by typhoid. "The following month is an utter blank," wrote Weeks later, "as I was at the point of death for a time."[67] The couple were

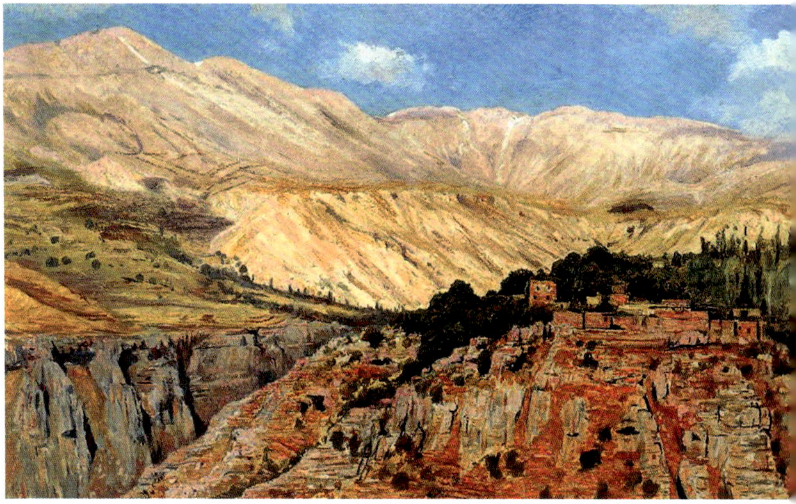

34. Edwin Lord Weeks, *Morocco, A village in the Atlas Mountains* (date unknown). Oil on canvas, 28.6 x 47.6 cm. Weeks traveled off the beaten track in the Atlas, visiting villages to which few, if any, Western visitors had been previously.

* A local colloquial term for foreigner.

nursed back to health by Gavin and eventually returned to Tangier on a British ship, but only after it had nearly capsized in a storm. Undaunted by these experiences, Weeks returned to Morocco within a year to try and reach the remote cities of the interior. He got as far as Marrakech, another coup for an artist who was constantly looking for new creative territory to claim as his own. His recollection of the two expeditions featured in "Two Centres of Moorish Art," published in *Scribner's Magazine* in 1901 and illustrated with his own drawings.

Fragile Equipment

As Weeks and many others before him had discovered, it was not easy being an artist on the road. Potentially sensitive equipment had to be transported over difficult terrain, and the heat and scorching sun made for arduous conditions. Frederick Goodall carried his art supplies around Egypt in a special sketch-box given to him by fellow artist Rosa Bonheur and which contained "all the appliances for holding a canvas, a board for sketching upon, all the mediums you may require, varnish, oil, and turpentine." The box was prodigiously heavy, however, and required its own pack animal and guardian: "I never went anywhere [in Egypt] without my two donkeys, one for myself, and the other for my dragoman, who carried my box and my portable tent to keep off the sun. The immense advantage of sketching in Egypt is that you have not to provide against rain."[68]

The popularity among some British artists of working in watercolor proved to be a distinct advantage to them, with the French artist Nicolas-Toussaint Charlet extolling the virtues of the medium in *l'Artiste* in 1850: "It is a pleasant, convenient technique: pleasant in that it involves little trouble or mess and that everything needed for it can be fitted in a six by four inch box—which makes it easy for the traveller."[69] Portability was essential and working in oils in the heat and dust of the Middle East was always going to be a challenge. Few artists attempted it out 'in the field,' most preferring to sketch or work in watercolor and then work up oil versions once back in the comfort and controlled conditions of their studios, either back in Cairo or Jerusalem—or, in many cases, London or Paris.

Amelia Edwards spent the winter of 1873–74 in Egypt, sightseeing, sketching, and painting. She ran into particular problems at Abu Simbel where, among other sketching issues such as the sheer immensity of the great temple and the fact that "everything, except the sky and the river, is yellow," she also found that "[the sand] fills your hair, your eyes, your water-bottles; silts up your color-box; dries into your skies; and reduces your Chinese white to a gritty paste the colour of salad-dressing. As for the flies, they have a morbid appetite for water-colours. They follow your wet brush along the paper, leave their legs in the yellow ochre, and plunge with avidity into every little pool of cobalt as it is mixed ready for use. Nothing disagrees with them; nothing poisons them—not even olive-green." Yet Edwards was keen to point out that none of this distracted from the charms of being in Egypt: "It was a delightful time, however—delightful alike for those who worked and those who rested—and these small troubles counted for nothing in the scale."[70]

Replacements for lost, damaged, or used art materials were often impossible to source locally and had to be sent from Europe. In 1831 Edward William Lane, back in England at that time (partly to pursue the publication of his book, see page 26), dispatched a box to Robert Hay, with whom Lane had worked in Egypt recording monuments and inscriptions. Lane was busy as Hay's "man in London," handling various matters and sending out supplies. He listed the contents of the box, which clearly contained art materials, in a letter to Hay:

> 96 sheets of drawing paper.
> A measuring chain.
> A measuring tape of 100 feet.
> Two scales for plans.
> A two-feet rule.
> A Mordan's pencil-case with Rhodian pen.
> Your old one repaired.
> A Greek testament.[71]

He also included a roll of paper for his good friend John Gardner Wilkinson, who was also conducting fieldwork along the Nile at that time.[72]

Later in the century the situation appears to have improved somewhat. Gustav Bauernfeind described a journey he made by sea from Damascus to Jaffa in 1889 in order to buy a fresh supply of paints, canvas, picture panels, and paper.[73] However, when William Holman Hunt's consignment of new canvas failed to arrive from England on one occasion a few years earlier, he had been forced "to search in the bazaar [in Jerusalem] for the best linen to be found there."[74] Unfortunately it only proved satisfactory for use in small pictures, tearing at the corners and edges when stretched to the required tension over a larger frame. Transporting sketches and other works from place to place, and ultimately back home at the end of a trip, could be equally problematic. Frederick Goodall offered fellow artists some useful advice in his *Reminiscences*: "Having accumulated much material, I began at last to make ready to leave Egypt; packing my sketches with thin buttered paper, the butter thoroughly wiped off, placed between each sketch to prevent sticking, a 'tip' worth remembering."[75]

Living alfresco for weeks at a time rendered travelers especially vulnerable to the elements. Heat, sun, wind, dust, and sand were all hazards with which to contend on a regular basis. In 1854 Hunt and Thomas Seddon were camping near the Sphinx when a storm blew up, threatening to overwhelm their tents. "Violent gusts were still battering and bellying the tent . . . by then several other fastenings had come undone, and the canvas was dashing backwards and forwards, up and down, beyond all control," recalled Hunt. "Seddon on his side was also holding on to the loose folds like an octopus; but it was too late, the tent was literally turned inside out, and we were rolled over and over as though in a blanket pudding."[76] Hunt subsequently wrote to John Everett Millais describing the event and including a sketch of himself and Seddon trying to stop the tent from being blown away.[77]

Another trial was the local wildlife, which ranged from the hyenas and jackals that raided desert camps at night in search of food to much smaller but often more pernicious fauna. David Roberts returned from the desert to Cairo and in a letter to David Ramsay Hay gave his verdict on the experience: " . . . with the exception of Mosquitos myraids of flys, fleas, bugs, lice, lizards and ratts, I was tollerably well off with these accompaniments you may Be shure all was not pleasure—add to which the Thermometer at 100 in the Shade and sometimes higher."[78] Roberts was often badly bitten by insects and

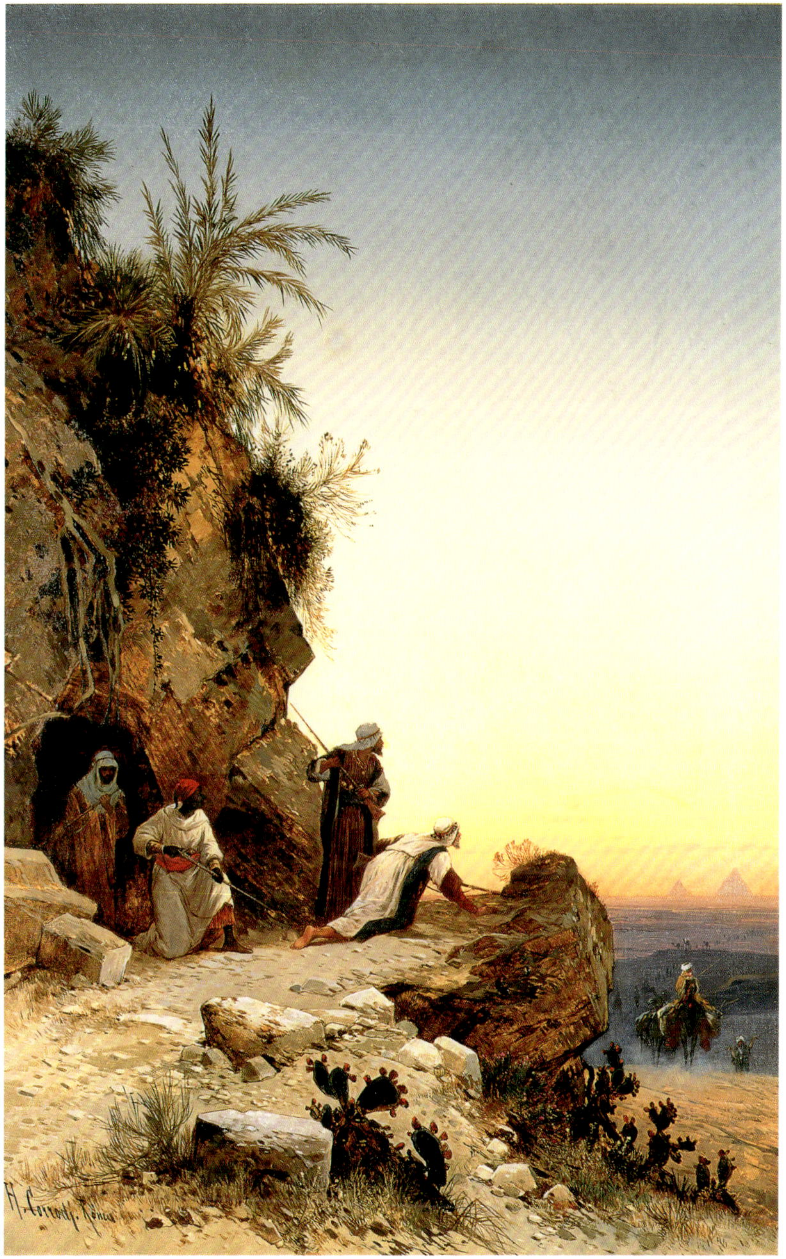

tried to avoid their worst excesses by wearing gloves by day to protect his hands and by sleeping under a gauze net at night.

Insects were sometimes the least of problems. There was also the very real risk of robbery or, in some cases, a worse fate. Even within cities, the security situation could be difficult. In 1832 Eugène Delacroix visited the Moroccan city of Meknès and encountered a very hostile reaction almost everywhere that he went. "Every time I go out I am escorted by a huge gang of curious onlookers," he explained in a letter home, "who lavish insults on me—dog, infidel, *caracco*,* etc., and jostle one another to get near me and make contemptuous grimaces in my face."[79] The situation was so bad that his safety could only be guaranteed when he was accompanied by an armed posse of soldiers.

Security outside the main population centers of the Middle East had always been a concern and, while the general situation improved considerably as the nineteenth century progressed, there were still frequent outbreaks of lawlessness. Wealthy foreigners presented an all-too-tempting target in more remote areas, often beyond the reach of what little central government presided, and David Roberts's expression of

---

* A local pejorative term for foreigner.

35. Hermann Corrodi, *The Ambush* (date unknown). Oil on canvas, 101 x 65 cm. Although Western visitors occasionally found themselves caught up in incidents of brigandry, skirmishes of the type depicted here by Corrodi were few and far between. Corrodi would almost certainly have based this work on his imagination and hearsay, rather than direct personal experience.

reassurance to his daughter Christine in a letter home that, "thanks to Mahomet Ali, travelling now in Syria is as safe as in England,"[80] was wildly disingenuous—if understandable. William Holman Hunt experienced the reality of the situation at first hand near the Dead Sea in the autumn of 1854, when he was working on the landscape setting for his painting *The Scapegoat* and was harassed and threatened by local tribesmen. Only by brandishing his double-barreled shotgun was he able to ward them off.*

In a letter dated 27 May 1858, Edward Lear reported how travel in Palestine was fraught with the risk of attack by bandits, who had recently robbed an American group and made off "with all but one large blanket, of which Mr. & Mrs T. made two garments & therein rode to the town . . . they took every book & drawing, & paper, & even Mrs. T.'s wig & spectacles."[81] The hotels and expatriate colonies in Jerusalem and Cairo were doubtless rife with hysterical speculation about such events, to a pitch quite likely out of all proportion to the real risk. Nonetheless, Lear had already experienced an attack by brigands on a trip to Petra earlier that year, when "about 200 of them came down on me, and every-thing which could be divided they took. My watch they returned to me, but all money, handkerchiefs, knives, &c., &c., were confiscated."[82] It is no surprise therefore that in an age when Europeans—of a certain class, at least—were quite accustomed to using firearms, artists were not unusual in packing weapons in their luggage. David Roberts describes how, before leaving Cairo on his trip to the Holy Land in early 1839, he "bought several items wanted on my journey to Syria—pistols and a sabre, etc."[83]

Over half a century later the risk of robbery in parts of the region was still very real, as Gustav Bauernfeind discovered when traveling with his wife Elise in the south Jordan Valley in 1896. Noting that "brigands from the south end of the Dead Sea had arrived in great numbers," he decided to leave everything of value at home—including, rather bizarrely, his revolvers—when going out to sketch each day. Instead he relied on an armed guard, who "amused himself by firing off his rifle over my head. Palette and sketches were buried in a shower of sand and dust."[84] Bauernfeind succeeded in escaping the attentions of the bandits on that occasion, yet there was no denying that the Orient could be a hostile and dangerous place in which good health and security could never be relied upon. It regularly claimed the lives of foreign visitors, although almost always as a result of disease rather than human violence. The artists William Bartlett, Paul Lenoir, Thomas Seddon, and David Wilkie were among those who succumbed and were never to return home alive.

Cultural Sensitivities

Among the issues faced by artists on a daily basis was the notion held by many Muslims that the portrayal of the human form was *haram* or sinful. In the eyes of many Arabs drawing was therefore a highly suspect activity, even when restricted to the depiction of landscapes or buildings, and any foreigner, whether an artist or not, attempting to wield a pencil and sketchbook in the crowded streets of Cairo or

* William Holman Hunt, *Pre-Raphaelitism and the Pre-Raphaelite Brotherhood*, vol. 1, 489–96. This notorious scene was later re-enacted by Hunt for a photograph.

Damascus, for example, was certain to attract attention. At best this would take the form of curiosity, both proactive and casual, but at worst it could be expressed in outright hostility or even acts of violence. With the ever-present risk of disturbance and disruption, or the unwelcome and obstructive attention of local officials, the simplest of excursions could become problematic.

In his diaries Gustav Bauernfeind indicates how, initially at least, he was charmed by the attention he received from the local people when exploring the streets of Damascus. "It is an absolute delight to see how inquisitively these folk follow the doings of Europeans," he wrote, "and what hilarious comments they often make regarding the subject."[85] *A Street Scene, Damascus* (*c.*1887) (Figure 36) brings into unusual focus the circus that would often gather around an artist trying to work in situ. In an unusual self-portrait, Bauernfeind depicts himself surrounded by a crowd and, with his pencil raised, appears to be explaining what he is doing to those assembled.

One of a mere handful of Orientalist paintings depicting an artist at work (see also pages 193–194), this painting relies on the interaction of the main protagonist with a group of locals as its focal point. Yet ironically this was often the very element that made such activity so time consuming and fraught with obstacles. Bauernfeind's apparently good-humored tolerance of the situation belies the reality of what must have been a constant and profound distraction. Although he carried a small notebook containing phrases in Arabic telling people to leave him alone or get out of his way or view, and later appears to have mastered some fluency in the language (see page 94), the situation did not improve greatly. In 1885 he wrote to his sister from Jaffa, complaining that "superstition, ignorance and indifference help together to make a painter's life a living hell."[86] The accounts of several of his peers are full of similar frustrations. In Bauernfeind's case, as with other artists working in the Orient, he was frequently forced to seek refuge on the rooftops of the cities in which he worked, from where he would attempt to photograph or sketch either the street scenes below, or the historic monuments that studded the skyline, without attracting attention.

Access to certain places and to particular types of building, notably mosques, was particularly sensitive. It was often dependent either on direct forms of superior protection, such as permission from the highest authority in the land, or on subterfuge. Religious sensitivities were such that the discovery of a Christian inside a mosque was likely to have the direst consequences. David Roberts almost discovered exactly what those entailed when, having entered the Mosque of al-Ghuri in Cairo disguised as a local, he noticed a group of weavers working on a large textile. Curious to inspect, he knelt down and touched it. The ensuing silence immediately alerted him to having caused grave offence, the severity of the error reinforced by his Egyptian escort putting his finger to his lip and drawing it across his throat. The textile was part of the hangings that adorned the Holy Kaaba in Mecca and regarded as sacred. "Had it been known that that sacred drapery had been polluted by the touch of an unbeliever—a dog of a Christian—and had I been caught, it is horrid to reflect upon what might have been my punishment for the unconscious sacrilege," Roberts wrote later.[87]

Later in the century the situation regarding Westerners visiting mosques appears to have eased somewhat, especially under French rule in North Africa. Yet tensions remained

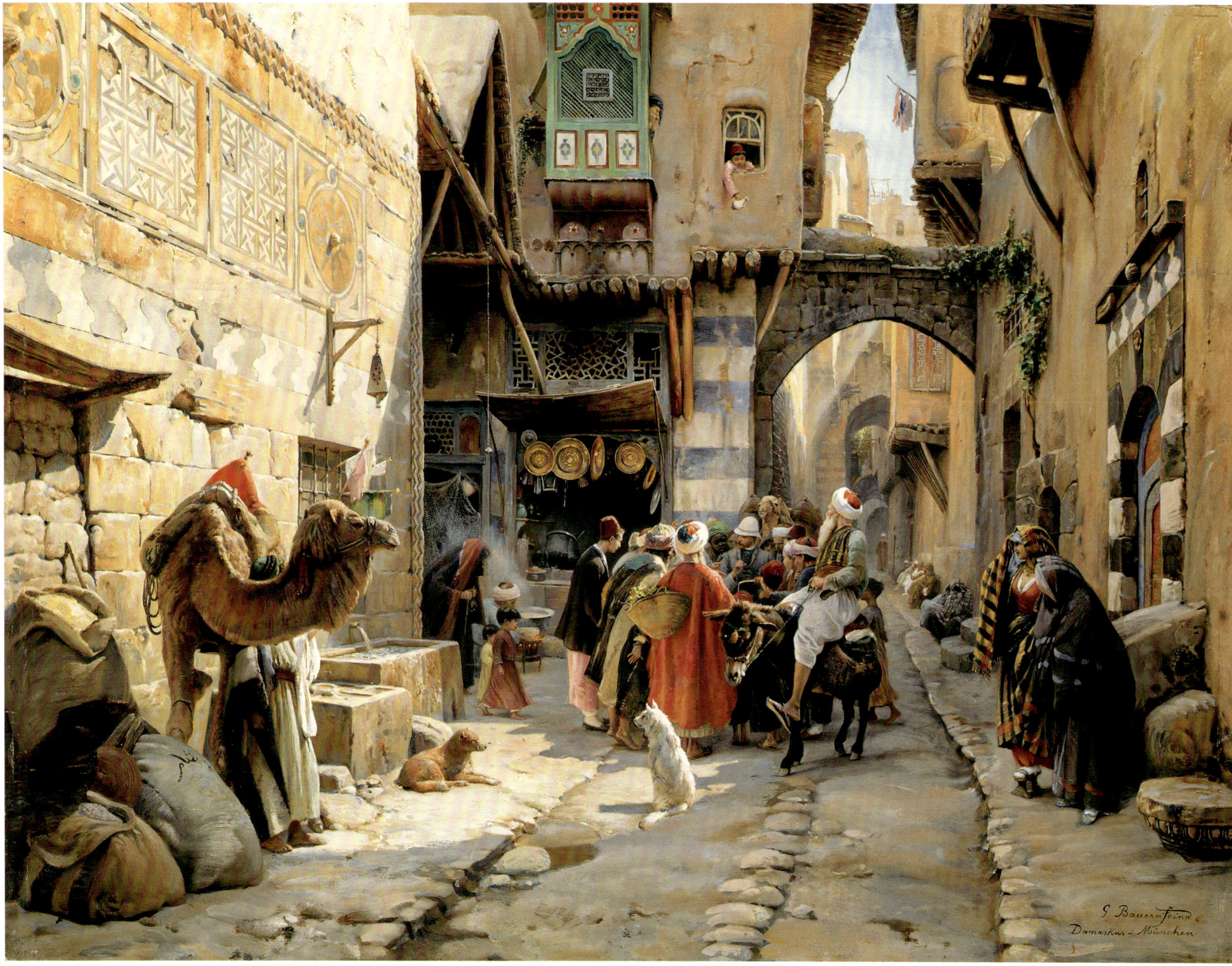
G. Bauernfeind
Damaskus - München

high, due in no small part to the arrogance shown by some of the colonial representatives, as Frederick Arthur Bridgman discovered in Algeria. "A French officer in top-boots once showed me a mosque, walking about as if the place belonged to him, and told me to keep on my shoes," recalled Bridgman. "As we came out, the offended Moslems looked at the officer with eyes that seemed to send out sparks of fire. Instead of sitting for hours without shoes on the cold, wet pavement, or even in the interior, when making studies, I adopted the plan of putting my socks outside of my shoes, which answered the same purpose. It does not make for a neat-looking foot, but that is of minor importance."[88]

Over thirty years earlier, David Roberts had only been able to enter mosques in Cairo when wearing local clothes and masquerading as a Muslim. Yet for a foreigner to do so was a risky business if he did not speak convincing Arabic, as discovery could result in unpleasant and difficult situations. Long-term expatriate residents such as Edward William Lane and John Gardner Wilkinson are known to have had excellent Arabic; John Frederick Lewis's proficiency in the language is less certain, but after a decade living in Cairo he can be expected to have developed at least a reasonable working knowledge. Particularly interesting meanwhile are the Arabic inscriptions in some of Lewis's paintings, notably in *An Intercepted Correspondence* (1869), in which three accurately reproduced quotes from the Qur'an are visible. These are evidence not so much of Lewis's proficiency in Arabic but of his observational skills. Cartouches containing poetic or Qur'anic inscriptions were a common decorative feature of Cairene houses of the seventeenth and eighteenth centuries and Lewis will certainly have encountered them, very possibly in his own residence (see page 73).[89]

36. Gustav Bauernfeind, *A Street Scene, Damascus* (*c.*1887). Oil on panel, 51.4 x 68 cm.

The linguistic situation with regard to other Orientalist artists is not always easy to deduce. A survey of nearly two hundred known to have traveled to the Middle East concluded that only 16 percent learned a foreign language (mostly Arabic or Berber, but also some Turkish), but their level of expertise was not assessed.[90] The presumption has always been that most artists barely bothered to make the effort, but there were some notable exceptions and obvious efforts to learn. Some artists demonstrated a distinct interest in local languages through their travel accounts; in her "Motley Images of Travel," Elisabeth Jerichau-Baumann gives many local terms for the objects and people about which she writes, but describes herself as having only "scant Arabic, with which I had prepared myself for this journey." A few of her fellow Orientalist artists are also known to have studied Arabic before traveling to the Middle East, among them Étienne Dinet, who studied it in Paris with fellow artist Paul Leroy, and Edward Lear, who certainly had Arabic lessons in preparation for his third trip to Egypt in 1866–67 and probably before then.

Certain artists had linguistic aptitude and were able to build up a good working knowledge of local languages. Thomas Seddon remarked toward the end of his first trip to the Orient in 1853–54 that "I know enough Arabic now to live among the Arabs without a dragoman, and could perfect myself very rapidly if I gave any time to the study."[91]

Jean-Léon Gérôme was adequately conversant with Arabic to be able to handle personally all the contractual arrangements with his dragoman and servants, and Gustav Bauernfeind was sufficiently fluent to be able to exchange witty retorts with people in the street. He writes about one occasion when he "went past the Snaniyeh [mosque] with Joseph (where I got in a sketch of the glazed ceramic tiles with inscriptions and ornaments over one of the windows) to the Meidân . . . . The spokesman [of a group of Arabs] addressed himself to Joseph! 'Let not the painter dare approach us here to make pictures of the Meidân!' 'Lesh?' [Why?] says I, 'Tabbak el Meidân?' [does the place belong to you?] He gave an embarrassed smile because he hadn't realized I understood him, and his companions were laughing at him."[92]

This last exchange reveals much about the nature of the Orientalists' experience when traveling in the countries they strove to portray. In most cases foreign artists visiting countries such as Egypt were unlikely to have mastered anything more than rudimentary instructions and basic vocabulary, their proficiency in Arabic as illusory as the persona created by the Oriental dress that some adopted. However, a few of these artist–travelers were able to break through that barrier, with Bauernfeind's brief bout of street banter a valuable insight into the world of cultural prejudice, language, and social solidarity, as well as the physical and emotional ownership claimed by both the visitors and the visited. It is significant that the incident culminated in shared humor, as it underscores the central dilemma posed by the Orient to the artist–travelers: how to engage with its people.

3. People

In 1881 Pierre-Auguste Renoir (1841–1919) paid his first visit to Algeria. Enchanted and inspired by what he found, he returned the following year, only this time he experienced frustration and annoyance. "Here I am installed in Algiers and negotiating with some Arabs to help me find some models," he wrote. "I have seen some incredibly picturesque children. Will I be able to get them? I'll do everything I need to for it. I've also seen some pretty women. If you knew the quantity of bad painters there are here. It's crazy, and above all the English, who spoil the few women who are available. It's insupportable."[1] The visit proved a difficult one for Renoir. After contracting pneumonia he spent several weeks convalescing and suffered permanent damage to his respiratory system.

His illness notwithstanding, Renoir's comments give an insight into issues faced by artist–travelers when visiting the Orient: the desperation to find models, without which future paintings risked being jeopardized; the resourcefulness and flexibility required to secure sitters; the presence of many artists of indifferent ability, anxious to ride on the bandwagon; and the petty jingoistic bickering that was often rumbling under the surface. As many artists were to realize, the success of their expeditions depended ultimately on developing productive relationships with local people.

Initial impressions were often less than encouraging. One of the most frequent observations made by visitors to the cities of the nineteenth-century Orient concerns the sheer volume of people they encountered on the streets. "Everything seems to roll like pebbles in a torrent," remarked Paul Lenoir about Alexandria in 1867, "your toes are trodden on through principle, and you are hustled and jostled . . . the dromedaries, asses, and horses appropriate the best part of the paved road and the foot-walks."[2] For artists, this seething mass of diverse and often bewildering humanity (and associated beasts) represented one of the greatest attractions of any visit, as well as posing some of the biggest challenges. As a potential source of subject material for paintings it was unrivaled, but social, cultural, and religious factors made access—whether physical or intellectual—immediately problematic.

Finding a way through the mêlée, in both physical and psychological senses, was a constant priority and one that most artists sought to achieve via their dragoman and other local contacts. The relationship between Western artist–travelers and the indigenous populations of the countries they visited was variously commercial, social, and cultural, and often took place on an accelerated timescale. This was especially so in the case of those artists who were visiting a destination only briefly and needed to see and do as much as they could in as short a time as possible. In such circumstances the chances of their achieving anything more than the most superficial of connections were slight, but for many this may not have mattered so long as they achieved their objectives of gathering adequate material to inspire their paintings. While forging longer-term understanding over repeated visits and/or periods of a few months' actual residency was not a guarantee of a more meaningful engagement, such bonds did develop between visiting foreigners and their Oriental hosts. This was in the face of what has traditionally been viewed as cultural intractability on the part of some Western visitors, specifically those who "usually remained thoroughly Christian and British, convinced that their culture was superior to the one they were observing. Their attitudes kept them apart from oriental life."[3]

Social Distinctions

Relations between all groups during the nineteenth century were underpinned, if not dictated, by prevailing values regarding race, class, and other factors such as religion. The opinions voiced by the majority of European visitors about

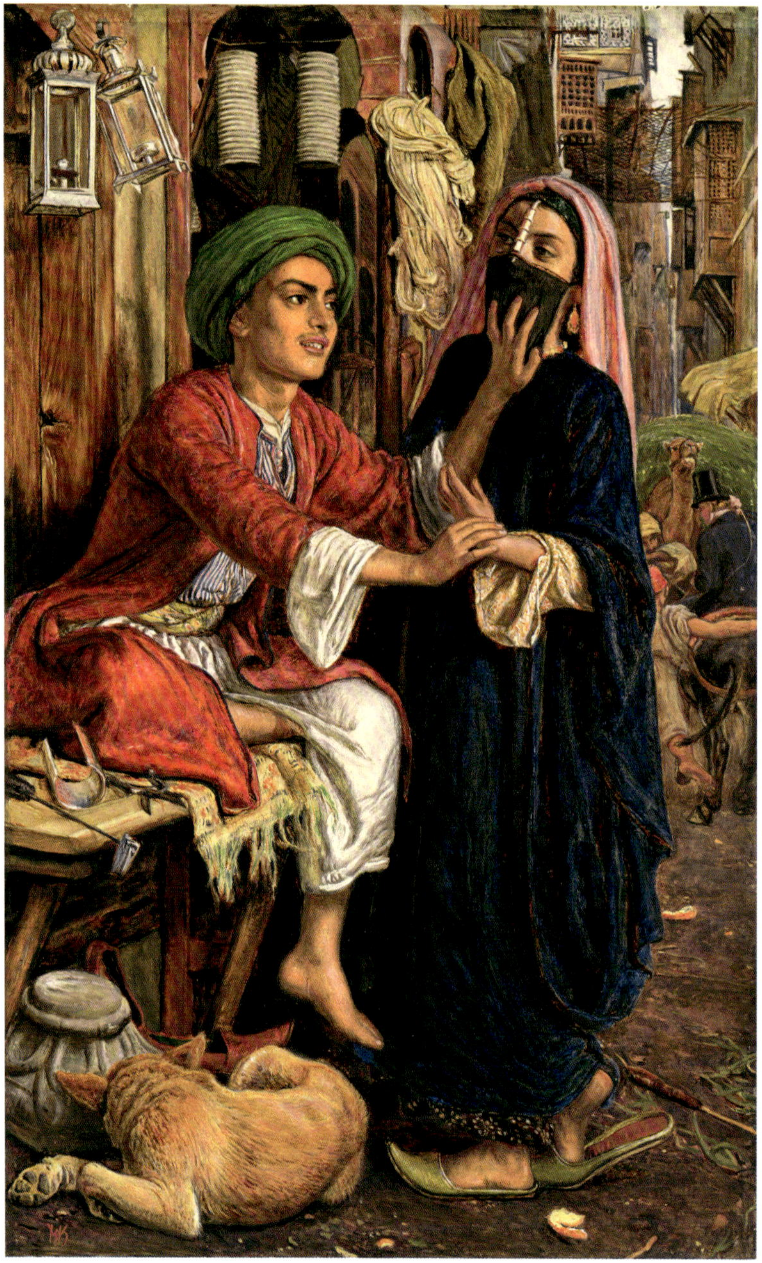

37. William Holman Hunt, *The Lantern Maker's Courtship* (1854–61). Oil on panel, 29.4 x 18.8 cm.

the Arab and Ottoman worlds typically included patronizing high-handedness, if not overt racism. One of the most revealing and shocking insights comes from the pen of Gustave Flaubert, in a letter written to his mother from Alexandria in November 1849. "One curious thing here is the respect, or rather the terror, that everyone displays in the presence of 'Franks,' as they call Europeans," Flaubert noted. "We have had bands of ten or twelve Arabs, advancing across the whole width of a street, break apart to let us pass."[4]

That native Alexandrians should have felt the need to give European travelers such a wide berth is sobering, and had obvious implications for those—such as artists—who relied largely on positive arrangements with local people in order to carry out their work. For an explanation of the "terror" cited by Flaubert one need look no further than the comments and behavior of William Holman Hunt, who took a decidedly robust and uncompromising approach when out on the streets. In a letter to Dante Gabriel Rossetti in March 1854, he observed that, "no stranger can have peace in the East unless he become the dictator of his own terms."[5] What this meant in practice is clear from his remarks regarding the people he encountered on the streets of Cairo, expressed in a letter to his patron Thomas Combe: "You would be astonished at their want of courage; when we in walking come upon a party of natives who do not at once get out of our way, at our expostulation with them, we raise our sticks, and lay about on ten or twenty altogether." While this may not have been universal or typical behavior by foreigners visiting Cairo and other parts of the Middle East during the nineteenth century, it was not exceptional either.

So strongly did Hunt believe in the need for Europeans to assert themselves vigorously when out in public in the Orient that he felt moved to depict this dimension in one of his most famous works, *The Lantern Maker's Courtship* (1861) (Figure 37). In the far right of the painting, a European wearing a top hat and sitting astride a donkey uses his riding whip to assail a cowering Egyptian, whose laden camel appears to be blocking the European's path. This particular outburst of racial bravado was not part of the original composition, which Hunt had started in Jerusalem several years earlier, but was added later in London with John Everett Millais as the sitter. Its juxtaposition with the tender scene that forms the main focus of the painting is symbolic of what has been described as Hunt's "complex response to the East, a blend of passion, prejudice and truth to nature."[6]

There was another approach, however; one followed by artists who were more immediately receptive to local people and customs, and as a result settled into their new environment with rather more grace and equanimity than Hunt found possible. This was particularly so with his erstwhile traveling companion, Thomas Seddon. That Seddon's approach bore fruit is revealed by comments made to him by Edward Lear and passed on by Seddon in a letter to a friend, with evident satisfaction: "[Lear] says that I have become accustomed to the language and habits of the people, and have settled down to work, in much shorter time than most persons, so my conscience is at ease."[7]

Seddon's ability to dismiss everyday trials and tribulations and focus on the positive aspects of his situation held him in good stead. One day he was attempting to work in the streets of Cairo but found the crowds so great as to be unable to continue. Having just sketched two dervishes he chose to leave, mentioning almost in passing in a letter home that "a stone was thrown at me," before going on immediately to report that "the storytellers, and men reading outside the coffee-shops, are very Arabian-Nightish."[8] On another occasion Seddon visited al-Azhar University, noting how "the older men are very polite, but the younger ones are dying to pelt you—in fact you are obliged to have men with long sticks to keep the boys off, or they would play you some trick; but two thousand turbaned boys, in every variety of colour and costume, make a most wonderful spectacle."[9] Clearly it took more than a tossed pebble to distract Seddon from the task at hand or from appreciating the artistic potential of the scenes before him. His remarks also betray the enduring power of the romantic mythology of the Orient and its Arabian Nights quality over those seeking to portray it.

Delicate situations like those mentioned by Seddon arose regularly on the streets. Most artists relied on their dragoman to deal with any problems, but inevitably they got involved personally at times. Gustav Bauernfeind's attitude to sketching and photographing in public varied from one of good-humored tolerance to bouts of extreme frustration (see page 91), but one particular episode reveals a degree of sensitivity and cultural awareness that other artists would have done well to emulate. On a walk through the streets of Damascus in April 1889, Bauernfeind found himself outside one of the entrances to the Sinan Pasha Mosque. An elderly warden was sitting on the *mastaba*, the raised bench next to the portal, through which Bauernfeind was able to glimpse the courtyard beyond. He took a photograph of the scene and returned later in the day, this time accompanied by his dragoman, Karam.

The events that followed give an insight into what were doubtlessly everyday episodes of cross-cultural misunderstanding between Western artists and the people in whose midst they were traveling and working. On this occasion Karam attempted to gain access to the mosque for his client, repeatedly trying to push open the door, which was then forced shut by those inside. Repeated attempts by both parties to have their way resulted in the door being damaged. In order to calm what had become a very inflamed situation, Bauernfeind offered to pay for the repairs and then adroitly used the opportunity to persuade the warden that, in return for a modest daily payment, he be granted permission to paint there. He returned regularly over the following days to make the detailed sketches he needed for his ultimate painting, *Warden of the Mosque, Damascus* (1891).[10] Through a considered and evenhanded approach, and a shrewd understanding of local ways of resolving disputes, Bauernfeind secured a positive outcome and one that appears to have kept honor intact on both sides. It is tempting to speculate on what result Hunt's doubtlessly more rambunctious approach might have produced in such a situation.

Achieving meaningful engagement with local communities required patience and sensitivity. One of the most successful such connections was made by Frederick Arthur Bridgman when he overwintered in Algiers. Arrangements were made by his guide for Bridgman to stay in the small courtyard house of a thirty-year-old widow called Baïa, who "had posed for artists a good deal; but since, with her youth on the wane, that lucrative occupation had become rarer, she gave her attention to weaving silk and woollen braid at three sous a yard."[11] By observing quietly and discreetly, Bridgman was able to record the everyday events and activities of the household and its women, a hugely privileged and almost unique position for a Western man (see page 134). A close friendship even developed, the artist and Baïa remaining in contact by mail for years after Bridgman had returned to France.

The formal nature of introductions and courtesies in the Arab world was also appreciated—eventually—by Edwin Lord Weeks. In 1877 he traveled to the Moroccan city of Rabat, then remote and visited by few foreigners, and described his first encounter with a group of the city's residents. "The circle of grave, and for the most part well-dressed, Moors which closed in around us expressed nothing of welcome in their attitude nor, in fact, any emotion whatever; they seemed to be simply awaiting events," Weeks wrote. "To say that the faces of these people expressed hostility, either open or concealed, might be going rather beyond the mark; but if any expression at all could be detected, it was of the nature of cold disapproval, and certainly not reassuring. But we were soon to learn that the Moor is not always to be read like an open book, and before many days most of the circle to whom we were indebted for this chilly reception hastened to offer their friendship . . . and they afterward improvised fêtes and tea-parties for us after the fashion of Moorish hospitality."[12]

Personal Relationships

For most artists visiting the Orient their single most important local relationship—beyond any high-level contacts—was usually with their dragoman. Yet despite the close proximity and degree of familiarity that one would expect to develop in such situations, many foreign visitors found their dragomans perplexing, infuriating, and even threatening. A description by Jean-Léon Gérôme of the selection process for a dragoman to lead him and his party on an expedition to Fayoum in 1867 confirms this stereotypical perception. "A veritable council of war, this ceremony had gathered together in our court a fantastic collection of physiognomies and of strange types," he wrote. "Nothing could be more singular than this legion of worthies, some of whom, armed to the teeth, recalled to us those types of brigands which till now we had only seen in the stories of Perrault and which spoil the comfort of travel like horrible nightmares . . . . Each one endeavoured to persuade us by *tours de force* of eloquence and bundles of certificates, forced from the victims who had honoured them with their confidence."*

Thomas Seddon's more equable observation, made on his arrival at Alexandria in December 1853, is both precise and revealing. He was met by his dragoman, who "interpreted in a language I have never discovered,"[13] a remark that crystallizes the degree of mystification, tinged with ironic suspicion, that characterized the relationship between dragoman and foreign visitor, at least from the latter's perspective. This cultural mismatch was doubtless compounded by the multinational, multilingual nature of the dragomans themselves. Many of those working in Egypt and Turkey were expatriates, often Greeks or Albanians, but there were also other nationalities, including Frenchmen, Italians, and Britons, of various religious affiliations, diverse social backgrounds, and multifarious skills. In a class-ridden and hierarchical society

---

* Hering, *Gérôme: The Life and Works of Jean Léon Gérôme*, 127–28. Charles Perrault (1628–1703) was a French writer of fairy tales based on traditional folklore.

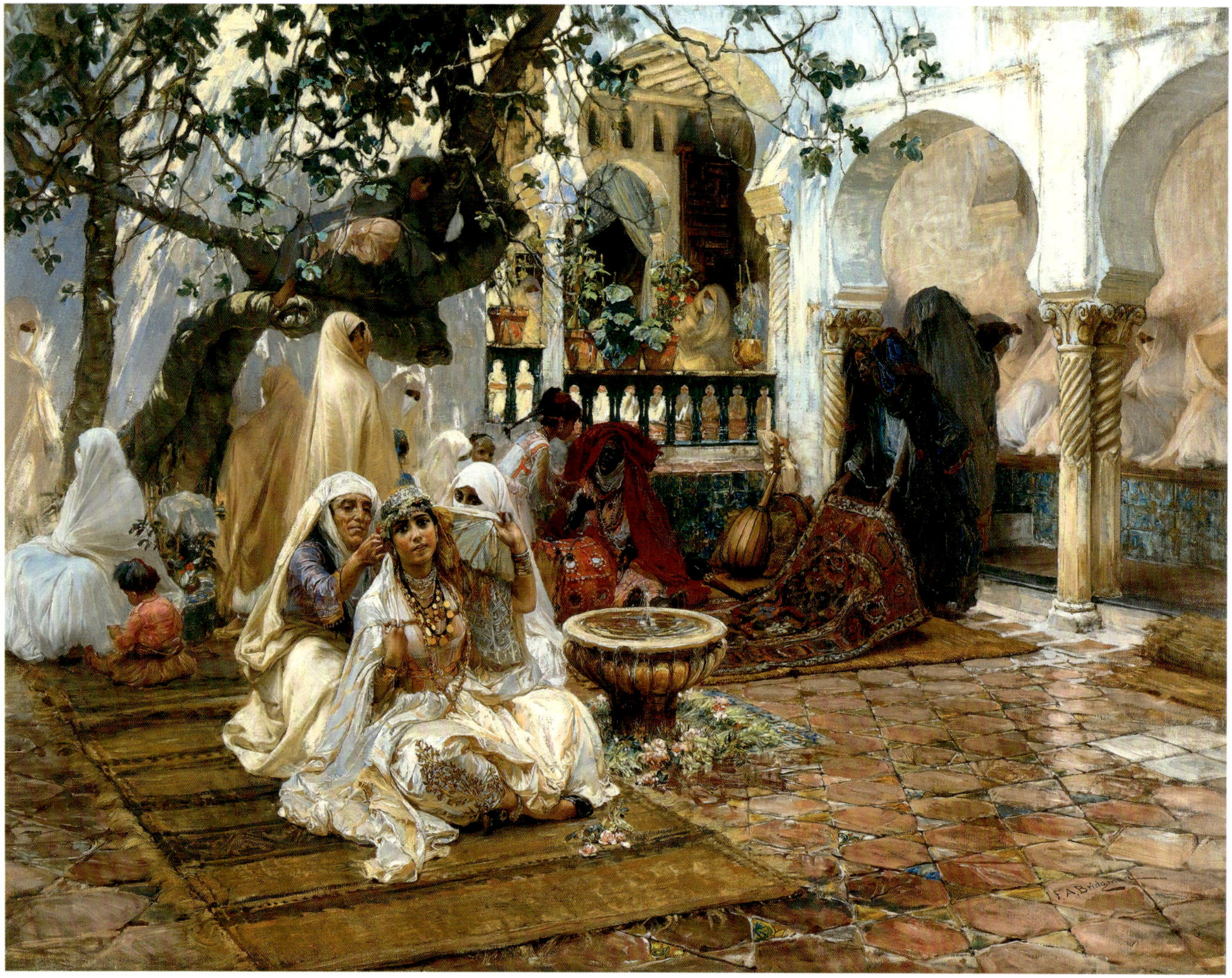

38. Frederick Arthur Bridgman, *Preparations for the Wedding, Algiers* (date unknown). Oil on canvas, 106 x 138.4 cm. Few artists, least of all male ones, were able to personally witness private scenes such as that represented in this work. Bridgman's close relationship with an Algerian family gave him unprecedented access.

like that of nineteenth-century Europe, this made it difficult for visitors to ascribe a social position to a dragoman: often impossible to pigeonhole, he was vulnerable to being viewed as suspect and destabilizing.

Despite any such misgivings, most visitors relied heavily on their dragoman. His absence, even if only temporary, left them feeling exposed and hopeless, as Viscount Castlereagh (whose party included the artist Antonio Schranz) revealed when his camp was approached by Turkish soldiers outside Hebron in 1842. "Very soon two sergeants entered the tent, and coolly sat down," he wrote. "I waited quietly for the attack, supposing it was an affair of quarantine. But no such thing happened. On the contrary, they were very quiet and well-behaved, with the exception of pulling about our swords, pistols, etc, and asking what each was worth. We had no dragoman with us, our baggage not having as yet arrived [the dragoman was presumably away arranging for it to be delivered]; therefore there were no means of sending them away, and as we were not very sure what might be in store for us, we did not choose to provoke any hostility."[14] On this occasion the moment was saved by the arrival soon thereafter of the district governor, but Castlereagh's account underlines how utterly dependent foreign visitors were on their dragomans. Life on the road in the Orient was certainly much more difficult, if not impossible, without one.

Managing one's dragoman was regarded as a constant process of negotiation and containment, as Frederick Goodall made clear. "My dragoman always asked for an hour at noon on Fridays for ablution and prayers," he recalled. "I granted it, for if the latter did no good I felt sure the former would, and in that respect I should not have objected if Friday had come round a little oftener; not that he looked dirty, on the contrary he was a very smart fellow, and, I thought, inclined to be honest, but this was not part of his religion. I must say I attributed his civility more to the fear of his not getting a good certificate from me when we parted than to any strong desire to do that which was right."[15] Despite such remarks Goodall clearly had a degree of confidence in his dragoman, whom he entrusted with the kitting-out of his rented house in Cairo.

In spite of their crucial role to visitors, dragomans remain elusive in the historical record as far as artists are concerned. To some extent this attitude reflects the social code of the day—dragomans were, after all, servants, as the guidebooks made clear (see page 66). Yet although some artists who left relatively detailed accounts of their travels—such as Goodall—refer only to "my dragoman," rather than to the individual by name, others are much more forthcoming. Two particular examples involve American artists, who perhaps displayed a more egalitarian approach than some of their European peers. Frederick Arthur Bridgman wrote warmly of his dragoman Miloud, whom he described as being "of much good nature and suavity of manner." Although his guiding skills were not necessarily of the highest order, Miloud was not backward in expressing an opinion—as Bridgman discovered when he queried why girls were not educated in Algeria. "Oh, *mais non*," replied Miloud. "The girls are of no consequence; they can help to do housework and wash the pavement of the mosques, and wait till they are married—good for nothing but man's use and pleasure. All misfortune in this world comes through the women; they are to blame for everything that goes wrong, and when a husband gets tired of his wife he has a perfect right to shunt her off." When

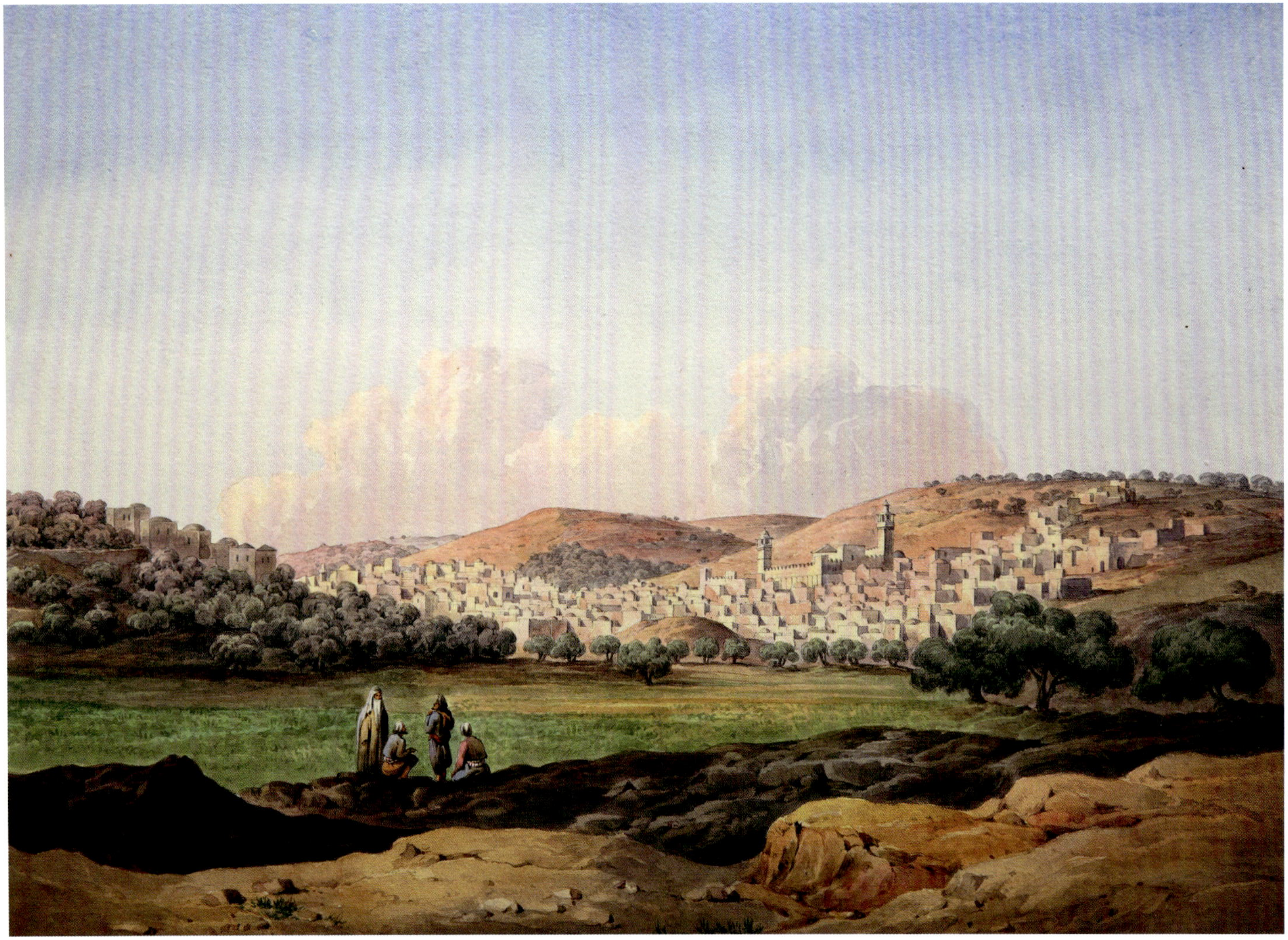

39. Antonio Schranz, *Hebron* (1841–42). Watercolor, 26 x 57 cm. It was outside Hebron that Lord Castlereagh's party, which included Schranz, had a potentially difficult encounter with some Turkish soldiers while their dragoman was away.

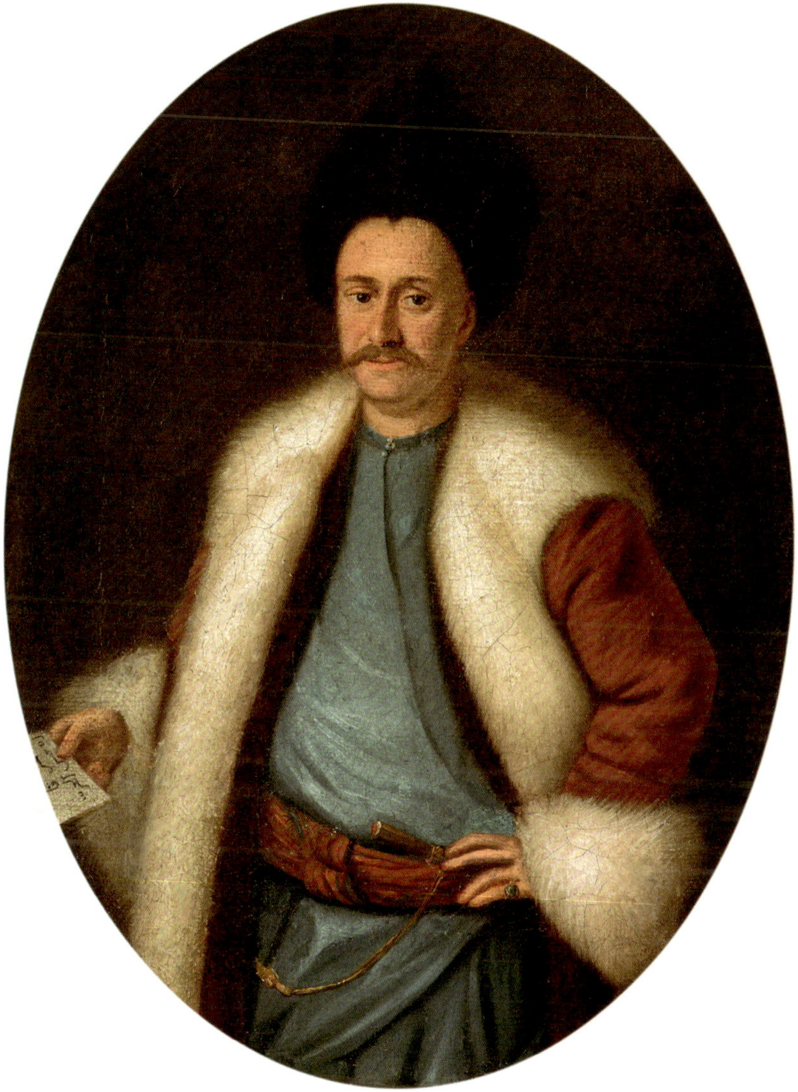

40. Jean-François Duchâteau, *Antoni Łukasz Crutta* (1779). Oil on canvas, 28.7 x 20.9 cm. The son of an Albanian father and Italian mother, Crutta was a highly successful dragoman in Constantinople and in the service of the Polish king, Stanisław August, from 1765 as a translator of Oriental languages. He was made a nobleman in 1775 and commissioned this portrait (and one of his wife) from Duchâteau, a French artist active in the Ottoman capital.

Bridgman ventured to suggest that a more enlightened view might be called for, Miloud was shocked. "Really, monsieur, it is incomprehensible," he retorted. "You look like an intelligent man, and seem to know a good many things and judge of them in a sensible manner, just as I do; but about the women I cannot understand how you can talk in this way."[16]

In 1892 Edwin Lord Weeks undertook an intrepid expedition from Turkey through Persia to India. For part of the route he and a journalist friend, Theodore Child, were guided by an Armenian dragoman called Artemis, whom they had engaged in Constantinople. Weeks refers regularly to Artemis in his account of the trip, noting how the "dapper dragoman . . . was compelled by fate to leave the flesh-pots of Pera and eat, drink and sleep in this tainted atmosphere." Life on the road proved even more taxing for the indecisive and hypochondriacal Artemis than it was for his American clients. Weeks relates how, when staying in a remote village on the Turkish–Persian border, he and Child even felt compelled to give up the best available sleeping quarters (warm and snug above a bread oven) to Artemis, who was suffering from one of his frequent chills. Eventually he was replaced and returned to Constantinople, but apparently with no hard feelings.

One dragoman who has emerged most convincingly from the anonymity of the shadows was Osman Effendi, born William Taylor in Perth, Scotland, in 1784. Even by the standards of British Orientalists, he led a remarkable life. Taylor ran away from home as a youth and enlisted in the army, arriving with his regiment in Egypt in 1807 as a part of a British attempt to depose the forces of local ruler Muhammad Ali. He was taken prisoner during the British defeat at Rosetta and subsequently sold into slavery. After an abortive attempt to escape, he was offered the choice by his owner of death or conversion to Islam. Taylor chose the latter, receiving the name of Osman, and was subsequently taken to Nubia and then Arabia by his owners before returning to Cairo. By now fluent in spoken and written Arabic and Turkish, he was generally well treated by his masters but remained a slave. He asked for the British consul-general, Henry Salt, to intercede on his behalf with the Egyptian viceroy Muhammad Ali to grant his freedom, but Salt only agreed to do so after an approach from the Swiss traveler, J.L. Burckhardt. A chance meeting in Jeddah had resulted in the two becoming friends and in Osman accompanying Burckhardt on his pilgrimage to Mecca in 1814, two years before he was finally made a free man.

Burckhardt died of dysentery in Cairo in 1817, with Osman at his side. In his will Burckhardt left Osman 2,000 piastres, all of his slaves, the contents of his house, and his wife. On the back of this bequest, Osman became a property magnate, buying houses in a part of Cairo popular with European visitors keen to experience the local atmosphere of the city. He was also appointed as dragoman and *mamluk* guard at the British consulate and was eagerly sought out by British travelers, businessmen, and officers, who had "often heard of him before they came to Egypt, and one of their first acts on arriving in Cairo was to contact him and ask his aid in any number of things."[17]

Despite his blue eyes, sandy-colored hair, and freckles, Osman passed convincingly as a Turk and served as the main mediator between European, especially British, visitors and Egyptian society. He was especially valuable to the coterie of expatriates that gathered in Cairo during the 1820s, people like Robert Hay and Edward William Lane, who rented a house from Osman on his first visit to Egypt. The two men subsequently became good friends and Osman was probably the source of much of the information that appears in Lane's *Manners and Customs*. The consummate entrepreneur, there was hardly any task to which Osman would not turn his hand, from orientation tours of Cairo and advice on the hiring of boats for expeditions up the Nile, to arranging fittings for local dress and settling disputes with customs officials. His vast knowledge and network of contacts made him an indispensable aide, supreme fixer, and a safeguard against the less savory aspects of Egyptian society. Hay noted how "nothing is to be accomplished without Osman, who keeps the rogues in order."[18] Evidence of the manner in which he bridged European and Oriental cultures exists in the nicknames conferred upon him, examples including the "Scotch Mameluke" and the "Caledonian Mussalman."

Osman died, probably of dysentery, in November 1835, his legacy appreciated in a very tangible sense by the Orientalists, notably David Roberts. In his journal entry for 22 December 1838, Roberts wrote, "Rented a house from Osman Effendi, an old Scotchman who built them and outfitted them for 8 piasters a day and for an outlay of 200 pt I made it really comfortable."[19] Osman had already been dead for three years by this point, but his larger-than-life personality lived on.

Coincidentally, within a couple of weeks Roberts had met a local man who also had a Scottish connection, an Egyptian called Hanafi Ismael. Apparently a convert to Christianity, and baptized in Glasgow in Roberts's native Scotland, Ismael worked as a manager in a government factory and was well educated and fluent in English. He and Roberts appear to have struck up an immediate rapport, and Ismael accompanied Roberts and his companion, Jens Pell,* when they and John Kinnear set out on their expedition to Sinai and Palestine, leaving Cairo on 8 February 1839. Roberts mentions Ismael several times in his journal, relating how he acted as their dragoman and proved to be a highly valued and congenial traveling companion. Later, *c.*1842–46, Ismael is recorded as being in Cairo, teaching Arabic to English visitors and also working as a dragoman on expeditions up the Nile.[20]

Not surprisingly, some dragomans found their way onto canvas and paper. Joseph Moussali worked for Jean-Léon Gérôme (who described him as "a very intelligent Syrian"[21] and appears to have held him in high esteem) and features in a travel journal drawing of Gérôme's party made by Willem de Famars Testas in 1868 (Figure 18). Elisabeth Jerichau-Baumann was impressed by the "elegantly dressed . . . handsome dragomans" she encountered at the Hôtel du Nil in Cairo, one of whom she later painted—although these men were more likely to have been doormen and attendants than true dragomans.[22] One of the most interesting examples of a dragoman appearing in an Orientalist painting

* The "Mr. Pell" referred to in Ballantine's biography of Roberts has been described in some sources as "Englishman John Pell." It appears, however, that he was in fact called Jens Pell, perhaps originally of Danish origin but living in England and with evidence suggesting that he was a frequent traveler overseas. Pell and Roberts corresponded regularly in the years following their time together in Egypt and Palestine. I am grateful to Briony Llewellyn and Krystyna Matyjaszkiewicz for bringing this information to my attention.

involves a man called Mahmoud, who features in John Frederick Lewis's *A Frank Encampment* (Figure 41)—described by John Ruskin as "among the most *wonderful* pictures in the world."[23] He is named in the work's full title, *A Frank Encampment in the Desert of Mount Sinai, 1842—the Convent of Saint Catherine in the Distance. The picture comprises Portraits of an English nobleman and his Suite, Mahmoud, the Dragoman, Etc., Etc., Etc., Hussein, Scheikh of Gebel Tor, Etc., Etc.* While his precise identity is unclear, a dragoman of the same name is mentioned in travel accounts as having worked for Lord Prudhoe on his two visits to Egypt,* as well as for the traveler Eliot Warburton[24] and for at least one other European visitor, so he was presumably well regarded. Whether this is the same Mahmoud who worked for Viscount Castlereagh as "our factotum" in Egypt and Palestine in 1842—and whom Castlereagh described as "possibly the best man in the world"[25]—must remain speculation, as Mahmoud is a common name across the region. However, reliable dragomans and guides were considered a precious commodity by traveling Europeans and were often referred on recommendation, so this could well be the same Mahmoud.

Relationships with servants more modest than a dragoman were usually not considered worthy of note by travelers. Stereotypes abound, with incidents of laziness jumped upon by foreign visitors as evidence of the ruinous indolence and sloth of the Orient and, by implication, the superiority of the industrious West. Accounts by Orientalist artists are littered with complaints about idle Arabs, servants or otherwise. Edward William Lane, certainly more attuned to local society than most other foreigners, still maintained that "indolence pervades all classes of the Egyptians," and David Roberts was scathing about what he saw as the descent of the country into a state of slothful barbarism: "During my progress I passed ponderous remains of places once inhabited by peoples and dynasties long, long forgotten; . . . splendid cities once teeming with a busy population, and embellished with temples and edifices, the wonder of the world, now deserted and lonely, or reduced by mismanagement and the barbarism of the Moslem creed, to a state as savage as the wild animals by which they are surrounded. Often have I gazed on them till my heart actually sickened within me."[26] Aspects of this sense of stagnation, decay, and lost glory were later developed by other Orientalist artists, including Jean-Léon Gérôme in paintings such as *The Snake Charmer* (*c.*1870).

Meanwhile, there were exceptions to the general rule of disparaging servants and helpers. Thomas Seddon wrote with affection and humor about Hippopotamus Jack, his "running footman," who had once accompanied a hippopotamus to London—a gift sent to Queen Victoria by the Egyptian pasha—and was also a seasoned snake charmer. "Hippo" proved both hardworking and entertaining, regaling all and sundry with tales of his travels to England. While maintaining the required social distinctions and patronizing paternalism of the day, Seddon appears to have become rather proud of his footman. "My ornamental servant, 'Hippopotamus,' I have rigged out in a blue blouse and white Turkish drawers," he wrote, "and having had his head shaved, and almost induced him to use soap, he is magnificent."[27]

* Lord Prudhoe was at one point incorrectly identified as the European character in the Lewis painting; see Weeks, *Cultures Crossed*, 133.

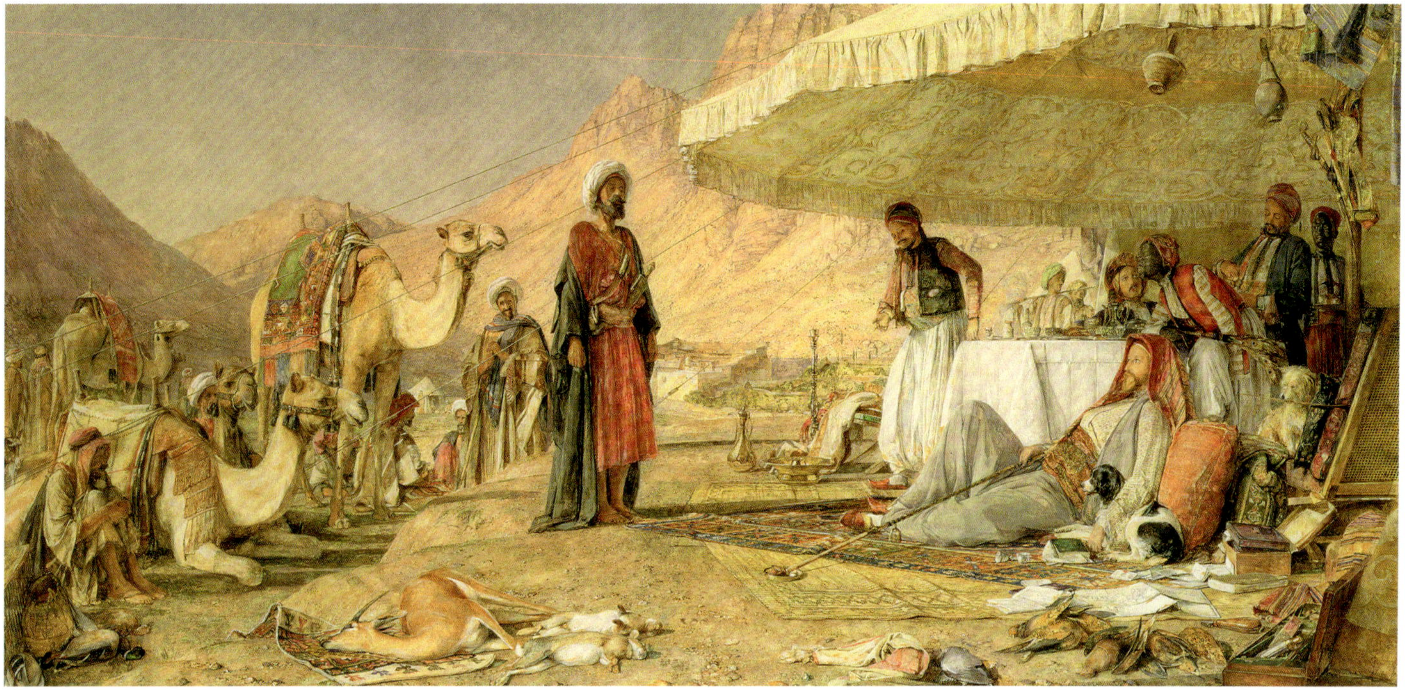

41. John Frederick Lewis, *A Frank Encampment in the Desert of Mount Sinai, 1842* (1856). Watercolor, gouache, and graphite, 66.7 x 135.9 cm. The work's full title (see facing page) includes a reference to "Mahmoud, the dragoman," most likely the figure standing alone under the canopy at the end of the table.

Amelia Edwards equally valued and respected the support of Salame, a member of her boat crew and who escorted her on all her excursions and particularly assisted when she was sketching or painting. "He is a native of Assûan, young, active, intelligent, full of fun, hot-tempered withal, and as thorough a gentleman as I have ever had the pleasure of knowing," she wrote. "Curled up in a shady corner, he . . . is ready with an umbrella as soon as the sun comes round; and replenishes a water bottle or holds a color box as deftly as though he had been to the manner born."[28]

More typical of Western attitudes, however, is the picture David Roberts felt moved to describe in a letter to his daughter, written after he had returned to Cairo in December 1838 after his trip up the Nile. "On the whole I was tolerably comfortable and as independent as any king in Christendom," he wrote. "There I sat, sketch-book in hand, smoking my long Turkish chabuk, with a servant to attend to all my wants, and a boat with eight men at my command to stop or go on, as I liked, and who never received an order without insisting on kneeling and kissing my hand."[29] It may well have been a royal lifestyle, but it gave Roberts little chance of supplementing his views of the Orient's architecture, landscapes, and monuments with anything more than a rudimentary understanding of the people who lived among them. This is ironic, given the enduring popularity of his works and their role in shaping Western perceptions of the region, but was probably of little concern to Roberts himself. He was not a portrait painter and, with a handful of exceptions, did not focus on portraiture during his Oriental travels.[30] People were usually presented as supporting vignettes to enhance the grandeur of his main act, and on at least one occasion he chose to include himself in the frame (see page 193).

Desert Nobility

One aspect of the human dimension to the Orient on which most artists were in agreement was the appeal of the Bedouin. Visually alluring, revered for their mastery of desert skills such as falconry and horsemanship, and with a reputation for nobility, honesty, honor, and hospitality, they were an immediately exciting subject. They feature prominently in works by many artists, from Théodore Frère and Eugène Fromentin to Carl Haag, John Frederick Lewis, Henri Rousseau (1875–1933), and Adolf Schreyer (1828–99), variously as individuals and as groups, and with their encampments a popular choice of setting for romanticized desert scenes. Particularly attractive for artists and their audience alike was the strongly developed martial culture of the Bedouin. This dimension served as a physical counterweight to their religious piety, a focus for artists like Otto Pilny (1866–1936), and to the spiritual qualities that many felt the Bedouin possessed—a characteristic often equated by artists and writers with the epic scale and energy of the Bedouin's desert environment, which many artists found equally inspirational.

On a more practical level, the Bedouin also fulfilled an essential function as guides, escorting parties of foreigners across the desert. Even the skeptical David Roberts was impressed when he met the Bedouin guides who were to lead him from Cairo on his journey to Mount Sinai in February 1839. "Introduced to Hassan, the sheikh of the Bedouins, and his followers," he wrote. "They seem a wild family, but I like their countenances, and am much mistaken if they are not trustworthy. Things are now in ship-shape, and I feel I shall enjoy the journey."*

This was high praise indeed by Roberts's standards, but his confidence was well placed and his Bedouin guides—members of the Beni Said tribe—led him and his caravan safely across the Sinai Peninsula to the Red Sea port of Aqaba, where the party was entrusted into the hands of another tribe, the Alawin. The respect accorded by Roberts to his Bedouin escorts is illustrated by the fact he painted one of them, the result—*Portrait of Besharah*—being one of his few single-figure works.

For those artists interested in finding material and inspiration for the production of Biblical motifs in their paintings, the Bedouin were a particular focus of interest.

* Ballantine, *The Life of David Roberts*, 114. The same sheikh features as "Hussein, Scheikh of Gebel Tor" in John Frederick Lewis's painting, *A Frank Encampment* (see page 106).

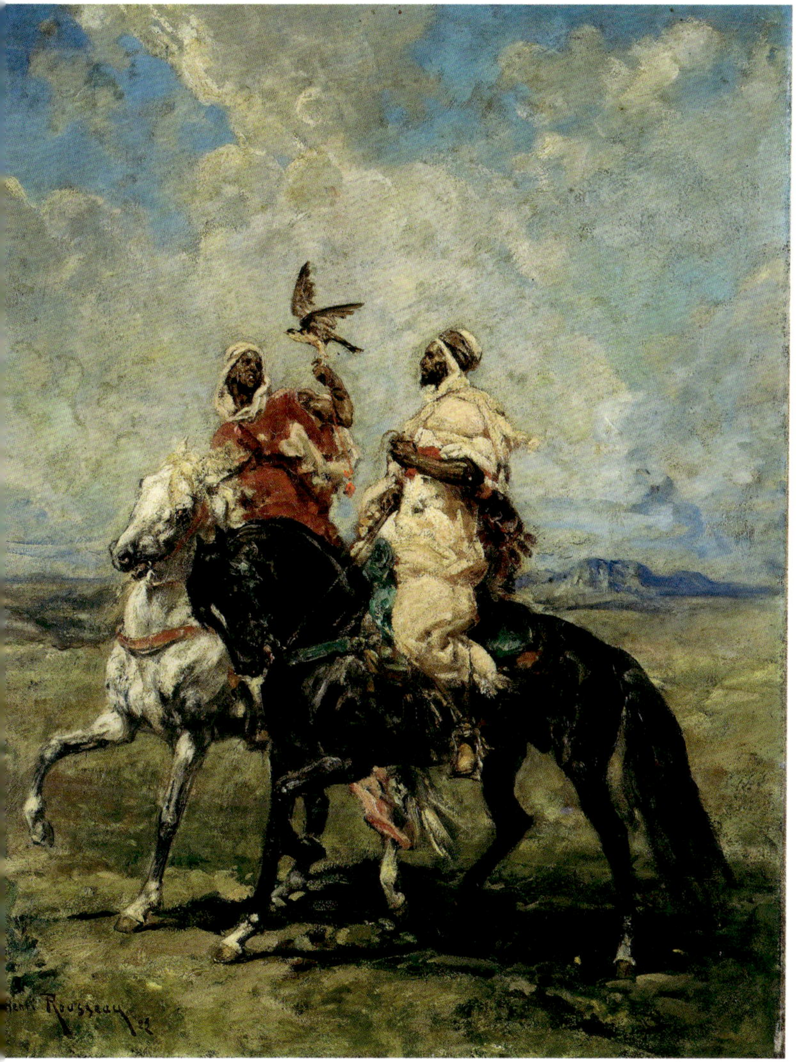

42. Henri Rousseau, *Chasseurs au faucon* (Falconers) (1922). Oil on canvas, 73 x 59.8 cm. Scenes of hunting and falconry were popular subjects among the Orientalists, not least because of their commercial appeal to European and American audiences.

Frederick Goodall had one of his first encounters with them when camping near the Sphinx in 1858, noting that he had made "some most successful studies of the Bedouin in their simple and, I might say, classical draperies, consisting merely of their long blankets wound round them—no two being wound exactly alike."[31] Draperies were an important aspect for many Orientalist artists, as they were seen to echo directly the robes of classical antiquity and thereby endorse the perceived longstanding nobility of the Bedouin.

Twelve years later Goodall traveled to Saqqara, where large numbers of Bedouin were gathered. "Early in my sojourn I was fortunate enough to come upon an encampment of pastoral Bedouin, with large flocks of sheep and herds of goats, besides breeding camels," Goodall recalled. "This was just what I wanted for the study of Scriptural subjects. With these Bedouin I stopped three months, painting the women weaving and the Arabs spinning the wheel, shearing sheep, taking their flocks to and from the pasture, grinding the corn with two stones worked by two women, all exactly as it is described in the Bible."[32] It was this timeless, authentic quality of a people seemingly unadulterated by what many foreign artists saw as the contamination of urban life and outside influences, that gave the Bedouin and their desert home such appeal.

Carl Haag—who camped with Goodall near the Sphinx in 1858—took a particular interest in the Bedouin, spending eighteen months living and traveling with itinerant tribes during 1859–60. Although probably accompanied by his dragoman, to all intents and purposes Haag would have lived much the same life as the Bedouin in whose company he moved, sharing the same food and at the very least observing, if not participating in, the daily routines of Bedouin life. It was an experience few other artists were ever able—or prepared—to undertake. The art critic Frederick Wedmore later described how in this way Haag was able to gather information on Bedouin customs and habits, from weddings and education to livestock care and funerals, and including how to throw a spear and use a sword.[33] It was an uncommon level of direct engagement and one that made Haag better placed than most of his peers to paint authoritative works on the Bedouin and their desert setting. These included portrait studies of subjects shown as individuals rather than as types, and of situations rarely encountered at first hand by Westerners, such as a Bedouin father holding his young son in his arms.*

Such depictions of local people as individual characters rather than as generic representatives of particular professions or ethnic groups was unusual. One of the greatest exponents of this craft was Amadeo Preziosi, whose long period of residence in Constantinople (see page 74) allowed him a rare degree of access to the lives and customs of the diverse communities living in the imperial capital and beyond, in the wider Ottoman hegemony. Although the majority of his figure subjects were undoubtedly "types," one group of watercolors stands out for its nuanced characterization of individual people. This is a series of thirty-one portraits of men and two of women that he created between 1852 and 1856, selected from a myriad of social, cultural, and professional backgrounds and the result of Preziosi "collecting exotic individuals much as a lepidopterist might collect rare and colourful butterflies."[34]

If Carl Haag was unusual in the amount of time he spent with the Bedouin, the experience of Étienne Dinet was truly remarkable. His association with Algeria spanned over four decades and he assimilated with the indigenous society and cultures more than any other artist in the Orientalist cadre. This gave him unparalleled understanding and access, placing him in a unique position as a non-native recorder and interpreter of everyday Algerian life. The main focus of his paintings were dancers, bathers, and children, but Dinet was also very interested in Bedouin culture, often traveling to tribal encampments on the fringes of the Sahara Desert. He especially admired the close affinity of the Bedouin with their environment, an unremittingly harsh context but one still able to provide them with the necessities of life, thanks to their inherited knowledge, skills, and resourcefulness. Bedouin bravery and hunting prowess were a particular focus of his interest, with several paintings—including *Le Guetteur (The Lookout)* (1906)—depicting hunters pitting themselves against the desert and their quarry.

Even by 1904, the year he made the desert-edge trading town of Bou-Saâda his base, Dinet's unique insight into, and relationship with, his adopted country was a source of respect and wonder to many contemporary critics. "No other painter has evidenced such an intimate knowledge of the East," declared Frederick Morton in the journal *Brush and Pencil*, "no one has caught and recorded with such fidelity the spirit of the Orient—people, topography, atmosphere, everything in his canvases is true to fact; no one has so vitalized his pictures with the breath that is not of the Occident." Morton attributed such

---

* *Bachist, a Howazee Bedawee, and Mabzookh, his little son* (Figure 43) is dated 2 August 1859, the same date as *Fadime, a Bedaween woman*. Both works are unusual in their intimacy. See Drewett Neate, *Watercolours by Carl Haag*, 54.

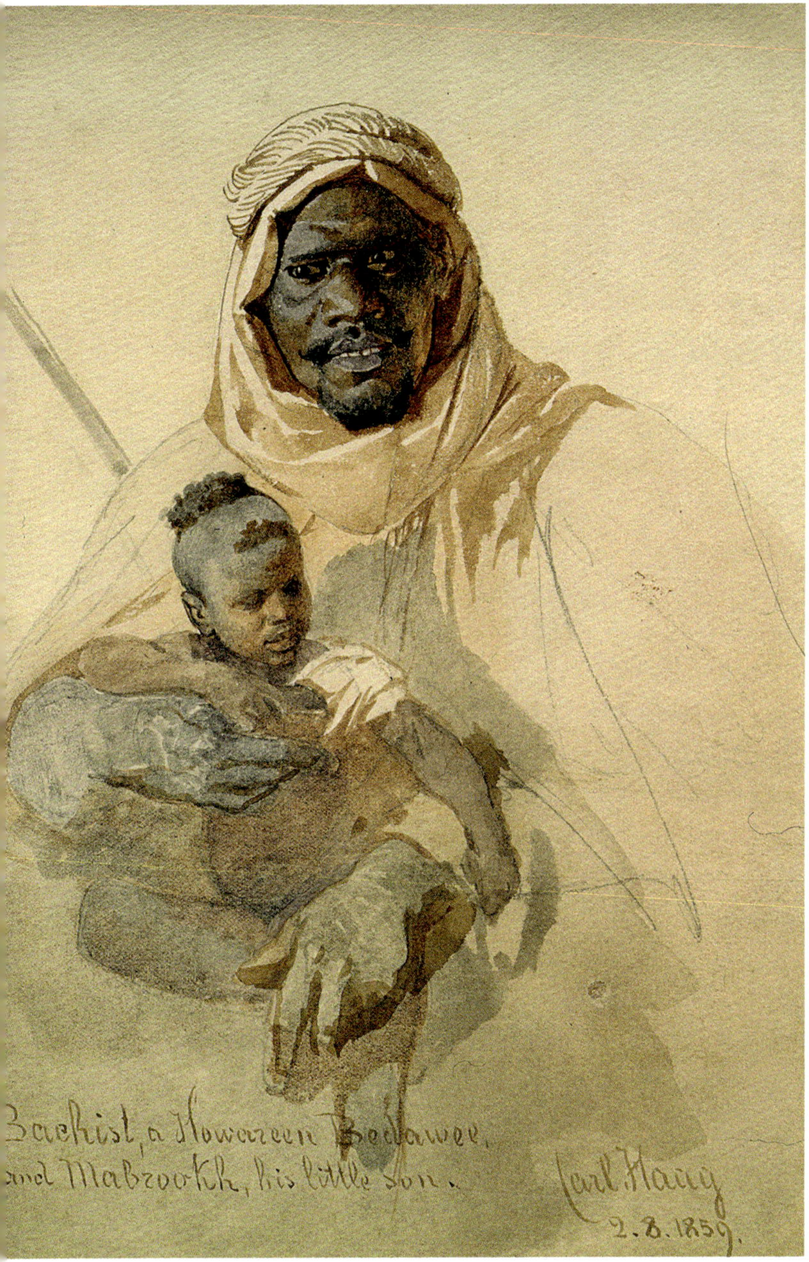

skill and insight to Dinet's ability to move seamlessly between East and West: "Dinet, in a large measure, has become one of the strange people he loves to paint . . . he has acquired the faculty of adapting himself to his shifting environment. In Paris he is modest and unassuming, companionable and thoroughly the man of the world; in the camps and towns of his favorite models he looks and acts the Arab chief."[35]

Central to Dinet's professional success was his close personal friendship with the Algerian writer and chieftain Sliman ben Ibrahim, a bond alleged to have been forged when Sliman saved Dinet's life during a tribal skirmish. Sliman taught the Frenchman about the folklore, legends, and history of the peoples of Algeria, particularly those of the Ouled Naïl, a Berber tribe with a strong tradition of music and dance. The two men collaborated on illustrated books, and Dinet painted portraits of his friend, both in Algeria and on a visit to Paris in 1896, with Sliman depicted walking across a wet and windy Place de la Concorde in his traditional robes (Figure 44). Theirs was a deep and very productive bond, and of a type not known to have been enjoyed by any other leading Orientalist artist (although recorded in the case of other Europeans active in the region, such as T.E. Lawrence). Morton understood the significance of the relationship and had a barb in the tail of his article for those artists hoping to join the Orientalist bandwagon on the back of a short visit.

43. Carl Haag, *Bachist, a Howazeen Bedawee and Mabzookh, his little Son* (1859). Pencil and watercolor wash on paper, 25.5 x 17.5 cm. The time Haag spent living with Bedouin families in Egypt allowed him to depict them both convincingly and with a depth of understanding rare among the Orientalists.

"An occasional glimpse of a new scene or an occasional contact with a new people cannot be productive of great art," he sneered. "The pictures of the Orient by the many artists who have essayed these subjects have sufficiently proved this . . . . They bear the same relation to the actual that a stage walk does to a natural gait, or stage tears to actual sorrow. Dinet, thanks to Sliman, became one of his tribe."[36]

Compatriots Abroad

The degree of cultural integration achieved by Dinet was exceptional. Most overseas visitors to the Orient stayed within their own tightly knit social milieu, but the camaraderie that one might expect to bond foreigners when traveling in such a demanding destination was not always forthcoming. The British applied their rigid class system as much abroad as at home, sorting themselves out into appropriate strata according to the social code of the times and often demonstrating a wariness of foreigners generally. Viscount Castlereagh was particularly exercised by the behavior of some of his fellow Europeans when he was in Cairo in 1842. "By way of change, one meets some straggling Franks, who are disreputable-looking vagabonds, and a disgrace to more civilized Europe. It is strange that most of these imports are of the worst description. . . . The better sort of Europeans, who pass through this place, stay so short a time that they are hardly known, and consequently the people judge of us, if they judge at all, by the specimens who gain a livelihood by cheating and robbing in every shape."[37] It is not clear toward exactly whom Castlereagh's ire was directed, but that shady European characters frequented Cairo is beyond doubt. Evidence suggests that respected foreign residents such as

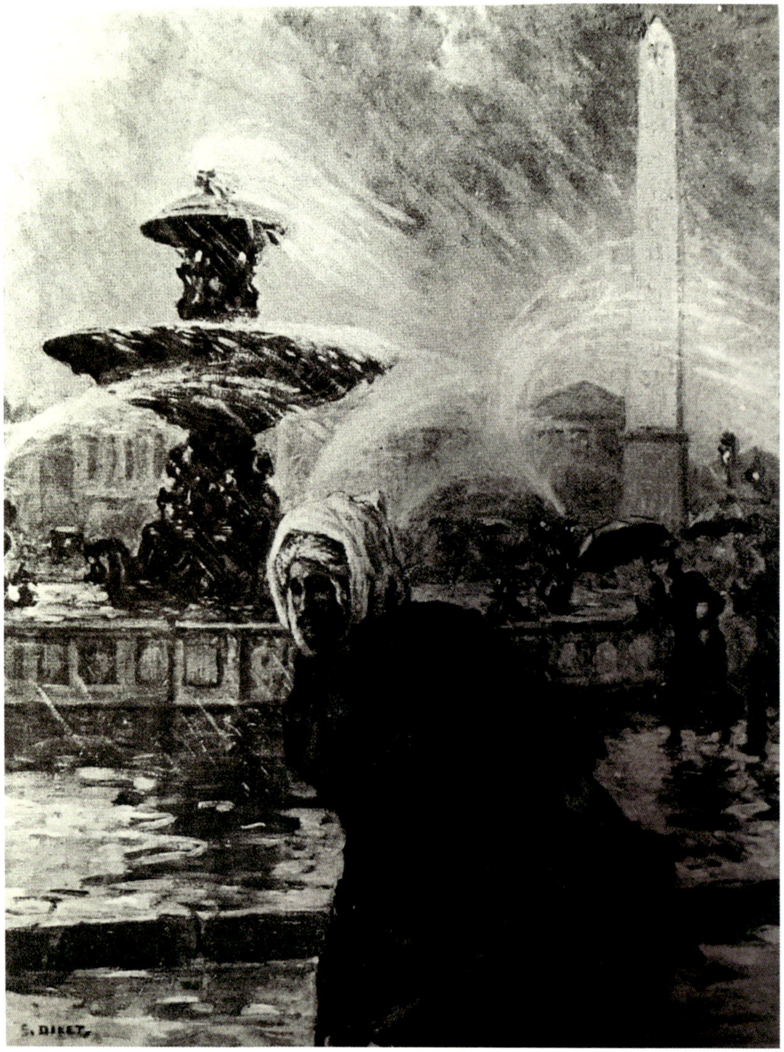

44. Étienne Dinet, portrait of Sliman ben Ibrahim at the Place de la Concorde, Paris (probably 1896). The whereabouts of the original work are unknown, but it was reproduced in Dinet and Sliman's 1908 co-publication, *Tableaux de la vie arabe*.

Edward William Lane and John Gardner Wilkinson shared Castlereagh's sentiments and sought to distance themselves from what they perceived as undesirable elements among the expatriate population.*

With so many Western visitors in places like Cairo and Luxor at peak times of year, it was difficult if not impossible for them to avoid each other. As early as 1835 Charles Gleyre was prompted to remark that "you no longer know where to go to get away from painters. There are at least a dozen here, all brilliant to hear them tell it. They have spoiled my Cairo."[38] William Holman Hunt found the company of his compatriots equally tiresome at times, describing how "the desert is beautiful; but . . . I could not settle down there, [and] I find a good deal of difficulty in doing so here [Cairo], for there are four or five other Englishmen in the hotel, and it is impossible to feel secluded enough to study."[39] Mid-century visitors to Egypt often remarked on how crowded the main sites were during the busy winter season, and how prices went up accordingly. The end of the American Civil War in 1865 saw a substantial increase in Americans traveling overseas, a development that Edward Lear found especially irksome. Writing from Cairo on 9 March 1867, he remarked, "you cannot imagine the extent of the American element in travel here! They are as 25 to one English. They go about in dozens & scores—one dragoman to so many—& are a fearful race mostly."[40]

* Many Europeans came to Egypt seeking opportunities under the pro-Western policies of the viceroy, Muhammad Ali. Not all such arrivals conducted themselves to the highest standards, Edward William Lane referring to them as "a most disreputable set of vagabonds." See Thompson, "Osman Effendi: A Scottish Convert," 90.

Some visiting Americans were not beyond making wry observations about their fellow nationals, among them Edwin Lord Weeks who, with his traveling companion A.P. Close, was received by members of the resident American community when visiting Beirut in 1872. The city was home to a large number of foreign missions, from American Protestants to French Jesuits, many of them running schools, colleges, clinics, and printing presses. Weeks wrote with some sarcasm about the eagerness of the Americans to entertain visitors and the grand style in which they lived. "We have received hospitable welcome from the resident Americans at Beirut," he noted. "Dr. Bliss,** the president of the American college, who looks like [indecipherable manuscript addition] called one evening and invited us to supper the next evening which was further seconded by a note from his wife the next morning inviting us to 'come early and see the sunset fade on Lebanon and the sea.' Here was another specimen of the houses in which missionaries learn to 'buffer and be strong' in a strange land; rooms twenty feet high opening into a marble hall as large as the [indecipherable manuscript addition] from the windows and balconies you look down over the roofs of square stone, villas with Moorish windows, gardens with tall cypresses, and occassional [sic] dates, way beyond the Moslem quarter with densely paved flat roofs and minarets, the purple and violet sea, and the muddy slope of Lebanon."[41]

**Dr. Daniel Bliss, founder in 1866 of the Syrian Protestant College, which later became the American University of Beirut (AUB).

There is evidence of periodic breakdowns among Western travelers into national stereotypes and accompanying prejudices, as Renoir's comments (see page 95) indicate. A particular flashpoint was Egypt, where the British and French enjoyed an often mutually antagonistic relationship shaped by the *Realpolitik* of the day and which dated back to before Napoléon's invasion of the country in 1798. Although the subsequent accounts by Vivant Denon and others had helped inspire a generation of British travelers to become interested in Egypt and its monuments, the French achievements had also been the target of criticism and ridicule in Britain. In his *L'insurrection de l'Institut Amphibie or The Pursuit of Knowledge* of 1799 the satirical cartoonist James Gillray had lampooned what some saw as French attempts to impose their values on the Egyptians. It proved to be an enduring image.

In November 1849 Gustave Flaubert and Florence Nightingale—the former still seven years from publication of his celebrated novel *Madame Bovary*, the latter five years before her famous endeavors during the Crimean War—may have been coincidental passengers on the same boat up the Nile from Alexandria to Cairo. They were not known to each other, but from a distance Flaubert scathingly described what seems to have been the Nightingale party as "hideous" and Florence's traveling companion Selina Bracebridge as "a sick old parrot."[42] There was often a degree of competition between travelers as they made their way between the various 'must-see' sites of Egypt in what could be testing conditions. This was an increasingly well-trodden route, with accommodation, reliable guides, and transportation often in short supply during the busy winter months, when prices rose considerably. Nightingale, for example, wrote of the "ruck" of English visitors at Aswan and of her frustrations with a group traveling with Lord Northampton a few days ahead of them and who "had devoured everything like locusts, even all the rice and milk."[43]

Nightingale also describes an impromptu encounter with John Frederick Lewis and his wife Marian. Arriving at the island of Philae at dawn on 23 January 1850, Nightingale and her party were surprised to find a European man and woman already there, the man busy sketching. It was Lewis. "He is making a series of drawings of the temple," Nightingale wrote, "and is a picture himself; he always wears the Turkish dress—a blue *gubbeh*, white kaftan, red turban, and a long white beard."[44] The discovery that she and the Lewises had friends in common, notably Charles Murray, British Consul-General in Cairo, and Dr. Abbott, an antiquities collector and long-time British resident in Egypt, ensured immediately cordial terms.

Each party entertained the other over the course of the next few days, with Nightingale's party hosting dinner on *Parthenope*, their *dahabiya*,* and the Lewises reciprocating in a tent described by Nightingale as "bitterly cold." For Nightingale and her companions this dinner must have been a highly unconventional occasion, with the guests swathed in blankets, chairs and carpets being transported from place to place and, when the time came for them to take their leave, Lewis leading the way to the beach, "shuffling first, in Turkish slippers, and losing one among the sand." During the course of the evening Nightingale was shown some of Lewis's works, noting dryly that "his figures are beautiful,

* A typical Nile boat favored by foreign visitors; see page 80.

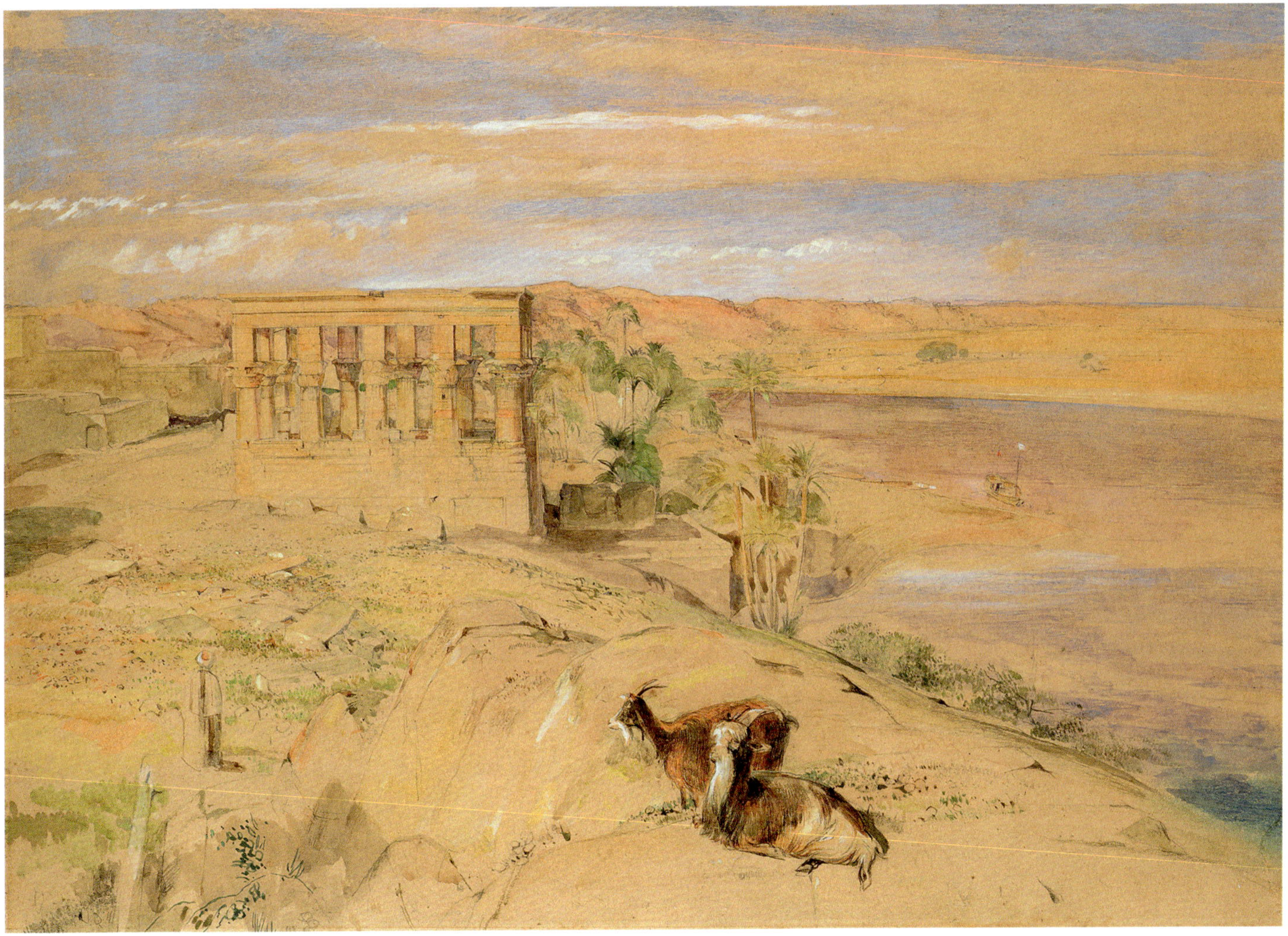

45. John Frederick Lewis, *The Hypaethral Temple at Philae* (1850). Pencil and watercolor on paper, 35.3 x 50 cm. It was while visiting Philae that Lewis and his wife met Florence Nightingale and her party.

his buildings commonplace."[45] Her account serves as an interesting counterpoint to that of Thackeray; hers rather prosaic and detached, his more lyrical and promotional in tone, as one might expect from a satirical writer who already knew the man about whom he was writing and may have had a particular agenda in mind (see pages 200–201). Both descriptions offer useful contemporary insights into the personality of the enigmatic Lewis and his time in Egypt, as well as shedding light on the psyche of the British abroad.

For those Britons traveling in parts of the Levant where French influence held sway, there is evidence of a greater sense of insecurity than they might have felt in British-oriented Egypt. Edward Lear was especially jittery, having already been attacked at Petra and with his muleteers suffering a similar experience on the road from Jaffa to Beirut. "But, cui bono!," he wrote in May 1858, "English people must submit to these things, *because we have no influence in Syria or Palestine, nor in the East generally*. I should like to hear of a French party being stopped or murdered!! The Arabs (& Turks) know too well that neither French nor Austrians can be touched with impunity."[46]

Model Problems

Whatever tensions and differences may have existed among the artist–travelers, they were united by one concern: the constant problem of finding local sitters. It must have been supremely frustrating to be surrounded by a myriad of colorful and exotic social types and yet find it so hard to make any detailed studies of them. For a few notable exceptions like Étienne Dinet, who had gained the confidence of the local community in which he lived, and the Turkish Orientalist Osman Hamdi, ostensibly a "cultural insider," finding models was not necessarily a problem. Yet for the vast majority of artists visiting the Orient it was anything but easy. In most places local religious and cultural concerns over pictorial representation and the status of women precluded both the sketching of crowds in public and the easy arrangement of private sittings. It was a hurdle over which many artists despaired of ever climbing.

The hunt for models was often underway on the journey out. In her account "Motley Images of Travel, 'Egypt 1870,'" Elisabeth Jerichau-Baumann describes how, on the ship taking her from Smyrna to Egypt in February 1870, she made impromptu sketches of her fellow passengers. "I had to use many small tricks to be able to sketch the Muslim men," she recalled, "as they were not supposed to know that I was drawing just them. It was, however, one handsome young man who became aware of my activities, but he ignored me and hence enabled my work." Sketching the women prompted a more animated reaction, however: "Under the tent, with the women, there was excitement while I was sketching them. All of them wanted to be painted so they came forward and stuck their heads out in front of the others. They wanted my sketchbook, and as it was passed from hand to hand, their dirty fingers put their marks on the pictures. They pointed at each other and laughed when they found likeness, and laughed even more when I laughed, but I was afraid my book would never be returned to me."[47]

The situation was potentially even worse once ashore. Working in public was never easy and often impossible (see pages 90–91), even when an artist was restricting him- or herself to drawing buildings and artifacts. Attempting to sketch passersby in anything but the most surreptitious manner would almost certainly provoke a negative reaction, so for most artists the only way a satisfactory study could be made of a person was by arranging a private sitting. Dragomans and other local fixers were usually able to arrange for models, for a fee naturally, but even within the context of such arrangements there was no guarantee of a satisfactory experience. Religious concerns, superstition, and misunderstanding over the implications of being sketched were rife; on one occasion Gustav Bauernfeind finally managed to get someone to agree to sit for him, only for the man to break his leg the next day. As a result, no one else would come forward, as the individual concerned had clearly been "punished" for agreeing to be sketched. On another occasion Bauernfeind did a watercolor of "a boy of about 14. The latter was awfully scared, and said at the end: He's been giving me the 'evil eye' for long enough now."[48]

It was sometimes possible to overcome such reservations by providing a suitable inducement, whether financial or in kind. In 1842 Viscount Castlereagh commissioned John Frederick Lewis to "paint a picture for me of ourselves, a party,"[49] as they traveled across Sinai. It was a work* that was ultimately to also feature Sheikh Hussein, the leader of the Bedouin who controlled the area around Mount Sinai. Hussein's initial misgivings about being sketched were dispelled by a well-chosen offering. "The Sheikh has been sitting for his picture," wrote Castlereagh, "much against his will, as it is forbidden by the Koran, and this has evidently weighed heavily on Hussein's mind. So that it is only by gift of a pair of pistols, that he has been prevailed upon to allow himself to be immortalized by Lewis."[50]

Even once a sitter was seemingly secured, there was often a problem over the venue. Women in particular were very loath to pose for an artist unless they were guaranteed privacy from the curious and potentially censorious eyes of their peers and neighbors. When staying in the Algerian oasis settlement of Biskra one winter, Frederick Arthur Bridgman had rented an empty dwelling as a studio "for the purpose of having models pose without the interferences of the populace." Securing such a space was only the start of a lengthy and uncertain process that might lead ultimately to a model physically sitting in the studio. Bridgman described how various ruses were required to entice the "half-frightened feminine natives" to attend, with them sneaking around corners and entering through holes in roofs to avoid being seen by anyone. More willing but potentially less desirable would-be models—"the halt, the maimed, and the blind, to say nothing of the healthy, ugly specimens of humanity"—were pounding meanwhile at the studio door, demanding that Bridgman paint them.[51]

Weeks described a similar scene when traveling in Lebanon in 1872: "The children as well as the grown up people were quite eager to be sketched, but then there was some difficulty in getting sketches of the women. Those who had any pretensions to beauty became suddenly bashful and hid their faces while the ugly ones were not at all backward in displaying their charms."[52] Regardless of any physical appeal or lack thereof, most local 'models' were unused to the requirements of the role and were prone to getting distracted or simply wandering off. Jerichau-Baumann recalled sketching a young woman who "collapsed in her powerlessness on

* *A Frank Encampment* (see page 107).

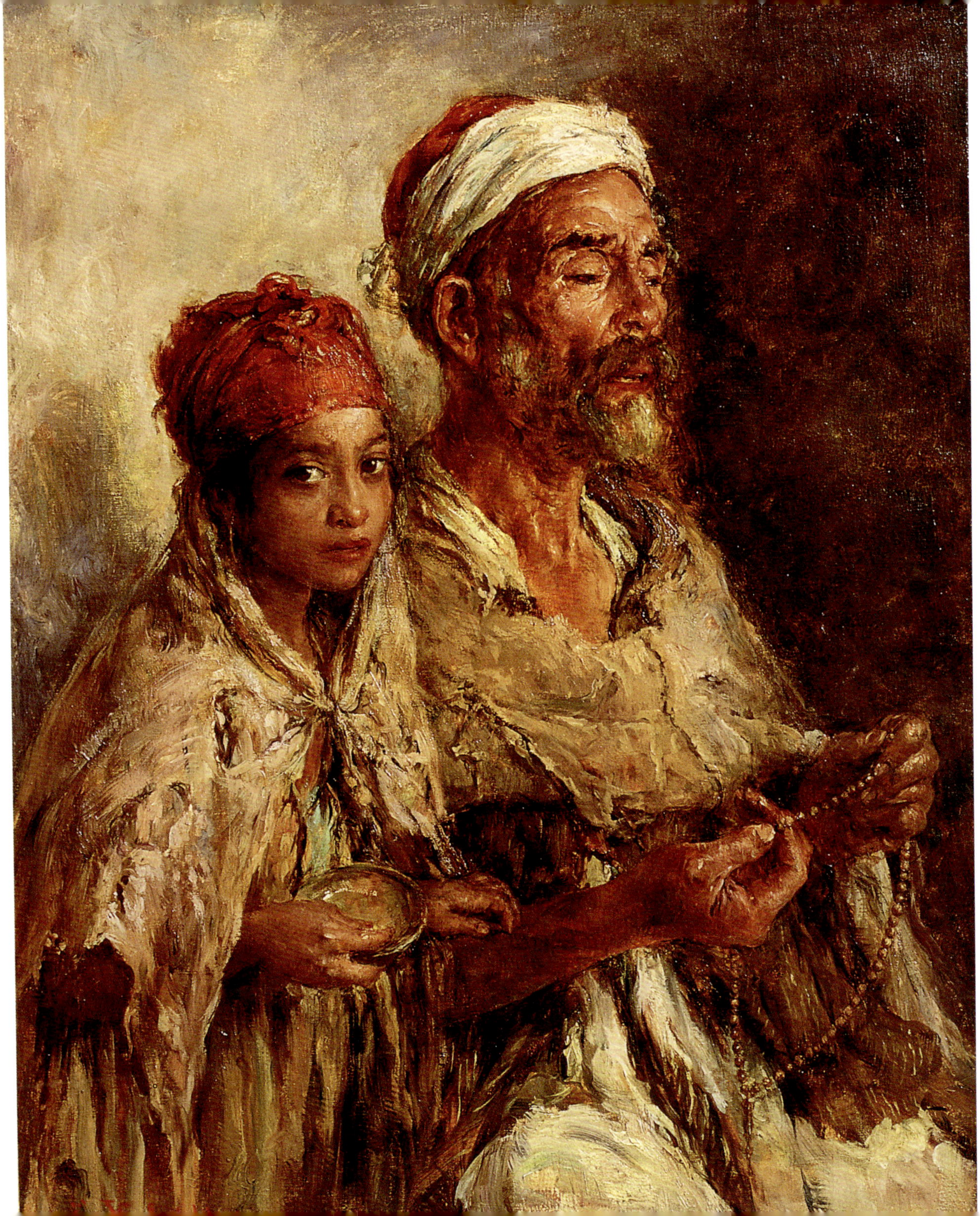

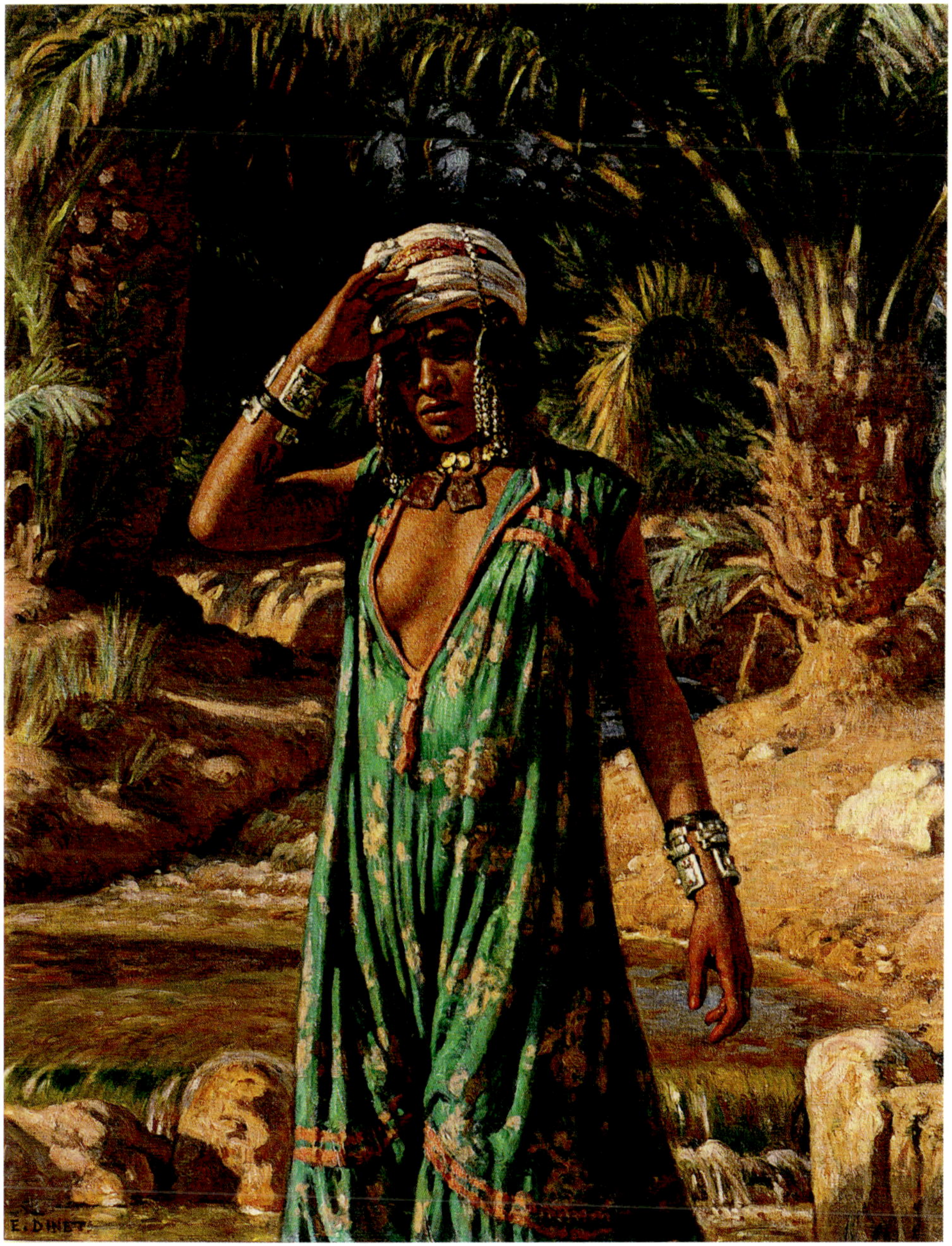

46. Édouard Verschaffelt, *Old Man and Young Girl* (date unknown). Oil on canvas, 100.3 x 80 cm. Verschaffelt excelled at portraits of the people among whom he lived following his marriage to a woman from the Ouled Sidi Brahim tribe.

47. Étienne Dinet, *Bather in Oasis* (*c*.1920). Oil on canvas, 100.4 x 81.3 cm. Dinet's long period of residence in Bou-Saâda, and the generally uninhibited attitude of the local people, allowed him to create works from real life which for other Orientalists could never be more than pure fantasy.

the floor, where she lay after only standing model for about fifteen minutes—something that can also happen to the strong men of the street,"[53] and Bauernfeind noted how he "was brought two Fellaheen women, one of whom I could only get down in colour very hastily, as they had a 3 hour journey home and were very restless."[54]

For those artists without their own studio space, one option was to organize a sitting at a private residence. Elisabeth Jerichau-Baumann relates how she arranged via an intermediary to pay a visit to a family house in order to paint some of the womenfolk. The 'models' proved difficult if not impossible to work with. One girl "became unruly and stuck her tongue out at me," while others repeatedly interfered with Jerichau-Baumann's painting equipment. The sitting came to an abrupt end when the master of the house—blissfully unaware of his family's clandestine commercial enterprise—returned home. To cries of "He is coming! Father is coming! Get rid of the giantess! He will kill us!" Jerichau-Baumann was bundled out of the house, clutching her sketches in her hands. "I was pushed down the stairs with my easel," she recalled. "But at least I had the study."[55]

As a woman, Jerichau-Baumann had obvious advantages over her male peers in terms of gaining access to female sitters. For most male artists this was usually very difficult to arrange. As a semi-resident foreigner with strong local links, Étienne Dinet was able to feature many female subjects in his works, an achievement doubtless helped by the less conservative attitude of the people among whom he lived for so many years. Other long-term residents were not necessarily so well favored. Over 250 Turkish and Egyptian subjects were included in the 1877 sale of John Frederick Lewis's works after his death the year before, but only a handful depicted women in Egypt, his home for a decade. While he certainly appears to have struggled to find female models in the years immediately after his arrival in Cairo in 1841 (see facing page), the situation presumably improved as his network of local contacts developed. Such access extended to using slave women from an Egyptian harem as models.[56] After his marriage in 1847 to Marian Harper in Alexandria, Lewis used his wife to pose for studies in Egyptian clothing and in all probability encouraged her to develop friendships with Egyptian women in the hope that they might agree to sit for him.[57]

The general lack of models was such that sometimes desperate measures were called for. Jerichau-Baumann confessed that she had been reduced to what she called "man-hunting"—basically combing the streets of Cairo on the lookout for likely candidates. On at least one occasion this led her into a potentially dangerous situation. "As I went out without a dragoman, a dark young fellow immediately came towards me offering his services. What an appearance! His skin, eyes and hair were wonderful! The eyes sparkled, the brown skin glittered, the hair had the colour of ebony, and a gleam of steel." Clearly impressed, Jerichau-Baumann followed her new acquaintance into the maelstrom of Cairene alleyways on the back of his promise to lead her to some suitable models in return for the inevitable financial reward. Such was his route that she was soon disoriented and lost, whereupon her guide presented her at the door of a house. "I assumed we had reached the destination," she recalled, "but a raw laughter, women's voices and the sight of many women and soldiers gave me goose bumps, and I ran off, through the irregular, dirty streets . . . I never again went 'man-hunting' in Cairo."[58]

William Holman Hunt ran into particular problems in Jerusalem in 1854, when he was looking for Jewish models for his work, *The Finding of the Saviour in the Temple*. Unfortunately his presence in the city coincided with concern among the Jewish community about the activities of Christian missionaries. A Jewish emissary was sent from Europe to investigate the situation and, according to Thomas Seddon, "His first step was to lay a heavy curse upon any Jew who held any communication with Christians; and Hunt, who had spoken to some about sitting to him, was put under a special curse."[59] Hunt had however enjoyed some success elsewhere with sitters, even if in unconventional and trying circumstances. "I prevailed upon the friends of a full-grown damsel to allow her to sit to me for an oil picture," he recounted, "but I had to undertake my work in an open cave under the plateau of the Pyramids, at times convenient for the girl, and at short notice. The increasing crowd of spectators testified to the survival in them of their ancestors' love of art. This trait would have been more appreciated by me had the amateurs been less bent upon attracting the girl's attention to the different points of the compass occupied by them, and had they not, on getting up from the ground (assuring me all the while that they would make no dust), shaken their sand-laden *abbias* on to my wet and too tenacious paint."[60] For foreign artists used to working with compliant models in controlled studio conditions, sketching alfresco in the desert with unruly subjects will have made for a novel challenge. It must also have raised interesting dynamics in terms of the accepted social and racial norms of the day—for in cases such as that of Hunt in his cave near the Pyramids, it was the impoverished local sitters that were calling the shots, and not the rich white visitors.

Creative Approaches

When it came to finding models, some artists were not averse to turning the misfortune of others to their advantage. When Edwin Lord Weeks found himself in Rabat at a time of famine, he offered food to "his impoverished new friends to pose for him; he called this 'interested charity.' They might never have sat for him under normal circumstances."[61] An even murkier story involves the alleged acquisition by John Frederick Lewis in 1842 of a slave whom he thought would make a good model, an incident described by Émile Prisse d'Avennes. The possession of slaves was commonplace in Egypt during the first half of the nineteenth century (particularly among Egyptians of a certain class) and while ownership of a female Muslim slave by a Christian was not permitted, European residents such as Robert Hay and Edward William Lane are known to have acquired female Greek—and presumably therefore, Christian—slaves. In both cases they subsequently married the women concerned.

Prisse relates how, on a visit to the slave market in Cairo, Lewis was struck by the beauty of an Abyssinian woman on sale there for fifty guineas. "What a head, what eyes," Prisse claimed Lewis had said, "what an unutterable expression of untamed beauty and voluptuousness! . . . I must have her at any price."[62] Prisse considered that the woman was not worth the sum demanded, and in any case the market dealer was refusing to sell her to Lewis on the basis that he was a Christian. So desperate was Lewis to acquire her, however—having already made an impromptu sketch of her in the market—that he prevailed upon Prisse, who spoke fluent Arabic and could pass as a Muslim, to buy her on his behalf.

Understandably the woman, named Husné, was a reluctant participant in the proceedings, only agreeing to go to Lewis's house after she had been "bribed by expensive gifts" and later causing so much trouble that Lewis soon tried to resell her and ultimately set her free. Meanwhile relations between Prisse and Lewis had deteriorated considerably.

It is unclear if Husné ever sat for Lewis in the way he had supposedly envisaged. Even if not, the incident could not have helped but inform what proved to be Lewis's landmark painting, *The Hhareem* (see page 136), although that did not appear until 1850, eight years after Husné's purchase. Lewis admitted to borrowing slaves from a harem to pose for him, and Prisse maintained that he had later bought another Abyssinian slave, but there is no evidence to support this claim. Meanwhile Prisse was to produce a watercolor, *Marché des esclaves*, showing an Abyssinian slave being examined at the market by a European bearing an uncanny resemblance to Lewis.[63] The whole sordid episode sheds light on the conflicted status of slavery at the time and on Lewis's own morals and scruples, as well as the often fractious nature of the relationship between the British and the French in Egypt.

Artists who struggled to find suitable models faced the real prospect of having to adjust their expectations regarding the type and amount of material with which they would be able to head home at the end of their trip. In Algiers in 1874 William Sartain (1843–1924) wrote, with evident relief, that "I have had finally a genuine Arab pose all day for me, & pose very well too. He is going to bring another one whom he says is very good. So I feel after all that I am not going to be confined to interiors & street scenes only."[64] However, a failure to secure sittings was not necessarily a total disaster. Almost all artists expected that they would only be able to produce preliminary works while traveling and that the production of the ultimate finished product would rely on intensive studio work to be carried out once back home. This extended regularly to the use of European, Arab, and African expatriate models (as well as the vast collections of artifacts that many artists acquired) to produce exactly the type of look or situation they were looking for (see chapter 4).

Even so, while abroad artists would often attempt to arrange set pieces designed to create a particular scenario they wished to feature in a work but which might prove problematic to capture in real life. Frederick Arthur Bridgman recounts how, on one occasion at Biskra when he was prevented from working outdoors by a sandstorm, his dragoman Achmed arranged for an indoor sitting with a female dancer of the Ouled Naïl tribe. She had been asked by Achmed to wear her "gala costume" for the occasion and, when she failed to turn up, the two men went to her house. "We naturally expected to find her in the act of putting the finishing touches to her eyebrows or her apparel," relates Bridgman. "Not at all. She roused herself drowsily from her bed." After the briefest of ablutions the woman accompanied Bridgman and Achmed back to the studio and a dancing scene was enacted for Bridgman to work from, with Achmed playing a drum and small children summoned off the streets to help create an ambiance by clapping their hands. Through such contrived situations it was possible for artists to glean at least some notion of local culture and customs which they could interpret for their largely unknowing audiences back home. Bridgman was able to combine these observations with genuine firsthand experiences, such as the wedding described and illustrated in his book, *Winters in Algeria*.[65]

Dancers were a consistently popular subject for artists for obvious reasons of color, drama, and ethnic interest, and in principle they were easier to make contact with than other potential models because of the often public nature of their performances and the fact that many of them were prostitutes. A rather more formal version of the impromptu scene Bridgman created in Algeria was witnessed by Leopold Müller in 1881 in Girga, a town halfway between Cairo and Luxor. Müller had been given an audience there by Crown Prince Rudolf of Austria, at which they were entertained by local dancers. The following day Müller wrote to his artist friend August von Pettenkofen, "and in the evening we saw Egyptian dancers. Take Gérôme as an example! I am so curious to know what [he] would do if he were here."[66] By this time the French artist was renowned for his portrayals of the Egyptian female dancers known as *ghawazee*, who performed unveiled in the streets. Müller would almost certainly have seen some of these paintings, either at the Paris Salon or in London, where he and Gérôme shared a dealer, Henry Wallis. Müller was to produce his own painting of a dancer, *Egyptische Tänzerin (An almée's admirers)* (Figure 48), a year after seeing the performance in Girga.

Women in the Landscape

Staged events such as dance ceremonies aside, artists were often forced to rely on serendipitous glimpses of invariably transient events to form the basis of sketches. Conjuring up the subject of a picture from something, or somebody, that had only been seen for a second or two was always a challenge, but a snapshot was often enough to spark the creative process. Elisabeth Jerichau-Baumann described traveling on donkey through the Egyptian landscape, swathed in a shawl and with a cotton towel over her cork hat. "I lifted the wrap every now and then to be able to observe some of the interesting surroundings," she wrote, "in the golden fog that spread out towards the Nile, which bent along flourishing palm woods like a broad belt of gold, with the seemingly golden flamingos and pelicans on their guard in this silent, vast African solitude. Sporadically, a single woman can be seen, walking soundlessly with her terracotta pot through the sandy fog towards the Nile."[67]

Léon Belly (1827–77) had also waxed lyrically about the pot-carrying women he had observed in rural Egypt during a visit in 1850–51: "They possess native gracefulness, nobleness of gesture and perfect balance in all their movements, as well as an easiness that quite possibly comes from their continuously engaging in the exercise of carrying large amphorae."[68] For Western artists the sight of women carrying these immense water jars conjured up a direct visual link with antiquity, the image of a woman with a jar or pot becoming a defining icon for many Orientalist artists.

Jerichau-Baumann acknowledged that it was such scenes that inspired her painting *Water-carrying Woman by the Nile*, but the same must also be true of *An Egyptian Pottery Seller near Gizeh* (Figure 49), in which the main subject embodies all the virtues, grace, and authority that so impressed the artist: "Woman, as if she were a lovely sculpture from ancient times [and] unaware of her great beauty, . . . becomes the more attractive because of the unawareness and virtuousness she expresses, often moves around naked while attending her

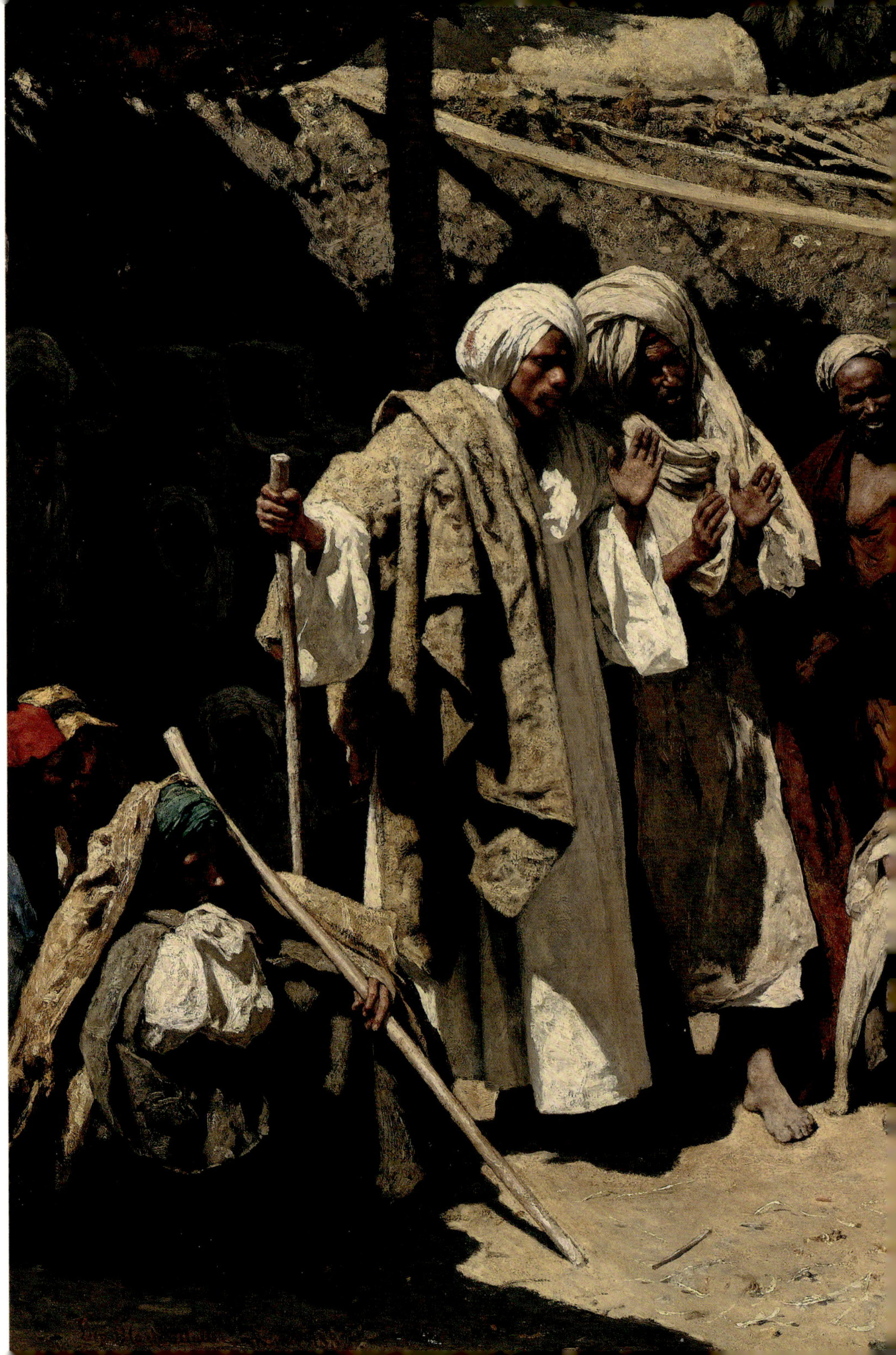

48. Leopold Carl Müller, *Egyptische Tänzerin* (An Almée's Admirers) (1882). Oil on canvas, 77.1 x 126.3 cm.

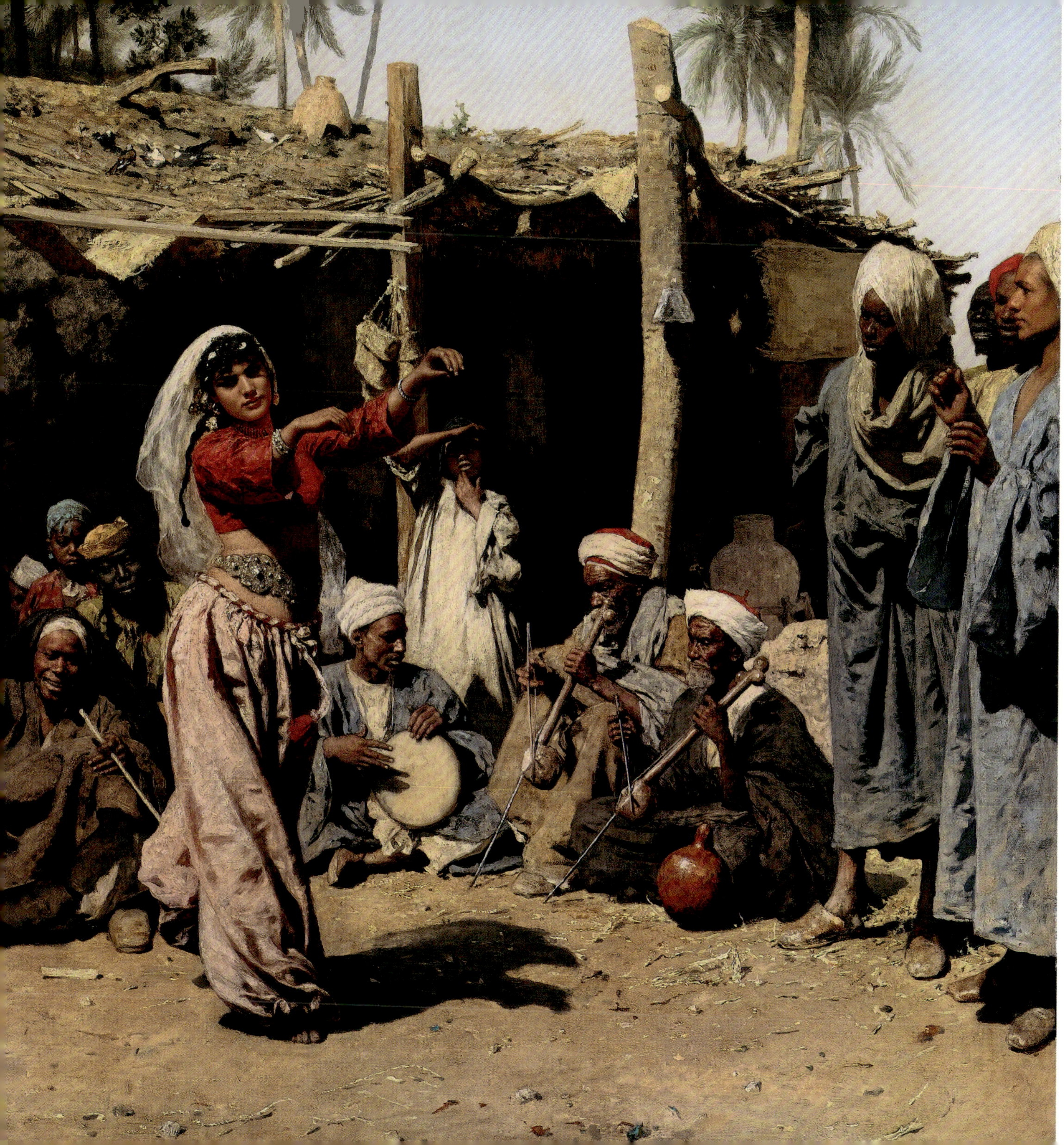

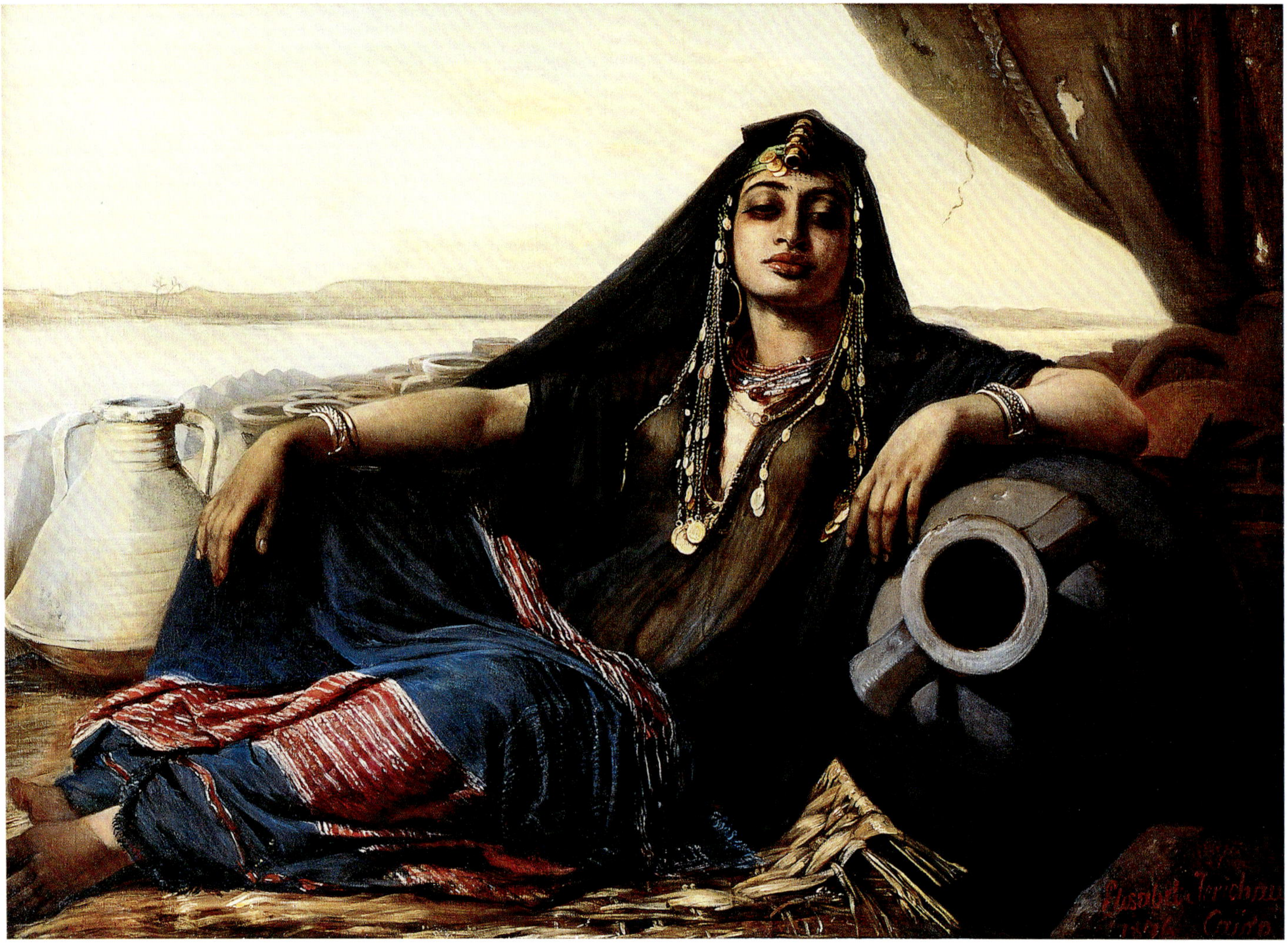

49. Elisabeth Jerichau-Baumann, *An Egyptian Pottery Seller near Gizeh* (1876). Oil on canvas, 98.4 x 138.5 cm.

daily chores, but without expressing shame."[69] Jerichau-Baumann's Egyptian women are a reflection of the artist's own free spirit and sense of confidence, and through portraying them in this way she helped move Orientalist women out of the harem and into the fields and onto the riverbank. While she was certainly not the first or only artist to do this—Frederick Goodall featured women prominently in such scenes, for example—Jerichau-Baumann's female subjects are presented as especially independent and sexually powerful, hinting at the irony of a liberation not yet attained at that time by the women of Europe and North America.

Whereas early Orientalist paintings had focused overwhelmingly on depicting locals of high status, the second half of the nineteenth century saw increasing appreciation of the artistic potential of the workers or fellaheen, who populated the rural landscapes of Egypt, especially along the Nile Valley. The appeal of what were seen as their simple, honest lives, led in a landscape unchanged for centuries (unlike in the cities, which were regarded as increasingly Westernized and corrupted), was strong, especially as these scenes delivered contemporary Western values such as the virtue of hard work and the demand for authenticity and realism. This made them especially attractive to the acquisitive *nouveau riche* collectors of Europe and North America, many of whom had made their fortunes in industry.

The different character of rural life was reflected in the attitudes of the people that lived there, regarded by foreign visitors and many urban Egyptians alike as being straightforward, without guile or pretension, and representing a direct visual and spiritual link with the country's ancient and illustrious past. The inspiration Jerichau-Baumann found in the countryside of Egypt was mirrored in the creative responses of other artists, eager to escape the crowded and often fraught conditions of the towns. Ernst Körner (1846–1927), for example, incorporated fellaheen figures in his Egyptian views in much the same way as classical European landscape artists populated their works with romanticized peasants and country folk.

An added attraction for artists and their audiences alike came from the fact that most female laborers in rural Egypt went about unveiled. In so doing they provided a physical and cultural antidote to their usually more conservative urban sisters and helped fuel the notion that the fellaheen were imbued with a timeless nobility and sense of liberty akin to that enjoyed by the Bedouin (see page 108). "It seemed to us that the wives of the fellahin were in truth the happiest women in Egypt," remarked Amelia Edwards. "They work hard and are bitterly poor; but they have the free use of their limbs and they at least know the fresh air, the sunshine and the open fields."[70]

This spirit was captured by artists like William Holman Hunt who, in his painting *The Afterglow in Egypt*, depicted a handsome woman agricultural worker glowing with vigor and health and surrounded by the plentiful bounty of the landscape in which she toiled. For others, the opportunity to make overt biblical references to such scenes proved irresistible. The themes of fecundity and inherent purity were developed in an obvious direction by artists such as Léon Bonnat, Émile Vernet-Lecomte, and Frederick Goodall, who in their depictions of fellah women holding their children aloft, strove to create popular—if somewhat clunky—metaphors for the Madonna and Child.

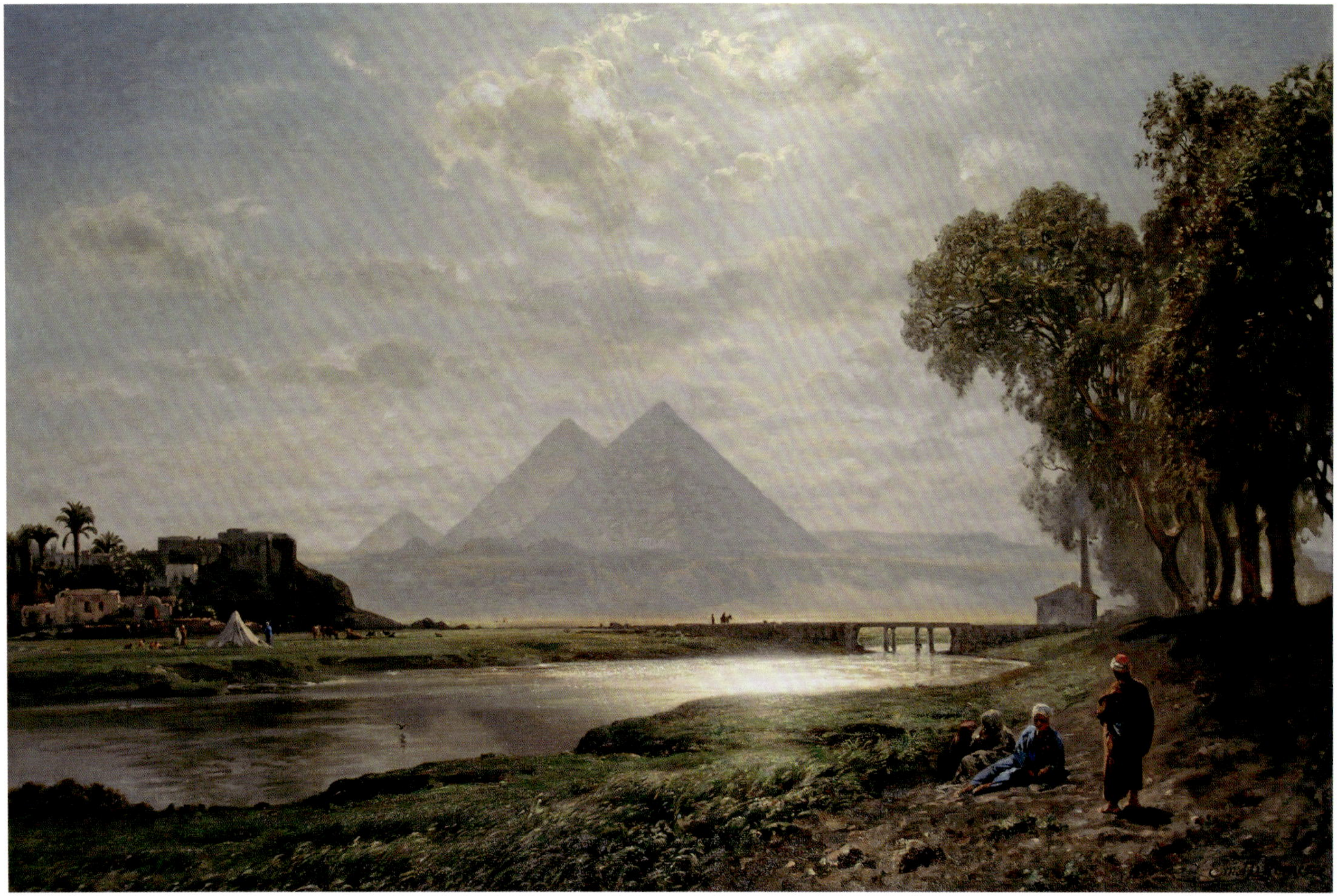

50. Ernst Körner, *Die Pyramiden von Gizeh* (The Pyramids at Gizeh, Morning) (1890). Oil on canvas, 100 x 150 cm. This work exemplifies the way in which Western artists sometimes applied the European landscape tradition to an Oriental context. Here the Pyramids are set as mountains behind a verdant and pastoral foreground.

Everyday rural scenes dominated by women were very much the forte of Marie Aimée Lucas-Robiquet (1858–1959), who traveled extensively in Algeria and Tunisia and specialized in compositions of women engaged in routine activities such as the preparation of food, cooking, weaving, washing clothes, and date harvesting. Her lavish use of vibrant color helped dramatize the value of these working women and their role as industrious creators in society, elevating them visually to a status unusual in Orientalist art and providing a powerful counterpoint to the idle, effete inmates of the harems and courtyards of Algiers or Tunis.

Artists such as Eugène Fromentin and Gustave Guillaumet took a less idealistic approach. While focusing their energies on the presentation of everyday folk as embodying the pure and enduring spirit of the Orient, they did not shy away from gritty portrayals of the harshness of rural life. In their works, the drawing of water, for example, takes on a decidedly workaday dimension, as described by Fromentin in his book, *Un Été dans le Sahara* (A Summer in the Sahara). "The women and children are there, leaning over the dark water, their backs in the sunlight, their *haïks** tucked up above their knees, veils tied back, filling and emptying the bowls, funnelling the water into the bulging goatskins which they then tie up. Everyone is milling around, bustling and busying themselves; but with so few words exchanged that one might think them mute. The flowing water fills the air with a sensation of coolness; and until dusk the wet dust gives off the deceptive aroma of a rainstorm."[71]

The intrinsic value of rural folk as the essence of their society was a view also endorsed by the so-called 'Ottoman Orientalist,' Osman Hamdi. Born in 1842 into the upper echelons of Ottoman society, at the age of eighteen Hamdi was sent to study law in Paris, where—against the wishes of his family—he was soon channeling his energies into art and painting. He enrolled to study art at the École des Beaux-Arts, where he was tutored by both Boulanger and Gérôme, and became thoroughly immersed in Parisian life—even personal letters to his father were written in French, and his first wife was a French woman whom he had met while a student in Paris. Evidence of his particular cultural attitude and sense of distance from the Ottoman Empire's population at large is clear from comments he made while working in Baghdad after his return from Paris. "It is not necessary to concern ourselves with the inhabitants of the big cities . . . these people, although they appear to bear a modicum of the civilization of the nineteenth century, are in fact far below the desert dwelling Bedouin, who, although they lead a primitive and patriarchal life, [are far better than the former,] who lead a life of infamy and corruption, to the point that in the whole of Bagdad and particularly among servants of the government you would not find a single honest man!"[72] As a Westernized Turk educated in Europe, Hamdi was clearly influenced by non-Oriental attitudes and therefore less of an "insider" than might intially be thought.

* A *haïk* was the traditional woman's attire in the Maghreb, a large rectangular piece of cloth, usually white, and wrapped around the entire body.

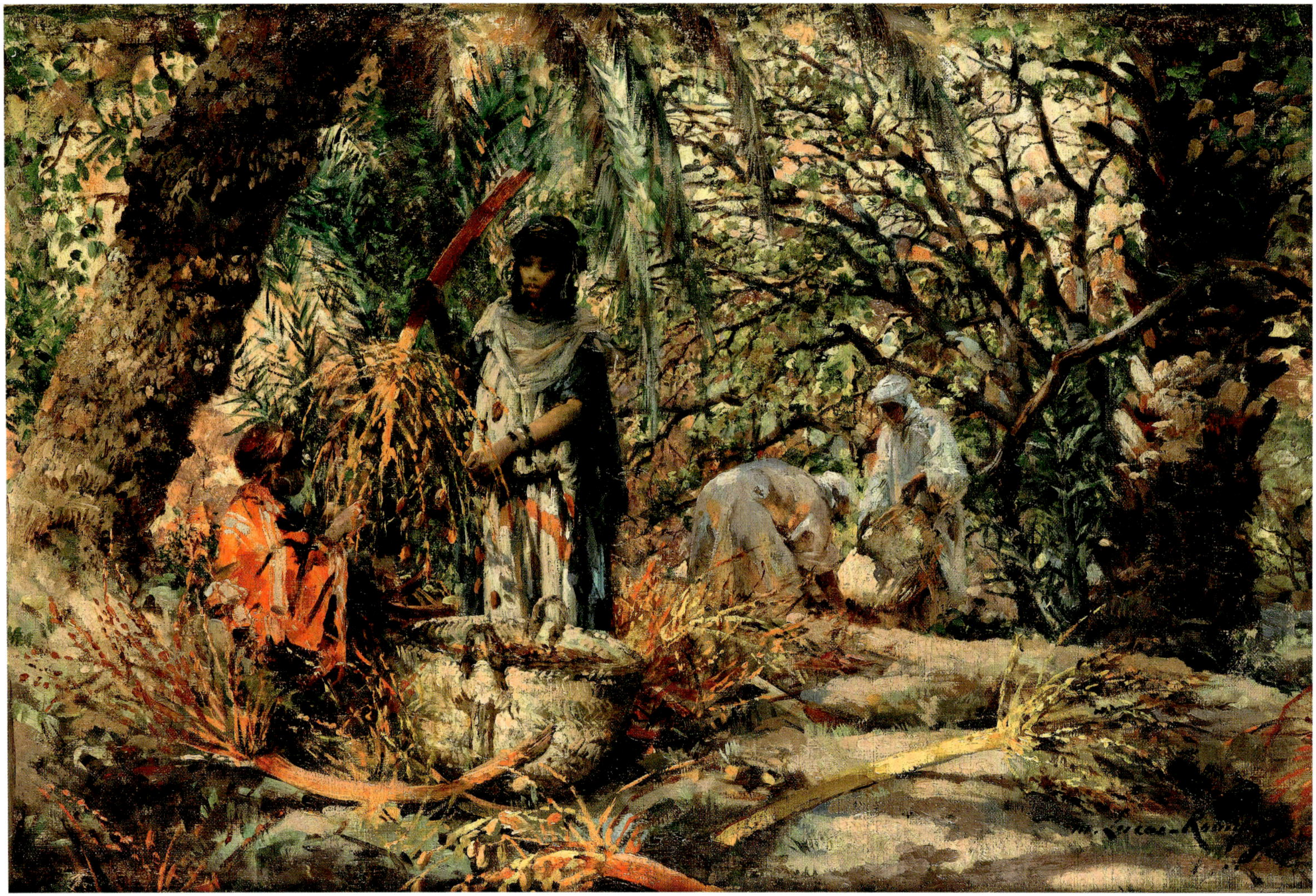

51. Marie Aimée Lucas-Robiquet, *Date Harvest in Touggourt* (date unknown). Oil on canvas, 31 x 45 cm. Lucas-Robiquet excelled at the depiction of women engaged in meaningful, everyday tasks, a subject far removed from the idling odalisques favored by other Orientalists.

The Power of the Seraglio

The frisson offered by unveiled rural women provided an interesting counterpoint to that most enduring of Orientalist subjects, the harem. The gaze of many artists inevitably strayed beyond the public streets and market places to the tantalizing private domains behind the forbidding walls and ornate portals of great Oriental cities such as Algiers, Cairo, Constantinople, and Damascus. Not only were opulent courtyard and domestic interior scenes highly popular with clients and audiences back home but they also provided the opportunity to portray the greatest prize of all, the ladies of the harem (often known as the seraglio in the Otttoman context). Interest in life within what was the preserve of the very highest echelons of Oriental society was virtually obsessive, hooked around a potent but clichéd cocktail of sexual despotism, sensuality, secrecy, enforced confinement, and voyeurism. So strong was the commercial appeal of this mix that many artists found themselves unable to resist trying their hand at harem scenes, however stereotyped. Often at the center of their fantasy was the voluptuous and usually scantily clad odalisque—the term used for a slave or servant in a Turkish harem.*

Needless to say, the reality of the harem was rather different. An alternative view had already been presented by Lady Mary Wortley Montagu in the early decades of the eighteenth century (see pages 21–24), and Edward William Lane's *Manners and Customs* had also attempted to dispel many of the myths surrounding the world of polygamy and concubines. Lane estimated that in the 1830s only 5 percent or so of men in Cairo had more than one wife and indicated that life in the harem was far removed from the common Western perception of immurement and misery. A similar situation applied in Turkey, where by the time of the abolition of polygamy in 1926 the taking by a man of more than one wife was already anachronistic and culturally defunct.[73]

Local cultural and religious conventions were such that this prism of the Oriental kaleidoscope was impossible for Western male artists to access direct. Many were forced to base their harem paintings on a combination of their imagination, second- or thirdhand reports, and the accounts of figures such as Lady Mary. The increasing number of women travelers during the 1800s led to more firsthand accounts of life within the mysterious seraglio. Doors firmly closed to men—foreign or otherwise—were in theory open to their wives and other female family members. Lane's own sister, Sophia Poole, wore local dress and veiled her face in order to gain access to harems and other female-only areas of Egyptian society. The information she gathered was quite likely fed back to her brother and certainly featured prominently in her own book, *The Englishwoman in Egypt: Letters from Cairo* (1844).

Female artists were clearly well placed to create unprecedented pictorial renderings of the inhabitants of the harem. Among the first to do so was Mary Adelaide Walker, who painted Princess Fatma Sultan, a daughter of the Ottoman sultan, in Constantinople in the late 1850s. Walker's association with her client was to last many years and included the provision of a temporary studio, set up within one of the rooms of the harem for use during the sittings. Walker

* From the Turkish *odalik*, meaning chambermaid.

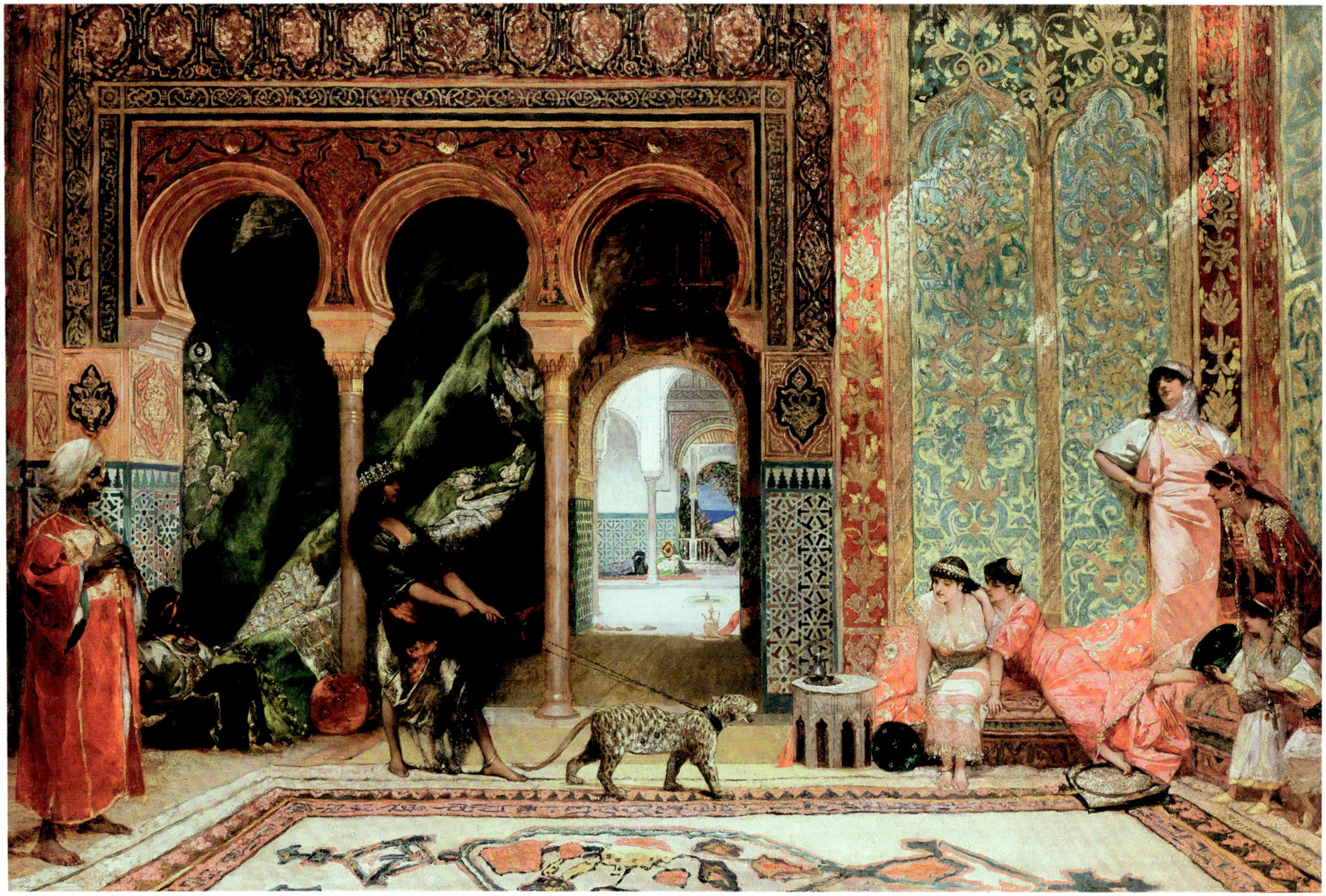

52. Jean Joseph Benjamin-Constant, *A Royal Palace in Morocco* (*c.*1880). Oil on canvas. Extravagant and fantastical depictions of life inside the palace walls remained popular with Western audiences until well into the late nineteenth century.

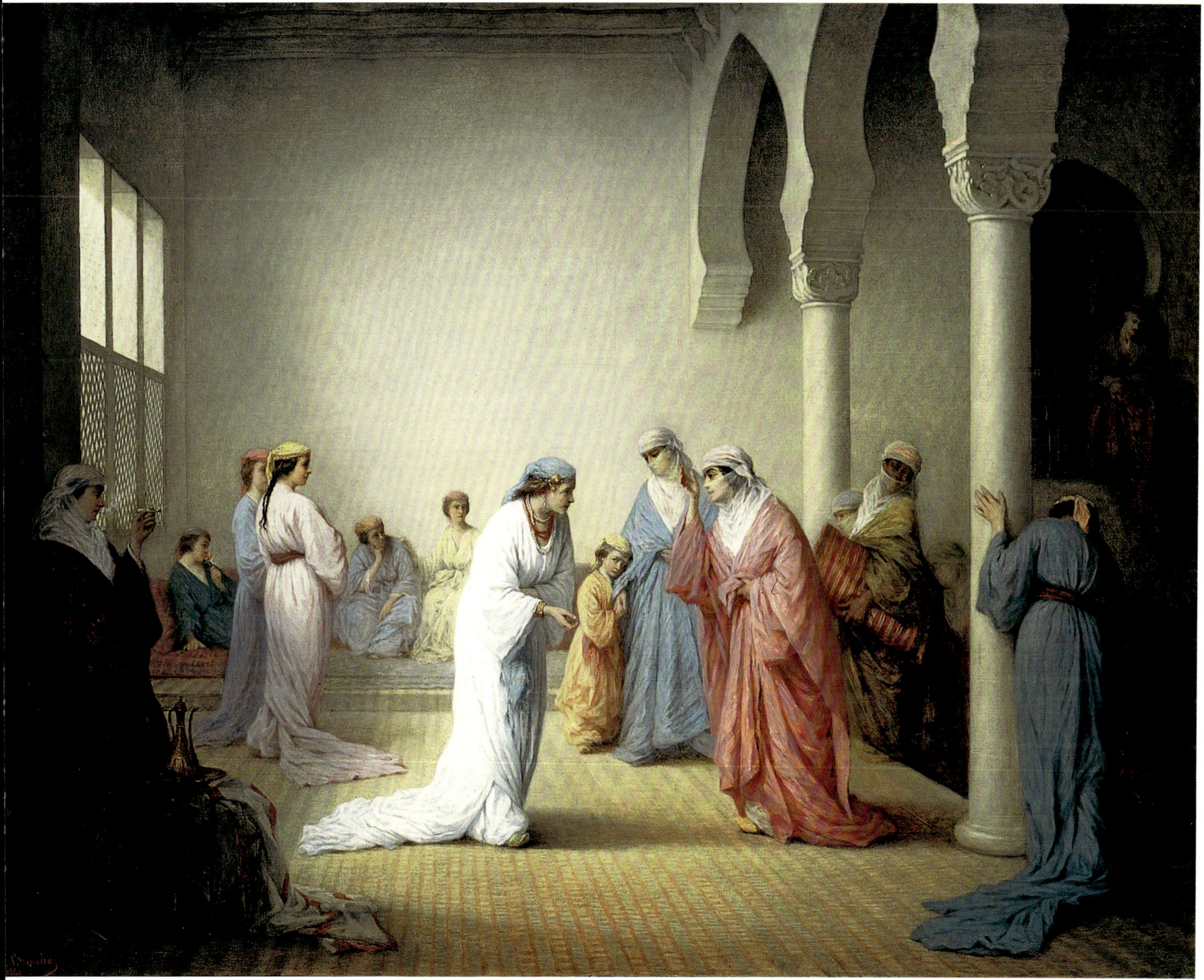

53. Henriette Browne, *A Visit: Harem Interior, Constantinople, 1860* (1861). Oil on canvas, 89 x 114 cm.

lived in Constantinople for three decades, but the current whereabouts of the portraits she painted—or even if they still exist—is not known. As an amateur artist she appears in no contemporary literature on the subject and it is only thanks to her memoirs that the story of the princess's portraits came to light.[74]

The earliest surviving harem paintings based on what is likely to be direct, firsthand knowledge are therefore two works, *A Visit* (Figure 53) and *A Flute Player* (both subtitled *Harem Interior, Constantinople, 1860*), by Henriette Browne, real name Sophie de Saux (*née* Bouteillier) (1829–1901). Browne visited Constantinople with her diplomat husband for two weeks in 1860. *A Visit* gives a rather gloomy and forbidding impression of the sparsely furnished seraglio, presented by Browne as fused with a paradoxical combination of tension and listlessness. Both works were exhibited at the Paris Salon in 1861, prompting the writer and critic Théophile Gautier to remark, "Only women should go to Turkey—what can a man see in this jealous country? . . . For a woman, on the contrary, the odalisque opens itself, the harem holds no more mystery. These doubtlessly charming faces, which the bearded visitor searches in vain to discern beneath the muslin of the yashmak, she is able to contemplate them stripped of their veil, in all the splendour of their beauty."[75]

Browne's lean and rather prosaic interpretation in *A Visit* was well received by critics such as Gautier as being a rendering of a harem "by someone who has actually seen it, something rare and perhaps unique." The painting certainly conveys the stultifying atmosphere and apprehensions of the women living there, perhaps the first such realistic insight of its type. What *A Visit* did not do was meet the traditional requirements for opulence, decadence, and eroticism in harem scenes. These were long-established expectations not easily dislodged by the brutal advent of reality—as in the over-lavish harem scenes created by Jean-Joseph Benjamin-Constant (1845–1902), for example—but Browne ensured at least that the inhabitants of "her" harem were shown as women rather than as fantasies.

Frederick Arthur Bridgman was one of only a handful of male Western artists to have gained any meaningful understanding of the domestic life of women in the Orient. His friendship with Baïa, an Algerian widow in whose home he lodged (see pages 98–99), gave him unparalleled access to the inner workings of the house. "Women friends were constantly 'dropping in,'" he wrote, "and seeing me there at work so often, they considered me as one of the family, and raised the veils from their faces and made themselves at home generally."[76] As a result of such displays of trust and acceptance, Bridgman was able to sketch scenes from real life which for most male artists had to be imagined or concocted from second- or thirdhand reports. These included preparations for weddings and religious feasts, as well as detailed observations of different types of female costume and the ways in which the domestic spaces within the house functioned. It was a unique insight for a male artist.

The View from Inside

Although their gender gave them privileged access in certain situations, foreign women artists were never going to be insiders in the Orient. Their ability to understand and relate to the lives of Ottoman women was constrained by their "otherness" and, like their male peers, they were

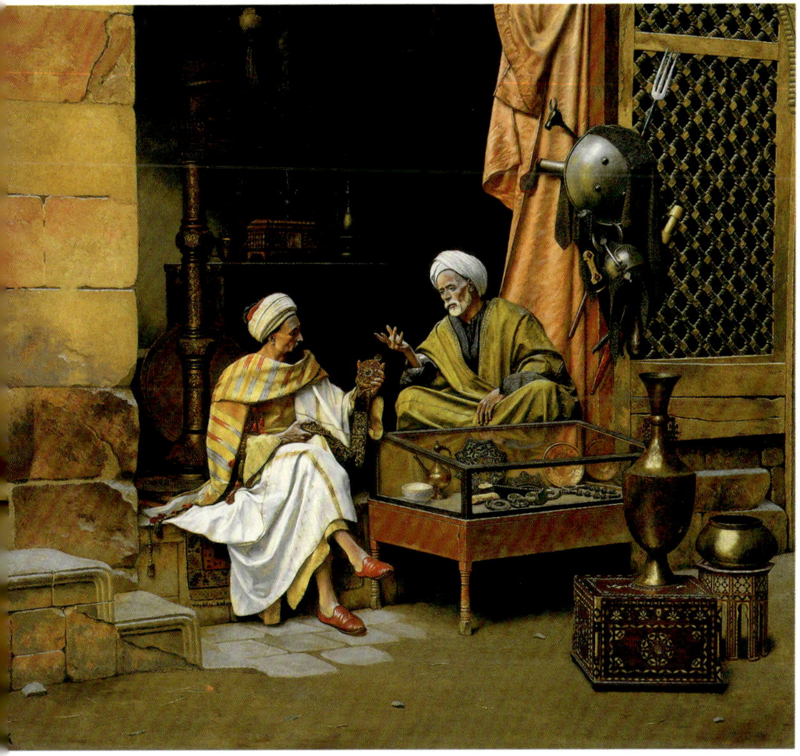

54. Ludwig Deutsch, *The Antique Dealers* (date unknown). Oil on panel, 72.4 x 81.3 cm.

primarily looking for subjects that fulfilled Western preconditions about the Orient as a picturesque world in an arrested state of development. Although artists such as Ludwig Deutsch and Arthur von Ferraris (1856–1936) made a point of acknowledging the advent of modernity by featuring in their paintings items such as newspapers, cigarettes, and glass display cases (the latter increasingly used by merchants in the Cairo bazaar to showcase antiquities and souvenirs aimed at foreign tourists, as in Deutsch's *The Antique Dealers*) (Figure 54), it was largely left to the handful of local artists painting in the Western style—notably Osman Hamdi—to try and express the rapid changes that were taking place during the second half of the nineteenth century in the lives of urban middle-class Egyptians and Turks, including their womenfolk.

Upon his return to Turkey from France in 1868, Hamdi was appointed to a position in Baghdad (then part of the Ottoman Empire), working with the governor, Midhat Pasha, a prominent reformist who admired the West for its progress and modernity and lamented what he saw as the backward and stagnating character of much of the Ottoman hegemony. While subscribing to this general view, Hamdi took a particular interest in the cultural traditions of his country—ironically the very elements that were coming under pressure from the modernizing forces he was also keen to promote. Hamdi's views on the subject were similar to those expressed by contemporary Western commentators and artists, centered around a romantic notion that the traditional costumes and crafts of countries such as Turkey embodied the truthful essence of their societies and represented the social and cultural integrity of a pre-industrial age. For Hamdi, such traditions were indivisible from his country's identity and were therefore a vital component in its future.

Hamdi's passion for indigenous crafts and textiles extended to an interest in fashion, all the more so at a time when sartorial and social values were shifting in response to wider changes in Ottoman society. The visit of Empress Eugénie to Constantinople in 1869 helped spark a vogue among the Turkish bourgeoisie for European, and especially French, styles of clothing. Conventional Turkish attire was adapted to accommodate elements of haute couture from Paris, and it became perfectly acceptable—if not necessarily fashionable among the populace at large—for a Turkish woman to wear an elegant and colorful bustle dress underneath a traditional plain *ferace* or coat.

Such a fusion was of little interest to Western artists—it was not, after all, what they had journeyed east to find. Indeed, many of them overtly regretted such expressions of European influence. For Hamdi, however, this was an important subject and one that he tackled in paintings such as *A Lady of Constantinople* (1881) and *Ladies Taking a Walk* (1887) (Figure 55). In both works, fashionable women are depicted in a symbolic synthesis of Western and Oriental dress, allowing Hamdi to offer both a revision of stereotypes and a socio-political statement about his country and its people.

The Quest for Accuracy

Interest in costume and dress was nothing new in Orientalism. Some of the early 'proto-Orientalist' artists, such as Jean-Baptiste Vanmour, had been crucial in shaping European visual perceptions of the peoples and cultures of the Middle East, but how to handle the complex ethnic and cultural composition of the nineteenth-century Ottoman Empire was an altogether bigger challenge. Costume studies required a particular skill and filled a limited niche, usually being intended for inclusion in larger publications and/or for reproduction as lithographs. Most mid-nineteenth-century artists therefore chose to explore ethnography—in the sense of portraying different societies and cultures—within the context of genre scenes. These were immediately more saleable and also offered greater flexibility in terms of an artist being able to respond to changes in what was a fast-moving art market.

An iconic example of its type is John Frederick Lewis's *The Hhareem* (Figure 56), painted *c.*1849–50 and described as "the most ambitious harem painting ever attempted by a British artist."[77] Leaving aside its artistic virtuosity and any sense of controversy stemming from the slave story connected to it (see pages 121–122), this work reflects prevailing interest in a harem's inhabitants in terms of their ethnography. The painting features a wealthy man with his three wives, designated by Lewis as Georgian, Circassian, and Greek. Two Abyssinians are also present, one of whom is a newly arrived concubine. The emphasis on the ethnographic dimension of the characters served to underline the painting's value as a realistic narrative on Egyptian life, a reason cited by some critics for its enthusiastic reception among the public. The painting is a construction, in terms of Lewis ever having been likely to witness such a scene with his own eyes, and is fused with subtlety and innuendo. As with Lewis's oeuvre generally, things are rarely as they appear. By such carefully crafted compositions, he was able to use ethnography as a vehicle for establishing his own authority and the authenticity of the scene he was representing.

The demand for ethnographic veracity continued to grow and by the 1860s Jean-Léon Gérôme was established as the artist-ethnographer *par excellence*. His precise drawing skills and crystal-sharp finish were deemed by critics (French ones, at least) as ideal for delivering authentic portrayals of the peoples and cultures of the Orient. "[Gérôme's] masterly studies as a painter of history," wrote Théophile Gautier in 1856 in

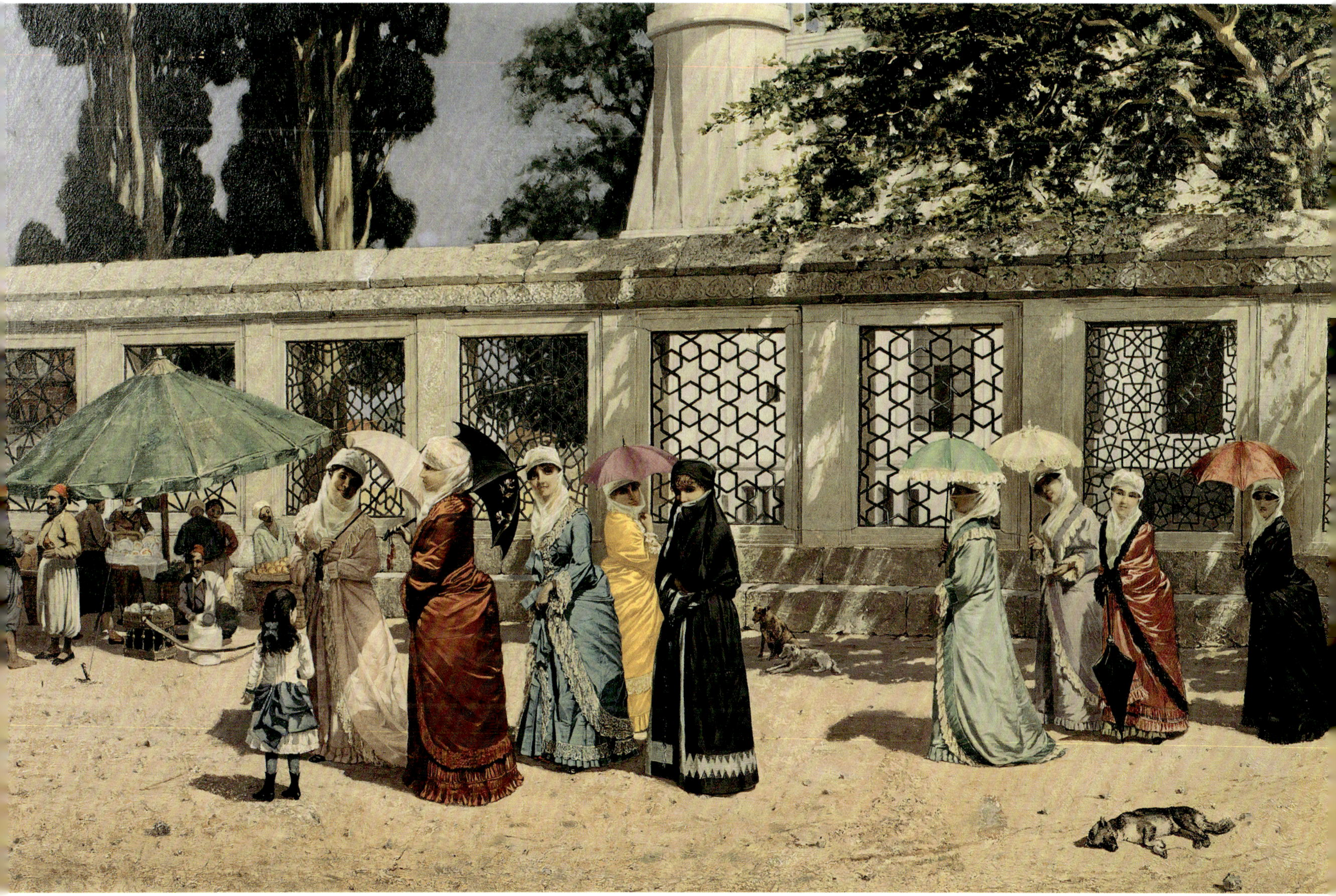

55. Osman Hamdi, *Feraceli Kadınlar* (Ladies Taking a Walk) (1887).
Oil on canvas, 81 x 131 cm.

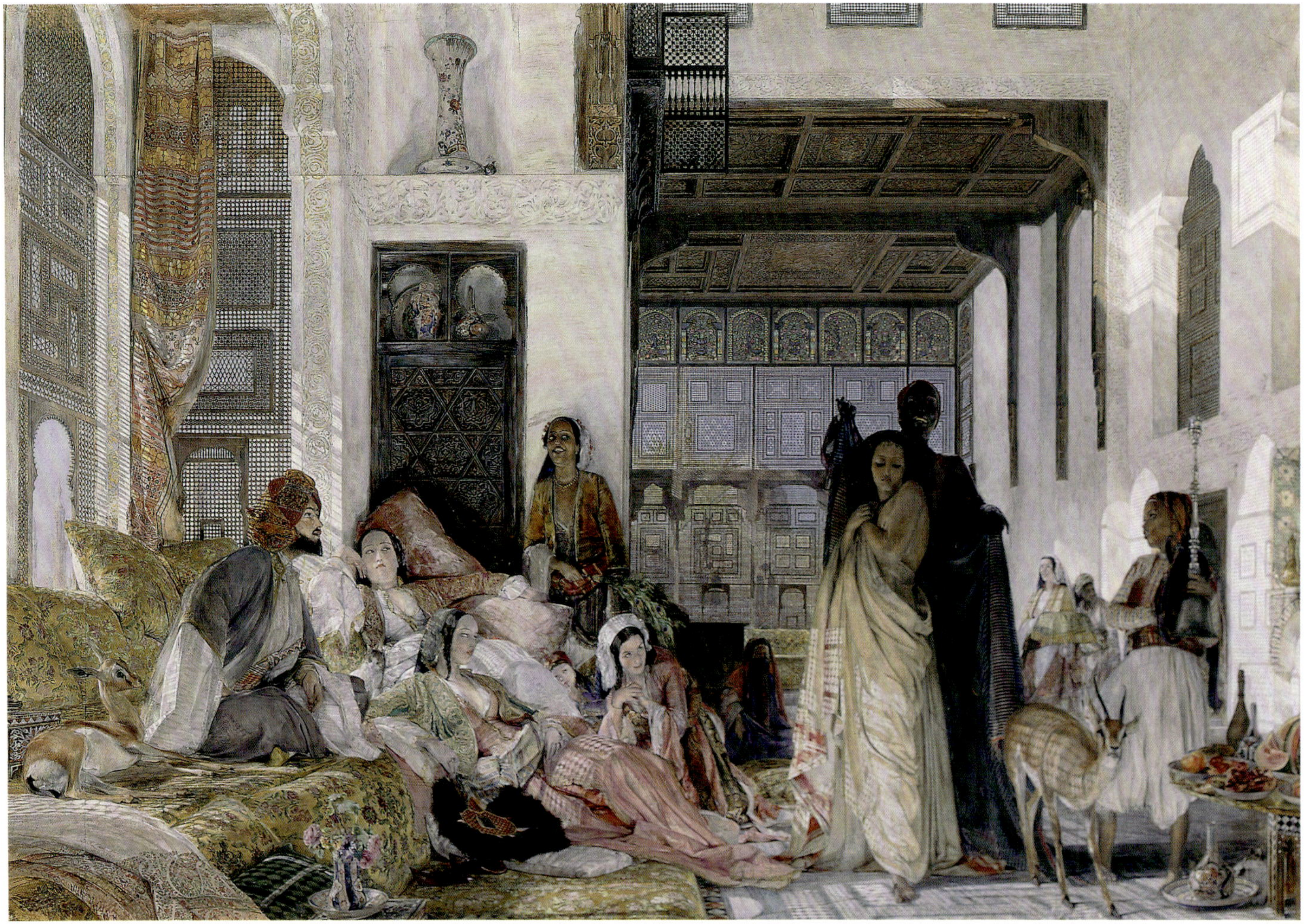

56. John Frederick Lewis, *The Hhareem* (*c*.1849–50). Watercolor and bodycolor, 88.6 x 133 cm.

the journal *L'Artiste*, "his talent as a draftsman—(refined, elegant, exact and yet full of style)—his personal talent for ethnographic perception . . . all this qualified him, better than any other artist to represent this simple interest which modern explorers of the Orient have till now neglected for the landscape, public structures and mere colour—I mean *mankind!*"[78] Gautier went on to explain how he had examined the drawings from one of Gérôme's portfolios, brought back from the artist's recent trip to Egypt, and found "numerous pencil portrait studies of different characteristic types . . . so exactly observed that they could be used in the anthropological treatises of M. Serres, so expertly drawn that they will guarantee the success of the painting in which they find a place."*

A year after Gautier had extolled Gérôme's ethnographic credentials in this way, the artist himself took to the pages of the same publication to reaffirm his documentary approach. "We are not of those who desire that art should have a purpose outside of itself; . . . we think that painting is useful when—respecting the requirements of beauty—it acquaints us with the types, customs, aspects and usages of distant countries."[79] Interestingly, drawings by Gérôme of ancient monuments appear only in the sketchbooks from his first visit to Egypt. Thereafter he concentrated entirely on depicting contemporary Egyptians and their lives.

Throughout the 1860s and 1870s Gérôme depicted a variety of different human characters and situations, from prayer scenes and guards at the palace gate to hammams and merchants in the bazaar. Some of these scenes—but certainly not all—were based on direct observation, but Gérôme achieved his high standards of ethnographic accuracy by recourse to a range of different applications. His highly developed eye for detail and exceptional draftsmanship were supported by other sources of expertise, not least his own extensive travels and experiences, but also including photographs and concentrated studio work that involved models and original artifacts from his own large collection (see page 146). Essential from the ethnographic perspective was Edward William Lane's *Manners and Customs*, which contained drawings showing a range of social customs, forms of behavior, and the accoutrements of daily life. These were a source used widely by artists eager to ensure cultural veracity in their works. Particularly relevant in Gérôme's case (and, indeed, that of other artists such as William Müller) were Lane's drawings of prayer posture, clearly discernible in paintings such as Gérôme's *Prayer in the Desert* (1864).[80]

The meticulous approach followed by Gérôme built on the work of artists such as Carl Haag in differentiating between different racial types. Indeed, Gérôme's presentation of ethnographic subjects established a benchmark that others strove to attain. Evidence of the standards he set emerges in the works of Ludwig Deutsch, for example: executed in a highly precise style, but one that in Deutsch's hand (and indeed those of his fellow Austrians, including Johann Discart (1856–??), Rudolf Ernst, Arthur von Ferraris, and Rudolf Weiss (1859–1930) favored an emphasis on the unerringly accurate presentation of the materials, textures,

* Gautier, "Gérôme: Tableaux, études, et croquis de voyage," 34. Étienne Serres was a professor of comparative anatomy and curator of an anthropological gallery at the Museum of Natural History in Paris.

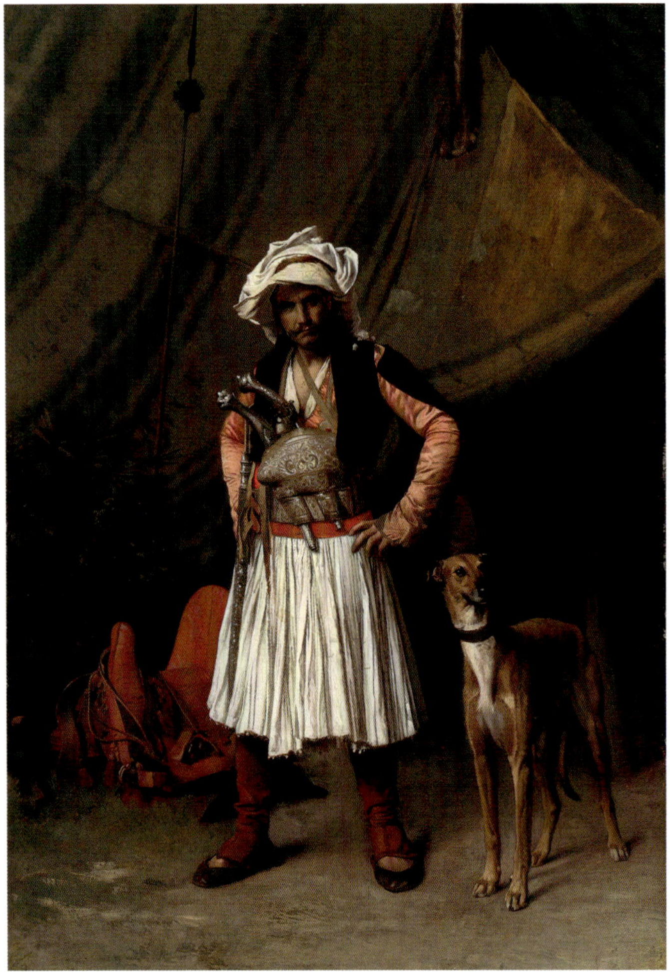

57. Jean-Léon Gérôme, *Bachi Bazouk et son chien* (A Bashi-Bazouk and his Dog) (1870). Oil on panel, 35.6 x 25.1 cm. The bashi-bazouks were a subject to which Gérôme returned several times. In at least some cases he probably dressed Parisian models in appropriate garments from his own extensive costume collection.

and surfaces of the objects that adorn the paintings, rather than an interpretation of the ethnographic dimension of the characters that feature in them. Although Deutsch experimented with a much looser style and interpretation late in his career (see page 234), his human subjects, however dramatic, were traditionally confined to a series of types. These included scribes, scholars, musicians, and—most notably—his celebrated palace guards, elaborately costumed and armed but ethnographically and compositionally stilted and repetitive. Deutsch's "people" were largely a product of his image-making, rather than a reflection of who and what he had seen when traveling in the East.

One other aspect of Gérôme's success as an ethnographic artist relates to some of the best known of his paintings, those featuring Cairo's legendary bashi-bazouks. These remnant and highly decorative figures were the descendants of the eponymous renegade Albanian mercenaries brought to Egypt by Muhammad Ali and were depicted by Gérôme at a time when, according to Paul Lenoir (who accompanied his tutor on two trips to Egypt, in 1868 and 1881), "these soldiers of ornament, these *opéra-comique* sentinels have no other duty than to pose for any itinerant photographer that might honour them with his patronage."[81] The days of the bashi-bazouks were clearly numbered, and while such works had obvious commercial appeal, Gérôme's accurate and powerful portrayal of the endangered mercenaries is an excellent example of 'salvage ethnography' through art: the recording of a traditional cultural type, custom, or activity threatened with imminent extinction.

For some artists the disappearance of historical types was of more than just aesthetic concern. William Holman Hunt's primary purpose in visiting the Middle East was to explore the Holy Land and use that experience to convey more accurately the authority of Christianity, and particularly of the Bible, to his audience back home. In *Pre-Raphaelitism and the Pre-Raphaelite Brotherhood* (1905) he explained how, "my desire is very strong to use my powers to make more tangible Jesus Christ's history and teaching."[82] Even when in Egypt—arguably less important to Hunt as a destination than Palestine—he was clear about his objective being to shed light on the value of the past rather than to illuminate the present for its own sake: "I had no ambition to illustrate modern Cairo, I was re-reading Herodotus, Sir Gardiner Wilkinson, the Bible, and Lane's *Modern Egyptians*, and what I saw was for the time studied only to make the records of ancient history clearer. All traditional manners were threatening to pass away, together with ancient costume and hereditary taste; I saw that in another generation it would be too late to reconstruct the past, save in rural and desert life, if even there."[83]

For Hunt the most pressing quest was to find and depict endangered scenes and subjects before they disappeared and what he perceived as the direct human link with biblical times was lost forever. Such harking back to a more glorious and, as he saw it, more spiritual past is a strand in Orientalism generally, with many artists seeking to document what they saw through the 'windows on history' that the Orient provided.

Étienne Dinet's paintings fulfilled a documentary function, although there is no evidence to suggest that he articulated his approach in quite the same way as artists like Hunt. Dinet's works spanned the full panoply of human life in the desert-edge villages that he came to know so well, ranging from scenes of children playing, women washing clothes, men praying, and couples flirting to depictions of dancing, hunting, and animal husbandry. In so doing he broke a string of taboos that had beset Orientalist artists in their depiction of people, ensuring a strong emphasis on human emotion throughout his work. He strayed also into territory with which few other artists felt comfortable, with some of his works handling difficult themes such as illness, rejection, and mourning. Such coverage helped shift his works away from any primarily ethnographic dimension and toward a more complete artistic representation of a people, both as individuals and as a community.

Dinet's presence in Bou-Saâda helped make it a destination for other overseas artists. One who made the journey there was Édouard Verschaffelt, who moved to Algeria with his wife to escape the chaos of Belgium during World War I. She died not long after they arrived in Algeria, and Verschaffelt subsequently married a woman from the Ouled Sidi Brahim tribe and became very integrated into local life. His wife sat regularly for him and appears in many of his works, this level of insider access allowing him to focus on family scenes and single-study portraits of girls and women in a way that would have been impossible for visiting foreign artists. Verschaffelt's impressionistic style was probably influenced by Renoir (who had visited Algeria in 1881 and 1882) and helped shift the portrayal of the peoples of the Middle East further away from the pristine and static ethnographic stereotypes of half a century earlier toward a more expressive interpretation.

It fell to another Belgian artist, Émile Deckers (1885–1968), to square the Orientalist circle on ethnography and contemporary artistic fashions and practice. A decorated war hero as a result of his service during World War I, Deckers

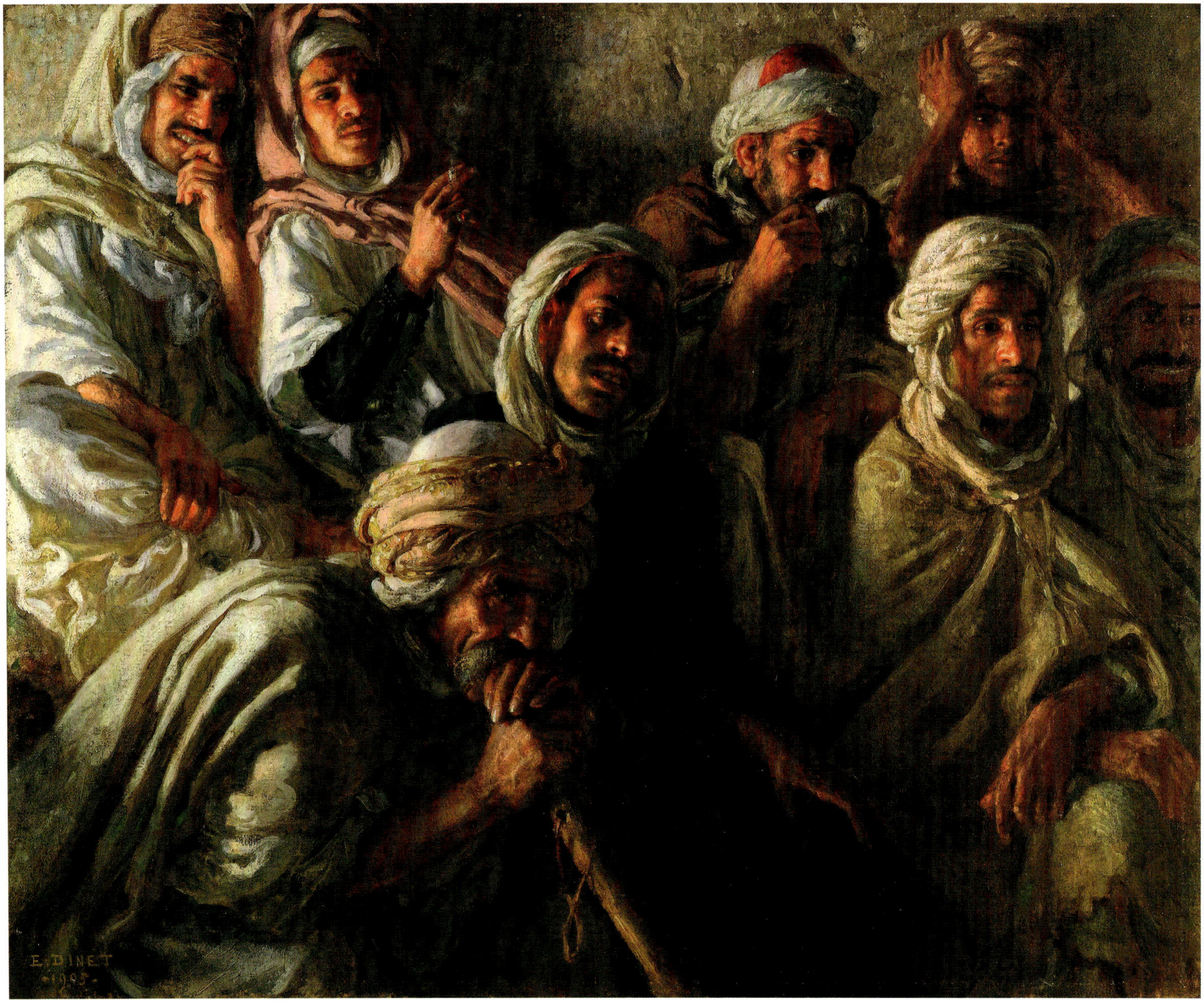

58. Étienne Dinet, *Spectateurs admirant une danseuse* (Spectators Admiring a Dancer) (1905). Oil on canvas, 84 x 102.5 cm.

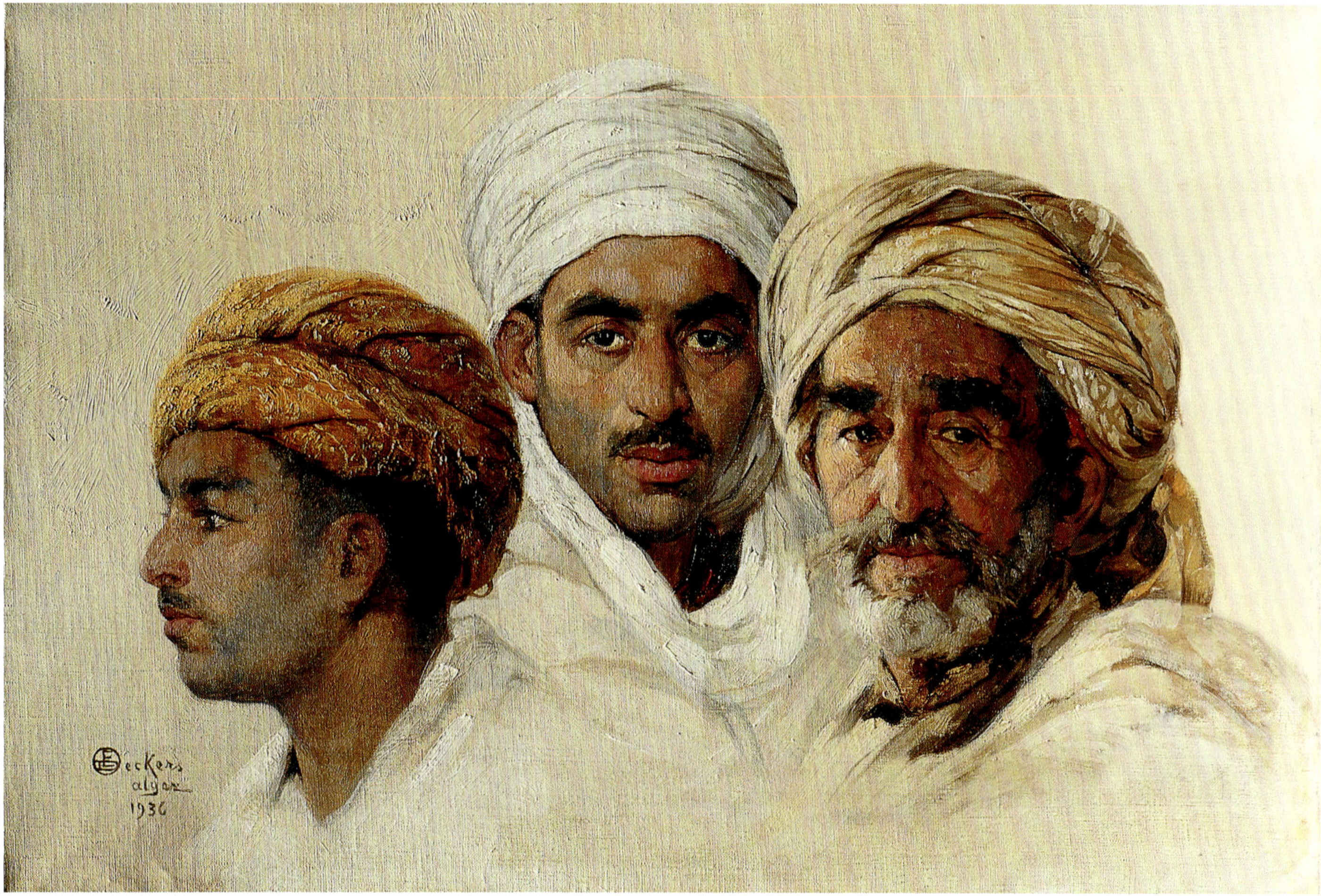

59. Émile Deckers, *Portrait of Algerians* (1936). Oil on canvas, 54.6 x 81.2 cm.

moved to Algiers in 1921. He was to spend much of the next forty-five years in the country, specializing particularly in portraits of both men and women from the Bedouin, Berber, and Tuareg communities. His trademark style was to feature three or four head studies in one composition, each of the subjects looking at a different angle and presented in a sketchbook format that gave the impression that they had been drawn from life, in situ—which many probably were.

Deckers took care to ensure that his portraits were clear likenesses of individuals, expressing elements of their personalities and so emphasizing an artistic departure from rigid ethnographic or anthropological types. He was able to portray a wide variety of physiognomies and his focus on personal characteristics not only avoided the duplication that came from the reuse of studio sitters (as with Ludwig Deutsch, for example) but also served to create a new 'badge of validation' for artists. Neither romanticizing nor patronizing his subjects, Deckers applied his approach to a wide range of different cultural contexts and was to produce a series of African studies when traveling in the Belgian Congo during the 1940s.

The experiences and works of Deckers have an interesting resonance with those of Rudolf Swoboda (1859–1914). After first visiting his uncle Leopold Müller in Egypt in 1879, Swoboda produced a series of Orientalist paintings notable for their attention to cultural detail. Thanks to the prominent and well-connected Austrian artist Heinrich von Angeli, he was subsequently introduced to Queen Victoria, who noted in her journal, "Saw a young Austrian artist recommended by Angeli. He is only twenty-six, of the name of Swoboda, and is full of talent."[84] The queen then commissioned him to paint some of the thirty-four Indian artisans brought to London in 1886 to demonstrate crafts in a "living display" at the spectacular Colonial and Indian Exhibition.

So impressed was she by Swoboda's studies of the artisans that Queen Victoria paid from her own pocket to send him to India later that year to produce sketches of the different nationalities and ethnic types found across her Indian Empire. In style and content these works presage the portraits of Deckers, with each subject conveying his or her personality through expression, clothes, and stance. Yet Swoboda's Indian studies pre-date the works of Deckers by over half a century. One can speculate on what Swoboda might have achieved if he had ever turned his attention to the Bedouin of Sinai or the Tuareg of Algeria, but the ethnographic content of his paintings and those of Dinet, Deckers, and Verschaffelt serve to emphasize how the portrayal of people and ethnicity by the Orientalist artists had by this time moved on significantly from the precision armlock of Gérôme and his followers. Such changes were a response to a raft of factors affecting Orientalist art in the final decades of the nineteenth century and early years of the twentieth, ranging from changes in the value attached to the concept of realism, the impact of the medium of photography, and also an evolution in terms of how artists perceived themselves, created their images, and saw their role as commentators and interpreters of the Orient and its societies.

4. Image

For most Orientalist artists a trip to Algeria, Egypt, or the Levant was just one stage on the often long road to a finished painting. Expeditions overseas were primarily an exercise in the gathering of experiences, information, and resources, to be examined, evaluated, and utilized in the calm and comfort of the studio environment back home. It was here that the end products were largely developed and refined, a process that relied not only on the bank of ideas and objects brought back from the Orient, sometimes over repeated trips, but also on other means of inspiration and support available more locally, including models and the advice and shared knowledge of fellow returnees.

In this carefully constructed environment, artists worked to create their images of the Orient. In so doing they sought to interpret a place which, although they had (mostly, at least) visited and witnessed at first hand, was now geographically and temporally at one remove, represented by their memories, sketches, and photographs and by the pile of artifacts sitting on their studio floors. There was an immediate fracture between the real and the imagined, a recurring quandary for some artists but a factor faced with equanimity by others, for whom artistic license was very much part of their oeuvre.

Eugène Fromentin highlighted the nature of the dilemma in his 1859 book *Une Année dans le Sahel* (*Between Sea and Sahara*). "The question amounts to knowing whether the Orient yields to interpretation, to what extent it is open to this and, if to interpret it is not to destroy it," he wrote. "The Orient is extraordinary . . . . It escapes conventions, it lies outside all disciplines, it transposes, it inverts everything . . . . I do not talk here of a fictional Orient." Fromentin's concerns were also relevant to the ways in which artists perceived their role. Many had enjoyed moments of whimsical fancy and freedom when traveling, but on their return were forced to reassess both their own understanding of what they had seen and also to consider how best to create for their audience a compelling image of the East in the face of the demand for realism and pressure from the rapidly expanding medium of photography.

Celebrity Studios

The nature of studio spaces belonging to successful and high profile artists was changing at this time, a development welcomed by the critic M. Phipps-Jackson in 1883. He lamented the traditional studio set-up favored by some British artists, at least: "A small room, frequently in the worst possible order, a lay figure, and here and there a few draperies scattered heedlessly about, formed the daily associations with which a painter attempted to nourish his artistic instincts, and produce works which were the chief occupation of his life." Phipps-Jackson went on to observe with relief that "all this, however, is now changed, and influenced possibly by the magnificence of modern continental ateliers, artists of the present day, more wise in their generation, seek to surround themselves with appliances suitable to an art finding full expression only in the highest refinement and the most cultivated skill."[1]

The Orientalists were at the vanguard of this change and some of those who traveled regularly came home to studios that were already lavishly decked out as a microcosm of the Orient. Vast collections of artifacts and antiquities, many of which would not have been out of place in an ethnographic museum, were amassed by artists such as Benjamin-Constant, Deutsch, and Gérôme. Benjamin-Constant's Parisian studio was particularly notable in this respect, resplendent with rugs and other textiles as well as armor, lamps, flags, and inlaid furniture, much of which had been acquired during his travels in Morocco. His collection included a vast Farahan carpet, which appears in an 1870s photograph of his studio and also features in several of his paintings, including *The Favourite of the Emir* (1879).[2] On Gérôme's death in 1904 an inventory of his possessions listed fifty-two pairs of ethnic footwear and 173 costumes, many of which doubtlessly featured in his paintings. Although in most cases such items were restricted to artists' storerooms and studios, in other instances they spilled out into the wider residence, a reflection of the passion of their owners for the Orient and its culture. As Phipps-Jackson observed, "for as surely as a painter's work is but the reflex of himself, with equal certainty his artistic tastes and sympathies are to be discovered in the abode he has chosen."[3]

In some cases, entire houses were built around the notion of "Orient." One of the most famous examples of an Orient-inspired interior of the period is Leighton House, where the eponymous lord set himself up as a London pasha in a house built to his own specification, extended to include an Arab Hall (1877–81) and designed to showcase his outstanding collection of Islamic ceramics and other antiquities. In the United States of America, artist Frederic E. Church (1826–1900)—a leading light in the Hudson Valley school and not noted as a specialist in Orientalist subjects—was inspired to build his extraordinary residence Olana (1870–72, with a later studio wing) following a trip to the Orient in 1867–69. A wildly eclectic mix of styles drawn from Andalusia and the Maghreb across to Persia and India, Olana (from the Arabic *'alana*, meaning "our place on high") housed Church's extensive collection of art and antiquities and served as "a dramatic opening up of the new world from the old,"[4] with its Islamic arches, balconies, and window surrounds framing the landscape views of the Hudson River and Upper New York State beyond.

Most Orientalist artists baulked at such architectural exuberance at home, but this was nonetheless a time of extravagant gestures. Many of these were ostensibly undertaken

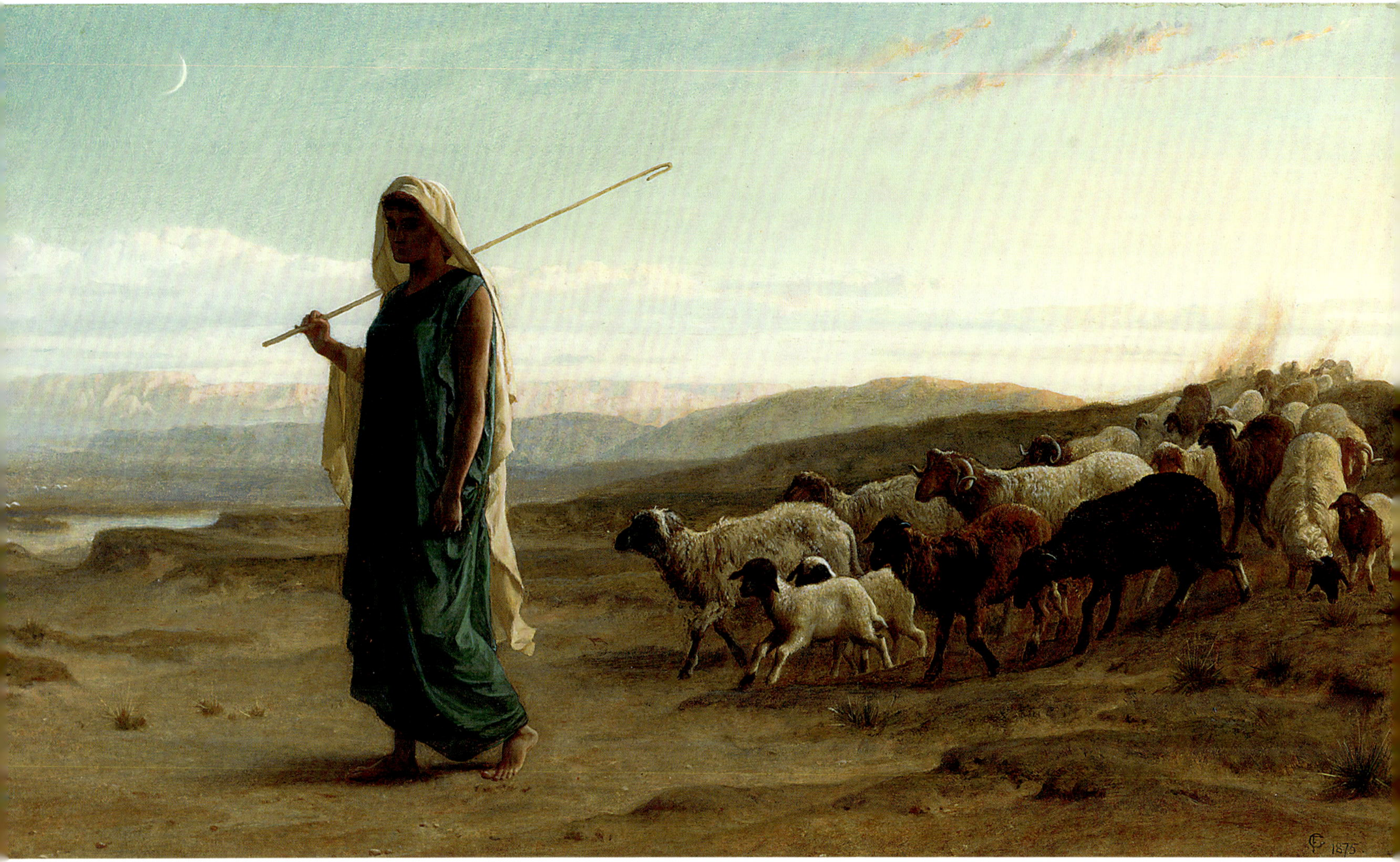

60. Frederick Goodall, *Rachel and her Flock, 'And Behold, Rachel his daughter cometh with the sheep'* (1874). Oil on canvas, 97 x 178 cm.

in the cause of artistic authenticity. Frederick Goodall even imported a flock of Egyptian sheep to England, with which to convincingly populate his biblically themed paintings, notably *Rachel and her flock, 'And behold, Rachel his daughter cometh with the sheep'* (1875) (Figure 60). The sheep spent some time living in the grounds of a new residence (named Graham's Dyke) that Goodall had commissioned outside London at Harrow Weald, designed by the eminent architect Norman Shaw and where the animals sat about on piles of gravelly soil and were fed dates by visitors. The new house included a "grand painting-room, where I painted some of my most important pictures," but Goodall later moved back to London and into a house formerly owned by the famous art dealer Ernest Gambart (see page 214). In his *Reminiscences* Goodall described this house and its furniture, which included "a very large cabinet of German Gothic, in the centre of which is a compartment six feet long, where I keep all my Egyptian costumes in sliding trays."[5]

Goodall also offered a detailed description of the layout and contents of his studio there, one of the few such accounts: "[It] is entirely hung with my Egyptian sketches painted on the spot—studies of camels, sheep, buffaloes, landscapes, fellaheen; the Bedouin spinning wool and weaving carpets and rugs; and a number of studies of heads in oil-colours of the women of the tents, besides several water-colour sketches of palm-trees, villages, and the customs of the natives . . . . The *Musharabea* lattice-work, as seen in the studio, is just as it appears in the houses of Cairo, with the original little windows or doors which the ladies of the Harem look out of occasionally into the street, or from which they drop a coin into the hands of a mendicant. Two very fine Egyptian doors—rare, of course, in England—are beautiful pieces of work, one inlaid and dovetailed, the other an exquisite design in latticework, and four ornamental carved and plastered windows, with stained glass let in. All this I bought from a house in the Mameluke quarter that was being pulled down when I resided in that locality."[6]

Goodall's studio was probably typical of those maintained by other successful Orientalist artists. His friend Carl Haag lived not far away in Hampstead, where he set up a lavishly furnished Oriental studio in his own house, described by *The Art Journal* of 1883 as resembling "Cairo in London" (see page 217).[7] However, not all Orientalists maintained such elaborate establishments or extensive collections of paraphernalia. Leopold Müller, for example, returned to Vienna from his first visit to Egypt (1874) to share part of the studio of his friend and fellow artist Hans Makart, only later (1878–92) moving to a larger studio of his own at the Vienna Academy of Art. Nor was Müller a great collector of Oriental artifacts, bringing back with him only a number of rugs—often old and torn—with which to adorn his studio and his home.[8]

Competing Media

However grand or modest in size and décor, it was the studio environment that provided the setting for the completion of many Orientalist works. A majority of the artists worked in oil, at least in terms of their final finished paintings. Watercolor had traditionally been regarded as a particularly English interest, but was nonetheless taken very seriously by some in continental Europe. One admirer was Eugène Delacroix, who wrote of the English Romantic landscape artist Richard Parkes Bonington (1801–28) that "no one in this modern school, and possibly even before, has possessed that lightness of touch, which particularly in the watercolours, makes his work a type of diamond that flatters and ravishes the eye, independently of any subject."[9]

It was this jewel-like quality that was striven for by many Orientalist artists and so admired by their clients and audiences. It traditionally relied on precise brushstrokes to create an intensity of saturated color and a burnished effect—all considered harder to deliver in watercolor than in oil. While watercolor's speed of application and portability led to it being regarded as particularly suitable for working when "on the road"—preliminary sketches and on-the-spot studies in watercolor were favored by many artists, from Delacroix to Lear—its credentials as the best medium for a finished work remained more dubious. Concerns revolved particularly around the instability of the medium generally, as well as the fugitive nature of individual colors.

Some artists took up the challenge. As early as the 1830s John Frederick Lewis was pioneering the use of gouache bodycolor to create a saturated effect in his watercolors, and further efforts in this direction were to come from Carl Haag. Attracted to England from Germany in 1847 because he was particularly interested in watercolor, Haag worked in this medium for the rest of his life. In order to overcome some of its perceived limitations, he used various methods—some of which he was forced to adopt following a pistol accident that severely damaged the tendons of his right hand. He concentrated on creating highlights by the application of multiple layers of wash, stippling over these with his brush, and then removing superfluous paint so that highlighted areas emerged. This helped create the density and depth that the traditional critics of watercolor felt the medium lacked. Haag also invented a fixative, made of wax and spirit of lavender, to apply to the finished paintings and help combat their supposed fragility. Through such practices he felt able to claim it was possible to achieve the "brilliancy of oil painting, combined with the tender-sweetness of water-colours."[10]

Despite such endeavors, most French, German, and Austrian Orientalists continued to work overwhelmingly in oil. Some artists made the transition from one medium to the other: Charles Robertson's early paintings were oils, for example, but by 1884 he was working almost exclusively in watercolor. John Frederick Lewis was equally proficient in both media, but faced concern from some of his clients and supporters that his watercolor paintings were less likely to stand the test of time than those in oil. Appraising *A Frank Encampment* (Figure 41), John Ruskin wrote to Lewis declaring that "Your picture is one of the wonders of the world. If it is in firm colour—it will one day be a thing that men will come from India to see. . . . I can't tell you how glorious I think it—*Are* you sure of your material—if one of those bits of white hairstroke fade—where are you?—*Why* don't you paint in oil only now?"[11]

Lewis's position was complicated by two factors. First, the market rate for watercolors was consistently inferior to that commanded by oil paintings; and second, Lewis's ambition was to become an associate of the Royal Academy, which at the time did not admit members of other artistic societies, including the Society of Painters in Water Colours. In 1858—shortly after resigning as president of the society, and by way of justification in the face of claims that he had betrayed his fellow watercolorists—he railed against what he saw as the disproportionate financial reward offered by that medium: "generally in spite of all my hard work, I find water colour to be thoro'ly [sic] *unremunerative* that I can stand it no longer . . . no rest, and such little pay!"[12] He became an associate of the academy the following year.

Endeavoring to reconcile his situation, Lewis's solution was in many cases to paint oil and watercolor versions of the same composition. This process began early in his career, but the first known Orientalist example is his oil on panel work, *The Greeting in the Desert, Egypt (Selamat Teiyibin)*, of 1855, the same year in which he exhibited a watercolor of almost identical composition. Several such "pairs" followed, including oil and watercolor versions of *The Dellál* (both dated 1875) (Figures 61 and 62) and *A Lady Receiving Visitors (The Reception)*, an oil on panel painting of 1873 with an almost identical (and larger) watercolor counterpart that does not appear to have enjoyed extensive public attention until after Lewis's death.[13] In this way, Lewis was able to satisfy his own desire to work in watercolor without sacrificing the greater commercial gains derived from painting in oil. In any case, many of his watercolors were to find eager buyers among the rich industrialists of the Midlands and north of England. Concerns about the durability of Lewis's watercolors (and particularly Ruskin's worries over *A Frank Encampment*) were to prove largely ill founded. Most have stood the test of time well.

Commercial considerations applied to all but the wealthiest artists, but were particularly keenly felt by Gustav Bauernfeind. With little or no private income, he lived from the proceeds of his paintings and on at least one occasion had to reschedule an overseas trip until he had landed a sale from which to fund it. Unlike the majority of Orientalist artists, he chose to base himself overseas for lengthy periods—his second expedition of 1884–87 lasted for almost three years, for example. In a letter to his mother in 1886, Bauernfeind outlined why he felt it was important for him to stay abroad for so long, in order to observe the passage of the seasons and the associated social customs and traditions. He concluded, "So you can see that you have to live in a country like this a long time before becoming even superficially familiar with all it has to offer."[14]

Bauernfeind's precarious financial circumstances meant that he needed to keep producing finished works while abroad and ship them home to potential clients and, hopefully, secure a successful sale. His situation contrasts for example with that of John Frederick Lewis, who lived in Cairo for nearly a decade before sending back his first finished work (*The Hhareem*, see page 136) in 1850; its success may have prompted his return to England the following year. The sensational subject matter of the picture may have been a strategic decision designed to help relaunch his career after years abroad. Lewis's ability to disregard repeated calls from the Society of Painters in Water Colours to send works back for exhibition also underlines the fact that he was wealthy enough to live comfortably in Egypt for almost ten years without apparently needing to sell any works.

In choosing to paint abroad full-time, Bauernfeind found himself hampered by all sorts of factors, not least the winter weather in Syria and Palestine. In early 1885 he was in Jaffa, complaining that "I have wasted a great deal of time in not being able to work as I intended, because of the insufficiency of sunlight in the winter. In Damascus I was unable to do any figurative work because I had no house

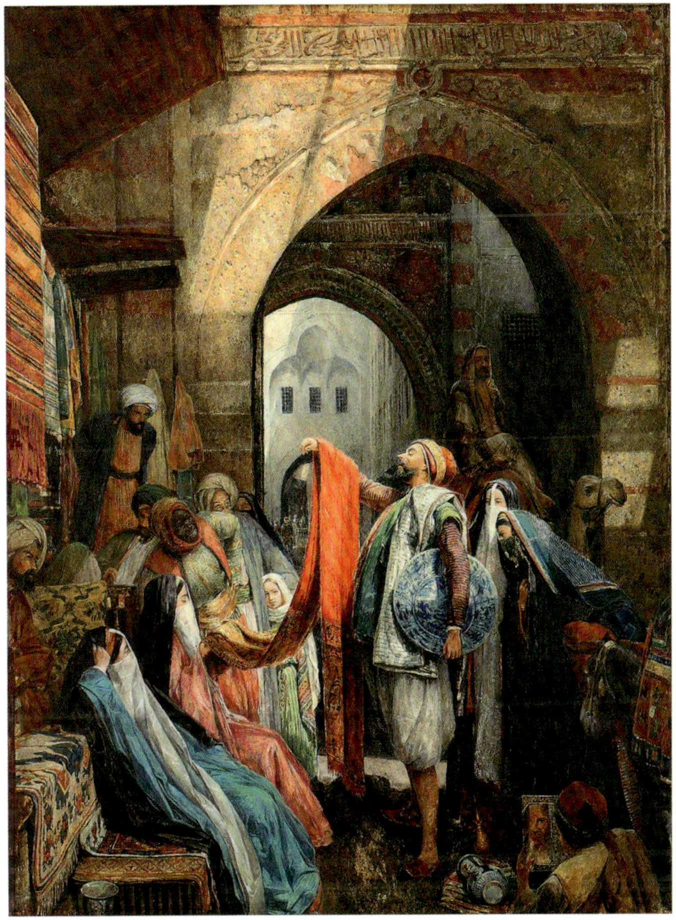

61. John Frederick Lewis, *A Cairo Bazaar; The Dellál* (1875). Pencil, watercolor, bodycolor, and gum Arabic on paper, 67.5 x 51 cm.

62. John Frederick Lewis, *A Cairo Bazaar; The Dellál* (1875). Oil on panel, 75.5 x 53.5 cm.

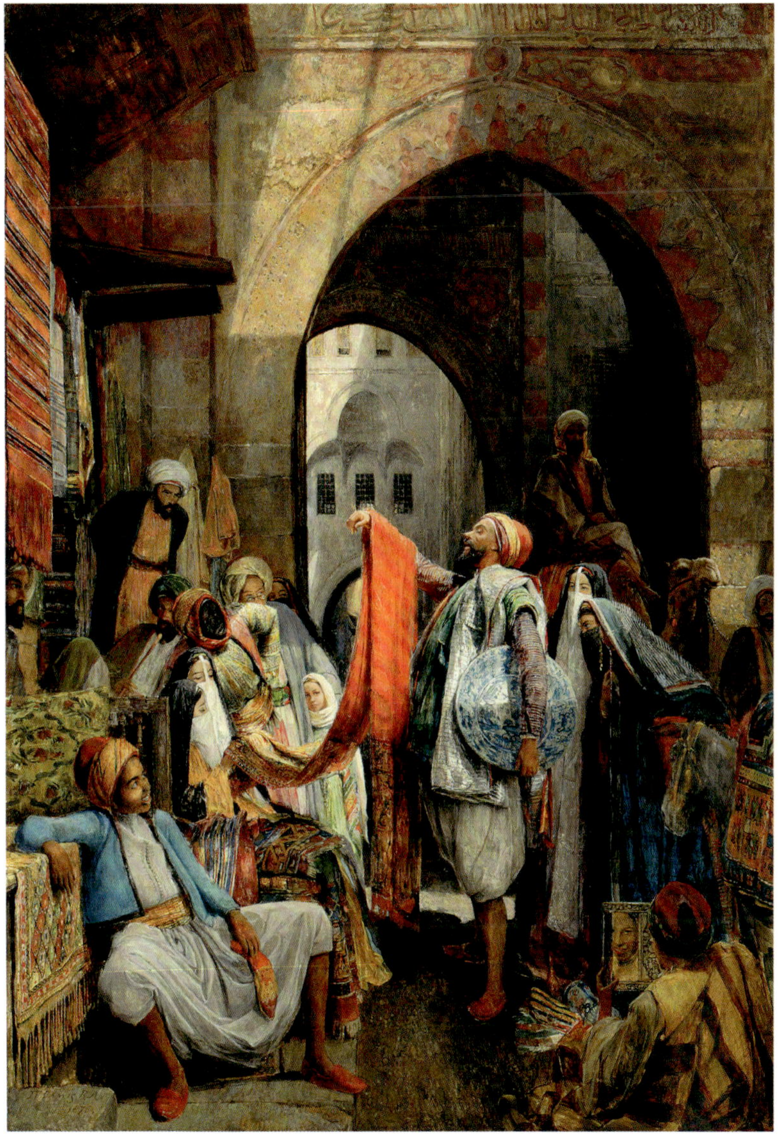

suitable for the purpose."[15] The lack of a satisfactory studio space in which to produce paintings proved a recurring problem, but one that he should have anticipated. It was, after all, why almost all other artists chose to return home to complete their works. Meanwhile, in Jaffa Bauernfeind was forced to repeatedly skim the airborne dust off his paintings as he worked. It was only in July 1885, nine months after he had arrived in the Middle East on the second of his extended visits, that he shipped his first completed work to his client in England.

Whether he had been producing his paintings in Europe or in Palestine, Bauernfeind would still have had to contend with similar market pressures to those about which Lewis had complained. Working alone, in difficult conditions and without being able to discuss his ideas or share his sketches with fellow artists or kindred spirits, Bauernfeind must have felt very isolated. Late in 1885 he wrote to his relations in Beirut, sounding them out about his concepts for a composition and bemoaning how he was being forced to compromise on format. "I have subjects enough for big pictures but not for small ones of the type that the Englishman [Arthur Sulley, a London art dealer and Bauernfeind's main client] would prefer," he explained. "I have just begun a new picture . . . I am not flattering myself when I say that the conception is very good indeed. A group of Jews stand at the gate . . . their heads thrust slightly forward as they peer into the paradisiacal sun-drenched precinct within, with its gleaming domes and coloured tiles and marble walls . . . . Within, Mohammedans dressed in vivid costumes stroll, sit, loll about, and the like. A fine contrast, don't you think? But alas my financial situation is not such as to allow me to realize such a picture as it should be realized, and in a manner that might make my reputation."*

Despite all the obstacles he encountered, Bauernfeind was convinced that he was better placed producing his finished paintings on location in the countries that he was depicting, rather than in a studio environment back home. He felt this gave his Oriental images more immediacy and accuracy, writing to Sulley in 1886 to explain that "I do not think I shall go to Munich [his base in Germany] this year as these pictures cannot be painted there."[16] The return home did not take place until 1889, when Bauernfeind set himself up with a studio in Munich and worked there—with limited success—until he sold virtually everything he had, including his collection of Oriental artifacts, and moved permanently to Palestine in 1896 (see page 224).

Even if his choice of working location often differed from that favored by most other leading Orientalists, the approach of Bauernfeind was essentially the same: he used the power of his own observation, expressed through pencil sketches and watercolor studies, as the basis for his paintings, enhanced by his props and the extensive use of photographs—many taken by himself—as source material. His approach to photography highlighted the transformation brought by the new medium to the ways in which the Orientalists worked, even if its advent was not universally welcomed.

* Carmel and Schmid, *The Life and Works of Gustav Bauernfeind*, 101–102. Bauernfeind did indeed complete the painting, *At the Entrance to the Temple Mount*, and sent it to Arthur Sulley the following year (1886). He received £500 for it. See Figure 96.

The First Photographs

The Orient makes a surprisingly early appearance in the history of photography. Less than three months after the announcement in Paris in August 1839 of the groundbreaking technique invented by Louis Jacques Mandé Daguerre to capture a photographic image, the artist Horace Vernet and his collaborator (and nephew) Frédéric Goupil-Fesquet were busy applying the new technology in Egypt. In front of an assembled audience that included the viceroy, Muhammad Ali, on 7 November that year they made a daguerreotype of the exterior of the harem at the Ras El-Tin Palace in Alexandria. After initially condemning the image as the work of the devil, Muhammad Ali soon became an enthusiastic advocate of the new practice and began welcoming European photographers to Egypt. Vernet and Goupil-Fesquet went on to take images of Cairo, Alexandria, and Jerusalem—"We were daguerreotyping as hard as we could go," Vernet reported[17]—and helped create a vogue for "Orientalist photography." They also established the tradition of artists gathering photographs as source material and *aide-mémoires* for their paintings, a practice that was to become a hallmark of the Orientalists.

Daguerre's invention was not the first image-recording mechanism that Orientalists had used in their work. Edward William Lane had illustrated his *Manners and Customs*, published in 1836, with engravings of drawings produced by his own hand using a camera lucida. First patented in 1807, this optical device used a mirror to superimpose a view onto a drawing surface, where it could be traced. The graphic telescope, a variation of the camera lucida, was patented four years later and allowed the user to increase the size of the image, thereby making it possible to draw more distant objects. Artists such as John Sell Cotman regularly resorted to the camera lucida and graphic telescope as a means of ensuring accuracy and perspective in their work, but the invention of photography opened up a whole new range of options.

Photographers flocked to the Orient in the years following Daguerre's discovery and Vernet and Goupil-Fesquet's trailblazing expedition. The themes expressed in Orientalist photography reflected those present in Orientalist art, with the same emphasis on sensuality, exoticism, and sumptuousness, although for obvious reasons it was rarely possible for on-the-spot photographers to produce quite the same level of extravagance in their work. The history of photography in the Orient was largely made by foreigners, either visiting or temporarily resident, and by indigenous Christian photographers. Islamic concerns over figural depiction ensured that very few Muslims felt able to take up photography.[18]

One of the earliest documented accounts of a photographic expedition to Egypt is that made by Gustave Flaubert and Maxime du Camp in 1849–50. Du Camp was on an official French government commission, charged with making a photographic record of monuments across the Middle East. He started in Egypt, traveling with Flaubert up the Nile on a trip that yielded the earliest photographs of many of the major valley sites. Du Camp's description of the expedition highlights what had drawn him to photography and what its advantages were to artists in particular. "During my earlier trips I had noticed that I lost precious time drawing the monuments and scenes I wanted to remember," he recalled. "I drew slowly and not very accurately and the written notes I took about buildings and landscapes seemed confused when I reread them later . . . . I wanted to be able to record as much material as possible, so I started learning from a photographer and began working with the chemicals involved."[19]

The accounts of both du Camp and Flaubert also give an indication of the cumbersome nature of the equipment involved and the time-consuming processes required to deliver a decent quality image. Du Camp regularly asked one of their boatmen, Hadji Ismael, to stand in shot to help indicate scale, and devised a seemingly successful strategy to avoid any fidgeting: "I told him that the brass tube of the lens jutting from the camera was a cannon, which would vomit a hail of shot if he had the misfortune to move—a story which immobilized him completely, as can be seen from my plates."[20]

As far as photography and art were concerned, there were obvious potential conflicts. Many artists worried that their careers and reputations might be threatened by the upstart new medium, and they were not alone in their concerns. The poet Charles Baudelaire launched a tirade against what he saw as the potentially negative impact of photography on art in his review of the Salon of 1859, the first Salon exhibition to admit photographic works. "If photography is allowed to supplement art in some of its functions," he complained, "it will soon have supplanted or corrupted it altogether . . . its true duty . . . is to be the servant of the sciences and arts—but the very humble servant, like printing or shorthand, which have neither created nor supplemented literature."[21] In 1862, a group of those French artists most hostile to photography signed a statement of protest affirming their opposition to "any assimilation of photography to art."[22]

Meanwhile, some artists were already embracing the new idea. Three years before Baudelaire's broadside, Jean-Léon Gérôme had traveled in Egypt with the artist–photographer Frédéric-Auguste Bartholdi. After training initially as a sculptor (he famously went on to design the Statue of Liberty in New York), Bartholdi took up photography and visited Egypt, South Arabia, and Abyssinia in 1855–56, sketching and taking photographs. In Egypt he was to spend time not only in the company of Gérôme but also with Narcisse Berchère and Léon Belly, and some of the pictures he took were subsequently used by Gérôme as source material for his works. Perhaps the most iconic image from that particular trip is a self-portrait of Bartholdi with Gérôme, both of them wearing local dress.

Theirs may not have been the first working encounter between a photographer and an Orientalist artist, if the claims of Claudius Galen Wheelhouse, a doctor and amateur photographer, are to be believed. In 1850 Wheelhouse recorded in his account that "at Ombos we passed the boat of the Englishman, Mr. Lewis, who is, I believe, preparing a set of Egyptian drawings for publication. He pronounced my Talbotypes to be very successful, so much so that he requested the use of them to aid him in finishing some of his more elaborate sketches."[23] Lewis's version of this story is not known, nor does his own work seem to reflect any of Wheelhouse's known images.

William Holman Hunt and Thomas Seddon met the photographer James Graham (1806–69) when traveling in Palestine in 1854–55. Graham lived in Jerusalem for two and a half years and was reputedly the first resident photographer in the city. Both artists were to use Graham's images as source material for their paintings. In September 1854 Seddon wrote to his fiancée from Jerusalem, "Mr Graham photographs, and

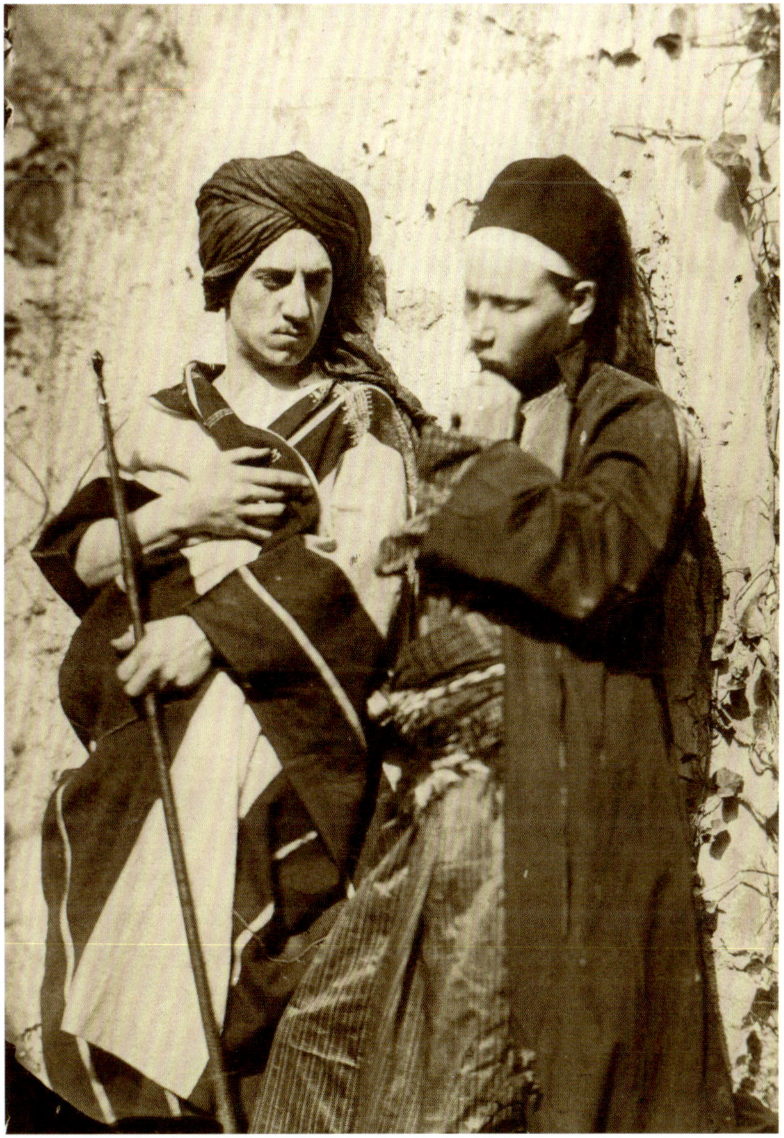

63. Frédéric-Auguste Bartholdi's photographic self-portrait with Jean-Léon Gérôme (the latter on the right), probably taken in Egypt, 1856.

I shall see his views in a few days. I hope to be able to shew [sic] them to you and supply my own want of sketches. They are extremely valuable, because perfectly true as far as they go; however, they will never supplant the pencil, for there is much in photographs that is false; the greens and yellows become nearly as black as the shadows, so that you often cannot distinguish which is shadow and which grass."[24] Seddon was to make use of Graham's photographs in his painting *Jerusalem and the Valley of Jehoshaphat from the Hill of the Evil Counsel* (1854) (Figure 30), which was completed in Brittany using his own field sketches and photographs by Graham of the same view. Graham also photographed the goat that served as the chief protagonist in Hunt's *The Scapegoat* (1855).[25]

Both artists visited Graham in the stone tower he used as a summer retreat on the Mount of Olives, and made excursions with him through the surrounding countryside, into Jerusalem itself, and to Jaffa and other towns and villages. Seddon even spent a week at Graham's tower recovering from an attack of his recurring rheumatic fever, described in a letter to his fiancée as "my old enemy."[26] Hunt, meanwhile, recorded how Graham's heavy photographic equipment was an impediment to progress when traveling, noting how at one point "Graham again was compelled to prolong his journey, for not an animal of any kind could be got to carry back his camera."[27] On another occasion they found themselves suddenly surrounded by unfriendly tribesmen. "It was time to consider our position," recalled Hunt. "We saw that Graham's camera was surrounded by five men apparently in great dread of it, but Graham was beating a retreat—if a very leisurely walk may be so described . . . . I tried to draw again, but it was evident to us that we could get no more out of our visit that day, and that we had first to rescue the camera."[28] The precious equipment was indeed retrieved from where Graham had left it, but only after the European visitors had fired a volley of warning shots.

Graham was living in Jerusalem at a time when the vogue for photography was sweeping Europe and North America. Overseas visitors to the Orient were increasingly interested in taking home images of their travels and, while commercial traveling photographers from the West continued to ply their trade, by the early 1860s photographic studios were setting up in most of the major cities of the Orient. One of the earliest was opened in Cairo by Antonio Schranz, an artist who had earlier accompanied travelers such as Viscount Castlereagh on their expeditions to the Orient (see page 101). Schranz may have established himself in Cairo as a professional photographer as early as 1849, and at Easter the following year he was visited by Florence Nightingale who, in a letter to her family, mentioned that she had been "to Schranz's, to get you some photographs."[29]

Schranz appears to have remained in Cairo until at least 1854, which was six years before one of most celebrated professional photographers in Cairo, Wilhelm Hammerschmidt, opened his studio there.[30] Around that time, or slightly later, many of the other great studios of the Orient also opened for business, including Maison Bonfils in Beirut; Pascal Sebah and the Abdullah Frères, both in Constantinople; Antonio Beato, in Cairo and Luxor; and Alary & Geiser in Algiers. Algeria was particularly well favored, with no fewer than thirty photographers listed in twelve cities across the country by 1865.[31] These studios provided a portrait service (including *cartes-de-visite*—small visiting cards with mounted photographs of the bearer), as well as selling views of local landmarks, scenery, and people, aimed specifically at the expanding tourism market. Business was not always brisk, however. The Bonfils studio, for example, was reported to have sometimes gone for a fortnight without a single sitter, even during peak season.[32]

Meanwhile, photography was beginning to have other impacts on the ways in which the Middle East was depicted. When Queen Victoria's son, Edward, Prince of Wales, embarked upon a tour of the Middle East in 1862, the decision was taken not to include an 'official' artist in his entourage—the traditional way in which such a formal visit would be recorded. Instead, the well-known and respected photographer Francis Bedford (1815–94) was invited to join the party, the first such appointment to a British royal tour. Bedford had enjoyed previous commissions from Queen Victoria, but the choice in favor of the new medium as a method of documenting the tour may also have been influenced by the interest generated by Roger Fenton's photographs of the Crimean War, an exhibition which the Prince of Wales is known to have visited twice.[33]

Bedford escorted the Prince throughout his travels to the Adriatic coast, Greece, Egypt, Palestine, Syria, Lebanon, Turkey, and Malta, producing almost two hundred photographs, which were subsequently exhibited and published to considerable acclaim. Despite the evident royal pleasure with Bedford's efforts—there are frequent references in the Prince's journal to the photographer's "very successful views"[34]—the artist Carl Haag, with whom the British royal family had an established relationship and who had traveled extensively in the region during 1858–59, was subsequently asked to produce his own renditions of the royal tour, despite not having been part of the actual visit. Clearly the appeal of more traditional visual souvenirs of such events had not been entirely diminished.*

Faster reproduction techniques and intense competition between studios saw a growth in nakedly commercial photographic work, a development of which figures such as John Ruskin—who was an initial convert to photography—were heavily critical, on the grounds that it commanded less artistic and aesthetic value. Artists, including the Orientalists, were nonetheless increasingly drawn to photographs as study aids for their paintings. While the wealthier artists could afford to commission professional photographers to accompany them on their travels, as Frederic Church did with Peter Bergheim in 1868,[35] most simply bought images in the photographic studios of Cairo and other Oriental cities. Here they could stock up on material to help them with their compositions once they had returned home.

In Europe, commercial photographers targeted the artist market by producing what were known as *études après nature*, images of a variety of objects, scenes, and people that were taken specifically to suit the requirements of artists looking for guidance on detail when preparing their sketches. This was such lucrative business that several Parisian photograph dealers chose to locate themselves conveniently close to the École des Beaux-Arts. A similar response can be detected in the Orient, especially in Egypt, where certain photographic dealers—notably G. Lékégian in Cairo—began to specialize in photographs of "types," such as street traders, which they knew were popular with artists as subjects in their paintings. Architectural views and details of decorative features were also in demand, as these helped provide accuracy with backdrops and settings such as market scenes.[36]

Artists Behind the Lens

Among the Orientalist artists who regularly took their own photographs was Gustav Bauernfeind, although this aspect of his working practice has received little attention. His letters and diaries reveal how he carried a camera with him on his first journey to the Orient, in 1880, and that photography was very much part of his research and preparation when out on location. In 1885 he described in a letter to his mother from Jaffa (where he had rented a house) about how he wanted to develop a composition featuring what he called "gypsy tents"—probably Bedouin encampments—in a "green landscape with a large prospect." He went on to explain: "For a start I took a number of photographs . . . and tomorrow I begin a study of same in either watercolour or oils."[37] This appears to have been his regular working style, which was to carry out a reconnaissance of a particular scene or situation, taking photographs, and then returning later to undertake sketches. Bauernfeind also appears to have processed his own material, traveling from Damascus to Jaffa on one occasion in January 1889 to obtain "utensils for developing the photographs." In December 1883 a letter to Bauernfeind from a Gottlob Paulus in Jaffa had included the following offer: "You can get all the chemicals you require for

* Haag produced two watercolor paintings inspired by the tour: one of the Prince of Wales visiting the encampment of Bedouin leader Agyle Agha, and the other of the royal party encamped near the temple at Baalbek. Haag was not present on either occasion. See Gordon, *Cairo to Constantinople*, 146, 167.

your camera from me,"[38] so Paulus could well have been Bauernfeind's source of photographic materials six years later.

Lengthy exposure times notwithstanding, a camera could prove especially useful in situations where the person behind the lens wished to obtain a snapshot of a particular scene or composition involving people. Yet this was not always the boon it might appear to be, as hostility on the streets to the use of the camera could be as commonplace and as intense as it was to an artist sketching openly. Frederick Arthur Bridgman described in *Winters in Algeria* how local people "will seldom consent to pose for an artist or photographer, so great is their superstition and their fear of abuse at the hands of their fellows. A miserable specimen of humanity hobbled past a photographer one day and muttered in Arabic, 'If he takes my portrait, I'll smash his machine!' In fact, it may be said that in Arab streets the 'camera is mightier than the cannon.'" Bridgman—a keen amateur photographer—went on to describe how one of his acquaintances was once beset by a hostile crowd while attempting to photograph group scenes. First showered with stones, he was then attacked with sticks and his camera broken before being rescued by the man he had employed to carry his equipment.[39]

Bauernfeind would have been very aware of the potential reaction of local people to being photographed in public. He is known to have possessed at least two cameras, a large one and his "photographic apparatus (*Dedectiv*),"[40] which arrived in Damascus from Munich in December 1888. He gives no detail about the *Dedectiv*, but it was almost certainly a portable hidden camera of the type famously used by undercover agents and private detectives. One of the most popular models at the time was the German-made Stirn's waistcoat camera, which was designed to be carried under a waistcoat or jacket with the lens poking surreptitiously through a buttonhole. Over fifteen thousand of these cameras were sold between 1886 and 1888.[41] They would have offered a seemingly perfect solution for anyone wishing to take photographs undetected in public, as Bauernfeind sought to do in cities like Damascus. Yet they were probably not infallible, as Bridgman once noted how local people had "a particular dislike to the camera, and have become acquainted with the noise of an instantaneous shutter."[42]

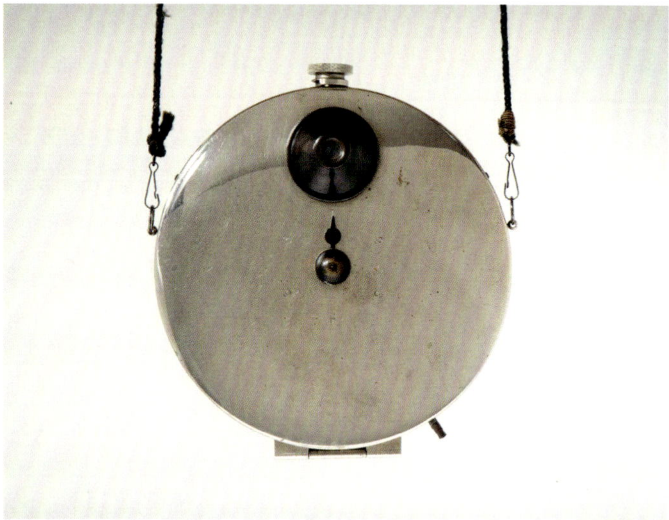

64. C.P. Stirn's waistcoat camera, probably the type of device used by Gustav Bauernfeind to discreetly photograph people and street scenes.

Not all artists were prepared to undergo the potential hassle of taking their own photographs. A firsthand account of how an artist specifically commissioned photography for use in his work comes from Mary ('May') Tyssen-Amherst, who visited Egypt for the first time in 1871 at the age of fourteen and continued visiting regularly for the next three decades and more.* On one occasion, while staying at Shepheard's Hotel in Cairo in 1873, she met the Russian artist Konstantin Makovsky (1839–1915). She recorded how "He allowed me to sit beside him and watch him paint the portraits of all sorts of picturesque models," and went on to relate a revealing episode regarding the procession that accompanied the return of the *mahmal*** to Cairo from Mecca. "[Makovsky] was very anxious to get a photograph of it as it passed through the streets," Tyssen-Amherst recalled. "This was before the days of snap shots and the Kodak was not known. He consulted my father about it one day, and as father was dining with the Khedive the following evening he promised to ask him about it. Nothing could have been kinder than His Highness's reply. The procession was to be ordered to stop at a certain point where the photographer was to be ready with a plate and focus fixed, and the photograph should be taken. Such a thing had never before been heard of; the greatest Mohamedan [sic] procession to be stopped so a Christian could take a picture of it."[43] The photograph was taken as planned and Makovsky duly completed his painting, *The Handing Over of the Sacred Carpet in Cairo*, in 1876 (Figure 65). Tyssen-Amherst saw it for herself some years later in the Hermitage Museum in St. Petersburg.

The halting of what was a procession of such special religious significance to Muslims just so that it could be photographed for a foreign artist is bound to have caused upset. Tyssen-Amherst acknowledged that it was viewed by some as "another example . . . of the Viceroy falling over himself to impress wealthy travelers, at the expense of his own people, and in this particular case, putting their religion second." Such incidents would only have helped make artists and photographers more unpopular on the streets and among the faithful.

Studio Images

The lengths to which artists and their photographers would go to obtain images is evidence of the value accorded to them as part of the research for a painting. Having access to a library of photographic images was increasingly important to artists such as Ludwig Deutsch, one of the most accomplished studio workers in the Orientalist pantheon, who had assembled a substantial photographic library by the 1890s. Brought up in Vienna, where he studied at the Academy of Fine Arts, Deutsch moved to Paris in 1878. Here he was part of a cabal of artistic Austrian émigrés, among them Rudolf Ernst, with whom he enjoyed a long and close friendship, Arthur von Ferraris, Johann Discart, and Rudolf Weiss. Deutsch was tutored by the history painter Jean-Paul Laurens and by 1881 was producing his first Orientalist works.[44]

* Mary Tyssen-Amherst came from a family with strong Egyptian links. Her grandfather was Admiral Robert Mitford, who had enjoyed good relations with the viceroy Muhammad Ali, and the family country seat of Didlington Hall in Norfolk had its own Egyptian museum. The celebrated Egyptologist Howard Carter was a close family friend, and May even led her own archeological excavations, near Aswan in 1901–04.

** The *mahmal* was a camel-mounted decorated litter, which was taken from Cairo to Mecca and back each year as part of the Hajj pilgrimage. Its journey was one of the most venerated rituals in Islam.

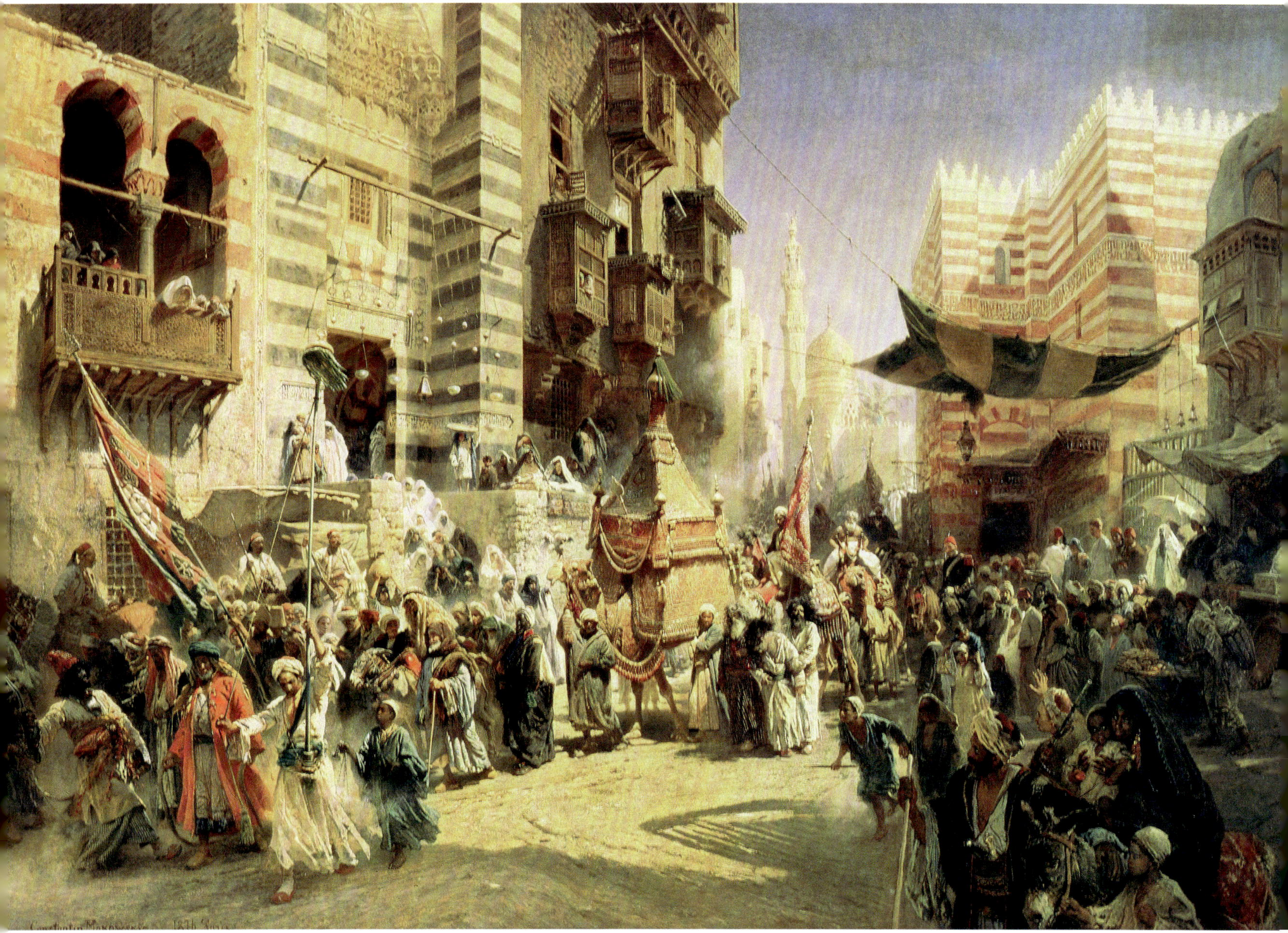

Yet the earliest of his three known trips to the Middle East was not until the winter of 1885/86, when he traveled to Egypt with von Ferraris,[45] with further expeditions following in 1890 and 1898. Deutsch may have undertaken other Oriental travels, both before and after these dates, but in the absence of any journals, letters, and other sources of data the detail of much of his life remains obscure.

This lack of firsthand accounts by Deutsch also renders his precise way of working unclear, but a series of oil studies by him of Egyptian men and women appear to be sketches produced during one or more of his trips there. Such studies would have formed the basis of his studio compositions, along with items and ideas drawn from his vast collection of decorative *bric-à-brac* and photographs—many of the latter purchased from the Cairo studio of G. Lékégian—with which he filled his studios in Paris and the south of France.

Deutsch produced his hallmark single-figure paintings in Paris using Arab and African (often Nubian or Sudanese) models, as did Gérôme. One individual reappears in several of Deutsch's most famous works, including *The Fortune Teller*, *The Mandolin Player* (Figure 73), *The Philosopher* (Figure 74), and *The Smoker* (Figure 66). Deutsch's great friend Rudolf Ernst also maintained a Parisian studio, eclectically and elaborately decorated in Oriental style and where he would don a tarboosh (or fez) when painting his models, presumably to encourage the appropriate ambiance.[46]

65. Konstantin Makovsky, *The Handing Over of the Sacred Carpet in Cairo* (1876). Oil on canvas, 214 x 315 cm.

The use by artists of such models—expatriate and otherwise—for studio work once back in Europe was commonplace. In 1855 Thomas Seddon used an Arab model ("a very handsome and fine fellow") in Paris to finalize figures in two works,[47] while in Munich Gustav Bauernfeind included in his list of expenses dated 9 January 1891 "M[ale] models for Mohammedans mendicants 2 hrs. apiece 1.50 [marks]."[48] In London, Frederick Goodall regularly employed the services of an Arab he called "Old Hasman," who was well versed in "winding turbans and putting on Oriental dresses" and whose daughter and son also appear to have sat for Goodall. One of Hasman's qualities was the ability to sit very still for long periods, thereby enabling Goodall to make careful studies of drapery, for example. It appears that Hasman was also happy to undertake more demanding roles, including one occasion when Goodall assembled a dummy camel from boxes, pillows, and bedding, positioned it on a table and asked Hasman to sit astride it in a pose. So comfortable was the false beast that Hasman fell asleep upon it, Goodall relating how he subsequently toppled off, apparently "without hurting himself in the least."[49]

Some artists also used lay figures or mannequins. Usually made of wood, often supplemented with cotton or wool padding to form musculature, and with articulated joints and limbs that allowed a range of postures, these figures were once a common studio tool. They were particularly used by artists when concentrating on poses that were hard for live models to sustain during a sitting—such as bowing or holding their arms aloft—as well as for the depiction of the drapery in robes and other forms of clothing. Usually an artist would first pose a live model in costume, make a sketch

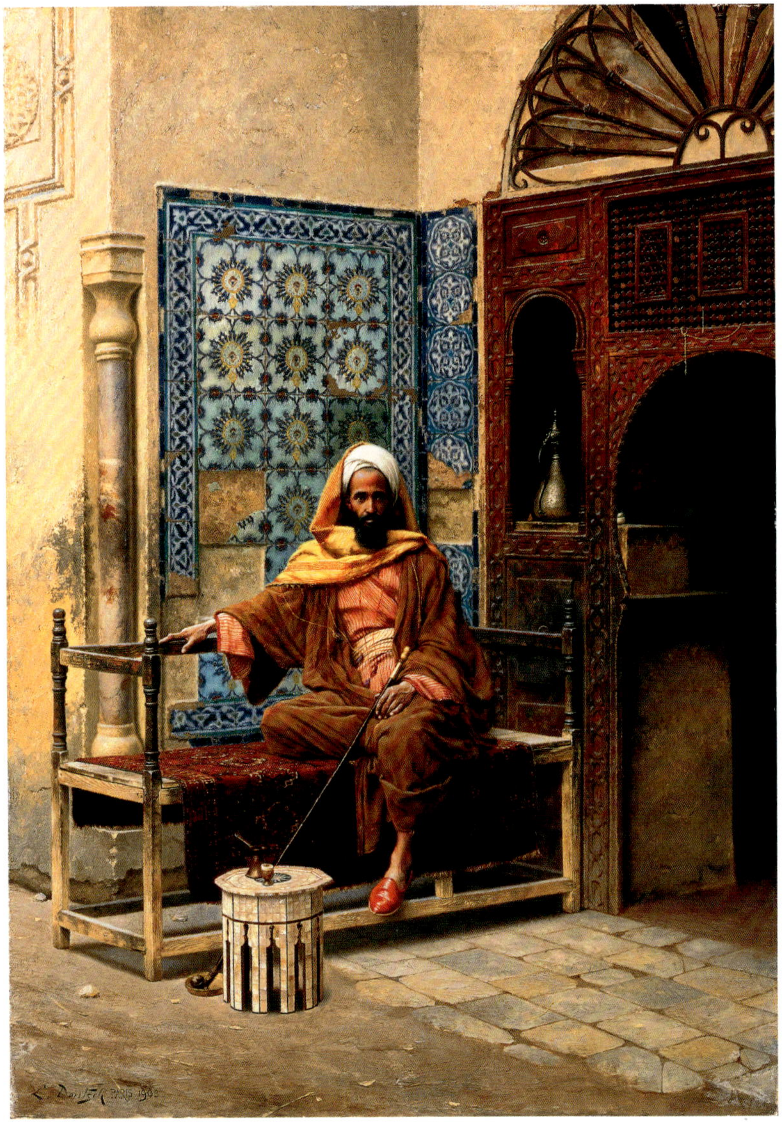

66. Ludwig Deutsch, *The Smoker* (1903). Oil on panel, 58.4 x 41.9 cm.

or working drawing, and then arrange the costume over a lay figure or mannequin configured in the same pose, from which he or she could work on the detail at their leisure. This was especially helpful for Orientalist artists painting complicated ethnic costumes, and most such studies will have involved the use of lay figures. Haag for example had in his studio at least one "life-size figure, which for the moment it is hard to believe not endowed with life, clad in the loose garments, the flowing kaftan, abajeh and handsome sash worn by the natives of the East."[50] However, the advent of the camera saw a decline in the use of lay figures, as it became easier to take a photograph of the live model when posed and then work from that (or from the increasingly large number of stock images that were available commercially).

Studio work with live models, lay figures, and assemblages of Oriental objects was underpinned with reference to on-the-spot observational sketches, notes, and photographs. The latter were especially useful when it came to generating architectural backdrops or depicting detailed decoration, but drawing direct correlations between individual photographs and Orientalist paintings is often difficult to do with conviction. Several artists are now known to have assembled extensive collections of photographic images, which could have been especially valuable for detail on aspects such as human physiognomy. Charles Cordier (1827–1905), for example, returned from Algeria in 1856 with an album of photographs of different North African people, which he classified as *Type Éthiopien*, *Race Soudanienne*, etc. and used as source material for his ethnographic sculptures.[51] On a more populist note, the proliferation from the 1850s onward of photographs of "Oriental" odalisques* was a significant source of ideas for artists specializing in paintings of that ilk. A small *Odalisque* by Eugène Delacroix dated 1857 appears to be the result of the artist working closely from a photograph, for in 1854 he had noted, "Worked a little at the *Odalisque* I am doing from the daguerreotype, but without much enthusiasm."[52]

While Delacroix (and also Gérôme, see below) may have been open about using photographs in their artistic practice, other artists were probably far more guarded. Such reticence is understandable given the lively debate at the time about the relative merits of the two media: "This tense atmosphere between photography and painting meant that the artist who decried every aspect of photography in public yet saved valuable hours by using photographs as copy aids in private, clearly had an interest in keeping his or her hoard of study photographs a secret."[53] It is likely therefore that artists preferred to use unpublished photographs as visual aids or, to help avoid accusations of plagiarism or derivation, would use only one aspect of a photograph in their work rather than copying an entire image wholesale. There are some instances of the latter, including Enrico Trenghi's *The Pottery Shop*, *c.*1880s, which appears to be an almost direct copy of a Lékégian photograph.[54] Yet artists and photographers were often traveling in the same places at about the same time, observing the same buildings and scenes, so the role of simple coincidence in the subjects portrayed in their respective works should never be underestimated.

Analysis of paintings by Gérôme has, however, produced direct evidence of his use of photographs to assist with particular areas of detail, something to which he was not afraid to admit.[55] His personal collection of images was extensive and known to have included photographs taken by Gustave Le Gray, for example, with whom he had trained in the art studio of Paul Delaroche, and Frédéric-Auguste Bartholdi, with whom he traveled to Egypt in 1857. An Ottoman house in Mocha (Yemen) that features in a photograph taken by Bartholdi in 1855–56 appears—almost to the last detail—in Gérôme's painting, *The Horse Market in Cairo* (1867) (Figures 67 and 68).[56] The artist never visited Mocha, so must have sourced the house from Bartholdi's photograph. His image collection is also known to have contained two photographs of men—probably paid models—dressed as bashi-bazouks (see page 140) wearing the traditional white arnaut skirts. These figures and their outfits (of which Gérôme had examples in his extensive costume collection) were a recurring source of inspiration and appear in many of his paintings.[57]

Gérôme visited Egypt with another photographer in 1868, this time his brother-in-law, Albert Goupil. A connoisseur of *objets d'art* and antiquities, Goupil took a series of photographs during that expedition that were to become part of Gérôme's increasingly large library of study sources, as did photographs purchased from what was probably a wide range of dealers. Gérôme appears to have also commissioned photography from other sources. In 1875 he was in Constantinople, where he was received by his former pupil

* Such images, showing (often Western) models in varying stages of undress and nudity and in risqué poses, were also popular in the less artistic context of gentlemen's clubs as well as other, more dubious, venues. Here they were often viewed on stereoscopes, which provided an easy and entertaining way of seeing printed visual material.

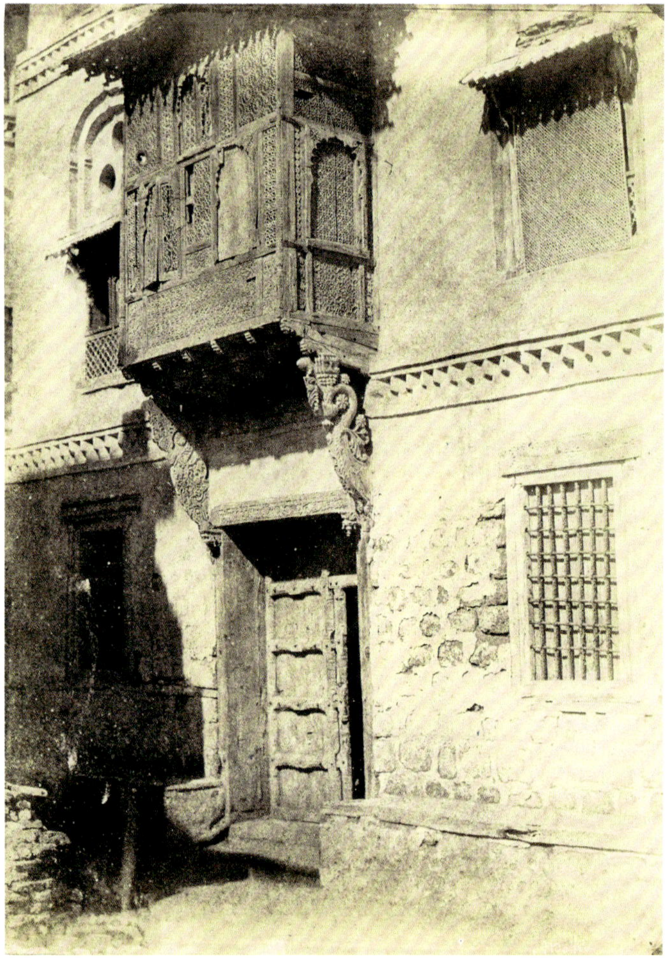

67. Frédéric-Auguste Bartholdi, photograph of a door in Mocha (present-day Yemen). Taken in 1855–56, this image appears to have been the direct source for the door depicted by Jean-Léon Gérôme in his *c.*1867 work, *The Horse Market in Cairo*.

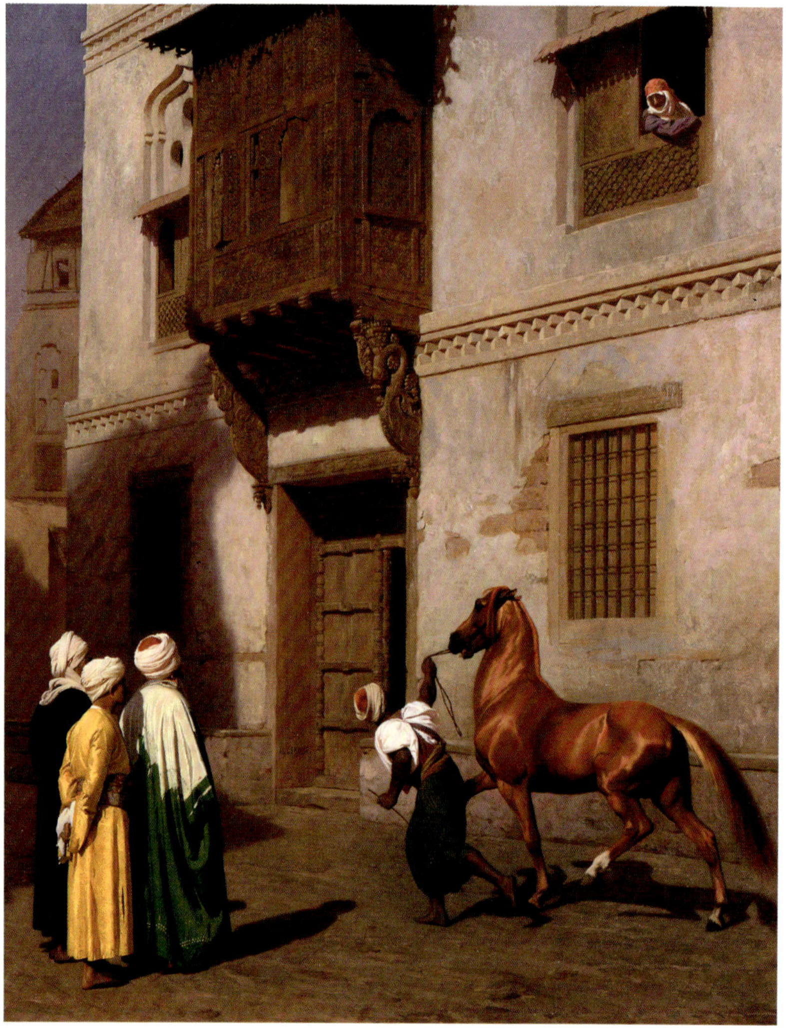

68. Jean-Léon Gérôme, *The Horse Market in Cairo* (*c.*1867). Oil on panel, 57.2 x 45 cm.

and friend Stanisław Chlebowski (see pages 58–59), and may well have made contact during this visit with a man called Abdullah Siriez who, two years later, was apparently arranging for photographs to be taken for Gérôme. It is not known whether these were of landscapes, architecture, or figures, but they may well have included interior scenes which the artist could use later for backgrounds in his paintings.*

Gérôme's photographic collection also included images by the Abdullah Frères in Constantinople, one of which may have provided the inspiration for the backdrop of tiled panels featured in his painting *The Snake Charmer* (*c.*1870).[58] The panels concerned were within a part of the palace inaccessible to visitors such as Gérôme and which he would probably only have been able to paint in such detail through reference to a photograph. What is less easy to explain in an age of monochrome photography is the accuracy he achieved with the color of the tiles. Meanwhile, the inscription in the frieze that appears above the panels in Gérôme's painting is faithfully reproduced from another building within the Topkapi complex, the Baghdad Kiosk,[59] highlighting the eclectic juxtaposition of elements that was typical of Gérôme in his architectural pastiches (see below).

The potential contribution made by reference to photographs when depicting intricate decoration and detail is also apparent in Rudolf Ernst's *The Fountain of Ahmed III, Istanbul* (1892) (Figure 69).[60] Although Ernst traveled to Egypt, Morocco, Tunisia, and Turkey, his paintings—like those of his friend, Ludwig Deutsch—were largely produced in a Paris studio. This particular work dates from two years after Ernst had visited the Ottoman capital and presumably seen the fountain, which stands just outside the gate to the Topkapi Palace. A complex and highly decorated structure, it must have presented a particular challenge to the artist and yet Ernst managed to achieve a very carefully rendered and accurate interpretation. Such a result was almost certainly achieved by the use of photographic *aide-mémoires*. Ernst is known to have taken photographs when traveling, although in Constantinople it appears he was prevented from so doing by officials. The city abounded, however, in professional photographic studios and that particular fountain was a popular subject, often featuring alongside images of the city in albums and other widely distributed publications. Ernst could have bought a photograph of the fountain while in Constantinople or sourced one from elsewhere, including when back in Paris. A monochrome image would not have been enough in itself, however; the accurate coloring Ernst gives the fountain pavilion must have come from his own on-the-spot notes and sketches. On other occasions, meanwhile—as with many Orientalist artists—Ernst was not averse to mixing up different realities and adopting a pastiche approach to his compositions. Indeed, while many artists extolled the virtue of their paintings being the result of sketches "executed direct from nature," Ernst took an unequivocal pride in his carefully crafted and more eclectic, wider-ranging studio work.

* Ackerman, *The Life and Work of Jean-Léon Gérôme*, 110. Little is known about Siriez, who remains an elusive character in the records. Ackerman speculated that he was the Ottoman court painter who received Gérôme in Constantinople in 1875, but more recent evidence confirms that this role was in fact filled by Stanisław Chlebowski. Gérôme and Chlebowski are known to have exchanged gifts of Oriental artifacts, some of which doubtless found their way into Gérôme's extensive collection.

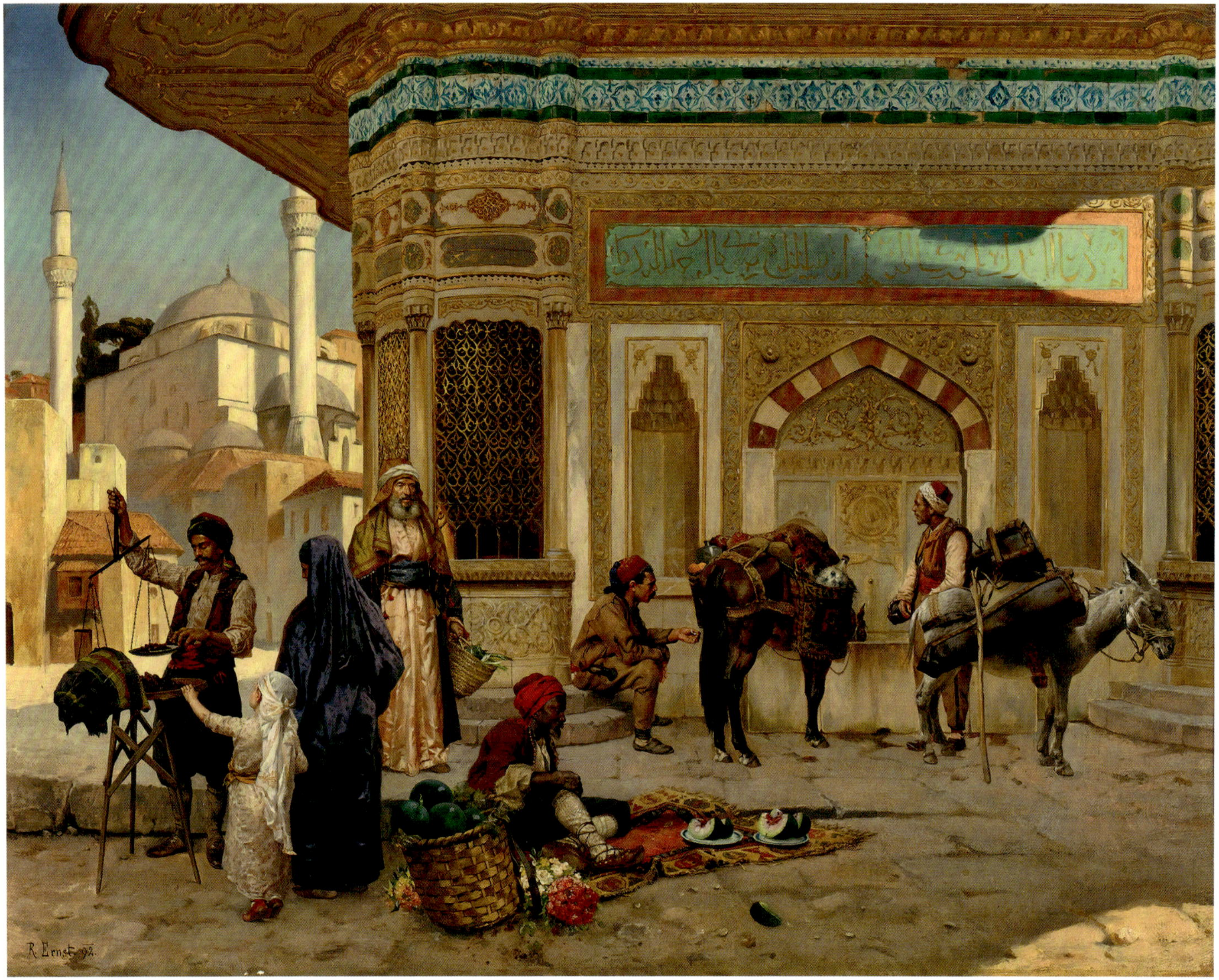

69. Rudolf Ernst, *The Fountain of Ahmed III, Istanbul* (1892). Oil on panel, 63.5 x 81.9 cm.

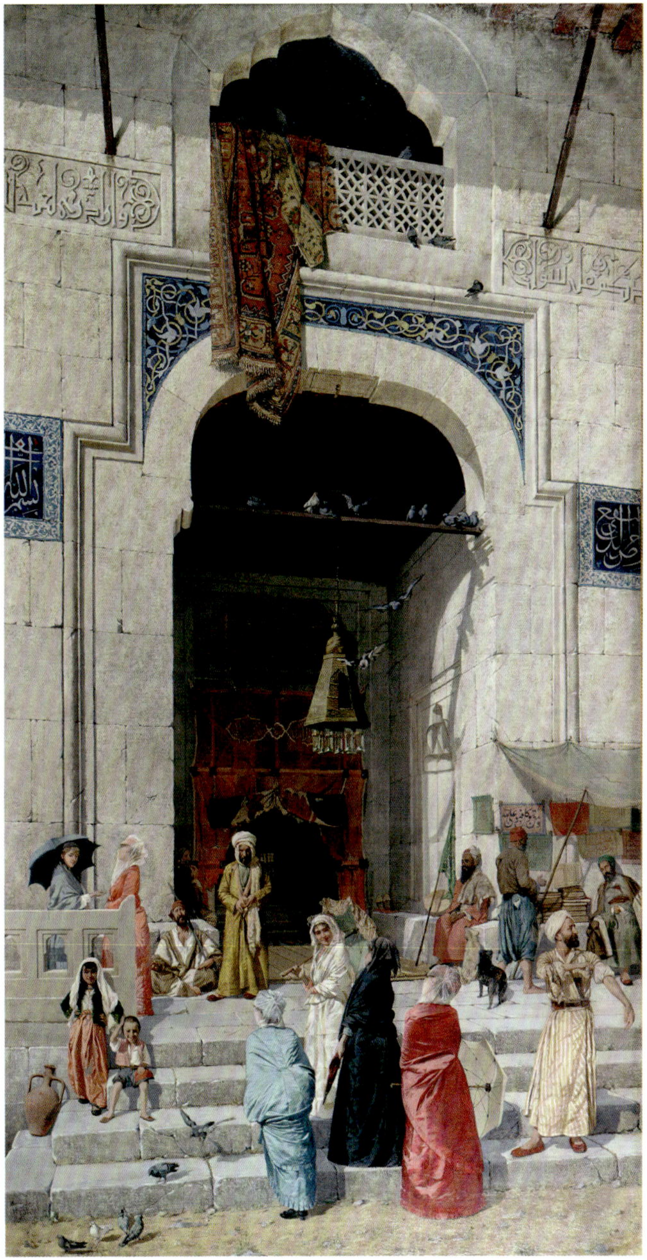

Osman Hamdi used photography in his art in a more directly personal way. Like other members of the Turkish upper-middle classes, Hamdi was an enthusiastic advocate of the camera and there are many surviving images taken by him (as well as of him) when visiting archeological sites as part of his role as director of the Imperial Museum of Antiquities after 1881. As commissioner for the Turkish submission at the 1873 Vienna World Fair, he had been responsible for the *Elbise-i Osmaniyye*, a photographic survey of traditional costumes from across the Ottoman Empire, on which he collaborated with Pascal Sebah, one of the most celebrated photographers in Constantinople. It is therefore not surprising that Hamdi made extensive use of photographic images—of which he is known to have had a large personal collection—in his works. He had himself photographed regularly in Ottoman dress, especially in later life, and even as particular characters, including as a dervish on at least one occasion. He would then use the images to create embedded self-portraits in his works, overlaying the print with a grid to facilitate the accurate transferral of the image to his canvas.[61] One of the most notable instances of this practice being applied is *At the Mosque Door* (1891) (Figure 70), in which Hamdi appears several times (see also page 199).

70. Osman Hamdi, *At the Mosque Door* (1891). Oil on canvas, 203 x 123.5 cm.

New Collaborations

The relationship between photography and the Orientalists was more profound than artists simply using the new images to inform their paintings. It was also manifested through links between some of the key personalities and photographers exploring the artistic opportunities offered by Orientalism. Through Gustave Le Gray there is a connection between Gérôme and Roger Fenton (1819–69), one of the most significant figures in the development of photography and who also produced a particularly important series of Orientalist images. Fenton's early career was as an artist; he trained in the same Paris studio as Gérôme, Le Gray, and Henri Le Secq who, like Le Gray, was to forsake painting in favor of photography in much the same way as Fenton. Although Fenton was accepted by the Royal Academy to show his paintings there in 1849–51, the critical reception was not encouraging. Perhaps as a result, and possibly encouraged by his contacts in Paris,[62] he traveled to the French capital late in 1851 to learn more about the Société Héliographique, one of the earliest organized groups of photographers. While there, Fenton also visited the photographic studio of Le Gray*, who had forged a career for himself as a professional photographer. Although there is little evidence surviving of the nature of the relationships between Le Gray, Le Secq, Gérôme, and Fenton, the three Frenchmen were certainly good acquaintances and it is likely that Fenton met Gérôme in Paris, possibly when he visited Le Gray's studio.

In 1855 Fenton set off on what was to become his most famous assignment. He traveled to the Crimea, where Britain, Russia, and Turkey were engaged in a brutal conflict that was to provide Fenton with the opportunity to produce the first ever comprehensive photographic documentation of a war. His images of the battle sites and detritus of warfare, as well as of the soldiers themselves, propelled him into the public eye and made his name—although curiously the photographs met with little commercial success.

His reputation nonetheless established, Fenton began to explore other photographic possibilities and in 1858 produced his "Orientalist suite," a series of prints of which fifty-one survive. These images depict domestic scenes inspired by the Middle East, but were all arranged and produced in the rather less exotic environment of Fenton's London studio. Featuring a range of subjects and settings, including various cameo groups, a reclining odalisque and a Nubian water carrier, the prints were exhibited in Edinburgh and London that year, and in Paris the following April. One of the most significant images is *Pasha and Bayadère* (Figure 71), in which Fenton appears as the pasha, alongside the artist Frank Dillon as a musician and with a female dancer whose arms were suspended in the required position by wires (carefully retouched as to become virtually invisible) for the duration required by the exposure. The images

* Gustave Le Gray later relocated to the Middle East, first arriving in Alexandria in the summer of 1860. He traveled to Syria and Lebanon before returning to Egypt, where he lived and worked until his death in 1884. However, by the mid-1860s he appears to have largely abandoned a career in photography in favor of being a drawing instructor. See Jacobson, *Odalisques & Arabesques*, 40.

71. Roger Fenton, *Pasha and Bayadère* (1858). Albumen silver print, 45 x 36.2 cm.

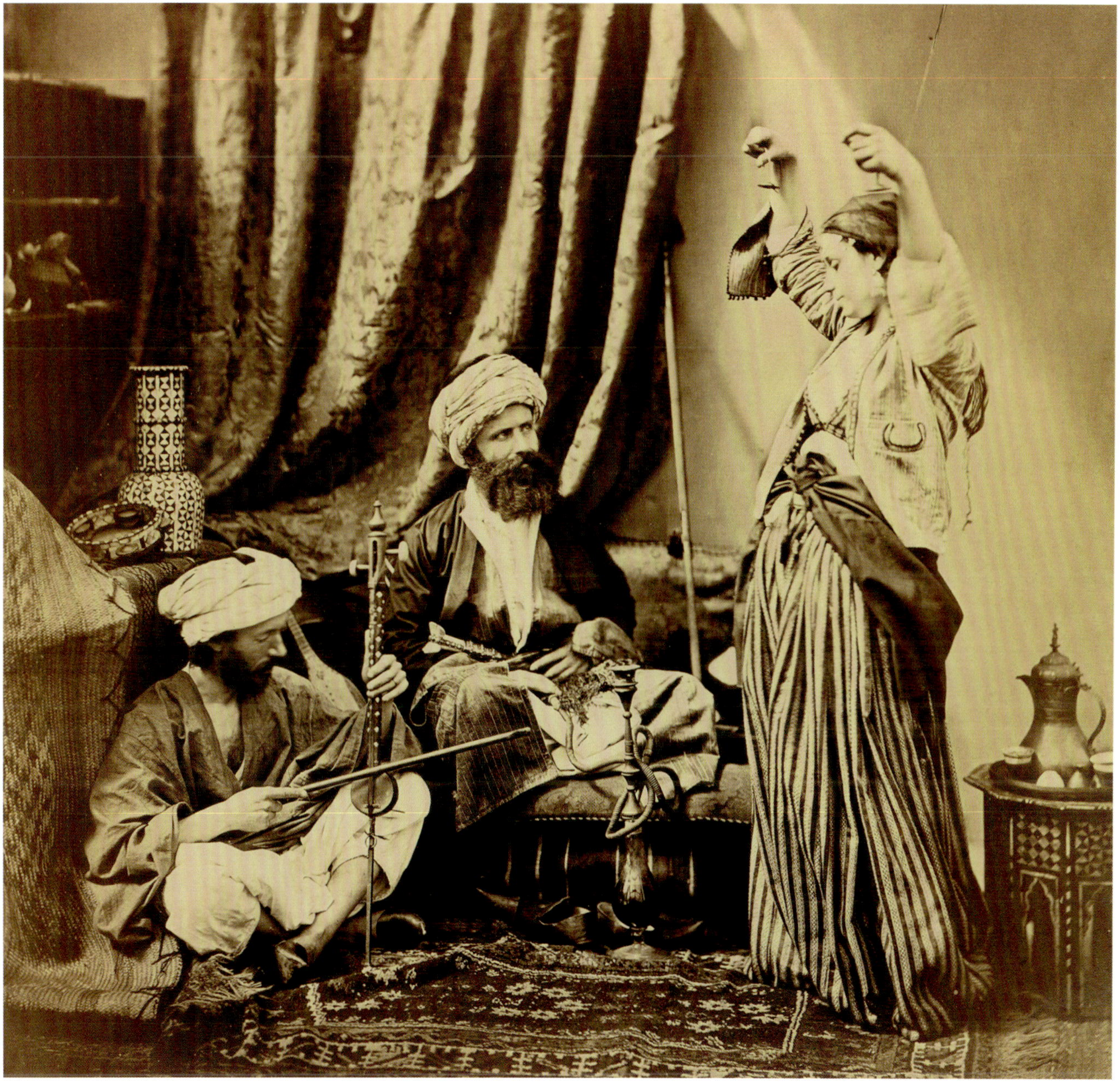

feature a rather motley collection of "Oriental" props, often randomly arranged—in one case, a European carpet can be seen peeping from underneath an Anatolian rug.[63]

Fenton's decision to produce this series was probably entirely commercial. He most likely had his first exposure to Orientalism while studying in Paris at a time when the Orient-inspired paintings of Delacroix in particular were attracting extensive attention. These works would have provided excellent source and concept material for Fenton, as would a volume of plates he owned from Vivant Denon's *Voyage dans l'Égypte* (1802), included in an 1870 sale of Fenton's collection of prints and engravings.

Through his close links with the Society of Artists and the Society of Painters in Water Colours, Fenton would have seen at first hand the growing commercial appeal of Orientalist art. However, the single most significant source of ideas and advice for Fenton in his choice of model poses, costumes, settings, and props is likely to have been Frank Dillon. Not only does Dillon appear with Fenton in *Pasha and Bayadère* but he also features in at least fourteen other images in the series, including costume studies and solo poses. Dillon was by this time well versed in the Orient, having traveled to Egypt in 1854–55 and exhibited his watercolors of Nile Valley landscapes and people at the Royal Academy in 1856–58. These works would almost certainly have been seen by Fenton, and it has even been suggested that the Orientalist suite may have been Dillon's idea.[64] Even if not, Dillon's figures—as well as his personal advice and experience—will have played an important role in shaping Fenton's own creative concepts.

There was a further important source of ideas for Fenton's Orientalist tableaux, and one more directly related to Fenton's own world: the photographs of Francis Frith (1822–98). A founding member of the Liverpool Photographic Society in 1853, Frith made an expedition to Palestine and Egypt in 1856, primarily to photograph biblical sites. The impact of the photographs and stereoscopic views he subsequently published was considerable and could well have played a part in Fenton's decision to bring out his own Orientalist series.

Fenton may well have created his images with a purpose beyond that of simply showing and selling. It has been suggested that he intended them to be used by artists as preparatory drawings, and that his *Nubian Water Carrier* provided the inspiration for Goodall's 1864 painting *The Song of the Nubian Slave*.[65] Fenton was also friends with Carl Haag, whom he had known since at least 1854, when Haag was commissioned to hand-color a series of photographs that Fenton had taken of the British royal family. These were presented as a bound portfolio to Queen Victoria on the occasion of her birthday in May of that year, Haag having already worked for the queen at both Balmoral and Windsor.[66] Soon after Fenton produced his Orientalist suite Haag left for Egypt, and, later, Fenton would almost certainly have visited Haag at his Egyptian-style studio in Hampstead (see pages 215–217), an arrangement which Fenton would have recognized following the staged set and props he had created for his own Orientalist tableaux. Fenton owned two works by Haag and his patronage was reciprocated, for Haag acquired four of Fenton's Orientalist studies. Whether the two had any sort of closer working relationship is not known, but they were both—along with Frederick Goodall and William

Müller, among others—members of the Clipstone Street Artists' Society, "a sort of artists' collective that hired street people, gypsies and singers to pose in the evenings."[67]

The Orientalist genre scenes created by Fenton received a mixed response from the critics, garnering some praise for his attempts to align photography with art but also attracting adverse remarks over the models' unconvincing "Orientalness" and clearly European looks. His images were not the first of their type by a British photographer, however. William Morris Grundy (1806–59) had traveled to the Orient *c.*1856–57, probably visiting Smyrna, Constantinople, Cairo, and Suez, and making a series of photographic Orientalist portraits that also featured decidedly non-Oriental models. Suggestions that both Haag and Goodall posed as sitters in these images have been discounted,[68] but Grundy certainly donned Oriental dress for a self-portrait, as did both Fenton and Francis Frith in similar attire for their own series. The fact that all three photographers chose to indulge in cultural cross-dressing in their works is an indication of the influence of similar behavior among artists such as John Frederick Lewis and of the appropriation of a promotional alter ego (see chapter 5). More than that, "The studio-bound nature of the whole enterprise merely confirmed that the photographer was trying to steal the painter's clothes: literalism (in photography all but inevitable, in painting a matter of choice) in the service of exoticism."[69]

Meanwhile, the success of Frith's photographs from his first trip to the Orient was such that he undertook further expeditions, in 1858 and 1859, to extend his portfolio. Many of the resulting photographs were reproduced in his two-volume book, *Egypt and Palestine*, which appeared in 1859. Frith's images were not only acclaimed for their contribution to knowledge of exotic lands and their people but also served to heighten appreciation of photography as a valuable—and truthful—form of artistic expression. A reviewer for the *Athenaeum* magazine lauded the educational and documentary importance of Frith's images: "There is not one of those views of Egypt but that teaches us some new feature of Oriental life."[70] *The Art Journal* review of the 1858 Photographic Society annual exhibition went even further: "The real value of photography is . . . most strikingly shown in the production of F. Frith, jun. His subjects in Palestine and Egypt impress us with a consciousness of truth and power which no other Art-production could produce."[71]

Photography as Art

This response to Frith's photographs was a direct challenge to the veracity and documentary value of contemporary paintings of the Orient, not least those of John Frederick Lewis. By this time well established as one of the leading British Orientalists, Lewis and his works were lauded by the artist's supporters in much the same way as Frith's photographs were by his. In 1851 an article in *Littell's Living Age* had positioned Lewis as the premier spokesman for "The East" following the exhibition of *The Hhareem*, which had "astonished every one by its wondrous presentment of local, national, and individual truth of character . . . marvels of minute execution, extraordinary delicacy as well as beauty of colour, dazzling effects of sun and shade . . . . The picture (which we rejoice to learn is now about to be engraved) gave us what we may call the most finished phase of Mr. Lewis' genius and studies—nature having been true to him throughout as he to her . . . .

We know of no traveller with pen or pencil who has brought back so much of exact truth from those distant scenes of travel."[72] The camera, however, was clearly a different matter, even if—at that stage, at least—it could not compete with the brush and palette on the presentation of color.

About this time the truthful storytelling potential offered by photography took the new medium to the cusp of usurping, or at least matching, the accuracy achieved by more traditional forms of artistic expression. The efforts of Fenton and others to elevate photography as a credible contemporary art form appeared to have been vindicated by the 1857 Manchester Art Treasures exhibition, which had photographs displayed alongside watercolors and oils. Yet resistance to photography as art proved hard to overcome, and five years later the International Exhibition in London saw photographs relegated to the engineering section, on a par with machinery and technical instruments. The adolescent medium was thus demoted from art form to tool, the inference being that it was more applicable to tradesmen than to artists. Perhaps in part as a reaction to this attitude, Fenton was later to turn his back on photography, selling his equipment and negatives and returning to law, a profession in which he had qualified some years earlier. Interestingly, some of his images were acquired by Frith, who by then had set up a highly profitable photographic publishing business that only closed down in 1971.

The two strands that emerged in the unfolding relationship between Orientalist art and photography—namely the taking of and/or using by painters of photographs as study aids, and the production by photographers of images that addressed the Orientalist themes being explored by art—came together during the winter of 1875–76 in a particularly interesting episode. Leopold Müller was on the second of what was to be a total of nine visits to Egypt, a country with which he became infatuated. On this occasion he was part of a group that included two fellow artists from Vienna, Carl Rudolf Huber (with whom he had visited Egypt previously, in 1874) and Hans Makart, the Munich painter Franz Lenbach, the Stuttgart architect Adolf Knauth, and Austrian Prince Karl Khevenhüller. The artists brought their own photographic equipment with them—Huber in particular was a keen amateur photographer—and, thanks to Müller's influential contacts, soon set themselves up in the sumptuous Musafirkhana Palace, which had been offered to them by Khedive Ismail. Here the group established a studio environment, decked out with carpets and other local artifacts, and for the next three months they lived a life of Oriental fantasy. Photography proved central to this masquerade, with the group hiring female models and making numerous photographic studies of them, both nude and otherwise. Müller appears to have assumed the role of harem master, writing to his sister Amalie that "I have spent much, but now live like a pasha."[73]

The productivity of the artists in the group in terms of sketches or paintings produced during their time in Cairo appears to have been mixed. This may have been in part a result of their enthusiastic engagement with photography and, in particular, the various sitters who became regular visitors to the palace. The resulting images have been viewed as being "thinly veiled as ethnographic documentation or artist source materials," and proof of [the] "artists' collective fantasy of Oriental female subservience."[74] Yet it is impossible

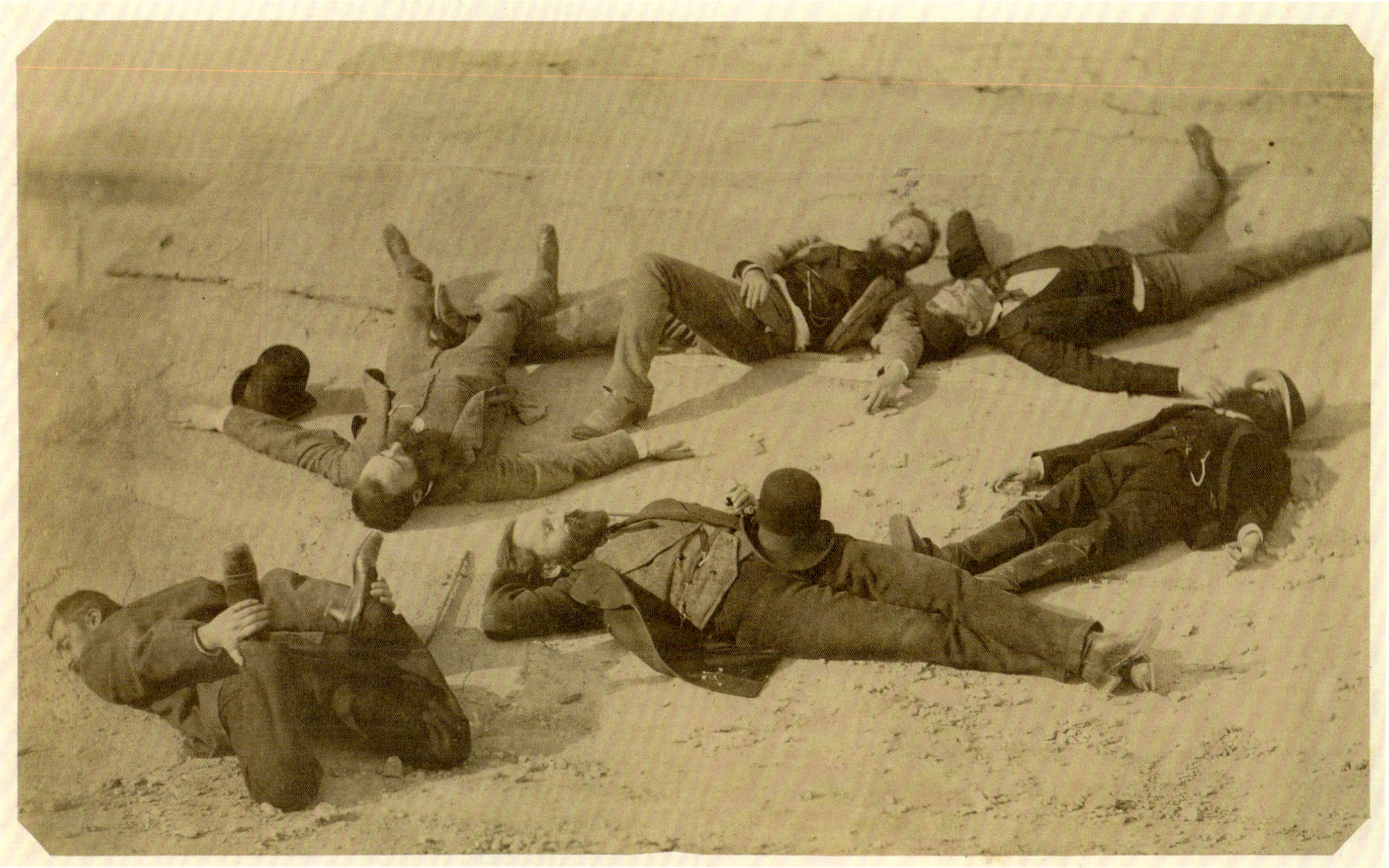

72. Ludwig Steiner (attrib.), untitled photograph of Leopold Müller and companions in prostrate staged positions, taken in Cairo in the winter of 1875/76. Müller is top right.

to discount the contribution made by these photographs as study aids for potential future paintings. Certainly, they read convincingly as evidence that on this occasion the camera had taken over from the pencil or brush as a means for artists to role play within the Orientalist fantasy. Other photographs taken by the group (probably mainly by Huber and Müller) included landscapes, architecture, animal studies, and Arab encampments.[75]

The group not only took their own photographic images but also did the developing themselves in their own darkroom, having brought the requisite equipment from Europe. It is interesting that they chose to do this, as by this time there were already several well-regarded photographic studios active in Cairo. The visitors even hired a professional photographer to accompany them on their excursions, the studio involved being that of Ludwig Steiner, a Viennese photographer who was based in Cairo for several years. The resulting series of images include some of the group in various posed positions, some quasi-comic in nature, at locations on the outskirts of Cairo, and were later published in a popular book by Georg Ebers.[76]

As a collection of images, the photographic enterprise undertaken by Huber, Müller, *et al.* during that winter in Egypt stands out as an intriguing expression of the different ways in which artists sought to empower themselves and expand their own creativity through a personal use of photography. In this particular case the resulting images went beyond traditional depictions of local landscapes and people toward a more integrated and subjective interpretation of what it meant to be a Western artist traveling in an Oriental land.

Different Realities

Meanwhile, the uneasy relationship between art and photography continued, with lingering suspicions in particular over the commercial practices of photographers. As early as 1856 William Holman Hunt had raised his concerns over the ways in which he felt the law in Britain was failing to protect artists and engravers against the rapacious new image-makers. "When in Syria I had received a proposal from two engravers of £300 for the copyright of *The Light of the World*, but I had not felt sure that they would do the work satisfactorily, and refused to close with the offer," he wrote. "Gambart* now asked me to make a price with him for the design. I asked him the sum hitherto mentioned; but he objected on the ground that there was the chance of the public not liking the print, and then no one would divide his loss, while if it became popular, photographers throughout England would pirate the work, and the prosecution of each would cost him £70; the only penalty to them would be the loss of a simple camera. In France, where the law treated piracy as a penal offence, the publisher was safe from such a violation of his rights, and so could pay the artist better."[77] This was a discussion that would rumble on, exemplifying how the tension between painting and photography went beyond purely artistic concerns.

The debate over the relative merits of painting and photography, and whether or not the latter could ever qualify as art, was primarily a preoccupation of the artistic establishment. Most artists simply got on with their work, forming their own conclusions over the potential value of photography to

* Ernest Gambart, the leading London art dealer of the day. See page 209.

them personally. There is no doubt that it had a profound impact on the ways in which Orientalist artists worked, both when traveling abroad and at home working in their studios. This influence was due largely to Orientalism's espousal of realism and its need for demonstrable authenticity.

In the 1850s the process of constructed realism in the Orientalist context was led in Britain largely by John Frederick Lewis, while in France Jean-Léon Gérôme was also moving away from the academic idealism favored by the French establishment toward a more documentary style. A timely confluence took place in 1855, a period of political détente between the two countries, when Lewis exhibited at the Exposition Universelle in the French capital as a part of a British contingent "that took Paris by storm."[78] He submitted four watercolors, including *The Hhareem*, which were applauded by French critics for their boldness of scale, presentation of truthful detail, and a vivacity of color that was traditionally considered to be the domain of oil painting alone.

These reviews may well have encouraged Gérôme in his resolve to establish the principle that in his own works he was tracing directly from reality. In this way he articulated and advanced the transition in Orientalist art from erstwhile fantasies, based largely on hearsay and speculation, to realist visions ostensibly rooted in empiricism and firsthand observation. The authority commanded by Gérôme at the Salon and the École des Beaux-Arts helped ensure that he not only influenced many other artists working on Middle Eastern subjects but was also able to set the mainstream Orientalist art agenda for the next quarter of a century at least.

Realism as a term applied to art was relatively new at this stage and not something with which many artists, Gérôme among them, would have immediately identified. What Gérôme did accept was the notion that progress relied on science and that the application of scientifically proven evidence could help improve the human condition on every level, including through art. His interest in the art of documentation meant that he sketched constantly while traveling, often in oil on paper, and working from local models wherever possible. Armed with hundreds of drawings, as well as notes and photographs, he would then return to Paris and his studio to work up the many-layered oil paintings that became his hallmark. His was a style that relied heavily on precise figure drawing, the posture and authority of his characters reinforced but not dominated by their architectural contexts and by the minutely observed and carefully crafted accoutrements with which they and their settings were dressed.

The results were a combination of architecture, portraiture, costume, and craft presentation that came to dominate Orientalist art during the 1870s and 1880s. Yet Gérôme did not consider himself a realist artist as such. In his preface to the 1889 biography written on him by Fanny Field Hering, he lambasted those artists whom he claimed had gone too far in that direction, complaining that "they have abandoned themselves to realism, to commonplace and indiscriminating realism: the letter has killed the spirit, and poetry has fled to the heavens."[79] For Gérôme it may well be that his desire for "poetry" was expressed through the license and artifice that he applied to his paintings. *The Snake Charmer* juxtaposes Balkan-costumed characters with Iznik tiles and Persian or Indian armor, featuring as its main subject a distinctly un-Ottoman tradition (snake-charming features little in the Turkish cultural canon).[80] Such incongruity was presumably irrelevant to Gérôme so long as a convincing level of detail was maintained, a strong story expressed, and visual impact achieved.

Ludwig Deutsch was similarly preoccupied with exactitude in his work. He presented his painstakingly rendered "types" within meticulously constructed tableaux composed of Oriental architecture, furniture, textiles, metalwork, woodwork, and ceramics. It is reasonable to assume that most, if not all, of the portable objects concerned would have been drawn from Deutsch's own extensive collection. He had a penchant for particular types of item, such as inlaid tables and chests and copperware basins and ewers, which appear in several of his paintings.

In some instances, Deutsch built an entire composition around a particular object, as in *The Mandolin Player* (1904) (Figure 73). In a level of detail typical of his precise hyper-realism, Deutsch painted his *'ud* with the correct seven strings—a lute (the closest European equivalent to the *'ud*, rather than a mandolin), would usually have eight. Both the instrument and its player are showcased against a wide variety of textures and surfaces, from the Damascene wall tiles and copper ewer, basin, and tray to the shimmering garments worn by the player and the opulent fabrics on the daybed. Beyond supplying a lavish context to the human subject in the painting, through these objects Deutsch was advertising his credentials as an expert and comprehensive purveyor of Oriental culture.

Yet the image of reality and knowledge that Deutsch strove to present in his works was a carefully prepared construct. In addition to drawing on his collection of artifacts, he is also known to have made extensive use of photographs when working up his compositions. These would have been particularly valuable to him when developing the architectural backdrops that were such a feature of his oeuvre. Analysis of the architecture and interiors depicted by Deutsch in his paintings reveals an interesting mixture of approaches. Some sections or features of buildings are so meticulously presented that they can be attributed clearly to particular buildings or monuments. One such example is the panel of stylized Kufic script that appears in *The Philosopher* (1905) (Figure 74). This is a very accurate copy of a panel in the Mausoleum of Sultan Qalawun, *c.*1285, in Cairo, and is precise not just in terms of content and layout but also color. This makes it likely that, rather than working purely from a (monochrome) photograph, Deutsch had in fact visited the site personally, making color notes and/or a sketch. The same painting also includes a small panel showing a section of an arcade, which is also identifiable as being very similar to a panel in the same complex as the Qalawun mausoleum—further evidence that Deutsch probably saw it in person.[81]

Similar levels of accuracy can be detected in *The Lamplighter*, where the architectural context has been identified as an iwan in the madrasa of Sultan Qansuh al-Ghuri (1503) in Cairo, clearly recognizable from the marble panels, border inscriptions, and wooden frame to the portal.[82] In other Deutsch paintings, however, more of a capriccio approach is in evidence, with architectural features that may be accurate in themselves (although are not always so) but which are not consistent with the elements around them, either in terms of date or style. For example, *At the Door of the Mosque* (1886) includes a door that is clearly identifiable as one taken from the madrasa complex of Sultan Hasan by Sultan al-Muayyad Shaykh for his own mosque complex (built 1415–20) just

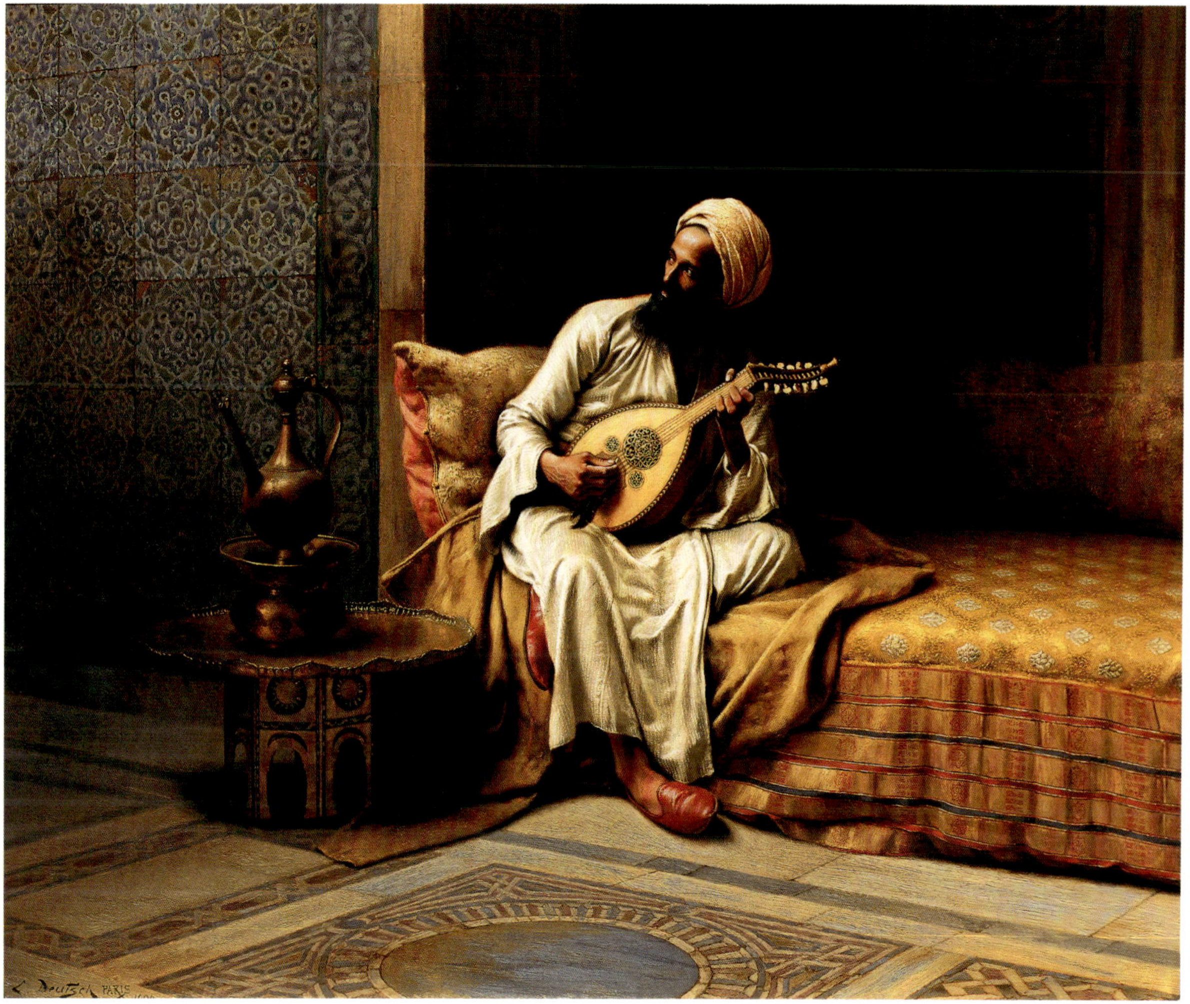

73. Ludwig Deutsch, *The Mandolin Player* (1904).
Oil on panel, 51.4 x 60.4 cm.

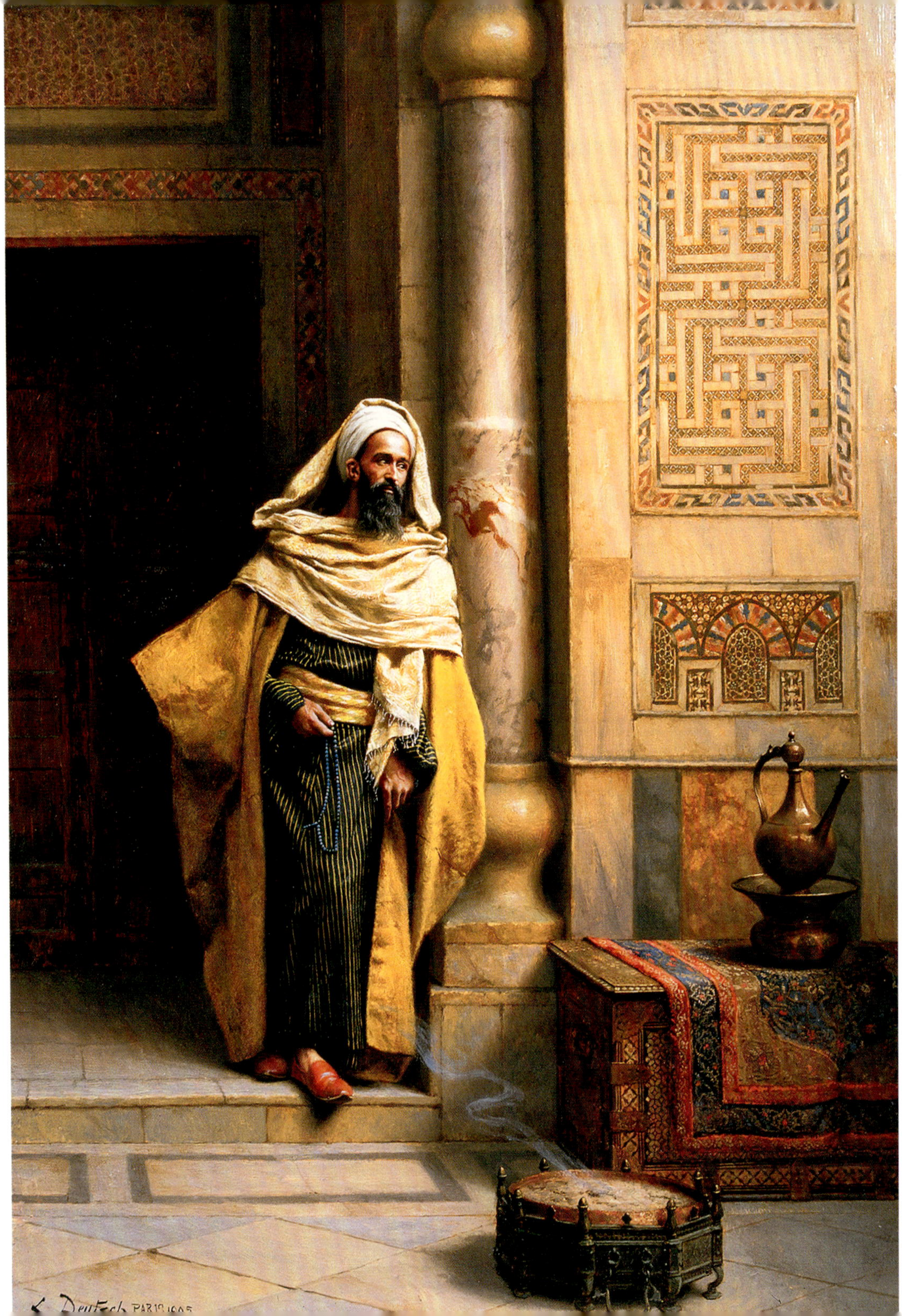

inside the Bab Zuwayla in Islamic Cairo. Deutsch has rendered the metal overlay very accurately, presumably based on notes or photographs taken on a visit. However, analysis of the door's setting—apparently convincing at first glance or to the untrained eye—reveals a clear pastiche, with the tympanum, stone bands, and corner column architecturally inaccurate and misplaced, both with each other and with the door.[83] The result is an architectural distortion masquerading as reality, a display of the artistic license so favored by many of the Orientalists.

A similarly hybrid eclecticism can be distinguished in the objects that feature in Deutsch's paintings. Palace guards and servants bear weapons from Arabia, Persia, and Turkey, and sport Ottoman robes juxtaposed with Moroccan slippers. Assemblages of objects include individual items of widely ranging provenance which, while convincing in contexts such as bazaar scenes—nineteenth-century Cairo was increasingly full of imported goods, many designed to appeal to foreign visitors—would not be accurate in other situations.

In the same way that Deutsch repeatedly used the same model, objects, and textiles in multiple paintings, he was not averse to reusing settings or individual architectural elements that he considered successful. A version of the corner column in *The Philosopher* of 1905 had already featured in his 1903 work, *The Smoker*, and a clearly identifiable corner of the portal of the madrasa complex of the Sultan Hassan Mosque (*c.*1360) also appears in two of his "palace guard" paintings, as well as in *The Offering* (1897) (Figure 102).[84]

74. Ludwig Deutsch, *The Philosopher* (1905). Oil on panel, 55 x 37.5 cm.

More widely, artists shared—inadvertently or otherwise—features or details in their works. For example, the doorway shown in Rudolf Weiss's *The Metalworker* (1889) (Figure 75) is clearly the same as that used by Deutsch in his undated painting, *Family at the Door*, while Deutsch's *The Sahleb Vendor, Cairo* (1886) and his undated *Outside a Café* both depict the same blue-and-red painted decoration on a wall as appears in Charles Wilda's *The Scribe* of the same year.[85] It is impossible to know how such duplication may have arisen, but it is perhaps not unexpected given the high footfall of artists in cities like Cairo and the savviness of local guides in leading artists to individual buildings or features that they knew would be popular with their clients. It is also likely that some artists shared local information and directed each other to sites of particular interest.

This situation comes into sharper focus when considering different treatments of the same building. Both Jean-Léon Gérôme and Rudolf Ernst featured Constantinople's Rüstem Pasha Mosque in their works, in some respects overtly and accurately, but in other ways more discreetly and with considerable artistic license. Gérôme's *Rüstem Pasha Mosque, Istanbul* (undated, but *c.*1876) (Figure 76) is at first sight a very accurate rendition of part of the interior of one of the city's most beautiful mosques, built in 1561–63. However, closer analysis reveals a rather less convincing presentation. Only a few of the key elements in that part of the mosque are depicted by Gérôme in exact detail, notably the inscription above the *mihrab* or prayer niche, and some (but certainly not all) of the patterns of tiles. The four tiled panels within the niche itself are closely modeled on the originals, but are not exactly copied. The *minbar* or pulpit is not a totally

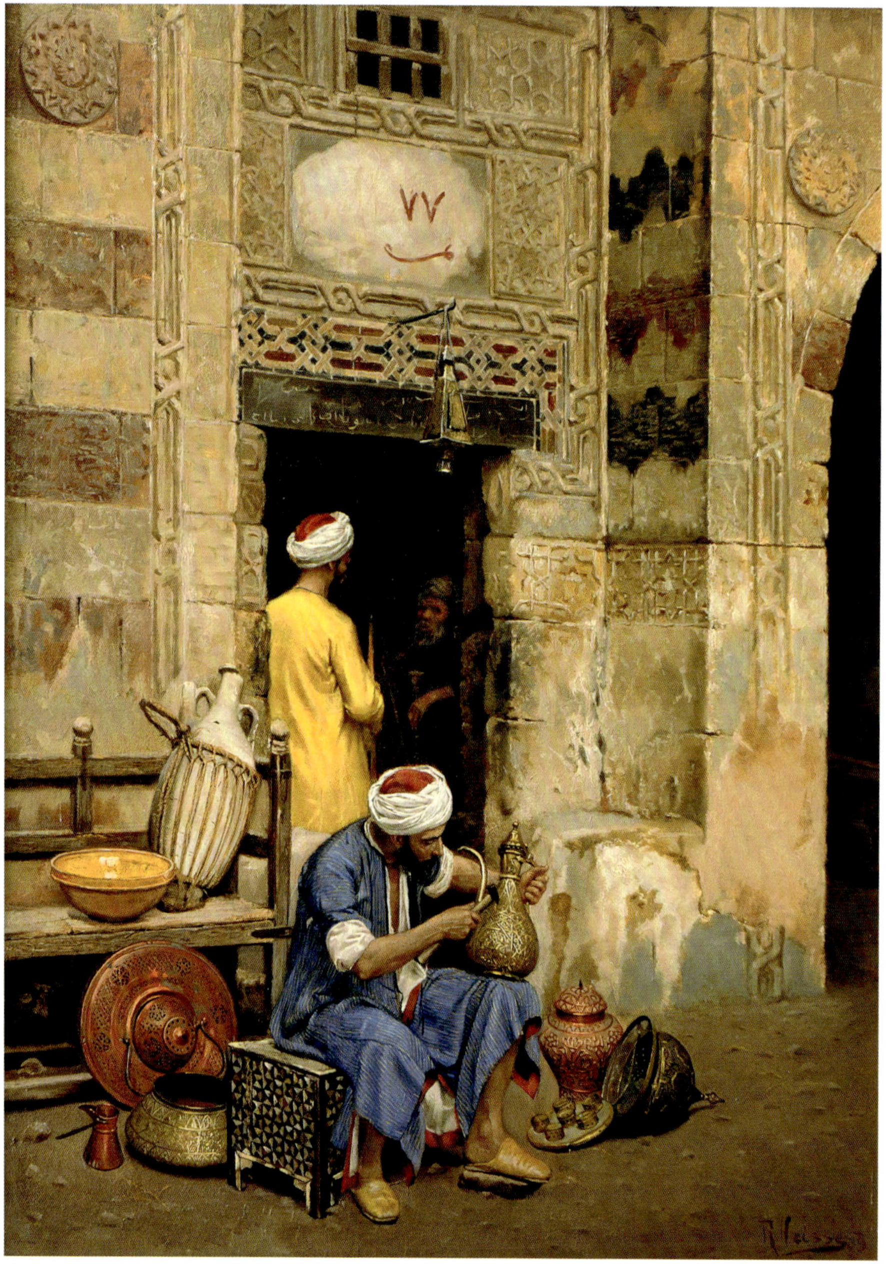

75. Rudolf Weiss, *The Metalworker* (1889).
Oil on panel, 48.3 x 34.2 cm.

accurate rendition either and nor is the window next to it, which Gérôme depicted as being glazed with colored glass, whereas it was in fact plain.[86]

A small preparatory oil sketch made by Gérôme when on a visit to Constantinople in 1868 was presumably the original source of the painting's composition, supplemented by the artist's own notes and possibly also by photographic references. That sketch, which is itself a less than completely accurate record, and the resulting finished painting in turn spawned a second work, *The Blue Mosque* (Figure 77), which dates from 1878. This also depicts a rendering based on the Rüstem Pasha and not, to add even more confusion, on the more famous "Blue Mosque" in Constantinople, of the Sultan Ahmet. In this second painting Gérôme added more worshipers, changed the inscription above the *mihrab*, altered the tiles (again) and restored the stained-glass window to a plain one. Both finished works showed a much larger view than did the oil sketch, so Gérôme was forced to improvise by inventing and/or copying details from elsewhere in order to fill the canvas.[87]

A Rudolf Ernst painting, original title unknown but now catalogued as *Interior of the Mosque of Rüstem Pasha*, is even more eclectically constructed. The *mihrab* appears to be based on that in the Rüstem Pasha, but a tiled pier that forms a major feature of the painting is actually from the nearby Yeni Yalide Mosque.[88] The overall composition of the painting is highly contrived and is neither an accurate reflection of the customary arrangement within an Ottoman mosque generally, nor of the Rüstem Pasha specifically. Yet to a Western audience the painting presented a convincing rendering of an exquisitely decorated mosque, and so Ernst was fulfilling contemporary expectations regarding authenticity.

Artists such as Deutsch, Ernst, and Gérôme, among others, specialized therefore in a constructed realism, one that mixed accurate renditions with collages and pastiches in a process characterized by a liberal use of "copy-and-paste." The artists' skillful presentation of these multiple elements was drawn from a mixture of firsthand experience and second-hand knowledge, the latter in turn based, in part at least, on photographs. The result is often tightly woven and difficult to unpick. In the case of Deutsch, the lack of detailed knowledge of his travels in the Orient make it impossible to distinguish between those places he knew personally and those that he was creating solely in his mind and on his canvas. In his case, reality truly became interwined with speculation and visual deception. The images Deutsch painted for his audience were arguably not so much the reality of the Orient as the exquisitely presented contents of his impressive collection of studio props, set against convincing—if manipulated—architectural backdrops. It was a realism of the sort that Eugène Fromentin had warned against when he observed, "The bourgeois Orientalist is going home to France to paint and to write about what he believes happens on the other side of the Mediterranean and in himself."[89]

The technical skill of Deutsch's paintings and their crystal clear cinematic quality, with each painting reminiscent of a film still, preclude his works from being anything other than outstanding accomplishments. Yet as early as the 1880s the impressive visual precision and sense of realism that Gérôme had pioneered, and which was the hallmark of Deutsch in particular and of the Orientalists generally, was attracting adverse comment. In 1888 the art critic Clarence Cook fired a salvo across the bows of the recently deceased (and hugely

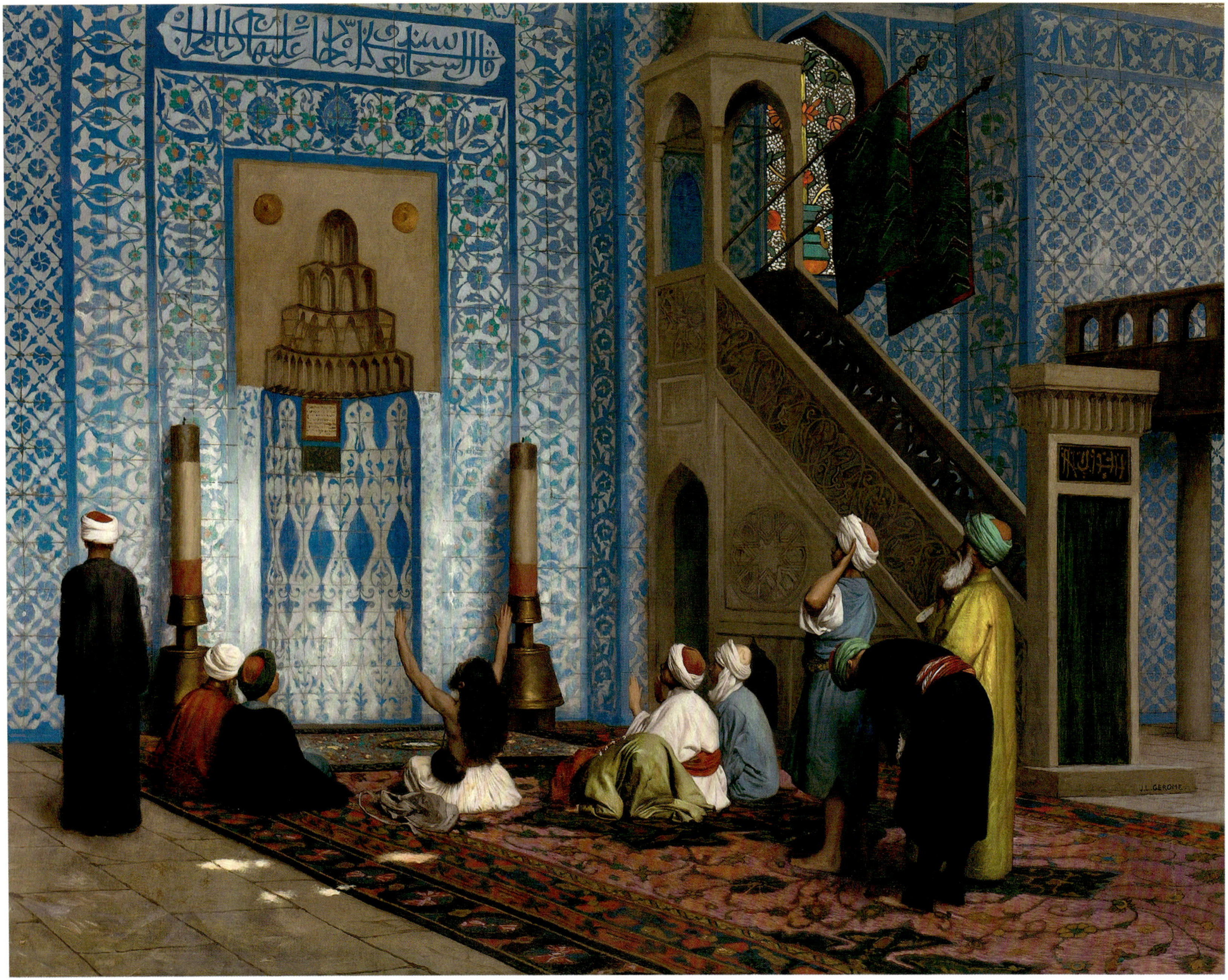
J.L. GEROME

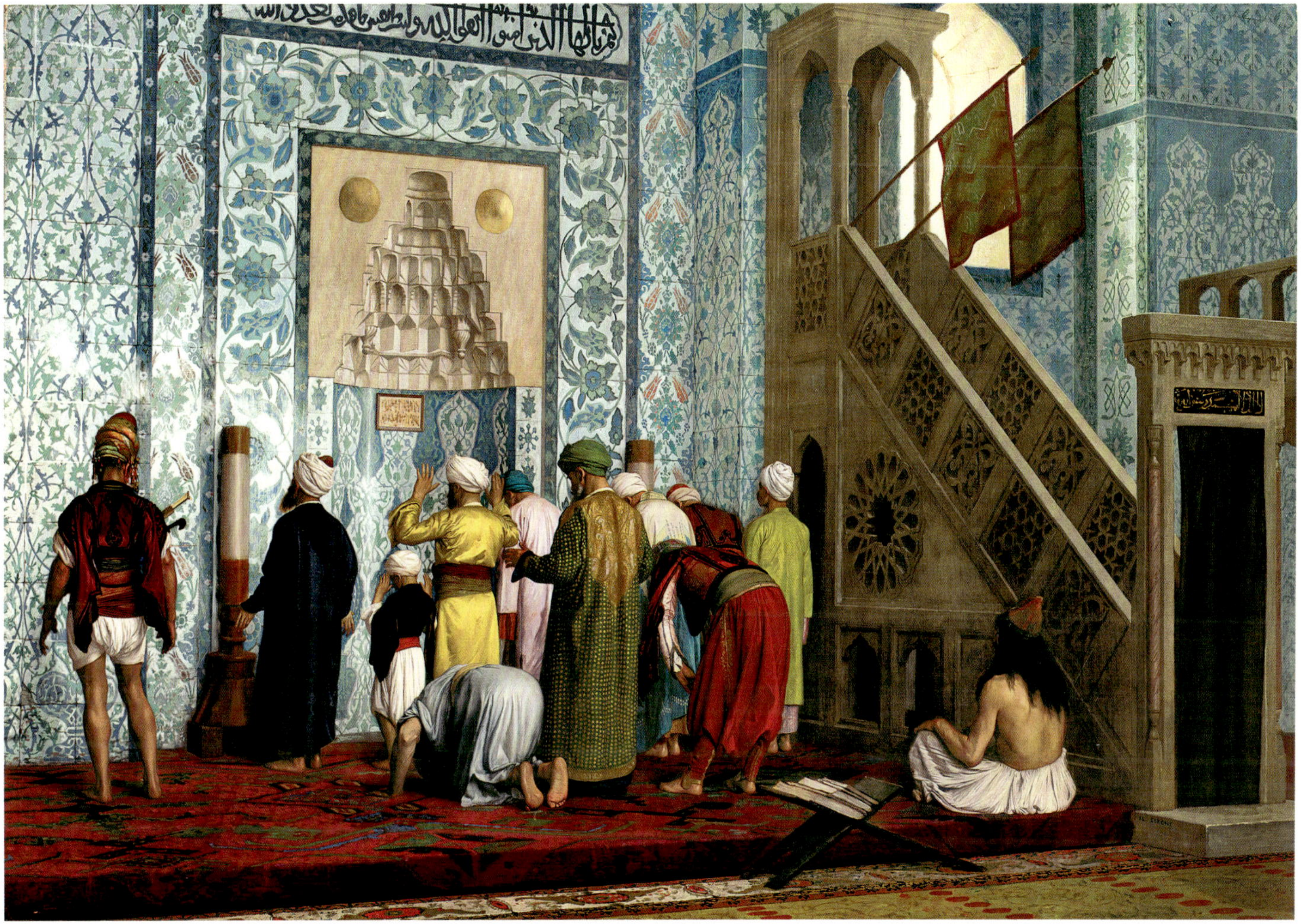

76. Jean-Léon Gérôme, *Rüstem Pasha Mosque, Istanbul* (*c*.1876).
Oil on canvas, 67.6 x 88.5 cm.

77. Jean-Léon Gérôme, *La Mosquée Bleue* (The Blue Mosque) (1878).
Oil on canvas, 72.4 x 102.2 cm.

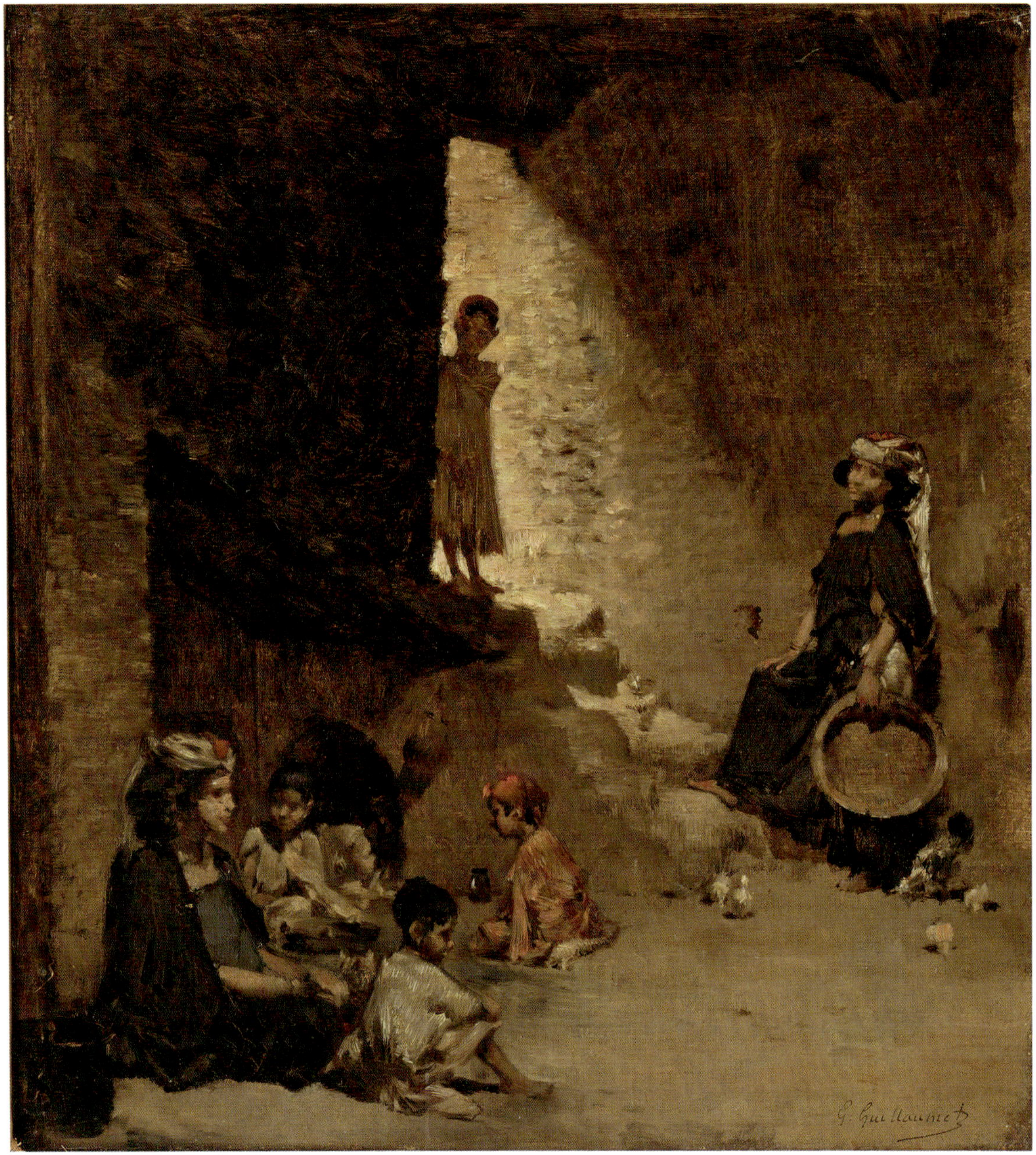
G. Guillaumet

successful in terms of reputation and sales) Théodore Frère, remarking that his pictures were "excellent in their way . . . the works of an industrious and painstaking career, which, if it have not added to the poetry or the charm with which the East is invested in our imagination, has at least helped us to a completer knowledge of the facts."[90]

Gustave Guillaumet, broadly contemporary with Frère (he died in 1887), had espoused a similar style of realism in his works but changed his approach during the last decade of his life, a time when Orientalist art was under pressure from Impressionism and other new and evolving styles. Guillaumet's melodramatic scenes of famine and dead camels—similar in concept to Eugène Fromentin's infamous 1869 painting *The Land of Thirst*—were largely replaced by quieter portrayals of the routine and character of daily life in the villages of Algeria. These works were still powerful in mood but more balanced and representative of the condition of the rural poor, whom Guillaumet strove to portray in works such as *A Cool Interior* (Figure 78) with respect and dignity rather than sensationalism. It was a sea change echoed in contemporary European art through the likes of naturalist painters such as Jules Bastien-Lepage, and was to be reflected across the Orientalist canon as artists sought to maintain their reputations as depicters of reality but via a style less impeded by the academic shackles and photorealism of artists such as Gérôme and Deutsch. A similar trend emerged in Orientalist photography, with the likes of Rudolf Lehnert and Ernst Landrock, who journeyed through North Africa in the early 1900s and were introduced by Étienne Dinet to the Ouled Naïl tribe, producing photogravures of the desert and its inhabitants that stand as a direct photographic counterpoint to Dinet's paintings of the same landscapes and people.

With the artistic climate changing, the period from *c.*1909 onward saw Deutsch experimenting with Post-Impressionism himself, using thicker brushstrokes and a much more liberated and expansive style that broke out of the studio environment and took him—metaphorically, at least—back into the 'real' Orient (see pages 234–237). With less emphasis on studio creations and on the direct power of photography as a tool for authenticity, the Orientalists were being forced to reassess how best to present their vision of the Orient and how to achieve—and sustain—success in an increasingly competitive and uncertain market.

78. Gustave Guillaumet, *A Cool Interior* (date unknown). Oil on canvas, 39.4 x 36.8 cm. This work exemplifies Guillaumet's ability to convey the power and integrity of rural North African life without resorting to the overdramatization that was characteristic of some of his peers.

5. Influence

In the summer of 1840 a portrait of David Roberts by his friend and fellow artist Robert Scott Lauder went on show at London's Royal Academy. Exhibited alongside some of Roberts's Oriental landscapes, the first of which were already taking the British capital's art scene by storm, the painting—now in the Scottish National Portrait Gallery—presents a swashbuckling incarnation of its subject. Swathed in an extravagant Middle Eastern outfit, a beturbaned Roberts stands confidently and with serene authority—albeit in front of a rather un-Oriental backdrop, the scudding clouds more reminiscent of his native Scotland. The portrait (Figure 79) was a promotional tool, conceived—and received—as an affirmation of Roberts's credentials as an intrepid and knowledgeable traveler to alien lands. Its purpose was clear from its title, *David Roberts Esq. in the Dress he wore in Palestine*, and Roberts evidently had high hopes that it would have an impact, remarking in a letter to his close friend David Ramsay Hay after his last sitting for Lauder that "I think it will tell in the Exhibition."[1]

The painting had been commissioned by Hay. In a letter to Roberts the previous autumn (Figures 80a and 80b), only a few weeks after the traveler had returned to Britain, Hay—with characteristic humor—had urged him to sit for Lauder without delay. "Now, as to your portrait for which you were kind enough to say you would sit for Lauder—have you arranged with Lauder regarding it," he asked. "I hope it will be set about while your Phiso Mahogany retains its Eastern bronze. What will you do for moustachios? Mr Kinear [sic] says you wore a pair of the most picturesque kind. Bye the bye he said he never met a more agreeable travelling companion—that you bore all hardships and privations, not only with philosophy but cheerfulness."*

Roberts later replied explaining that he had "arrainged [sic] with Lauder for the sitting or rather Standing in my Arab

* Letter from Hay to Roberts, 22 November 1839, private collection (Figures 80a and 80b). The final sentence in this excerpt is interesting, given the perception of Roberts as one prone—at times, at least—to complaint and criticism while on the road in the Orient.

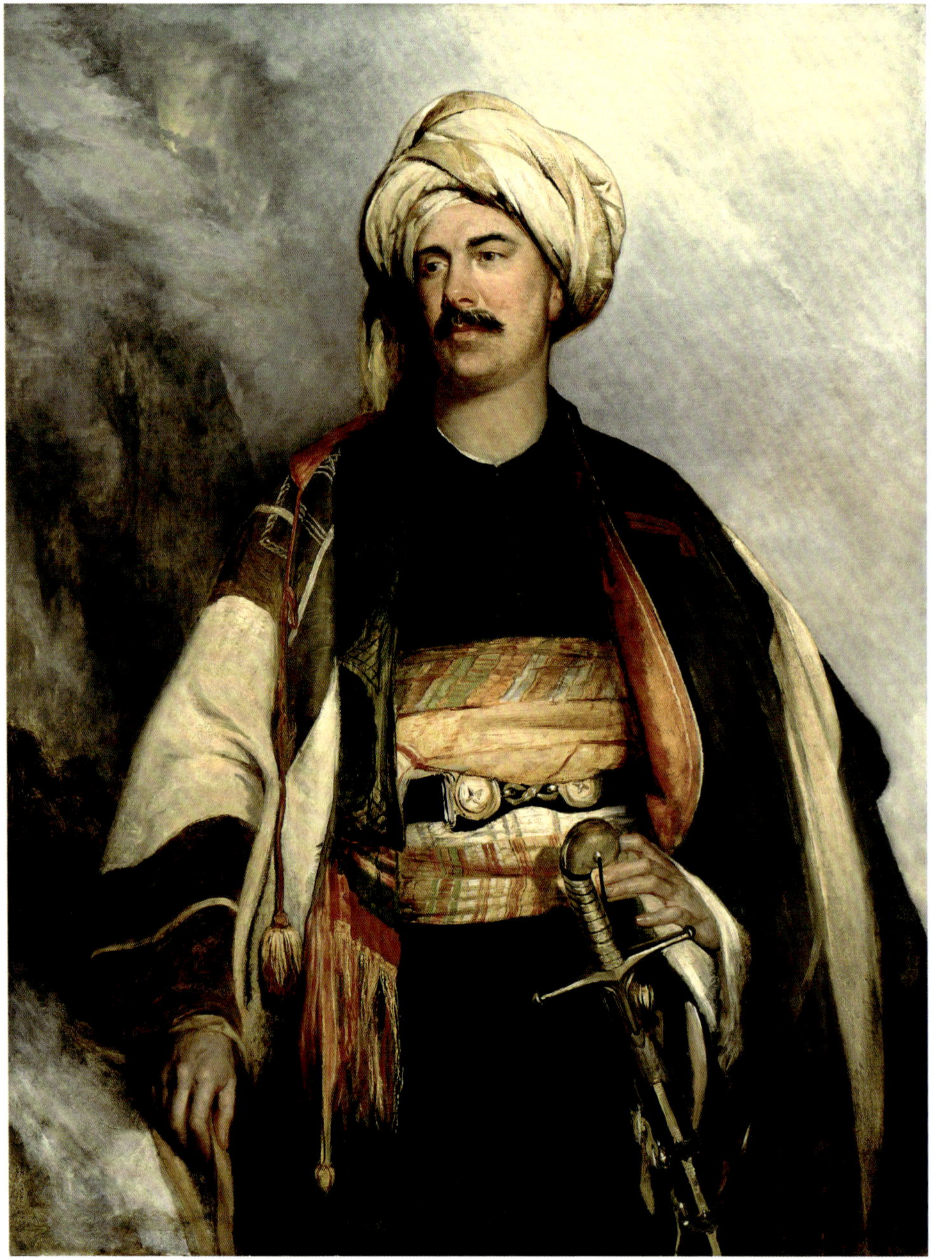

79. Robert Scott Lauder, *David Roberts Esq. in the Dress he wore in Palestine* (1840). Oil on canvas, 133 x 101.3 cm.

dress—I put it on the other day and he was much pleased with it. I regret the loss of the mustachious [sic], as it is essentially in character with the dress I must endeavour to get a loan of a pair I suppose."[2] He agreed to sit for two hours a week for Lauder until the portrait was finished, which was early in 1840.

Clearly, considerable thought and effort went in to this highly staged event. Roberts initially responded positively to the portrait, but later appears to have changed his mind, questioning "the representation of the Edinburgh callant [chap] in that outlandish dress."[3] When traveling in the Orient he had not worn local clothes as a matter of course, donning them only in particular situations such as when visiting mosques (see page 91), which may explain his unease about being shown in such an atypically extravagant manner. Roberts was always concerned to present himself as a Western authority on the Orient, rather than risk appearing as someone who had "gone native." A more accurate representation of him therefore was the lithographic portrait that appeared on the frontispiece of his *Holy Land* volumes, in which he sports traditional Western attire and looks every inch a member of the artistic establishment. It was an equally powerful piece of propaganda.

Accuracy was not the real point of the Lauder portrait, however. Whatever Roberts's views may have been about being depicted *à la turque*, and indeed the artistic license taken by Lauder (with, one assumes, the sitter's acquiescence) over the Oriental outfit itself,* as a piece of pictorial advocacy the portrait was hugely successful. It marketed Roberts as a commodity, as an expert authority on a fashionable subject and with something new and interesting to impart. More to the point, the portrait was timed to perfection. Roberts was busy at that time raising funds to support the publication of illustrated volumes of his travels, and the painting created a specific visual identity around which he could base his pitch to potential subscribers and buyers. More widely and longer term, this romanticized image of Roberts as an Oriental connoisseur gave him a status and influence over his audience that helped ensure continued fame (and sales) for many years to come.

Such self-promotion also helped Roberts steal a march on the competition. Observers, both then and since, could be forgiven for thinking that Roberts was the only Western artist exploring the Orient in the late 1830s. Yet his own much-trumpeted travels in Egypt were directly contemporary with those of the young English artist William Müller who, after spending six weeks in Greece during the autumn of 1838, set sail for Alexandria. He landed there in November, a few weeks after Roberts had passed through the city. Müller then spent two weeks in Cairo before—like Roberts—chartering a boat up the Nile and traveling as far as Luxor before returning northward. The two men must have passed each other on the Nile at some point without realizing or acknowledging the fact. Müller arrived back home in England in March 1839 (by which time Roberts had reached Petra), and set about producing paintings inspired by his Egyptian travels. These works were exhibited at the Royal Academy and British Institution and saw him lauded by the *Art-Union* journal as "one of the ablest and most rising artists of the country."[4] Such accolades

* While the individual garments Roberts is shown wearing appear authentic, they would not have been worn together in such an ensemble. See Llewellyn, "'Solitary Eagle?' The Public and Private Personas of John Frederick Lewis," 171.

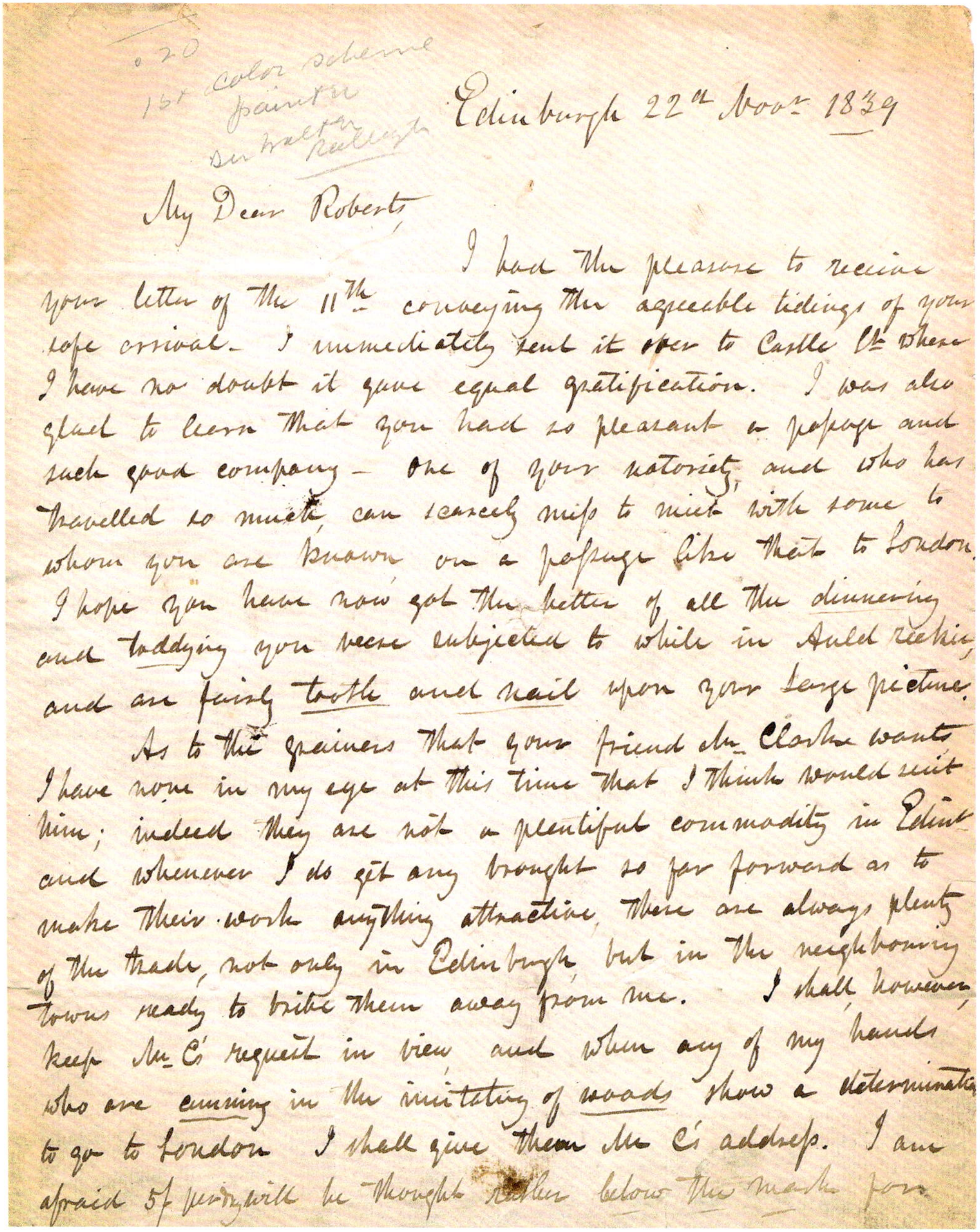
1st color scheme painter Sir Walter Raleigh

Edinburgh 22d Novr 1839

My Dear Robert,

I had the pleasure to receive your letter of the 11th conveying the agreeable tidings of your safe arrival. I immediately sent it over to Castle St where I have no doubt it gave equal gratification. I was also glad to learn that you had so pleasant a passage and such good company. One of your notoriety and who has travelled so much, can scarcely miss to meet with some to whom you are known on a passage like that to London. I hope you have now got the better of all the dinnering and toddying you were subjected to while in Auld Reekie, and are fairly tooth and nail upon your large picture.

As to the grainers that your friend Mr Clarke wants I have none in my eye at this time that I think would suit him; indeed they are not a plentiful commodity in Edinr and whenever I do get any brought so far forward as to make their work anything attractive, there are always plenty of the trade, not only in Edinburgh, but in the neighbouring towns ready to bribe them away from me. I shall, however, keep Mr C's request in view and when any of my hands who are cunning in the imitating of woods show a determination to go to London I shall give them Mr C's address. I am afraid 5/ per day will be thought rather below the mark for

80a and 80b. Letter from David Ramsay Hay to David Roberts, dated 22 November 1839. This hitherto 'lost' piece of correspondence, discussing Hay's commission of the now-famous portrait of Roberts by Robert Scott Lauder, was discovered by the author in 2014.

excuse me for attempting to show you how to do it, but sometimes the same idea does not strike two people altho' writing on the self same subject. — Now as to your portrait for which you were kind enough to say you would sit to Lauder — have you arranged with Lauder regarding it. I hope it will be set about while your phiz Mahogany retains its Eastern bronze what will you do for moustachios? Mr Kincar says you wore a pair of the most picturesque kind. By the bye he says he never met a more agreeable travelling companion — that you bore all hardships and privations, not only with

P.S. Have you sounded Sir David yet regarding his picture let me know. And let me know at your convenience if Lauder has made a beginning. I should prefer a Kit Cat to match your friends Allan, Duncan, McCulloch. My kind regards to Fraser, Leitch &c &c ever yours &c
D.R.H.

Add!
David Roberts Esquire A.R.A.
24 Mornington Place
Hampstead Road
London

1798–1866

philosophy but cheerfulness. — I have sent over to Castle Street and my servant brings me word that your Father and Mother are just the same as when you left them, and of course along with your Sister send their Love.

I have had a visit from Mr Hawes the M.P. who in looking at and admiring your Seville cathedral asked me if ever I had seen your daughter, of course I said I had but some years since "for" says he "she is one of the prettiest little creatures I ever saw" There is a compliment for Miss Roberts from an M.P. but I suppose she is so much accustomed to compliments that she will think nothing of this one. Give my kind regards and believe me Yours sincerely D.R. Hay

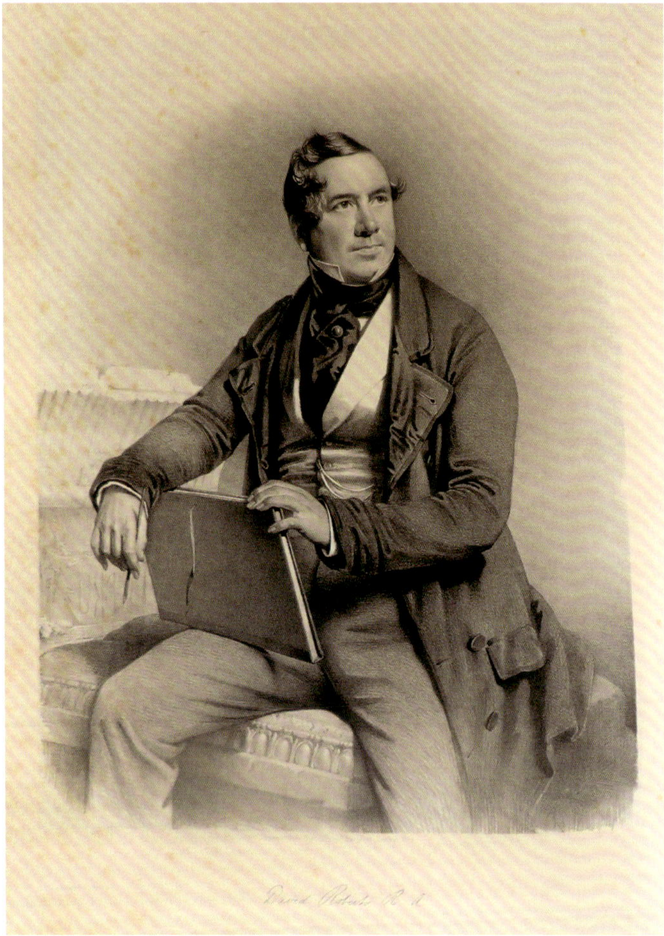

81. Charles Baugniet's 1844 portrait of David Roberts, lithographed by Louis Haghe, appeared on the frontispiece of Volume One of Roberts's *The Holy Land*. This image of a conventionally attired Roberts is an interesting counterpoint to his extravagant appearance in the Scott Lauder portrait, painted very soon after his return from overseas and later downplayed by Roberts.

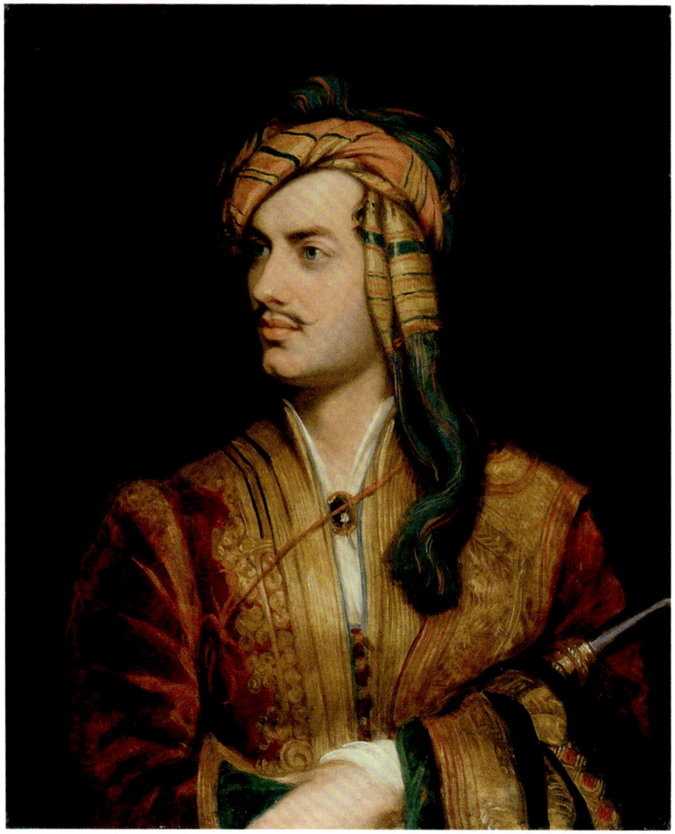

82. Thomas Phillips, *George Gordon Byron, 6th Baron Byron* (*c*.1835). Oil on canvas, 76.5 x 63.9 cm. Phillips painted two portraits of Byron in 1813–14, one of which was the original of this painting. Showing the ostentatious poet in Albanian costume, it first met with a mixed reception but its longer-term impact proved seminal. Phillips was to produce several versions, of which this was among the last.

notwithstanding, Müller's achievements failed to secure him the recognition accorded to the more established Roberts, the latter dominating the Oriental limelight by virtue of his shrewd and persistent networking and through such potent symbols as the Lauder portrait.

The gold standard in promotional portraits had been set over a quarter of a century earlier by a series of paintings of Lord Byron in Albanian costume painted by Thomas Phillips (1775–1845). The first of these was *Portrait of a Nobleman in the Dress of an Albanian*, exhibited at the Royal Academy in 1814.

Overtly stylized, this flamboyant representation of the poet was to define his public image and its success was such that Phillips continued painting variations on the same theme into the 1830s, well after Byron's death (Figure 82). His portraits established around Byron what would today be recognized as a cult of celebrity, and Lauder's portrait of Roberts was predicated on much the same premise, showing its subject in a decidedly Byronic pose. The success of the painting as a marketing device would not have been lost on other artists, including returning Orientalists seeking to promote their own endeavors overseas and advance their careers accordingly. For most, their journeys had an ultimate commercial objective alongside any purely artistic aims, and upon their return it was therefore important for them to stake an early claim to credibility as a cultural commentator. Reputations and fortunes were there to be made on the back of such enterprises, but marketing, promotion, and networking were just as important as the quality and content of the finished paintings.[5]

Artists in View

Portraits of artists depicted when traveling or working in the Orient are relatively few. In a formalized sense, the most obvious include David Roberts's *Interview of Mehemet Ali in his Palace* (1839), a group portrait around the Egyptian ruler and in which the artist depicts himself in formal Western attire, sitting and holding his hat; Jules Didier's portrayal of fellow artist Jules Laurens painting the Euphrates in 1857;[6] a possible self-portrait painted in Cairo in 1863 and signed

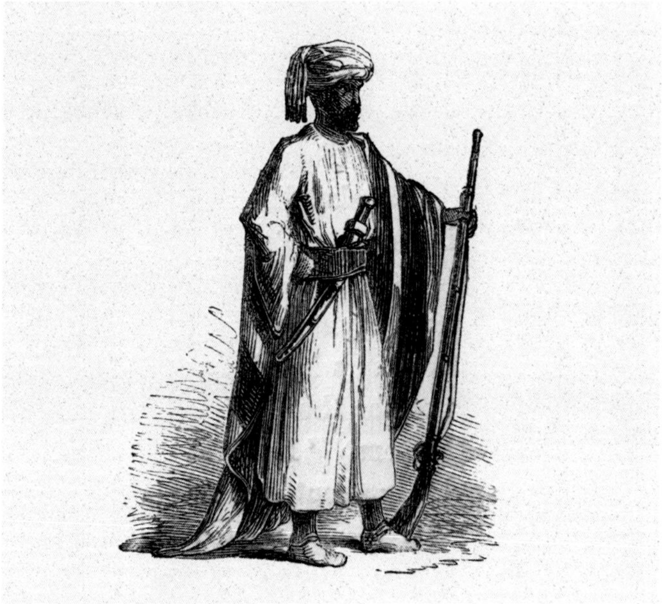

83. Thomas Seddon, self-portrait sketched while in Cairo in January 1854. Seddon was an enthusiastic wearer of local dress, much to the amusement of his traveling companion, William Holman Hunt.

"Émile Lecomte," which shows a European artist sitting under a tree and sketching an encampment;[7] and Gustav Bauernfeind's *A Street Scene, Damascus* (*c.* 1887) (Figure 36). More informal depictions include a self-portrait study by Vivant Denon as he sketched the ruins at Hieraconpolis in 1799 (Figure 7); Roberts's *Portico of Deir El Medina* (1838), which shows an artist—wearing Oriental attire—sitting at his easel with his back to the viewer and which must be assumed to be a self-portrait, even if Roberts is not known to have said so explicitly;* crayon studies by Eugène Fromentin, dating from his 1852–53 visit to Algeria and which have been identified tentatively as self-portraits in Arab dress;[8] two sketched self-portraits by Thomas Seddon, both sent in letters, one from Cairo in January 1854 (Figure 83) and the other from the Pyramids in March of the same year;[9] two sketches by William Holman Hunt from the same expedition, one a self-portrait of him painting *The Afterglow in Egypt* at Giza in 1854 (Figure 84), and the other a quasi-caricature of his traveling companion Seddon (Figure 27); a pencil sketch by Willem de Famars Testas of Émile Prisse d'Avennes "at work in the remains of a Christian church at Qasr Ibrim, Nubia" in 1859;[10] and a colored drawing by Testas of Jean-Léon Gérôme, Léon Bonnat, Paul Lenoir, and their traveling companions near Aqaba in 1868 (Figure 18).

Hunt's sketched self-portrait is especially interesting because the most immediately noticeable feature is that he is armed—holding a rifle in his left hand while he paints with his right, and with a holstered pistol at his belt. Even if this drawing were not intended for public display (it appears in a letter to Thomas Combe), it was an image of himself that Hunt did not shirk from advertising. His account of his Middle Eastern travels is riddled with references to incidents when he was called upon to carry firearms and use them to deter would-be attackers, none more so than when he was working on *The Scapegoat* in 1854 (see page 90). He even felt moved to reenact the *Scapegoat* incident for a quasi-comic photographic shoot some forty years later.

Despite generally refusing to wear Oriental dress when traveling in the region, once back in England Hunt began to see the promotional advantages it might bring. *A Portrait (Self-Portrait)*, which he started in 1867 and finished eight years later, shows him wearing a striped *qumbaz*, a typical Oriental man's robe and described in a 1906 catalogue entry as "the common one worn in Syria which [Hunt] constantly used in his painting room." Hunt was dressed in the same garment when photographed by Julia Margaret Cameron in 1864 and for his portrait by John Ballantyne the following year, and similar robes appear on figures in other Hunt paintings. Not only did this outfit endorse Hunt's credentials as an artist–traveler with a profound knowledge of the Orient but it also helped confer upon him a sense of historical pedigree—the Earl of Denbigh had been painted by Van Dyck wearing a striped Eastern jacket and Hunt is known to have seen a copy of this portrait.[11] Even more pertinently, this garb—and the Nebuchadnezzar-style

* Roberts usually wore Western clothes when traveling in the Orient, so this possible presentation of himself in local garb may well be a deliberate act of self-promotion as an authority on the Orient.

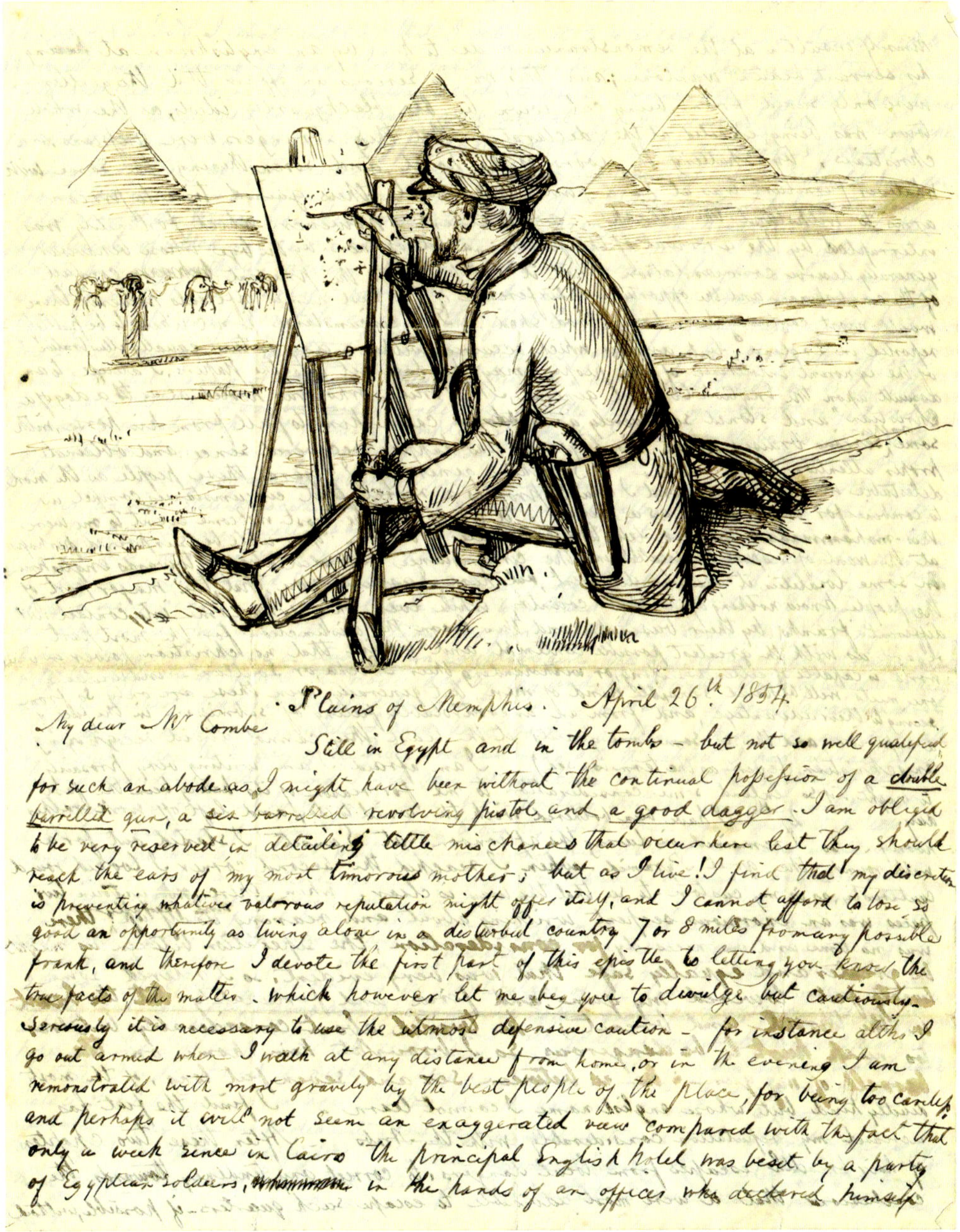

Plains of Memphis. April 26th 1854.

My dear Mr Combe

Still in Egypt and in the tombs – but not so well qualified for such an abode as I might have been without the continual possession of a double barrelled gun, a six barrelled revolving pistol and a good dagger. I am obliged to be very reserved in detailing little mischances that occur here lest they should reach the ears of my most timorous mother; but as I live! I find that my discretion is preventing whatever valorous reputation might offer itself, and I cannot afford to lose so good an opportunity as living alone in a disturbed country 7 or 8 miles from any possible frank, and therefore I devote the first part of this epistle to letting you know the true facts of the matter – which however let me beg you to divulge but cautiously – Seriously it is necessary to use the utmost defensive caution – for instance altho I go out armed when I walk at any distance from home, or in the evening I am remonstrated with most gravely by the best people of the place, for being too careless and perhaps it will not seem an exaggerated view compared with the fact that only a week since in Cairo the principal English hotel was beset by a party of Egyptian soldiers, [illegible] in the hands of an officer who declared himself

84. William Holman Hunt, self-portrait while painting at the Pyramids and holding a rifle. From a letter to Thomas Combe, 26–27 April 1854. Hunt was well aware of the power and value of such imagery among his audience at home.

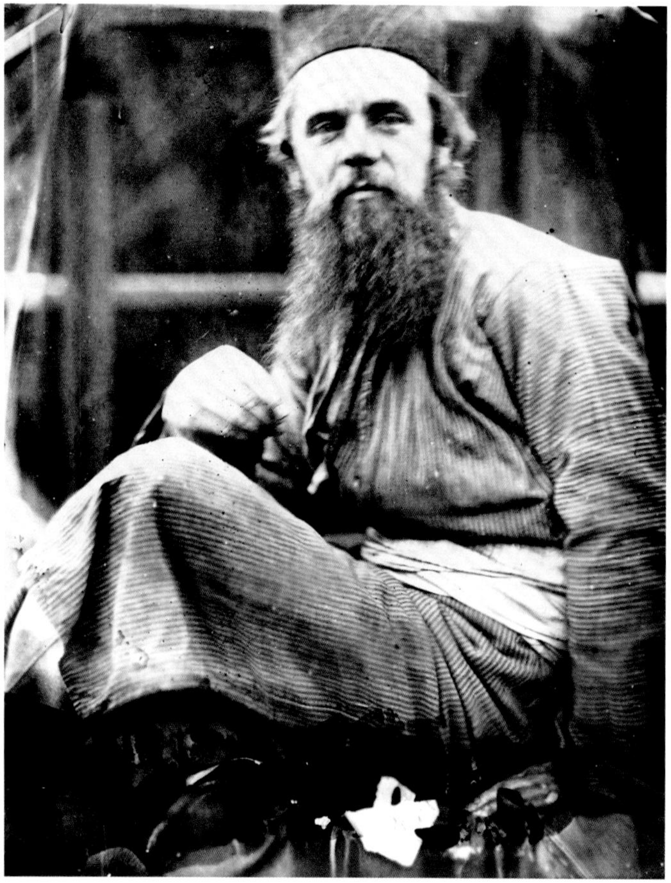

85. Julia Margaret Cameron, *W Holman Hunt in his Eastern dress* (1864). Albumen print.

beard sported by Hunt—made him look decidedly biblical, striking precisely the required note when the portrait was exhibited alongside works such as *The Scapegoat* (1854–56) and *The Miracle of the Sacred Fire, Church of the Holy Sepulchre* (1892–99).

Easy to read as an act of overt self-promotion, Hunt's self-portrait might also have a more sympathetic dimension as a statement of his affection for the Orient and its ways. While at first sight this stands in curious opposition to the robust views he expressed on Arabs and Islam, Hunt's relationship with the region was nothing if not complicated. His sense of wonder at what he found there was never in doubt and, whatever his misgivings may have been about wearing local dress when traveling abroad, when back in England the opportunity to rekindle his experiences by donning Oriental attire on special occasions or, as in this instance, for a particular purpose, may have been eagerly embraced. Certainly his earlier combative attitudes showed signs of mellowing as the years passed (see page 233).

Hidden Presences

A particularly nuanced—if not downright cryptic—approach to self-promotion through cultural cross-dressing emerges with John Frederick Lewis. Returning to London in 1851 after almost ten years' residence in Egypt and on the heels of the tremendous success of *The Hhareem* (see page 171), Lewis found himself firmly in the limelight and acclaimed as a meticulous and reliable eyewitness of Oriental life. The years that followed saw him consolidate this position to the point that a critic was moved to write in 1865 that Lewis was "in knowledge of Orientals quite one of themselves."[12] Lewis was doubtless as aware as anyone of the significance of reputation and networking in securing market success, but his tactics—and personality—were markedly different from those of David Roberts. Lewis eschewed the latter's direct high-profile approach in favor of a more subtle strategy that arguably proved just as successful.

Lewis's ambivalence about his quasi-celebrity status is clear. He chose to live outside London, away from society, in the bourgeois backwater of Walton-on-Thames. If not exactly a recluse, he showed little inclination to seek out company, prompting Ruskin to observe that Lewis "never dined with us as our other painter friends did."[13] Such social reticence was in stark contrast to Roberts, a noted *bon viveur* and regular (and popular) guest at society dinners, previews, and other public functions. Such events were rarely attended by Lewis, despite their forming the hub of the London art scene and a place where much business was done. Visibility was important, and a failure to put in regular appearances made it difficult for an artist to promote himself, either among his peers or to gallerists, dealers, and potential clients. In such situations professional survival depended on ensuring that some form of compensatory "absent presence"[14] was in place. The Oriental Lewis alter ego that had emerged as a result of his appearance in William Thackeray's 1846 *Notes of a Journey from Cornhill to Grand Cairo* (see page 73) had provided such a vehicle from Cairo and had the potential to work just as effectively from Walton-on-Thames.

Lewis chose to develop such a presence through inserting himself in his works via a series of loosely disguised representations.[15] Assuming the form of white- (or sometimes brown-) bearded gentlemen, of varying stages of middle age and apparently European physiognomy but wearing Ottoman or Bedouin dress, this character appears in several Lewis paintings and in a variety of different contexts. In no instance is the representation an explicit self-portrait in the sense that Lewis admitted it as such, but the resemblance between the bearded gentlemen and the known appearance of Lewis at that time is such that it is hard to refute. Among the earliest Orientalist paintings in which the connection can be made is *The Greeting in the Desert, Egypt (Selamat Teiyibin)* of 1855/56, in which either—or, intriguingly, both—of the two bearded men could be read as Lewis. More convincing still is the figure depicted in standing prayer in *Interior of a Mosque, Afternoon Prayer (the 'Asr)* (1857), the subject in *An Arab of the Desert of Sinai* (1858) (Figure 86) and the carpet vendor in *In the Bezestein, El Khan Khalil, Cairo* (1861). The latter figure in particular has provided the most direct evidence of self-portraiture by Lewis, based on two photographs (undated, but probably taken at about that time) that show him in Oriental dress. The similarities between those images and the Khan Khalil carpet seller speak for themselves.*

Further such convergences can be identified throughout Lewis's oeuvre. Indeed, the majority of his male figures conform to a distinct ethnographic type, arguably invented by Lewis as an idealized incarnation of himself in his Egyptian heyday during the 1840s. The idea that, via this self-promotional device, he was busy imposing himself on his audience and his peers is simultaneously engaging and intriguing, perhaps representing a teasing gesture on the part of Lewis himself. In some senses, it may also be seen as subversive. Most curious is the fact that at the time Lewis was producing these works there seems to have been no

---

* See Llewellyn, "A 'Masquerade' Unmasked: An Aspect of John Frederick Lewis's Encounter with Egypt," 133–51. It is possible that there was a further photograph in the series that showed Lewis in the same pose as that adopted by the carpet seller (Llewellyn, *pers. comm.*); see also Weeks, *Cultures Crossed: John Frederick Lewis and The Art of Orientalism*, 21.

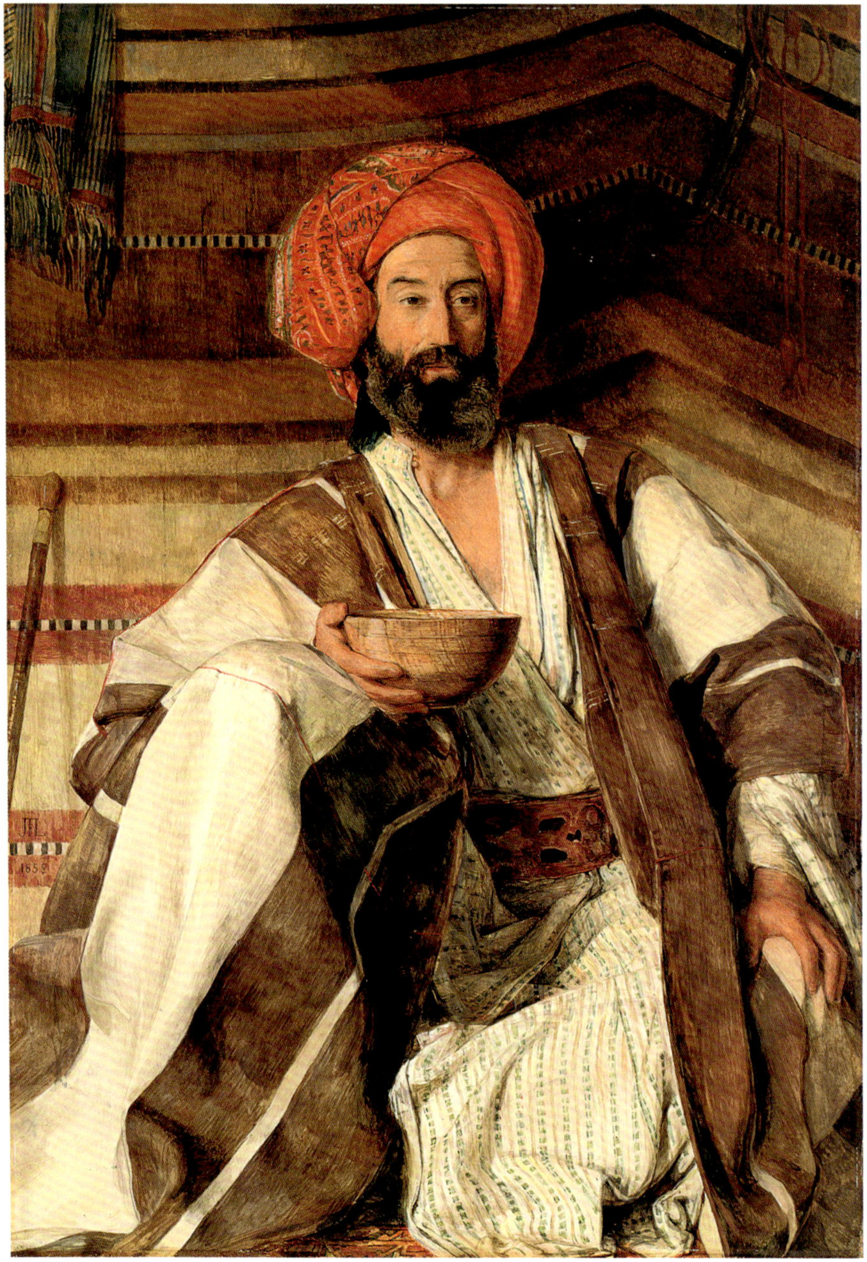

86. John Frederick Lewis, *An Arab of the Desert of Sinai* (1858). Oil on panel, 43.5 x 30.5 cm.

speculation on the possible identification of these subjects as being representations of the artist himself. Such discussion is a purely modern preoccupation, so if this were an attempt by Lewis to maintain and enhance his profile among his contemporaries, its effect at the time is hard to assess.

Lewis's cross-cultural interventions have been interpreted as "an attempt to perpetuate the cultural traverse"[16] and as part of his "project of self-fashioning."[17] He was a complex and often contradictory personality, deeply affected by his years in Egypt—a period which he appears to have striven to rekindle at home in Walton-on-Thames.* His attempts at self-portraiture—thinly veiled, to modern eyes at least—are perhaps best seen as a semi-private conceit and evidence of what has been described as his two personae: a "conventional 'Western' face and a more outré 'Eastern' obverse."[18] The two photographs of him in Oriental dress appear never to have been intended for public display and so cannot be considered an act of self-promotion on Lewis's part. They, and his apparent self-portraits, were perhaps more a means of Lewis reliving the Oriental experiences and atmosphere he needed to create the type of paintings that—subject to a few hiccups here and there—were garnering him both critical acclaim and a handsome income.

The practice of embedding character self-portraits into Orientalist paintings was not restricted to Lewis. Osman Hamdi also did so regularly and had himself photographed in Ottoman costume so that he could use his own likeness in his works (see page 167). He appears in a variety of different guises and characters, including alongside other members of his family, such as his son Edhem.[19] One of the most obvious instances is *The Arms Seller*,** in which father and son—dressed in elaborate costumes—pose as vendor and purchaser respectively of a range of weapons in a basement setting with background figures based on photographs in Hamdi's own extensive collection.

The reasons behind his choice of this particular scenario are not known, but as a Westernized Turk who favored European dress in his everyday life (as did most of his class and background), the donning of Ottoman or Arab costume can be considered a self-fashioning device similar to that espoused by Lewis.

Hamdi would have had easier access than his Western counterparts to "real" local models, so his decision to populate his works with images of himself (often multiply, as in *At the Mosque Door*) seems to have been a premeditated choice rather than one borne of necessity. As someone whose major passion was archaeology, and in particular the excavation and protection of Turkey's classical past, the decision may reflect a desire on his part to reaffirm his credentials as an equally expert commentator on the country's Islamic heritage. By introducing himself into the *tableaux vivants* of his paintings, surrounded by the crafts, costumes, and architecture

* Two of Lewis's friends, Thomas Woolner and Edward Coleridge, refer separately to the Oriental character of time spent at the Lewis residence. See Llewellyn, "'Solitary Eagle?' The Public and Private Personas of John Frederick Lewis," 173.

** The painting's original name, as it appeared in the 1908 Paris Salon catalogue by Ludovic Baschet, was *Le tranchant du cimeterre (The cutting-edge of the scimitar)*. It became known as *The Arms Seller* or *The Arms Dealer* during the 1970s–80s. I am grateful to Edhem Eldem for this information.

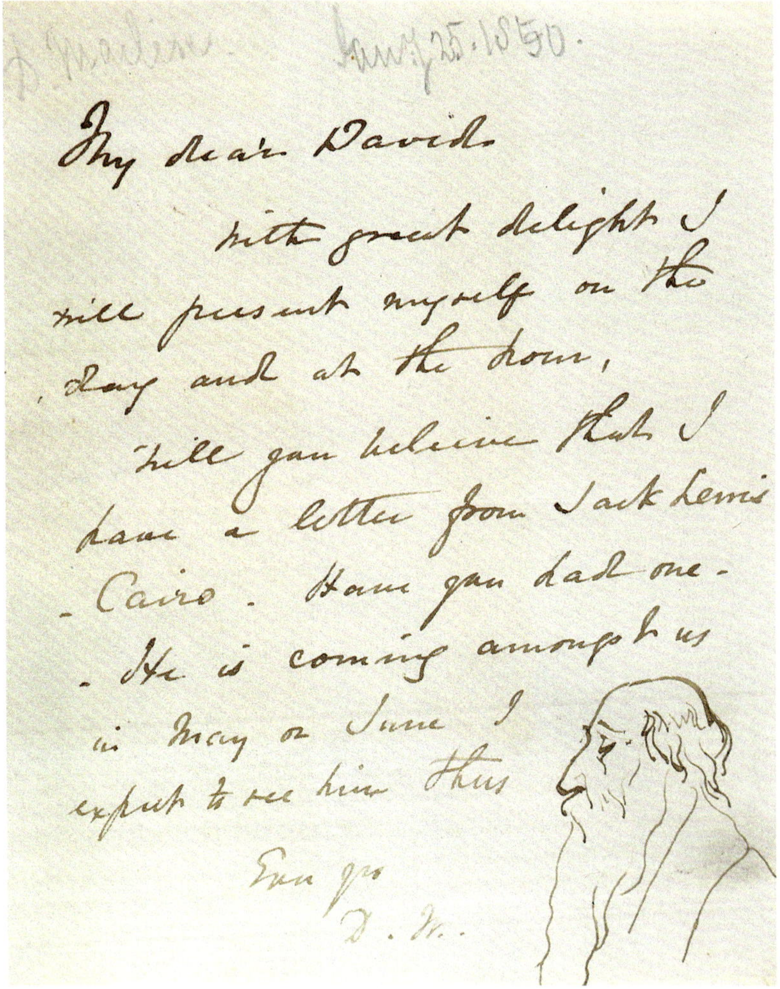
D. Maclise. Aug 25. 1850.

My dear David.

With great delight I will present myself on the day and at the hour,

Will you believe that I have a letter from Jack Lewis – Cairo. Have you had one. – He is coming amongst us in May or June I expect to see him thus

Ever yrs
D. M.

87. Daniel Maclise, sketch of John Frederick Lewis in a letter to David Roberts (1850). Ink on paper. The London-based Irish artist Maclise was friends with both Roberts and Lewis.

with which he was involved through his position at the Imperial Museum of Antiquities, Hamdi was also creating a cultural persona for himself and forging a connection with an Ottoman past, perhaps partly imaginary or invented, that may have been as remote to him as it was to truly outsider Orientalists from Europe and North America.

Maintaining connections was important on a range of different levels. John Frederick Lewis's decade living in Cairo, away from British society (expatriates and visitors excepted) and the London art world and in the state of seemingly suspended animation described so lyrically by Thackeray, had raised questions about both his artistic commitment and his professional future. "He seems indeed to have been somewhat out of mind as well as out of sight," remarked John Roget in *A History of the 'Old Water-Colour' Society*. "What has he been doing all the while? It may naturally be asked. How was he spending his time? And why were the talents of so great an artist as he had proved himself to be thus hidden under a bushel?"[20] Lewis's friends and erstwhile colleagues were equally unsighted on precisely what he had been doing and even as to his appearance after so many years abroad. On receiving a letter from Lewis announcing his impending return to England, Daniel Maclise conveyed the news in a letter of his own to David Roberts, complete with a sketched caricature of a balding, long-bearded Lewis with the comment, "I expect to see him thus."[21]

Lewis was presumably aware of the growing sense of professional and personal estrangement from his former life in England. He did receive some European visitors, however, most famously Thackeray in 1844 (see page 73). Thackeray's *From Cornhill to Grand Cairo* was primarily a promotional vehicle for the author and one from which he hoped to make money and enhance his reputation. The book's commercial success—it immediately sold very well and was quickly reprinted—and associated publicity benefits were an obvious wagon on which others could ride. Thackeray appears to have appreciated the additional monetary opportunities this presented, and there is a hint that he may have offered to "push" Lewis in this way. When in Cairo, he apparently handed Lewis a note that is alleged to have read: "I don't want much money—but any trifle you can bestow will be thankfully received by yours truly Thackeray."[22]

Such an offer may well have appealed to Lewis. Whether or not a deal was actually struck, Thackeray's account of his Cairo meeting with Lewis, the "languid Lotus-eater"—whose identity was so thinly disguised in the book as to be quite obvious—painted a beguiling portrait of the exoticized expatriate Englishman and one that would have sparked comment in the clubs, galleries, and drawing rooms of London. Not only could this have served to revive Lewis's waning profile in England but it could also have flagged up his credentials as an Orientalist and thereby the niche that awaited him professionally on his return from his protracted sojourn overseas. Yet the importance of Thackeray's book as a launch pad for the next stage in Lewis's career should not be overstated; five years were to pass between publication and Lewis's return to England and it is not clear that the "Thackeray effect" lasted that long. Perhaps Lewis intended to return sooner but, as with many aspects of his life, it is impossible to be certain about what his intentions were.

The Publicity of Self

Promoting oneself and one's art relied on much more than a mention in an amusing book. The need to cultivate a network of influential contacts was taken as read, but in terms of sales and remuneration there were other strategies to employ. Foremost among these was the reproduction and publication of copies of original artworks. Not only was this a way of maximizing financial return—the sale of prints helped enhance the income derived from the sale of the original painting (even if the market value of the latter was usually constrained by the release of a print run)—but the dissemination of the image to a much larger audience brought obvious promotional advantages in terms of visibility and reputation. Not least, it was a convenient means of keeping an artist in the public eye without the need for him or her to be constantly producing 'new' paintings.

David Roberts was well aware of the opportunities offered by supplying artworks for print reproduction. The experience of his friend David Wilkie, who had been having engravings made from some of his works as early as 1809, showed that prints offered a steady and reliable income. The paintings resulting from Robert's own trip to Spain in 1832–33 were sold widely as prints in illustrated publications such as the *Landscape Annual* (1835–38) and *Picturesque Sketches in Spain* (1837), the resulting exposure helping him to secure many private commissions. He cut what he thought was an excellent deal for twenty drawings and a vignette for the 1835 *Landscape Annual*, which earned him a total of £420—a very handsome sum at the time. "This I incline to think is the highest price any artist, with the exception of Turner, has received for drawings of a similar nature," he crowed. "My journey has been expensive, and my risks not few; but the subjects I have selected and drawn stagger all who see them."[23]

Robert's entrepreneurial skills were well developed and the main purpose of his trip to the Orient was to make money and enhance his reputation. Before setting off in August 1838 he offered a previous publisher, Messrs Finden, first refusal on the paintings he planned to produce as a result of the expedition. Roberts had a clear vision for how these should be published: in an illustrated account of Egypt and the Holy Land, each volume featuring lithographic illustrations of his original paintings, in folio size, and with the investment costs supported by pre-publication subscriptions. It was a hugely ambitious and expensive project, and one that few artists would ever have contemplated.

At this time lithography was fast becoming the premier means of reproducing original artworks. Invented in 1796, the process relied on the mutually repellent qualities of oil and water to enable the lithographer to create a mirror image of an original painting onto a smooth stone tablet, which would then be inked and from which a new image could be printed. Although complex and highly skilled work, lithography offered a relatively quick and inexpensive method of accurately reproducing artworks, thereby making them accessible to a much wider audience than would ever be able to afford an original painting.

On his return from the Orient in 1839 Roberts found that Messrs Finden had gone cold on the idea. After four months waiting in vain for a response from them, he sounded out another of his former publishers, John Murray, who had published Roberts's *Picturesque Sketches in Spain* two years earlier. Initially positive, Murray redid his calculations and then baulked at the estimated £10,000 investment he considered that the project required. Undaunted, Roberts—who had a defined sense of what he and his paintings were worth financially and had turned down offers from elsewhere to create more modest publications—subsequently agreed terms with F.G. Moon, who "agreed to bring out the work in the manner I had proposed—viz. two volumes on Syria . . . two volumes on Egypt . . . and one volume on Modern Cairo." Roberts agreed to supply Moon with three hundred drawings in total, for which he was to be paid £3,000.[24] It was, however, a condition of the contract that adequate funds be raised to cover the production costs before publication went ahead.

A consummate and confident networker, Roberts then undertook a promotional tour of Britain, exhibiting his Oriental works in London, Edinburgh, and other cities, as well as to leading society figures, as a means of raising awareness of the project and attracting financial support. His network of contacts and senior figures held him in great stead, with Queen Victoria agreeing to be the first subscriber and to have the publication dedicated to her. Subsequent subscribers included the tsar of Russia and the emperors of Austria, France, and Prussia.

By May 1841 Moon had mustered almost four hundred subscribers, twice as many as had been expected, and a few months later was able to issue formal notice of publication: "The Holy Land: Views in Palestine, Egypt and Syria, from drawings made on the spot by David Roberts, R.A., with historical and descriptive notes by the Rev. George Croly, LLD., Rector of St. Stephen's, London. This work will be published in parts, each containing six facsimiles of the original drawings, executed in lithography under the inspection of the artist, at £ sterling 1.10.0; proofs £ sterling 1.11.6, and a few copies, coloured and mounted in imitation of the original drawings in a portfolio at £ sterling 2.2.0."

Moon was charged with the task of selecting a lithographer for the job, but Roberts almost certainly played a role in the decision to overlook the original choice of J.D. Harding in favor of Louis Haghe, with whom he had already worked on some of his Spanish sketches. "[It] was ultimately arranged that [the drawings] should all be done by Mr Haghe," Roberts later recalled, "and there can be only one opinion as to the masterly manner in which he executed the work. The notices given by the public journals, wherever the drawings were exhibited, were highly laudatory; the work, when completed, was equally favourably noticed; and the success of the publication was all that could be desired."[25]

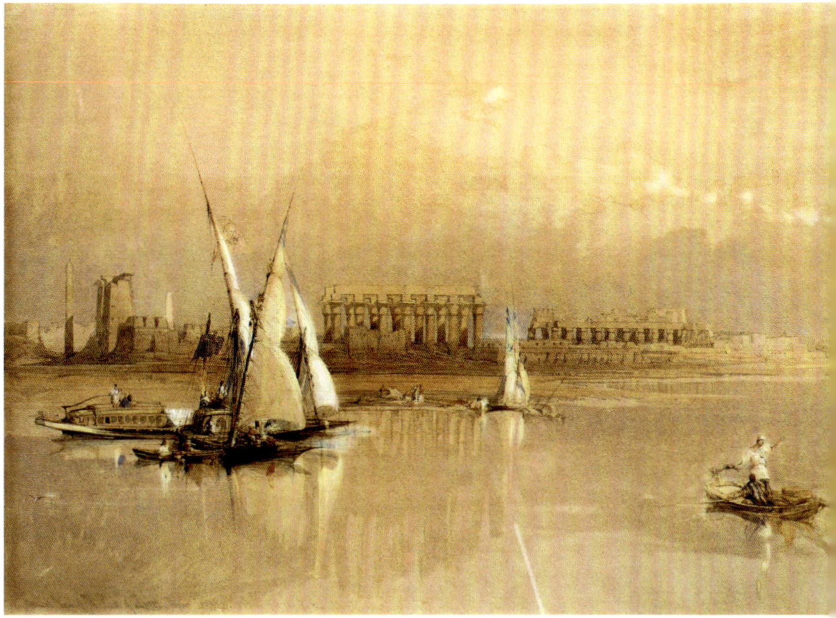

88. David Roberts, *A General View of the Ruins of Luxor, from the Nile* (1843). Pencil and watercolor heightened with white on buff paper, 32.4 x 8.9 cm.

Masters of Their Trade

Louis Haghe (1806–85) was one of the most respected lithographers of his day. Born in Belgium, he trained first as a watercolorist and then as a lithographic draftsman in his hometown of Tournai. With lithography emerging as the foremost medium for the reproduction of artworks, Haghe subsequently moved to London and *c.*1830 set up in partnership with the printer William Day. Their company of Day & Haghe became one of the leading publishers of pictorial lithographs in Europe and was appointed lithographer to the British king and queen.

Roberts redrew all the sketches he had brought back from his travels and it was from these that Haghe prepared the lithographs. This process lasted several years, with publication taking place between 1842 and 1849. A talented artist in his own right, Haghe's skill is apparent in the accuracy of the artworks he prepared, which are virtual facsimiles of Roberts's originals. This is all the more remarkable given that Haghe only had the use of his left hand, the right having been paralyzed since birth. He appears to have been personally responsible for each master lithograph, with those prints destined for inclusion in the deluxe edition—reserved for the original subscribers who provided the funds to support publication—subsequently hand-colored by a production line of workers, each adding a particular tint or shade.

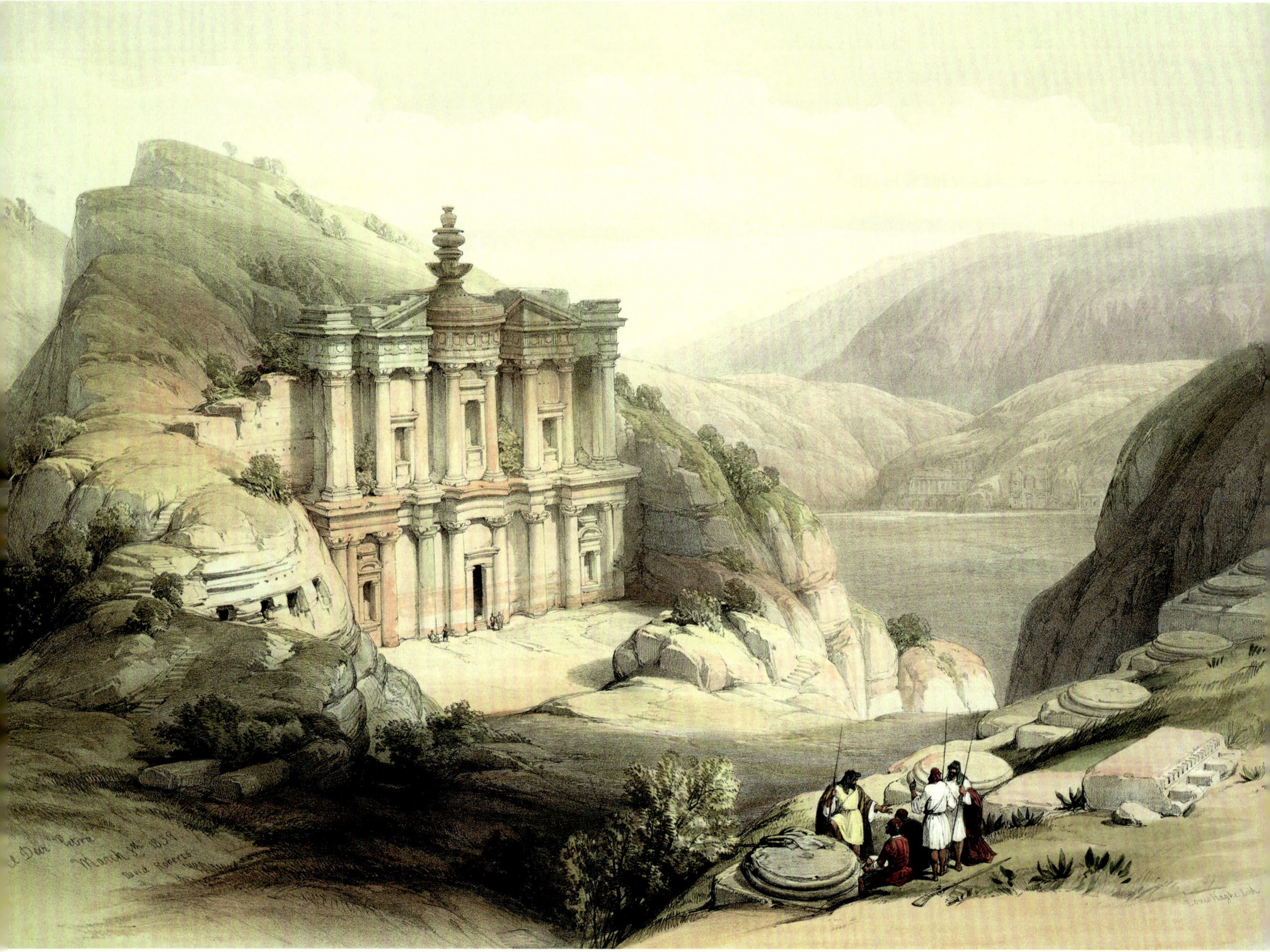
l Deir Petra
March 8th 1839
David Roberts
Louis Haghe lith

Roberts had a high opinion of Haghe's skills, affirming how "[he] has not only surpassed himself, but all that has hitherto been done of a similar nature. He has rendered the views . . . with a masterly vigour and boldness which none but a painter like him could have transferred to stone."[26] It is perhaps a sign of Roberts's confidence in Haghe that in the later prints in the series both his and Haghe's signatures appear side by side and of equal size. Such a public statement was perhaps Roberts's seal on what proved to be one of the greatest partnerships in the history of Orientalist art. Not every response to Haghe's efforts was so generous, however. John Ruskin—who was one of the subscribers to the publication—labeled the lithographs as "unsatisfactory in every way" and "a libel on Mr. Roberts,"[27] but the general acclaim and commercial success of the published volumes must surely have outweighed such peevishness.

After retiring as a lithographer in 1852, Haghe enjoyed a second successful career as a watercolorist. Roberts's star continued to rise, sustained by a prolific output on a range of fronts and by a constant presence on the art scene, both at home and abroad. Fêted by institutions and societies, he spent much of his time "be-dinnering," as he called it,[28] attending functions and, initially at least, reveling in his fame and fortune—in stark contrast to the more subtle (but equally effective) path chosen by his contemporary and friend, John Frederick Lewis (see page 196). Commissions for new paintings of the Orient continued to arrive for Roberts, as the impact of the *Holy Land* and *Egypt* volumes generated sustained interest in the region generally and in him personally.

89. David Roberts, *El Deir, Petra, March 8th 1839*, plate 90 from Volume III of *The Holy Land*, engraved by Louis Haghe. Color lithograph, 35.2 x 50.5 cm. The subject of innumerable reproductions, official and otherwise, this view remains one of Roberts's most iconic and best known.

Issues of copyright were an immediate concern, with unauthorized (and often poor quality) versions of *The Holy Land* appearing very soon after its publication and at a substantially lower price than the original work. To try and reduce the impact of these pirated copies, cheaper authorized editions were published in 1855–56, as well as an American edition with the plates lithographed in small size. These publications ensured that Roberts's name reached an even wider audience, prints of his paintings proving very popular with those on more modest incomes for whom the original volumes were out of reach financially. Yet, ironically, by this time what was ultimately the short-lived heyday of lithography was already on the wane, partly as a result of the rise in the popularity of photography.

Gérôme and Goupil

The successful partnership of Roberts and Haghe is not the only such example in the Orientalist canon. From 1859 onward Jean-Léon Gérôme and art dealer Adolphe Goupil forged a similarly productive alliance that saw both their reputations and fortunes hugely enhanced, at a time when artists, dealers, and publishers alike were struggling to keep abreast of rapid changes in the techniques used to reproduce artworks. Improvements that allowed the mass production of prints without compromising on the quality of the reproduction opened the door for huge profits and the type of exposure that would have been unthinkable only a decade earlier.

The Paris firm of Goupil was set up in 1829 by publisher Adolphe Goupil and a print seller, Henry Rittner. It made and sold prints of paintings, initially produced by engraving or lithography, and later (from 1853 onward) through photography. The company was soon at the forefront of rapidly evolving techniques such as photogravure, a method of printing photographs by copperplate engraving. In 1869 Goupil set up a state-of-the-art printing house, which was kitted out with the latest printing equipment and where 107 people were employed by 1882. Most of the prints sold were of Old Masters, but in 1846 Goupil started purchasing original artworks and the right to reproduce them, reselling the originals after he had completed reproduction. This enabled him to move into the contemporary art market, expanding his company hugely to become an international operation with offices across the world and selling hundreds of thousands of prints annually. From starting out as a print factory processing works by the likes of Murillo, Raphaël, and Veronese, Goupil's became a showcase gallery for some of the most respected and popular artists of the day.

The exposure offered by Goupil was understandably hugely attractive to artists. Among the first to link up with him were Paul Delaroche and Charles Gleyre, in whose ateliers Gérôme had trained—doubtless providing a smooth transition for him to also start working for Goupil. A seminal moment came in 1863, when Gérôme married Adolphe Goupil's daughter, Marie. This union cemented the professional relationship between the artist and his dealer, and

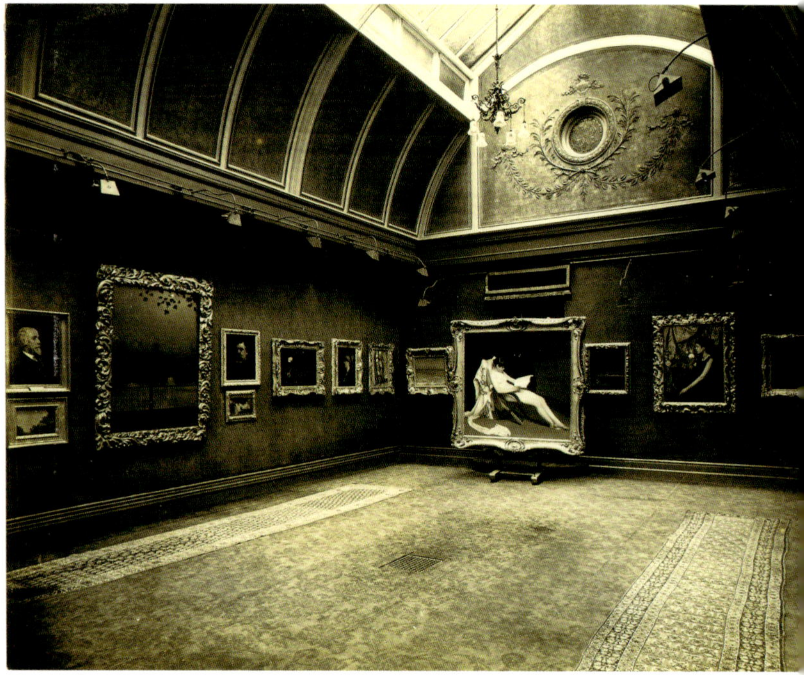

90. Interior of Goupil Gallery, London, October 1927. Photograph by A.C. Cooper. Adolphe Goupil had first opened a London gallery in 1857, following the success of his enterprise in Paris. Located on Regent Street after 1893, the gallery sold paintings, drawings, and prints and was an important link between the art markets of the British and French capitals.

Gérôme became particularly friendly with Marie's brother, Albert. The two men traveled to the Orient together (Figure 18 and page 163) and when Albert died prematurely at the age of forty-four in 1884, he left his vast collection of antiquities and *objets d'art*—including many items of Oriental provenance—to Gérôme. Although some of the best objects were passed to French museums, much of what remained probably found its way into Gérôme's already extensive personal collection of Oriental paraphernalia. A reception room in the Goupil family's Parisian residence is shown in a painting by A.E. Duranton (sometimes confusingly referred to as being of Gérôme's house or atelier) as a lavish Oriental showcase, with many of the items on view probably well known to Gérôme and possibly later passing into his ownership.[29]

The exact terms of the commercial deal between Gérôme and Adolphe Goupil are not known, but while it does not appear to have been a sole agency contract in terms of sales —the artist seemingly at liberty to sell his paintings to other clients—there is evidence that Goupil had insisted on first refusal in terms of reproduction rights. In 1862 Gérôme wrote, "Goupil is harrying me about the reproduction [of *The Prisoner*] which belongs to him like the reproduction of all my paintings, as he has a contract to that effect."[30] In the event, the vast majority of Gérôme's paintings went straight to Goupil, an arrangement that prompted Émile Zola's acerbic observation, "Mr Gérôme works for Goupil. He paints a picture for it to be photographed and printed and sold by the thousand."[31]

The first of what were to be many thousands of such prints appeared in 1859, when Goupil bought his first six paintings by Gérôme. The company ledgers reveal that between 1859 and 1914 (the last date being ten years after Gérôme's death) Goupil bought 337 different works by Gérôme.[32] The actual number of transactions related to these works was considerably greater, as some works were sold, reacquired, and then resold. These records indicate that the most prosperous period of the Goupil–Gérôme relationship was during 1865–85, peaking in 1880 when twenty works were bought and nineteen sold, the highlight of which was *The Snake Charmer*, sold to Albert Spencer for 75,000 francs.

Many of the collectors interested in Gérôme's works were, like Spencer, from the United States. Wealthy American magnates such as William Henry Vanderbilt and Alexander Turney Stewart bought his paintings, as did British industrialists and trade tycoons such as Samuel Mendel, John Grant Morris, Sir John Pender, and Henry James Turner. The Turkish collector Khalil Bey was also interested in Gérôme and is recorded as buying *The Old Clothes Merchant* in 1867. However, these people rarely acquired works direct from Goupil. Many of the British collectors for example bought from the Manchester dealer Thomas Agnew, who was supplied by Goupil, as was the London dealer Ernest Gambart and the Americans Samuel P. Avery and William Schaus, among others. In this way Goupil was able to offer his artists exposure and promotion to an international network of foreign dealers and their clients, the first time such access had been available on such a scale.

Gérôme is estimated to have painted over 350 Orientalist works. Many of these were second originals or versions of particularly successful originals, painted on commission for collectors or at the request of Goupil, who often asked Gérôme to paint smaller replicas of paintings as these would reproduce more easily. The artist's Orientalist works appear to have been particularly favored in this respect, probably a reflection of their popularity with buyers. Anxious not to miss an opportunity, Gérôme was clearly happy to paint whatever was required. On one occasion he wrote to Michael Knoedler (who worked for Goupil)* reassuring him that, although he had sold the particular work in which the dealer was interested, "I am about to start work on the other one, that you saw a sketch for, and it will be as good as the first, if not even better."[33] It appears that Gérôme was equally prepared to accede to specific requests, even if that meant altering a composition and compromising on his much-vaunted authenticity. In the same letter he recalled that in a version of his painting *Prayer in the Mosque* he had added a figure *facing* the viewer (the other figures were all shown praying away from the spectator), because the client felt it would make the work more attractive to buyers. While this change rendered the painting technically incorrect, as all those worshiping should have been facing the same direction, toward Mecca, "I did as he wanted because his reasons were commercially sound."[34]

In October 1858 Goupil launched his first series of photographs of paintings. This proved to be one of his most successful enterprises, as customers rushed to buy prints of famous paintings. Particularly popular were the inexpensive but decorative "cabinet cards" and *cartes-de-visite*, which took works by celebrated artists like Gérôme, Delaroche, and Vernet into the homes of a less wealthy but more numerous audience for the first time. Goupil also published collections of single artist images, and in the late 1860s produced *Selected Works by J.-L. Gérôme*, a deluxe photogravure version of which was issued a decade later in folio volumes complete with eighty-four plates.

The promotional and commercial impact of Gérôme's relationship with Goupil was profound. Not only did it make both men very wealthy but their professional reputations were also enhanced greatly. For Gérôme the link was particularly important as he sought to move his career on from the increasingly tainted Second Empire patronage he had enjoyed previously, Goupil offering Gérôme and other living artists a new sense of direction and dynamism as he turned art publishing into a lucrative and powerful industry. The dealer's fame and influence extended well beyond the world of print-rooms and galleries, with his annual masquerade ball one of the most eagerly awaited highlights of the Parisian social season, for example.

Boosted by his success with Goupil, Gérôme was lionized in his native France and showered with decorations, medals, and awards. The number of students attending his atelier at the École Nationale des Beaux-Arts rose from thirteen in 1864 to over a hundred in 1879,[35] when he was at the peak of his fame and authority. Among those who studied under him were future Orientalist stars in their own right, including Frederick Arthur Bridgman, Stanisław Chlebowski, Eugène Girardet, Osman Hamdi, Vasily Vereshchagin, and Edwin Lord Weeks. Many of his protégés were also to find themselves working for Goupil, doubtless on their master's recommendation. However, it was in America where the impact of the Gérôme–Goupil axis was most dramatic,

* The trusted twenty-three-year-old Knoedler (who later became a highly successful art dealer in his own right) had traveled to New York in 1846 on behalf of Goupil to open up the American market for the company's reproductive prints. Goupil, Vibert & Co opened a print shop and gallery on Broadway in May 1848, which served as a launchpad for French artists, initially focusing on Paul Delaroche but later showcasing Gérôme in particular. Goupil never actually traveled to the US himself, relying instead on Knoedler and on his business partner, Théodore Vibert. See McIntosh, "Goupil and the American Triumph of Jean-Léon Gérôme," 31.

a success that was due in part to the ever-entrepreneurial Goupil working in concert with another dealer who also helped change the art business and worked to promote some of the leading Orientalists: London-based Ernest Gambart.

The London Art Scene

Born in Belgium, Ernest Gambart arrived in London in 1840 as an agent for Adolphe Goupil. He soon set up his own print publishing business, but maintained good relations with his former boss and by the mid 1850s had established the French Gallery on Pall Mall, one of London's most elegant and expensive thoroughfares. Until that point exhibitions of contemporary (usually referred to at the time as "modern") art were organized on an ad hoc basis in a variety of temporary venues and by various groups and individuals. Some of these were decidedly dubious in terms of their art knowledge and business practices, and were used by their detractors to give art dealers generally a bad name. The official art scene was dominated by the Royal Academy and other exhibition societies such as the Society of Painters in Water Colours and the British Institution, largely conservative structures dominated by vested interests and generally resistant to change. Gambart's French Gallery helped transform the nature of the London art scene, breaking the lock held by the Academy in particular and establishing the concept of permanent gallery spaces that were dedicated to the display of quality art by living artists and run on professional lines by knowledgeable and trustworthy staff.

The gallery system that was to emerge in London in the years that followed, challenging the monopoly of the Royal Academy and helping turn the British capital into one of the most important international centers for art, owed much to Gambart's pioneering efforts. Orientalist artists who had traditionally pursued their careers largely through the Academy or the Society of Painters in Water Colours took advantage of the new opportunities provided by this innovative cadre of professional middlemen, who covered a range of functions from framing and selling to the arranging of exhibitions. Gambart in particular successfully fashioned a role for himself as a professional dealer, distinct from being an idle speculator (with all the reputational baggage that entailed), and presenting himself as an altruistic promoter of art generally and not as a biased trader in a single commodity. His approach worked, and artists responded accordingly. In the early stages of his career David Roberts, for example, had relied mainly on private commissions, print reproductions, and the largesse of the Royal Academy—he was elected a Royal Academician in 1841 and sat on the Hanging Committee, a typical example of the route by which reputation and influence were secured at the time. Yet by the 1850s he was dealing with Gambart, selling him "the cream" of his Spanish sketches in 1857. Gambart paid Roberts £1,338 and sold the works three years later for £3,000,[36] a not atypical profit by the standards of the day.

One of Gambart's major assets was his level of access to the emerging new collectors, wealthy middle-class men who had made their fortunes in commerce and industry and had largely swept away the traditional aristocratic patronage of the eighteenth century and early 1800s. Their tastes as collectors were often different from those of their predecessors and they showed a decided penchant for works by living artists. As the art critic and historian Lady Elizabeth Eastlake eloquently but tartly put it, "one sign of the good sense of the *nouveau riche* consisted in a consciousness of his ignorance upon matters of connoisseurship. This led him to seek an article fresh from the painter's loom, in preference to any hazardous attempts at the discrimination of older fabrics."[37] In such a charged environment, with much debate around what constituted taste, and over the validity of "modern" art, it is little surprise that would-be collectors lacking confidence and the knowledge of what to buy—and which artists to follow—would have welcomed the advice of reassuring figures such as Gambart. Yet while almost all collectors acquired works through dealers at some point, very few relied on them exclusively, adding to their collections by buying variously at auction, from commercial galleries and exhibitions, or direct from artists or other collectors.

The buying power of the new order of collectors was prodigious and artists were anxious to reach them, even if some of these patrons were rather unconventional in their ways. Frederick Goodall recounted how one morning a huge delivery of coal turned up at his house, arranged by a wealthy fuel merchant who had commissioned a painting and sent the gift of coal "to seal the bargain."[38] The American tycoons were among the richest of all and eager to acquire European (especially French) art, traveling periodically from their homes in cities such as New York, Boston, Baltimore, and Philadelphia on buying sprees to Europe. Gambart saw the commercial and strategic advantage in bringing his wares to them, and from 1857 onward took several exhibitions from his London gallery to the United States of America. He had already co-published prints with Goupil, but Gambart's touring shows of French art provided American audiences with their first opportunity to see Gérôme's original paintings. Gambart also landed the artist's first sales in the States, including one work to the Baltimore financier, William T. Walters.* For the first time, American collectors were able to inspect and buy works personally without making the journey to London or Paris.

The Dominance of Paris

Paris was the accepted center of the Orientalist art world in the mid-nineteenth century. In large part this was due to the presence of the Salon, which fulfilled a role similar to that played in London by the Royal Academy. Both institutions had traditionally held a virtual lock on public taste in their respective countries, but the diversification that the British art market was undergoing in the early decades of the century was paralleled by changes in France. New ways of buying and selling art were emerging and a gallery system similar to that developing in London appeared in the French capital also, with independent dealers and gallerists opening up premises on and around Rue Laffitte.[39] Avant-garde artists such as the early Impressionists were particularly drawn to these new opportunities as they often struggled to find a home for their

91. The picture gallery at the Baltimore residence of leading art collector William T. Walters, *c.*1884. A portrait of Walters by Léon Bonnat hangs top right, and Jean-Léon Gérôme's *The Duel after the Masquerade* (1857) is the fourth painting from the right, bottom row.

* The painting, *The Duel after the Masquerade* (1857), was bought by Walters for $2,500 and appears in a *c.*1884 photograph of his picture gallery (see Figure 92). It is now part of the collection at the Walters Art Museum.

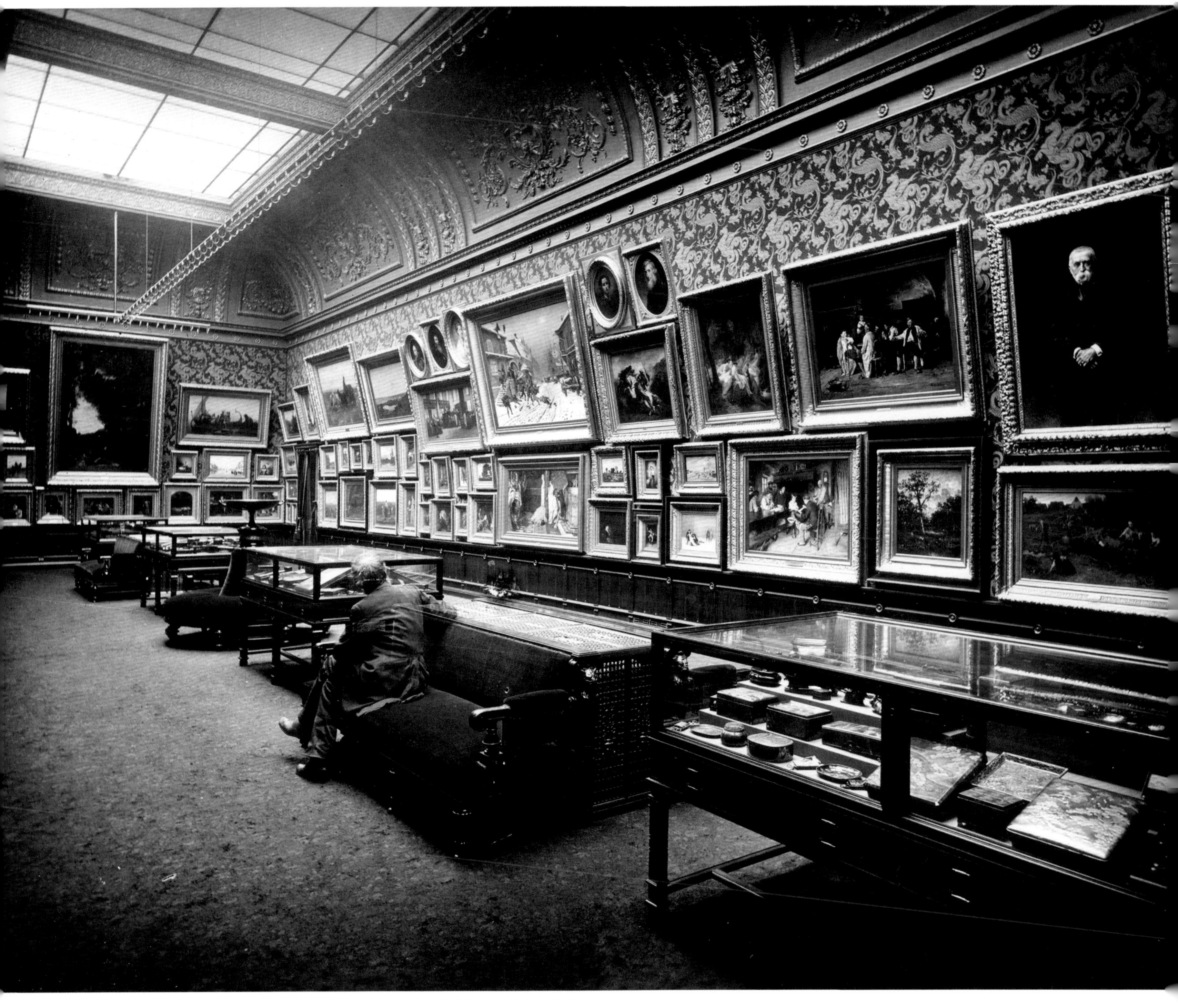

art at the Salon, their applications to exhibit usually rejected by the conservative Salon jury.

Permission to show at the Salon's annual exhibition was usually less of a problem for the Orientalists. With their style and subject matter regarded as part of French art's academic tradition, Orientalist artists found admission to the Salon relatively straightforward once they had received official recognition through accredited attendance at ateliers or having attracted the attention of members of the Salon jury. More of an issue for individual artists was finding a way of ensuring that their paintings stood out from the crowd of similar works. Every Salon from 1850 to the end of the century and beyond featured Orientalist paintings, and it was around the Salon and the influential École des Beaux-Arts that major luminaries such as Gérôme—who exhibited at the Salon for fifty-seven years and taught at the École for over forty—congregated and fostered the Orientalist ethos.

Paris was a gathering point for Orientalist artists of all nationalities, proving especially attractive to the Americans and Austrians. Although London had a consistently strong market for Orientalist paintings, especially for those involving Egyptian subjects, it was rather more conservative in character and arguably less diverse—there were fewer outlets for artists specializing in more risqué portrayals of subjects such as the harem, for example.

The preeminence of the French capital was confirmed by the establishment in 1893 of the Société des Peintres Orientalistes Français, the first formal recognition of Orientalist art as a distinct concept and one that came curiously late in the day. Its fourteen founding members included Étienne Dinet and Paul Leroy, and the Société's mission was "to inspire love for indigenous races, to penetrate and understand their civilization, their customs, their history, their arts, which now belong to them like so many provincial riches."[40] This declaration helped locate Orientalism within the context of the expanded French colonial mission in North Africa especially, and also served to reinvigorate the style at a time when it was coming under increasing attack.

Playing the Market

In Britain, there was no such formal structure for Orientalism and those artists specializing in Orientalist subjects took their chances with the rest. In such a competitive scrum the new breed of dealers were highly influential, particularly in terms of their relationships with art critics and commentators. Artists were naturally anxious to court favor and avoid negative reviews, and so were understandably drawn to dealers whom they thought could secure positive publicity or at least a benign commentary on a painting or a show. Ernest Gambart, for example, was on very good terms with many of the key figures in the art world and maintained cordial relations with John Ruskin, one of the most influential critics and commentators of his day. Most artists were eager therefore to socialize with Gambart and become part of the circle with which he surrounded himself, which included both Frederick Goodall and William Holman Hunt.

Gambart and his wife Annie were renowned for their hospitality, hosting glittering dinners, parties, and balls at which the leading artistic figures of the day would gather. Early in the morning on the day of one such event in 1866, with the Gambart residence full of guests, a gas explosion destroyed a large part of the house. One servant was killed and another

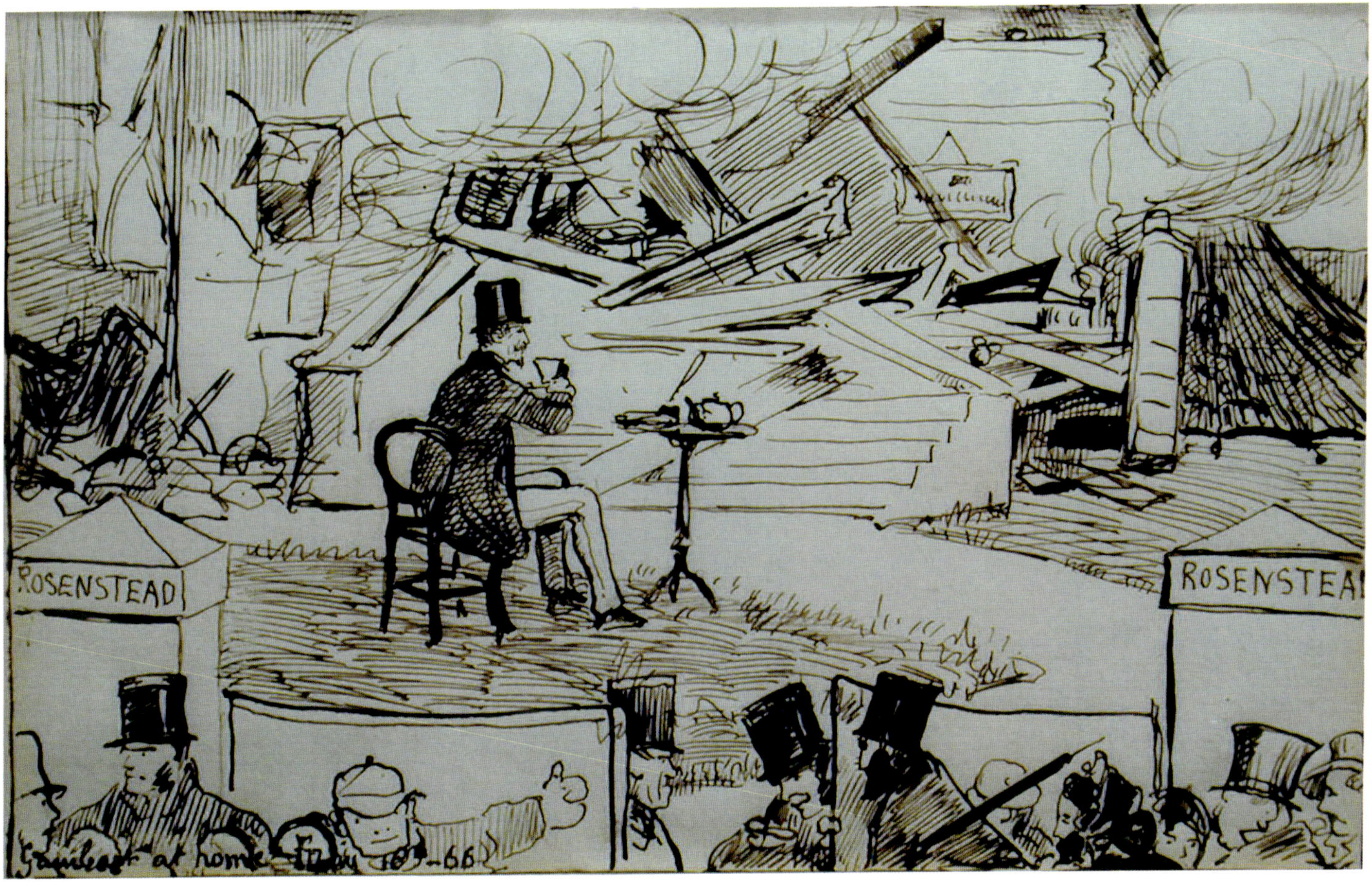

92. Philip Hermogenes Calderon, *Gambart at Home* (1866). Pen and ink. Rosenstead, Ernest Gambart's opulent villa in the affluent London area of St. John's Wood, was torn apart by a fatal gas explosion in May 1866. Calderon's sketch appears to be extolling Gambart's *sangfroid* in what was otherwise a tragic event.

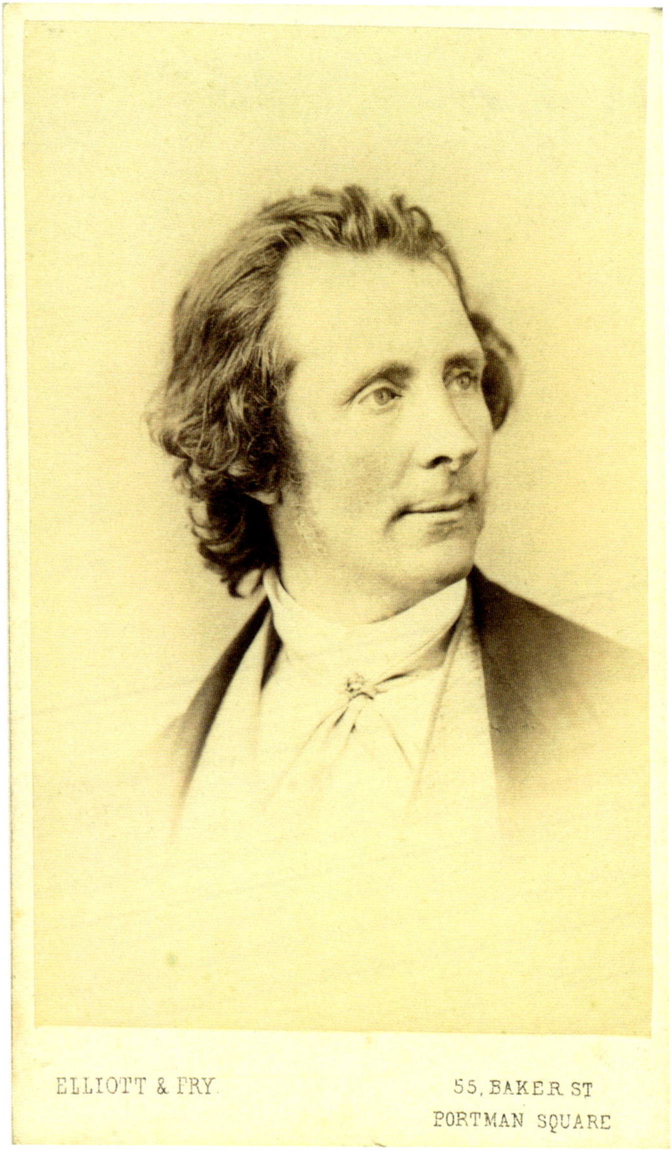

seriously burned. The artist Lawrence Alma-Tadema and his wife narrowly escaped injury and a painting by David Roberts was found lodged in an apple tree, pierced by branches and having been blasted across several gardens.[41] Somewhat curiously, Goodall was to buy the same house a few years (and two owners) after Gambart—by now retired and separated from his wife—had moved to an opulent villa on the Côte d'Azur.

During the 1860s Goodall was one of the bestselling British artists, allegedly earning over £10,000 per annum. Much of his reputational and commercial success was down to the promotional efforts of Gambart, by now the preeminent London dealer of the time. In a typical example of Goodall's sometimes overbearing *amour-propre*, the artist later remarked that Gambart was "one of the greatest admirers of my works."[42] The canny dealer certainly understood the commercial potential of Goodall's art, particularly once the artist was focusing on the Orientalist subjects that were to propel his popularity to greater heights than might otherwise have been the case. In 1859 Gambart had proposed to pay Goodall £5,000 for the contents of his "box of sketches" on his return to England from his first visit to Egypt. There were 130 oil studies inside the box (which had been given to Goodall by artist Rosa Bonheur; see page 87), as well as some

93. *Carte-de-visite* of Frederick Goodall, *c.*1865. Albumen print by Elliott & Fry. In the 1860s Goodall was at the peak of his popularity and very adept at self-promotion. However, his star waned in later life and he died virtually penniless.

watercolors, but Goodall declined the offer, saying that he "wanted them for pictures."

Exactly what Gambart had planned to do with the sketches if Goodall had agreed is not clear, but he may have had the publication of an album of prints in mind. The box had very nearly not made it back to England anyway, having gone astray during the rail journey between Trieste and Vienna. Goodall was fraught with worry while awaiting its reappearance, suffering "unutterable torture lest I should have nothing to show for my seven months' labour in Egypt." The box turned up after a day or so, the lid having been forced open by persons unknown but with the contents safe and sound.[43] Gambart did eventually get his hands on all of the oil studies, paying £6,000, and in 1869 he exhibited fifty of these at the Royal Academy. All were sold, including fifteen works to the Duke of Westminster.

The new emphasis on marketing and promotion in the art market, changes largely wrought by Gambart and his peers, helped ensure that—once established—"superstartists" like Goodall generated a sustained momentum of their own and there was apparently little they could do wrong. This was a period when "more money is probably spent on pictures in a year than was spent during the whole reign of George III," according to critic Francis Palgrave,[44] and in 1868 the *Art Journal* reckoned that in the preceding fifteen years "the dealers in modern pictures have shared a million of money between them."[45] Demand for Goodall's works was so high that he could not produce them fast enough and the number of paintings he exhibited at the Royal Academy—170 over a period of forty-six years, with only a handful of years in which he did not show there at all—is remarkable.

The Gilded Elite

In such a red-hot market and with intense public interest in art, at least among the chattering classes of the major cities, it is no surprise that the stirrings of quasi-cult status developed around certain individuals and groups of artists. The Pre-Raphaelites are the most obvious example of the latter, their personalities, relationships, and working environment providing an irresistible focus of media attention. Dealers like Agnew and Gambart actively promoted their artists through press reviews and features, but for the Orientalists there was also the opportunity to use the exotic appeal of their personal travels and experiences to market themselves. The extravagantly decorated studios established by some of the Paris-based artists were a showcase for their work and Oriental credentials, with their fame extending beyond purely artistic circles. Frederick Arthur Bridgman had a large extended residence on the fashionable Boulevard Malesherbes, part of which he developed as a lavish studio. One room was decorated in ancient Egyptian style and another as an Algerian house, complete with a divan, *mashrabiya* and mosaic flooring, as well as staff dressed at all times in pseudo-Moorish attire. John Singer Sargent laconically remarked how Bridgman's studio ranked with the Eiffel Tower as one of the French capital's top visitor attractions.[46]

Among the grandest of the "super-studios" in London was that of Carl Haag, described by John Lewis Roget in *A History of The 'Old Water-Colour' Society* (1891) as "a notable example of the luxurious artist-habitations which in the present day contrast so nobly with the straitened surroundings of the struggling draftsmen who founded the now Royal Society of Painters in Water-Colours."[47] As Roget's reaction indicates,

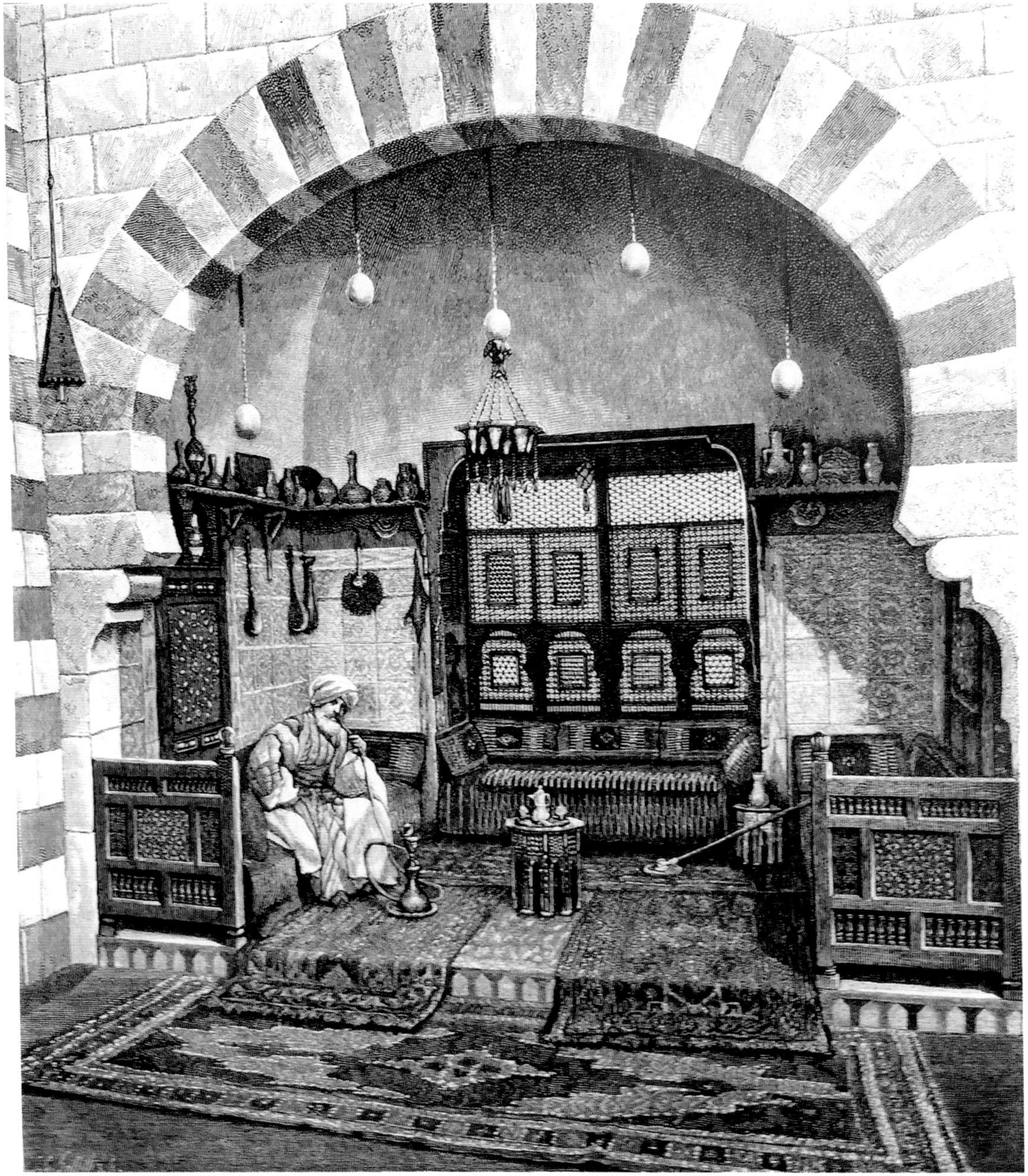

such studios did more than simply house collections of decorative *objets d'art*—they were important promotional vehicles, advertising the authority, celebrity, and success of their owners as expert interpreters of the Orient and its ways. The studios also formed part of an artist's public persona, through which his or her personality and character were scrutinized and appreciated by critics and the public alike.

Haag's studio had been showcased a few years earlier in the *Art Journal*, the author of that article enthusing about how, upon "entering the room, the visitor is at once impressed with the idea that it is scarcely possible he can be in an English home, in our great metropolis, so instantaneous is the change to that of rich, but not oppressively sumptuous, Eastern existence."[48] The article was accompanied by several engraved illustrations of Haag's Orientalized house in an early example of the celebrity home-style features that have since become an inescapable fixture in popular publishing. This was precisely the sort of proactive public relations that Gambart and other top dealers sought for their artists.

Promoting oneself and one's art on the printed page in personal words as well as pictures could also yield positive results. Some artists ventured successfully into travel writing, with Frederick Arthur Bridgman's *Winters in Algeria* immediately popular upon publication in 1890. His engaging prose, coupled with illustrations of his paintings, allowed him to further enhance his status as an expert Orientalist insider, and the book has proved to be an insightful and enduring view of a lost world. Edwin Lord Weeks's written accounts of visits to Morocco and his expedition from Turkey to India (published in 1896 as *From the Black Sea through Persia and India* and previously as a series of articles in *Harper's Magazine*) gave a more wide-ranging overview of the intrepid character of life "on the road" in the Orient, in contrast to Bridgman's more domestic perspective. Weeks described the challenges faced by the artist–travelers and, by inference, what he personally had endured in order to bring his exclusive views of the Orient to his audience back home. Even the irritatingly smug and self-indulgent reminiscences and memoirs of Frederick Goodall and William Holman Hunt were designed to serve a promotional purpose and can be viewed alongside the bowdlerized biographies of figures such as Roberts (by James Ballantine, and published after Roberts's death) and Gérôme (by Fanny F. Hering, and published during the artist's lifetime), which were equally designed to bolster the reputations of their subjects.

Standing head and shoulders above his peers in this aspect of the Orientalist canon is Eugène Fromentin, whose rare combination of literary and artistic talent attracted the respect—and in some cases envy—of his artist peers. He traveled to Algeria three times, subsequently distilling his experiences into two books, *Un Été dans le Sahara* (A Summer in the Sahara), which first appeared in the *Revue de Paris* and then in book form in 1857, and *Une Année dans le Sahel* (Between Sea and Sahara), which was published in 1859. Fromentin's purpose in turning his attention to publishing books was purely to earn money. He would write in the

94. Engraving of a room in Carl Haag's London house, reproduced in *The Art Journal* in 1883. Haag's home in Hampstead was elaborately decked out in Orientalist furnishings and artefacts, serving to underline his professional credentials as an expert on the region.

evenings, after spending the day painting, and his passionate and colorful prose reflects his tremendous eye for detail and extraordinary recall of sights seen and experiences undergone. Through his lyrical but forthright narrative Fromentin positioned himself not just as a rapporteur on Algerian life but also as a commentator on social and political issues—not least the nature of the unfolding colonial relationship between the French and the Algerians. It was a resourceful and successful attempt to occupy a unique patch of territory among the Orientalists and affirmed his reputation as a leading member of the clan.

The Peak of Fame

With their status and reputation ascending fast or already established, some artists saw the value of their work hit new heights. William Holman Hunt had a high opinion of his worth and invariably tried to drive a hard bargain. On one occasion, his negotiating tactics—on which he had sought the advice of none other than Charles Dickens—saw Hunt hold out for a huge fee from Gambart for *The Finding of the Saviour in the Temple* (Figure 95), for which he had probably made the first sketches when traveling along the Nile to Damietta in 1854.[49] The two men agreed on a price of £5,500, at the time (1861) the highest sum ever paid in Britain for

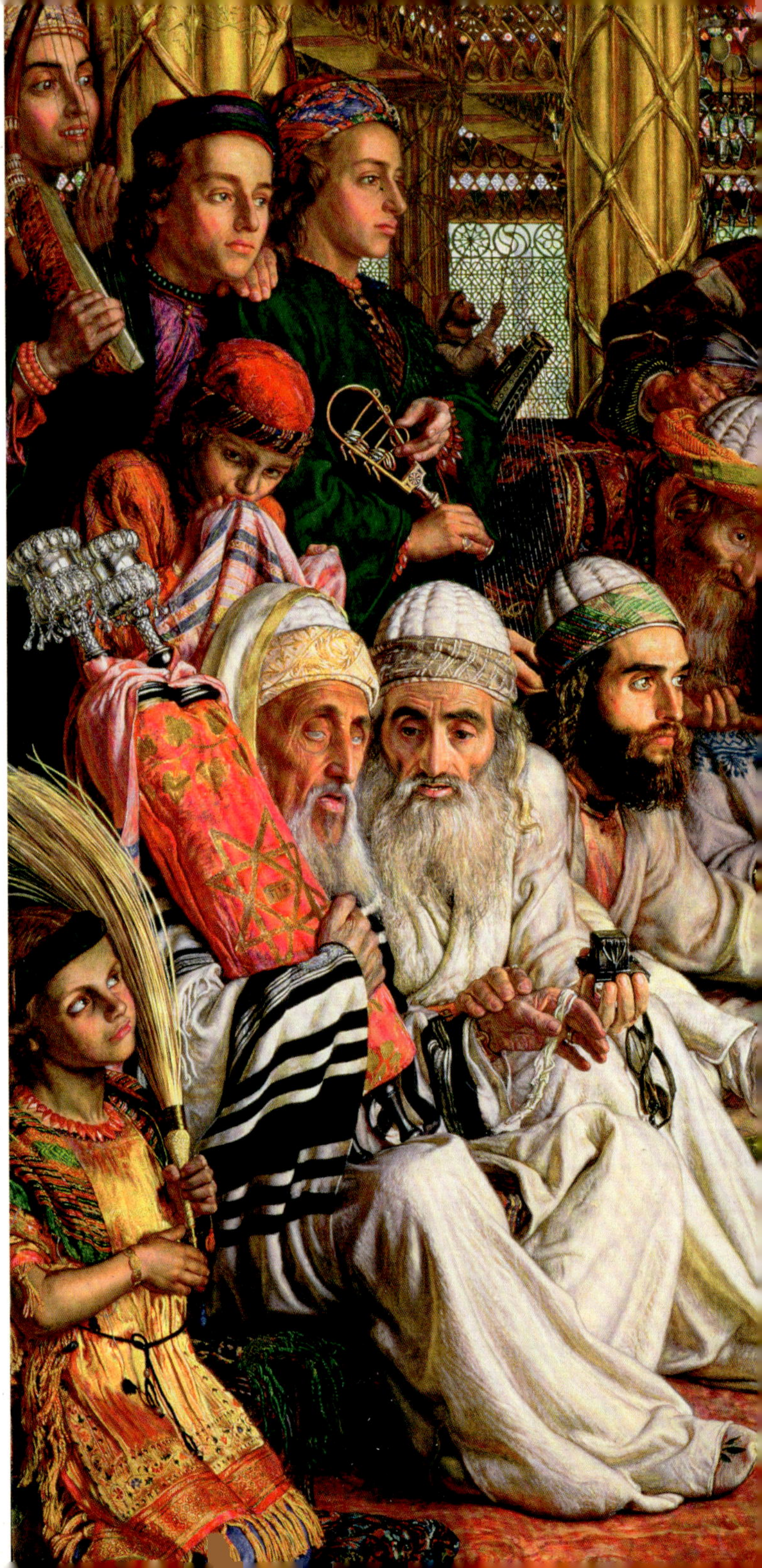

95. William Holman Hunt, *The Finding of the Saviour in the Temple* (1854–60). Oil on canvas, 85.7 x 141 cm. Hunt struggled to find appropriate models for this work, but ultimately it became a celebrity in its own right and earned vast sums for both Hunt and his dealer, Ernest Gambart.

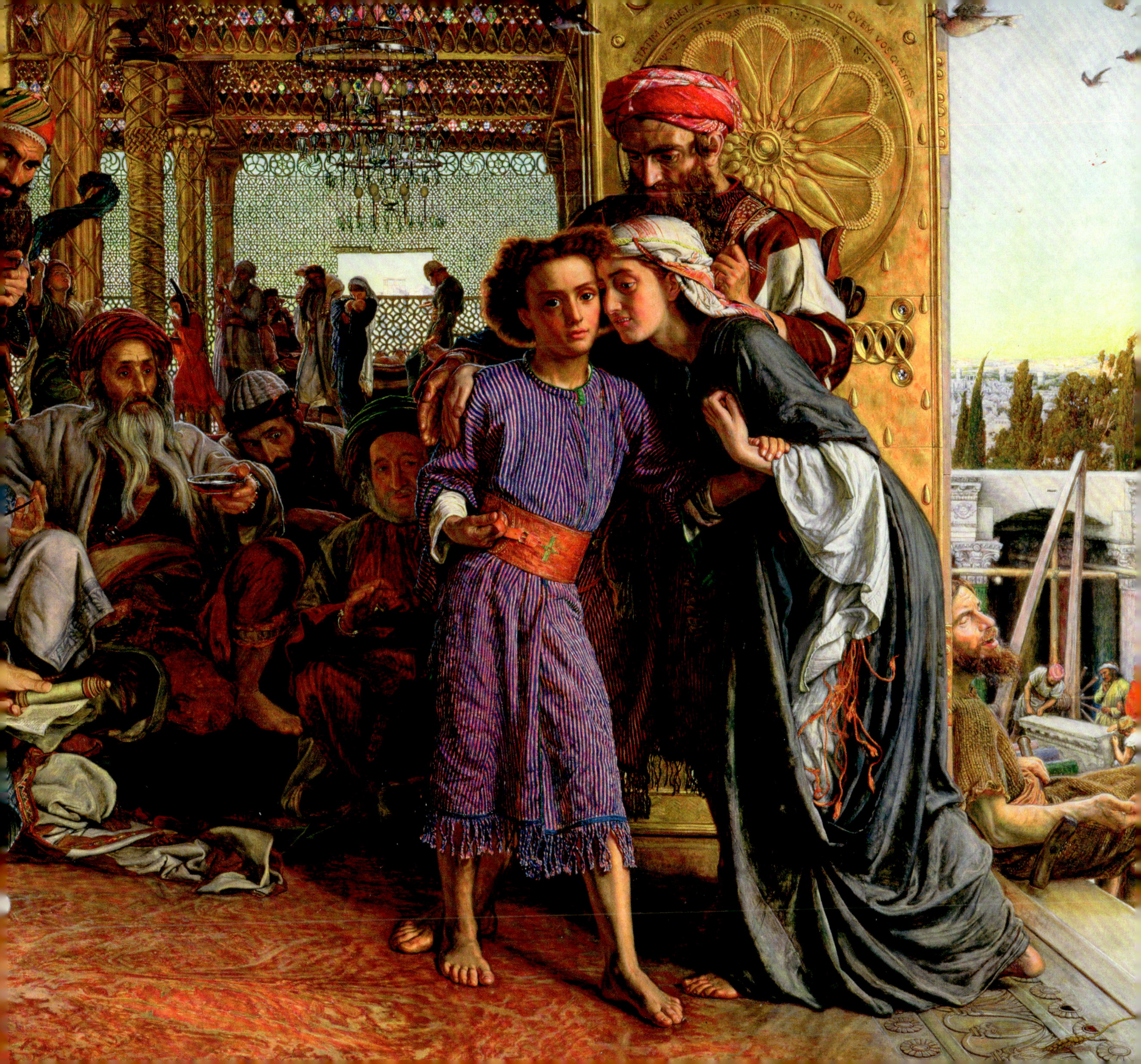

a single work by a living artist. The painting subsequently went on tour, attracting large crowds and with thousands of prints sold within a matter of weeks, thereby extending Hunt's reputation and profile even further. Described by the artist himself as "ever shrewd and entertaining,"[50] Gambart knew when there was good business to be made and while always treating his artists with charm and courtesy, he was no pushover. He understood the sort of works that spoke best to the art-buying public and politely but firmly resisted pressure—whether vainglorious or simply over-enthusiastic—from artists desperate for him to take paintings which he felt had little commercial appeal, whatever their artistic merit might be.

Upon first being shown *The Scapegoat* (1854–56) by Hunt, Gambart was less than keen to acquire it, fearing that it would not sell owing to the biblical story it portrayed being unrecognizable or meaningless to most people. Hunt demurred, but was proven wrong by Gambart's wife and her friend who, unprompted, were led to the painting, told its title, and asked for its significance. When they were unable to say anything beyond "Are you intending to introduce any others of the flock?," Hunt was forced to conclude that "the dealer was proved to be right, and I had over-counted on the picture's intelligibility."[51]

Along with *The Finding of the Saviour in the Temple*, *The Afterglow in Egypt*, and *Street Scene in Cairo: The Lantern Maker's Courtship*, *The Scapegoat* ended up in the collection of Charles Matthews, a brewing magnate from Essex. Gambart is known to have sold him *The Finding of the Saviour in the Temple*, but not necessarily the other works. At one point Matthews also owned seven John Frederick Lewis paintings, which he may have bought direct from the artist, as he was complimented by the *Art Journal* on one occasion for not using dealers. The role of middlemen was still suspect in the eyes of some, based on the crude analysis that, as a result of their presence, the buyer paid more for a painting and the artist received less than might otherwise be the case in a direct transaction. Press exposés on unscrupulous or crooked dealers were commonplace, although on several occasions the *Art Journal* lauded Gambart and Agnew for their high standards and professionalism.[52]

When Lewis used the services of a dealer, he favored William Vokins over Gambart. He was also content to deal direct with clients, as a series of letters between him and the collector John Noble in 1854–55 reveals. The artist starts by expressing his gratitude to Noble for coming to him direct and not buying via a dealer, and then enters into some astute bartering over the price of the commissioned work. He suggests first that he paint it in oil (more costly than watercolor) and then proposes a larger painting than initially agreed, claiming that the suggestion came "from no wish to *increase* the price, but *really* to give you more satisfaction."[53] Not all artists were as confident and as skilled at negotiation as Hunt and Lewis, however. Many of them valued the role of dealers, whom they felt both softened the edges of what could be a brutal market and also sheltered them from the whims and caprices of overly demanding clients.

The fact that very few collectors bought exclusively direct from artists suggests that that the role of the dealer was mutually valued. Even so, there were occasional incidents of a more fractious nature. Gérôme once challenged a dealer to a duel, receiving a bullet in his right arm as a result and only escaping probable death by turning sideways at a critical moment. It appears however that the disagreement may have had more to do with a conflict over the attentions of a woman than a painting.[54]

Meanwhile, artists such as Hunt, who did rather well out of his relationship with Gambart, still took metaphorical potshots at dealers generally. In Hunt's case this was because he felt that they coerced artists into producing endless replicas and versions of the most popular "pot-boiler" paintings and were preoccupied with publishing prints and engravings. Hunt conveniently ignored the fact that these were, after all, the financial mainstay of the art market, and his reservations on this front do not appear to have held him back from enthusiastically joining the fray, as his numerous copies and variations confirm. In 1874 he was in the record books again when William Agnew (who had taken over from his father Thomas in 1861) paid him £11,000 for the right to exhibit and engrave *The Shadow of the Cross.*

As David Roberts had correctly understood two decades earlier, image reproduction—now increasingly achieved via engraving—was the most lucrative aspect of the whole art industry. The proliferating ranks of print-sellers formed the vehicle that "carried an artist's reputation into every home in the country and to all four corners of the globe."[55] Before the advent of photography, it was engravings, not lavish oils and watercolor paintings, that interpreted the landscapes and people of the East for the man and woman on the streets of London, New York, and Paris. While figures such as Hunt may have been sneering about this inescapable fact, other artists immediately understood the impact and value of mass-distributed engravings. Some were concerned, however, about the quality of the reproductions and how distorted and inaccurate they could be. This was a particular problem with the large number of pirated versions, over which the creator of the original work had no control. Thomas Seddon was especially exercised over the low standard of representations of the Holy Land. "I told you when I first came how untrue all the engravings I have ever seen of Jerusalem are, but I scarcely knew how incorrect they were until now," he wrote in a letter home dated 4 September 1854. "In the books on Syria published by the Christian Knowledge Society, very few of the places are recognizable, and many are entirely false . . . . I intend, when I return, to write to them, and protest against their pretended 'Christian knowledge,' which is most unchristian story-telling."[56]

Competition to acquire the right to engrave a work was understandably fierce and, given the intense rivalry within the art world, it is surprising that relations between the dealers themselves were often warm. Goupil and Gambart were certainly on good terms, as were William Agnew and Arthur Sulley, another London-based dealer. Cooperation on engravings was not unusual, Gambart sometimes collaborating with Agnew, for example. Perhaps the most interesting relationship was between Gambart and Louis Victor Flatow, an ex-chiropodist who after dabbling with Old Masters turned his hand to modern art and became a major player in the London art market. Illiterate and considered vulgar by some, he was the antithesis of the suave and cultivated Gambart. Nevertheless, he soon gained a reputation for his artistic judgment and business acumen, which locked him into a "fierce (but probably friendly) rivalry" with Gambart.[57]

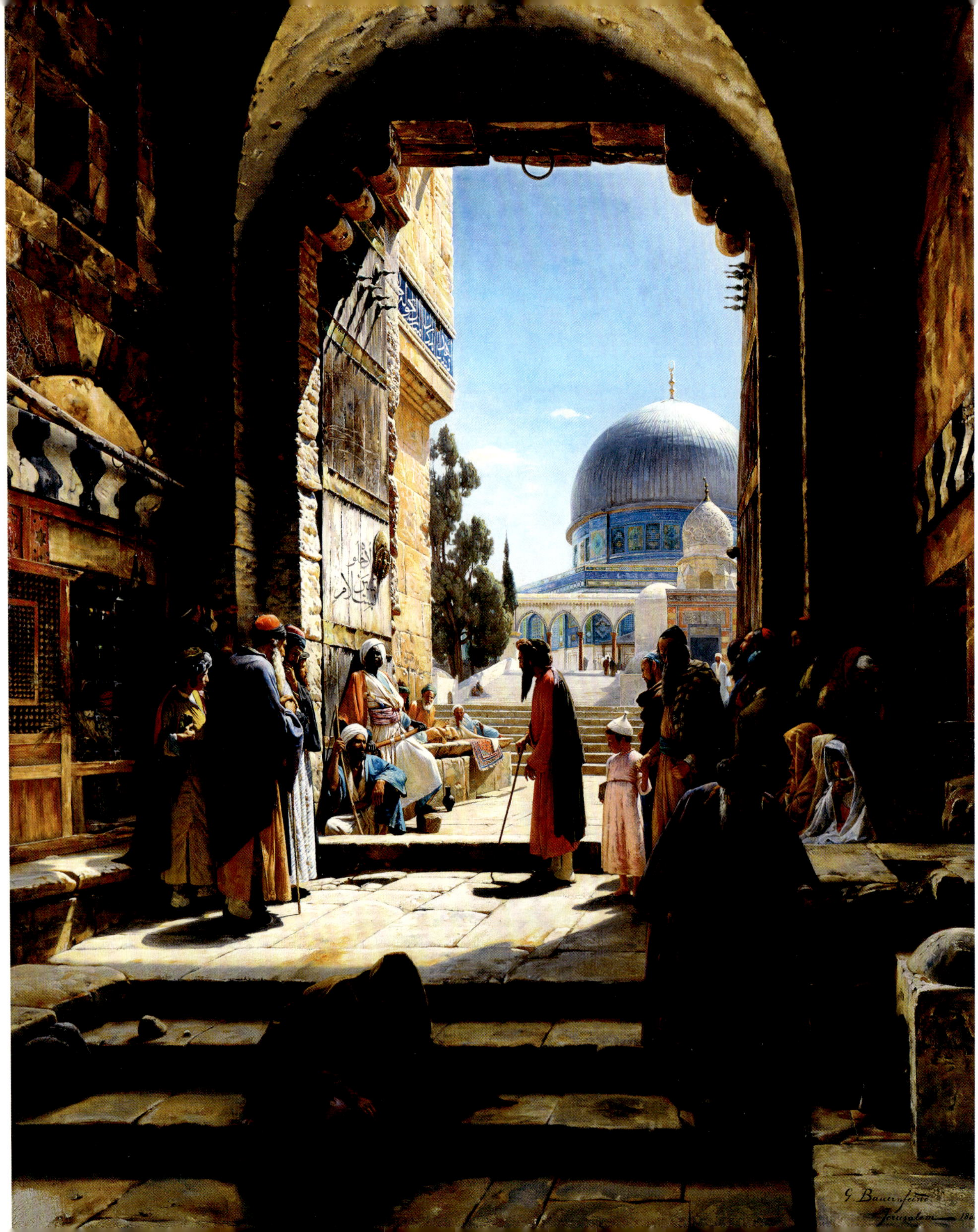
G. Bauernfeind
Jerusalem 186

Overseas Dependents

Arthur Sulley played a little-known but important role in the history of Orientalist art through his involvement with Gustav Bauernfeind. Returning to Germany in 1881 from his first visit to the Orient, Bauernfeind struggled to work up the sketches he had made while in Damascus into the finished paintings that he hoped—and needed—to sell. His journal notes and correspondence reveal that the few openings that came his way during this period were the result of the suggestion and intervention of friends such as Adolf Gnauth, who had traveled to Egypt with Leopold Müller in 1875–76. Bauernfeind continued to struggle financially until September 1883, when, thanks to his friend and fellow artist Christian Mali, he sold a painting for 6,500 marks to an American client resident in Germany.

This sum enabled him to fund his second trip to the Orient, during which he completed a picture that had been commissioned by Sulley. How Bauernfeind first came into contact with Sulley is not known, but over the next few years he wrote regularly to the London dealer about further commissions, asking for payments on account as "a token of good faith" and sending lists of the works on which he was currently engaged and with descriptions of possible subjects. On at least one occasion such a letter elicited an ironic reply from Sulley that he would much rather see the finished painting than a description of what might come, having already paid the artist an advance.[58]

Despite his arrangement with Sulley, Bauernfeind continued to endure financial woes. In 1885—one year into his three-year-long second trip to the Orient—he was forced to ask his family to settle his debts and pay the rent on his Munich studio, but his situation improved the following year when he sold his long-awaited *At the Entrance to the Temple Mount in Jerusalem* (Figure 96) to Sulley for £500. The painting was exhibited that year in London, but Bauernfeind was deeply upset by a comment in the *Athenaeum* magazine that the shadows in the painting were "too black for those of sunlight." He even wrote to Sulley attempting to refute the charge. While Sulley appears to have been far from bothered by the criticism, even asking Bauernfeind for more such paintings as quickly as possible,[59] this episode illustrates the artist's sensitivity and the precarious nature of his position.

There is no evidence that Bauernfeind ever visited London to meet Sulley in person, although there is a reference in a letter to a potential meeting in Munich.[60] For much of the time, however, the artist was working in Syria and Palestine, over two thousand miles away from his main—indeed, often only—client. At a time when the professional value to artists of networking and forging relationships with their dealers was growing, this physical and psychological distance left Bauernfeind particularly exposed and unsighted. This contrasts with the approach of Leopold Müller who, on the advice of the Prince of Wales (whom he had met in 1875), targeted his works at British collectors, often through

96. Gustav Bauernfeind, *At the Entrance to the Temple Mount, Jerusalem* (1886). Oil on canvas, 155.4 x 123.4 cm. Bauernfeind labored long and hard over this painting, sending it to his London dealer, Arthur Sulley, with the uncharacteristically confident assertion, "I think the picture will find your approbation."

contacts he had made in Cairo, and followed up with a personal visit to London in 1882.*

In late 1889 Bauernfeind returned to Munich from his third visit to the Orient and set about supplying Sulley with new pictures. Among them was *Gate of the Great Mosque of Damascus*, shown in London the following year and acclaimed by *Punch* magazine as "wondrous."[61] At this point Bauernfeind might have thought that his reputation, if not definitively made, was at least secure enough to guarantee him continued sales and a degree of financial confidence. Yet the next two years proved very lean indeed, and on 4 April 1892 came a letter from Sulley advising that he would not be buying any more modern paintings and that Bauernfeind should no longer regard him as a client. Although friendly in tone and concluding with an expression of best wishes for the future, the letter was little short of a disaster for the artist.

Bauernfeind's career—always erratic and uncertain—never recovered. Although he continued to sell some works, they brought in nothing close to the income required to support himself, his wife, and—after 1894—their young son. Presumably quite desperate by this point, in 1895 he petitioned Luitpold, Prince Regent of Bavaria, for a position in the royal establishment as the curator of one of the palace art collections. His petition included a poignant mention of the impact of the heart defect from which he suffered, as well as an explanation that "material reward has not been commensurate with the sacrifices that have been made, and has moreover greatly declined over the years . . . my art can no longer provide for my family." Bauernfeind's plea never received a reply.

One last attempt (by mail) at reviving his business relationship with Sulley having failed, in spring 1896 Bauernfeind resolved that the best way forward was to relocate permanently to the Middle East. His sister and brother-in-law were still living in Beirut and his wife had family in Jerusalem. It was to the latter city that the Bauernfeinds headed in the autumn of that year. They paid for their fare from the proceeds of a large studio and house sale, which included the disposal (for relatively modest sums) of the bank of paintings that had been sitting unsold for years in the artist's studio, as well as of the large collection of Oriental artifacts that he had acquired on his previous three visits to the region.

The decision of Bauernfeind to leave Germany for good was most likely driven as much by emotion as by practicality. After having struggled for so long to succeed in terms of reputation and sales, Bauernfeind may simply have wanted to withdraw from the fray, as he saw it, and return to a land he had grown to love. His sister Maria recognized the power of the Orient over her brother, affirming that "you should finally find your heart's desire," but suggesting that he might prefer to discover it somewhere closer, such as Italy.[62] In the event, the move to Palestine did not signal a change in fortune. It proved even more difficult for Bauernfeind to sell works there and he was reduced to offering art classes to expatriate residents in Jerusalem to try and keep his family clothed and fed. His sense of professional estrangement was doubtless compounded by the social barriers he encountered—as a

* Müller's network of contacts proved equally fruitful for some of the younger artists whom he taught, including Rudolf Swoboda, Charles Wilda, and Franz Kosler, all of whom were to depend largely on British patrons.

former atheist, he was an uneasy fit into the heavily religious nature of the German colony there.

Bauernfeind collapsed from heart failure on Christmas Eve 1904, shortly after returning home from a trip to Beirut to see his sister. According to his son Otto, he died under the half-decorated Christmas tree.[63] In the weeks that followed, Elise Bauernfeind attempted to sell as many of her husband's paintings as possible, advertising viewings at the family residence by means of English-language flyers aimed at tourists and their guides, who were offered 10 percent commission on every work sold to a tourist in their group. While she baulked at touting the paintings around the city's hotels, there is an irony in the fact that such a marketing campaign only took place after Bauernfeind had died. Similar promotional effort during his lifetime might have rescued his parlous financial situation, but—in stark contrast to David Roberts, for example—his journals and letters betray no indication that he understood how important networking was. By relying on favors from (ever more distant) friends and attempting to sell via a dealer whom he may never have met, Bauernfeind helped consign himself to a professional fate unworthy of his considerable artistic talents.

The Star Wanes

The failure of Bauernfeind contrasts with the reputational glories and financial success achieved during their lifetimes by some of his contemporaries. Particularly outstanding were the American artists Frederick Arthur Bridgman and Edwin Lord Weeks, who garnered widespread acclaim and considerable fortunes during their long careers. Both resided in France and led opulent lifestyles, exhibiting regularly at the Paris Salon and elsewhere in Europe and North America, their works selling regularly to top collectors and for prodigious sums. In the 1890s the two men, who were friends, were at the height of their powers, basking in the admiration of their peers and an adoring public. Yet already the storm clouds of a changing art world were spilling over the horizon, presaging the dramatic impact that shifts in taste and fashion were to have on the hitherto largely charmed world of the Orientalists generally and on specific individuals among them—not least Bridgman and Weeks.

Orientalism had always had its detractors and these had become increasingly vociferous from the 1870s onward. In France, figures such as the journalist and critic Antoine Castagnary—who launched his first attack on Orientalist art in a review of the Salon in 1857—derided the Orientalists as being obsessed with foreign lands and "unpatriotic . . . [and] guilty of a failure to believe in the beauty of France and its people."[64] Such criticism was robustly refuted by Léonce Bénédite, who had been instrumental in setting up the Société des Peintres Orientalistes Français in 1893 (see page 212). The previous year Bénédite had been appointed acting curator at the Musée du Luxembourg and he spent the next three decades acquiring artworks on behalf of the state. With hindsight, he can be seen to have missed major opportunities to develop the collection in his care, passing up the chance to buy works by the emerging Cézanne, Matisse, and Picasso.[65] Instead Bénédite channeled his energies into more traditional artistic spheres, including Orientalism.

The Universal Exposition in Paris in 1889, with its showcase Moorish palace serving as the Algerian pavilion and a variety of other crowd-pulling cultural exhibits from Arab and Islamic lands, was a rallying point for the Orientalists led by Bénédite. Through demonstrating the close relationship between the Orient and Mother France they were able to counter the accusations of unpatriotic behavior leveled at them by Castagnary and others, presenting their works as a vehicle for the promotion of the greater glory of France and its beneficial colonial influence overseas. Even those Orientalists who were uneasy about the more brutal aspects of colonial rule, such as Gustave Guillaumet and Étienne Dinet, fell short of doing anything but support and endorse what they saw as the civilizing mission of French colonialism in North Africa, particularly when expressed via the creation of an arts infrastructure in countries such as Algeria. Meanwhile, Bénédite was to undertake a series of expeditions to the region, traveling to Tunisia in 1897, to Algeria to visit Dinet in Bou-Saâda in 1905, and to open the municipal museum in Algiers in 1908 (which subsequently became the Museum of Fine Arts in 1930), and accompanying the artist Charles Cottet in 1911.[66]

In spite of the efforts of Bénédite and the Société des Peintres Orientalistes Français, by the early 1900s Orientalist art was at the very least approaching a crossroads and, at worst, a crisis. Among older artists particularly there was an increasing feeling of nostalgia, a sense of loss for an Orient that many felt was disappearing before their eyes under a wave of Westernization. Guillaumet was particularly concerned by the destruction of the traditional architecture and atmosphere of Algiers in favor of new development dominated by commercial premises. "They are demolishing without letting up," he lamented, "the Moorish peristyles, the gateways of sculpted marble, to make space for businesses or workshops . . . . Life here no longer seems as before, held together by dreams and bringing life to the shadows."[67] It was a similar story elsewhere in the Orient. Certainly by the 1880s Egyptian cities like Cairo and Alexandria had been transformed by European influence, with their Western-style main thoroughfares and elegant residential districts. Frank Dillon, who visited Egypt at least four times between 1854 and 1874, was fascinated by the traditional domestic and civic architecture and decoration of Cairo in particular. Through his paintings, which presented carefully rendered exteriors and interiors of Cairene houses, Dillon endeavored to highlight the plight of the city's traditional buildings and campaigned—largely in vain—for their protection.*

Leopold Müller also bemoaned the rapid rate of change and the disappearance of the local built heritage. "For only too soon everything still remaining of the traditional Arab architecture will have disappeared," he wrote in a letter dated 12 March 1875. "This means that houses and whole streets are being demolished with a fury. Today one

97. Frank Dillon, *Exterior of the House of the Memluk Raduan Bey, Cairo* (1870). Watercolor, 40.6 x 29.5 cm. Dillon exhibited his paintings of Cairene houses at the Royal Institute of British Architects in London to try and raise awareness of the fate of traditional architecture as the Egyptian capital was being redeveloped.

* Dillon was an avid conservationist. He campaigned in the 1890s against the construction of the dam at Aswan because of the impact it would have on antiquities such as those at Philae.

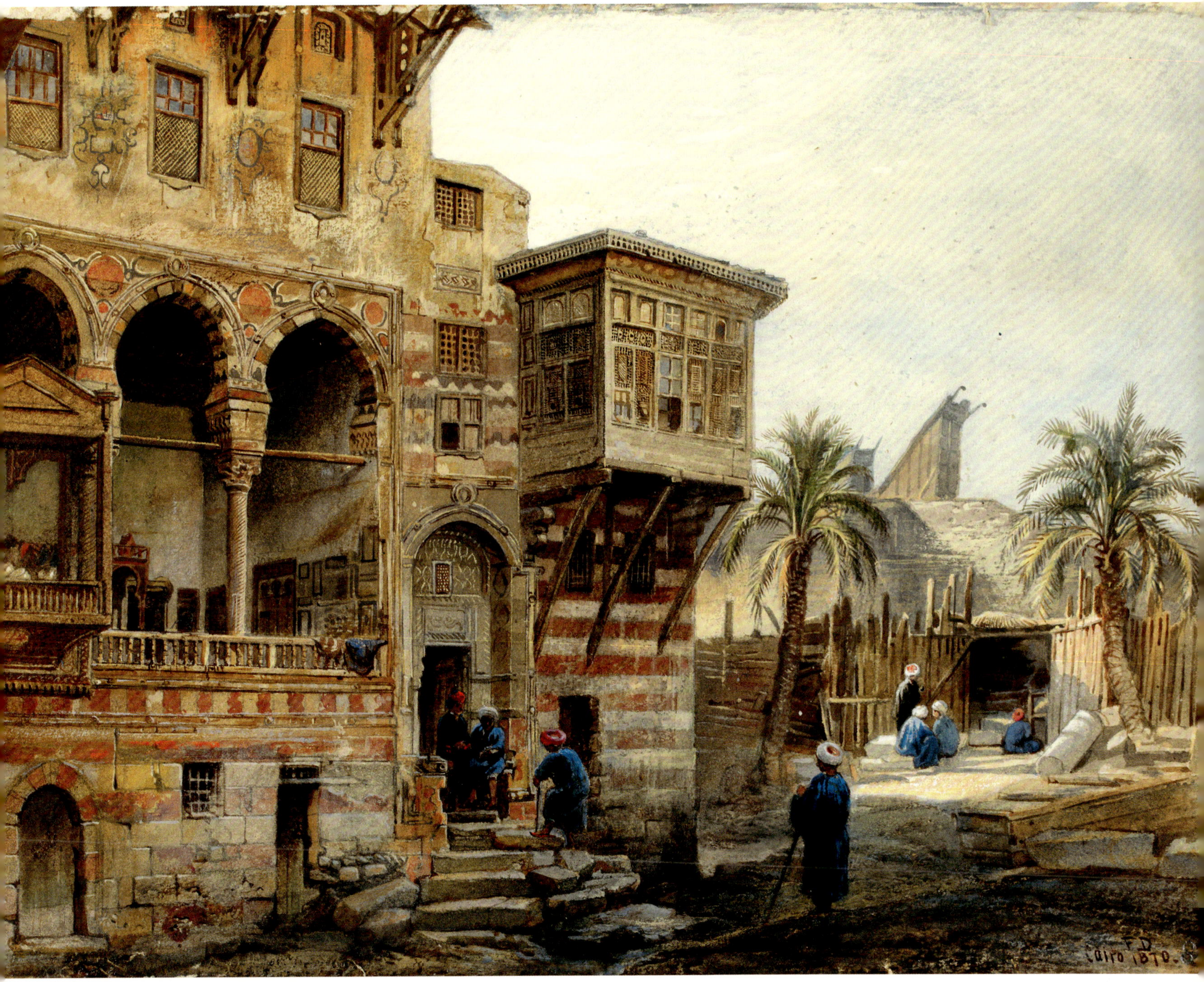
FD
Cairo 1870.

could call Cairo a huge heap of rubble. What is extremely strange is that no buildings have been erected in place of what has been pulled down. One does not see much construction—only destruction."[68] In an act of crass irony, sections of demolished Cairene buildings were relocated to Paris to create a pastiche "Cairo Street" for the Universal Exposition of 1889.

The modernization of Egypt was something that certain foreign visitors had been regretting for some time. Edward William Lane had been aware of its impact in the 1840s, while in 1843 Gérard de Nerval wrote to Théophile Gautier about what he articulated as his betrayed dream. "I have already lost, Kingdom after Kingdom, province after province, the more beautiful half of the universe," he lamented, "and soon I will know of no place in which I can find a refuge for my dreams; but it is Egypt that I most regret having driven out of my imagination, now that I have sadly placed it in my memory."[69] For de Nerval, as a Romantic, the loss was irrevocable: "For a person who has never seen the Orient, a lotus is still a lotus; for me it is only a kind of onion."[70] Edwin Lord Weeks expressed similar concerns, his writings wracked with a sense of frustration at the impact that the relentless march of progress was having on the traditional cultures of the Orient, with Egypt unnamed but perhaps central in his sights as the country most compromised by outside influence. Morocco, Weeks felt, had at least acted as a bulwark against external forces. "No other Moslem country has so long resisted and successfully baffled the aggressive progress of modern civilization," he proclaimed, marveling that "there is not yet a single road over which wheeled vehicles may pass in the whole empire of Morocco." For Weeks the country represented "a museum of antiquity, a working model of the Middle Ages," which he pleaded should be maintained and celebrated.[71]

Such a Western view did not, of course, take into account the potential gains to those living in such medieval paradises of improvements in the fields of trade, health, education, transport, and other infrastructure, and nor did it make any accommodation for the possibility of independent self-expression by the local population. Instead, it helped reinforce the sense of estrangement that many of the Orientalists felt as the advent of the twentieth century approached. Not only was their world shrinking, as journey times between Europe and the Orient became ever shorter (Bénédite remarking in the early 1900s that "a trip of forty-eight hours suffices to throw us headlong into the most profound distancing of space and time"[72]), but the very subjects in which the Orientalists specialized were disappearing too, as traditional societies became more urbanized and centuries-old customs and ceremonies dwindled in importance and frequency. In less than a generation, hitherto remote regions and places that intrepid artist–travelers had previously spent weeks or months risking life and limb to visit and capture on canvas were now destinations that tourists could reach themselves easily in a fraction of the time, and increasingly—doubtless to the horror of Edwin Lord Weeks—by motor car.

Some artists took a more sensitive view and were in particular uncomfortable about the Western plundering of the Orient's antiquities and cultural heritage. William James Müller was especially scathing about the exploits of foreign archaeologists in Turkey. "I have truly taken away much," he wrote on his return from a trip to Lycia in 1844, "but not, like those armed with authority, torn from earth the monuments of the past, and made spots dear to us from historical association a wilderness, that but records the evils they have done. Their sins be upon their own heads."[73]

Meanwhile, audiences back home were at risk of becoming jaded and blasé. As early as 1851, the *Illustrated London News* carried an article lamenting that "every now and then a young gentleman returns from Greece or Egypt with a beard and a M.S. In a week or two, the new journal of Travels in the East is announced and a new 'oriental traveler' takes his place among the 'wise men' who have preceded him. . . . It is a sad thing to reflect on, that, with regard to the East, Europe's honeymoon is over."[74] Eight years later, John Ruskin sounded a similar note of exasperation when reviewing John Frederick Lewis's *Waiting for the Ferry-boat—Upper Egypt.* "Well, of course, it is very nice," Ruskin wrote. "Housings and camels—palm trees—clouds, and sheikh. But waiting for a ferry-boat is dull work; and are we never to get out of Egypt any more? nor to perceive the existence of any living creatures but Arabs and camels?"[75] For many, the unconditional love affair with the Orient was finished, and the novelty and excitement of those earlier encounters had faded and passed.

The craft practiced by the Orientalist artists was also under intense pressure. New ideas about art and taste were sweeping Europe and North America, not all directly challenging the ethos of the Orientalist approach but serving nonetheless to undermine it and, equally significantly, distract and divert the all-important collectors, patrons, and audiences. At the vanguard of the changing art world were the Impressionists, whose free-flowing and bold expressive brushstrokes were in such stark contrast to the minutely executed and labored way in which many of the Orientalists worked. Locked into a formal academic style that drew heavily on the disciplines of earlier decades, the painters of the East now seemed hopelessly dated and archaic.

Ironically, Impressionism considered aspects of the Orientalist canon to be significant, at least in an historical sense. Many of its protagonists held Delacroix, one of the early flag-bearers for Orientalism, in high esteem and expeditions to North Africa in particular were still an artistic rite of passage for artists such as Renoir, who went on to produce his own interpretation of the odalisque theme. Claude Monet was a particular admirer of Théodore Frère, and had pronounced himself "intoxicated" by Algeria during the year he spent there in 1861–62. Yet he was not inspired to develop any aspect of his oeuvre around his North African experiences. Indeed, the Impressionists mostly rejected the high drama of exotically staged Oriental subjects in favor of everyday urban life and domestic landscapes, subjects much closer to home than those with which most Orientalists felt either comfortable or competent. Even their desire to travel was ridiculed. Paul Cézanne once famously carped, "All these chaps taking off to the East, to Venice, to Algeria in search of the sun—don't they have a little country house on their father's land?"[76] His snide dismissal of the great spirit of ambition and adventure that had so mobilized the artist–travelers of the mid-nineteenth century presaged how the heyday of Orientalist art was soon to find itself eclipsed in the early years of the twentieth, an *ancien régime* struggling to survive in a changing world that largely regarded it as outmoded, inarticulate, and irrelevant. One of the

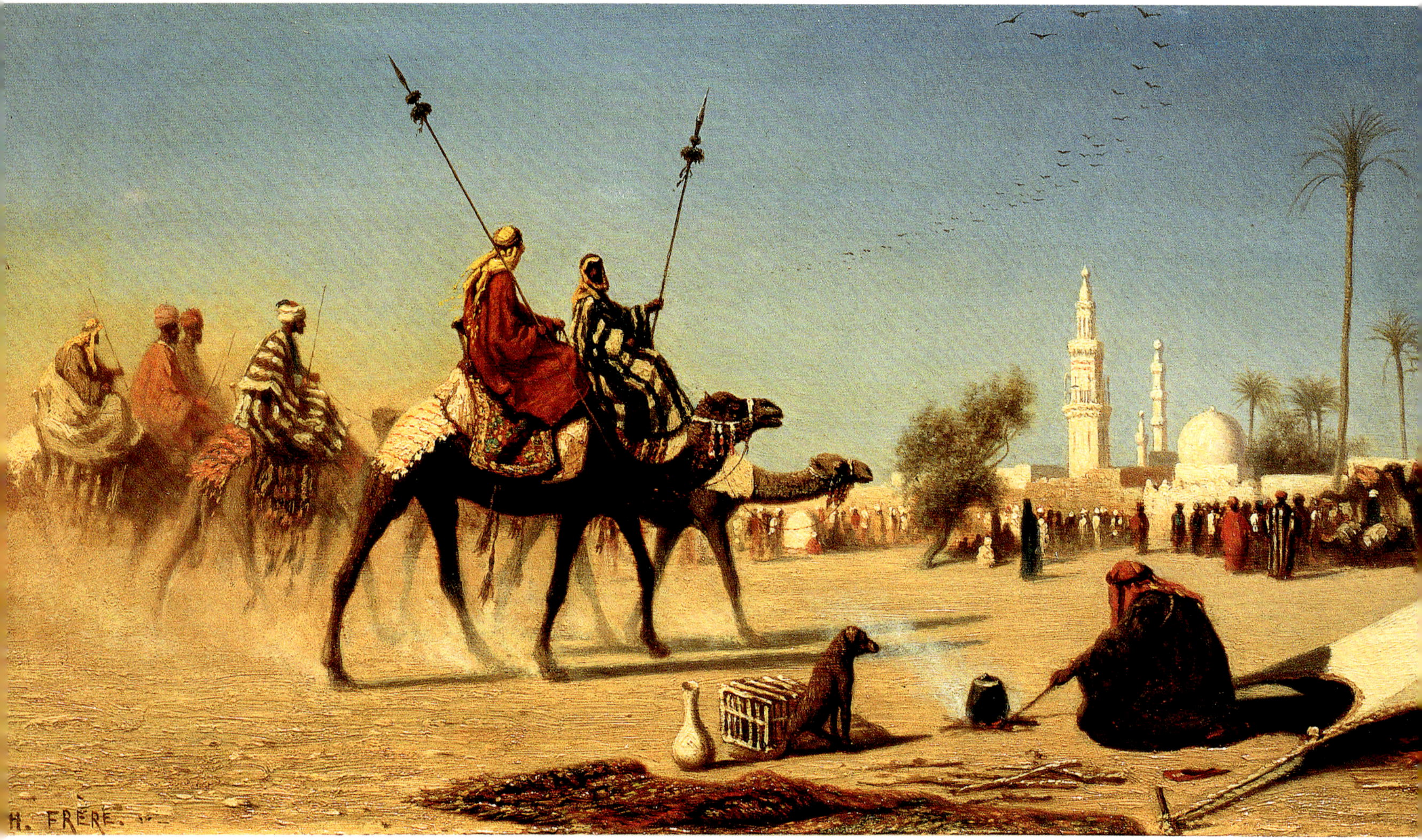

98. Charles-Théodore Frère, *Market Day, Assiout, Egypt* (date unknown). Oil on panel, 22.2 x 36.7 cm. Frère was one of the most admired and commercially successful artists of his day, but by the time of his death (1888) his style was coming under attack from groups such as the Impressionists.

bitterest blows of all came in 1890 from the pen of the art critic Albert Aurier. Writing about Vincent van Gogh, he lamented that the artist had not tried his hand at depicting the Orient: "Would not he—that intense, fantastic crusher of gold and precious stones—have been the worthy painter of these resplendent lands, with their dazzling suns and blinding colours? Rather than the Guillaumets, the dreary Fromentins, the muddy Gérômes?"[77]

Reputations Challenged

The impact of this artistic earthquake on individual Orientalist artists varied, but few were to emerge unscathed from its repercussions. Some of the older protagonists passed away before their world was overwhelmed, with their careers completed and reputations apparently secure. David Roberts died in 1864, much lauded and lamented, revered as a pioneer in the depiction of the Orient and with his laurels rooted in his magnum opus, *The Holy Land, Syria, Idumea, Arabia, Egypt & Nubia, 1842–1849.* His magnificent architectural and topographical views had stunned London and Edinburgh when first shown, yet Roberts created only a handful of new Oriental works after 1850. Instead, he consolidated his reputation through the production of bestselling paintings of Italy, Scotland, and London, and by landing commissions from Queen Victoria. By the 1890s volumes of the *Holy Land* were changing hands for only a few pounds apiece, a victim of changing tastes and a far cry from the price and admiration they had commanded nearly half a century before.

The enigmatic John Frederick Lewis died in 1876 in equal esteem to that accorded to his friend Roberts twelve years earlier, and revered for the extraordinarily detailed paintings which he had continued to create for nearly a quarter of a century after his return from Cairo. Lewis did not always get an easy ride from the critics, however. He was censured by some for producing copies that were perceived to fall short of the composition and quality of his originals, as with an 1863 oil version of his rapturously received watercolor of seven years earlier, *A Frank Encampment* (Figure 41).[78] A decade later, and toward the end of his career, *The Reception* (1873) attracted much acclaim but also some adverse comment over its "wooden damsels."[79] However, Lewis's star sparkled long enough to confirm his credentials as one of the best-regarded British artists of his day, his paintings later garnering the admiration of some adherents of the Aesthetic movement that gained ground toward the end of the century. In 1896 the critic F.G. Stephens said—approvingly—of Lewis's *Lilium Auratum* (1871), "it illustrates no story and is possessed of no passion; its subject is the beauty and brilliance of nature set forth by means of exquisite execution."[80] Such praise may not have met entirely with Lewis's approval, but it confirmed a degree of perhaps unexpected longevity twenty years after his death.

The younger generation of Orientalists had an even rockier ride. In the case of Weeks and Bridgman, they and their works were to pass into shadows from which they were not to emerge until several decades later. Weeks died in 1903 at the age of fifty-four, probably from a disease contracted when traveling in India. He left 277 paintings in his estate to his wife, Frances Hale Weeks, who two years later sold the entire contents of his Paris studio, including almost all of his paintings and collection of Oriental objects. She gifted one painting to the Metropolitan Museum of Art, but her late

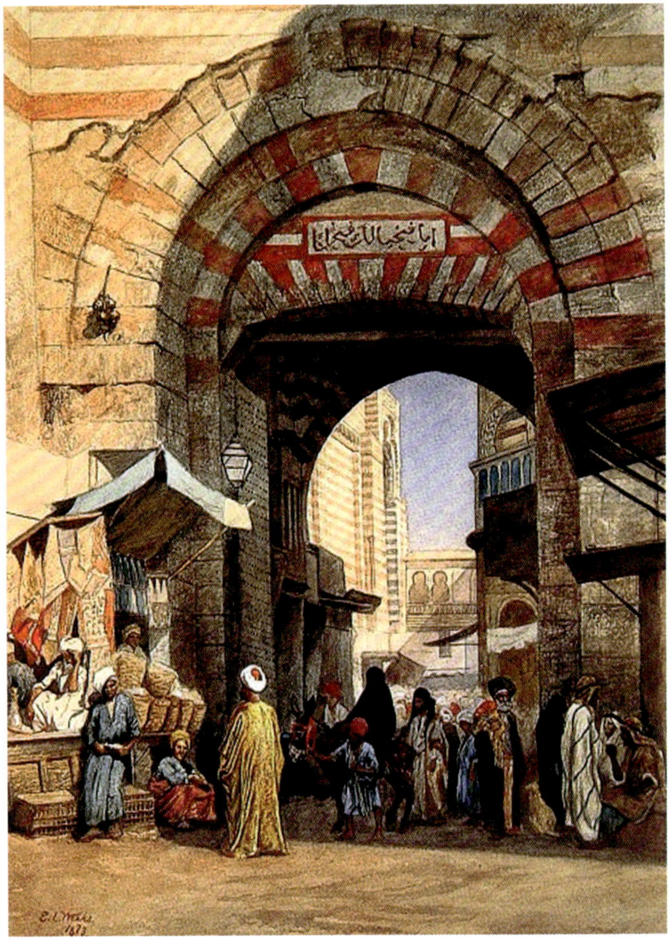

99. Edwin Lord Weeks, *The Moorish Bazaar* (1873). Watercolor, 63.5 x 43.7 cm. Hugely successful in his day, like many of the Orientalists Weeks lapsed into virtual obscurity in the years after his death. Works such as this disappeared from view and have only reemerged in the last three decades or so.

husband's other works were acquired by private collectors and largely disappeared from view. Apart from an exhibition featuring some of his paintings at the National Gallery of Art in Washington DC in 1926, Weeks was effectively forgotten about until fifty years later, when an exhibition of his works was held at the University of New Hampshire. The authors of the catalogue noted then how "our research turned up not one word written about [Weeks] or his work since the 1920's."[81] Remarkably, at the time of writing there is still no catalogue raisonné or monograph on Weeks, or indeed on many of the other leading Orientalists.

Weeks did at least die with his reputation still intact, his last painting (which was unfinished) being exhibited posthumously at the Salon of 1904. Bridgman's star was, however, already well on the wane by the time of his death in 1928. At his peak he had held one-man shows in New York City and Chicago that featured up to four hundred paintings and had customers queuing out of the door, evidence of his stature as one of only a handful of Orientalist artists who were able to command such attention and prestige. His first wife, Florence Mott Baker, was a wealthy heiress and for much of his working life Bridgman did not need to sell his works in order to live very well. Yet an unhealthy interest in gambling, the death of Florence in 1901, and plunging sales as Orientalist subjects became increasingly unfashionable all combined to drive him into severe financial difficulties. Forced to sell his Paris residence, he relocated to Normandy, a far cry from the glamorous metropolitan life he had enjoyed for so long, and where his death at the age of eighty "was not a matter of great notice to the general public."[82]

Frederick Goodall found himself in similarly ignominious circumstances in the last few years of his life. Once one of the highest earning of all Orientalist artists (see page 214), by the late 1890s he had fallen on decidedly hard times. Not only did his works no longer command the appeal and prices they once did but the critics also increasingly had him in their sights. His obsession with biblical subjects and with churning out the same compositions led one exasperated reviewer to refer to them as "the stories Mr Goodall has, we trust, finally abandoned," while the Egyptian-themed paintings he submitted for the 1896 Academy Exhibition were derided by at least one commentator as being unoriginal, little different from those he had been showing for all those years previously, and "nothing more than new arrangements of [his] one set of props."[83] It was a far cry from the halcyon days of the 1860s.

During 1899–1902 Goodall's annual income amounted to little more than £1,000, a tenth of what it had been three decades earlier and insufficient to cover his yearly household expenses of £2,000. He was declared bankrupt in 1902 and, by now in ill health, forced to sell his lavish London residence and downsize to more modest accommodation, although only after a "pathetic auction sale"[84] of his paintings and household effects. He died two years later, before he was able to check the proofs of what he had hoped would be his salvation from financial disaster and a flagging reputation: his *Reminiscences*. In the event, the book, which appeared shortly after his death, caused barely a ripple of interest. Even Goodall's final artistic triumph, the purchase by public subscription of his 1897 Egyptian-themed painting *The Ploughman and the Shepherdess* and its subsequent presentation to the Tate, was described witheringly in one obituary as "really a gift to a deserving artist who had outlived his popularity."[85]

Goodall's contemporary, William Holman Hunt, fared rather better. His role as a founder and leading member of the Pre-Raphaelite Brotherhood helped ensure a sustained public profile and he remained one of the bestselling living British artists until his death in 1910. His 1905 two-volume memoirs—*Pre-Raphaelitism and the Pre-Raphaelite Brotherhood*—not only allowed him to set out his stall as the definitive historian of the brotherhood but also contained much about his travels in the Holy Land, rekindling interest in the travels of an artist whose Orientalist dimension was often obscured by other elements of his oeuvre. Interestingly, the abrasive and bigoted bravado of the younger Hunt when swashbuckling his way around Egypt and Palestine appears to have mellowed in later years. Not only did he rescind his earlier opposition to Westerners donning Oriental dress (see page 68) but he also embraced a more accommodating attitude to Islam. When working on his third version of *The Light of the World* c.1900 he chose to add a crescent moon—the symbol of Islam—to the lantern held by Christ, something that would have been unthinkable twenty years earlier.[86]

Meanwhile, Hunt's popularity with the public continued with a series of successful retrospectives in London and other British cities during 1906–1907. Even so, he was not immune to the cold wind of opprobrium, with one critic remarking of his paintings, "We are bidden to admire them because the making of them has been so laborious and because of their moral beauty, although beauty itself, the great essential, evaded him in his pursuit of unnecessary fact and irrelevant detail."[87] This slight bears a close resemblance to that passed on a Lewis painting a few years earlier (see above), and the perceived slavish adherence to authenticity and the academic tradition was, after all, what had led to the Orientalists as a group falling out of favor. Yet Hunt's career was largely unaffected. His creative and emotional horizons extended considerably further than the Orient and helped ensure that he neither depended on the fortunes of the Orientalists nor could ever be accused of belonging to the "old school."

Emerging Faultlines

In France, even the mighty Jean-Léon Gérôme eventually found himself eclipsed by events. The Orientalist icon Eugène Delacroix had died in 1863, showered in plaudits, with his artistically and financially successful peers Fromentin, Frère, Guillaumet, and Boulanger following during the 1870s and 1880s. These last four lived to witness the growing criticism of Orientalism by figures such as Antoine Castagnary, but remained nonetheless popular with the buying public and held in high official esteem. Gérôme meanwhile proved to be rather longer-lived and also to become personally embroiled in an increasingly acrimonious debate over Impressionism and the direction of art in France. A vehement opponent of the Impressionist movement, avant-garde painters, and Modernism generally, he staged a public protest against Édouard Manet's posthumous retrospective in 1883 and in 1894 organized a petition to the French Senate opposing the acceptance by the French government of Gustave Caillebotte's collection of Impressionist paintings for the Louvre, denouncing the works as "junk" and "a collection of inanities."[88] Such bitter and obsessive behavior was understandably viewed as little short of a public scandal and served to underline how reactionary and anachronistic Gérôme—and, by unfair implication, the Orientalists generally—had become. Gérôme died aged eighty in 1904, having outlived his popularity and compromised his own reputation.

100. Johann (Jean) Discart, *L'Atelier de Poterie, Tanger* (date unknown). Oil on panel, 35 x 45.5 cm. Italian-born Discart traveled to Paris with Ludwig Deutsch from Austria after the two had been denied permission to study under Leopold Carl Müller. Like Deutsch, he settled in the French capital but the precise details of his career are unclear. This work probably dates from the 1920s, by which time Discart's precise, documentary style was already out of fashion.

Meanwhile, some of the other Paris-based Orientalists continued plying their trade as if nothing had changed. The Austrian cabal of artists such as Johann Discart, Arthur von Ferraris, Rudolf Ernst, and Rudolf Weiss carried on producing their trademark portrayals of palace guards, bazaar craftsmen, and cameo street scenes, for which there was still a willing market—even if by the 1890s the style was regarded as hackneyed and predictable. Their painstaking studio-based craftsmanship continued to command respect. However, in the case of Ludwig Deutsch there was an impending revision in style that must have been inspired or at least prompted by the wider changes he saw taking place around him. Deutsch had won a gold medal at the Universal Exhibition in Paris in 1900 for one of his classic detailed compositions, but a decade later his style had transformed in favor of a Post-Impressionist approach, with looser brushstrokes and a much freer application. He was also tackling new subject

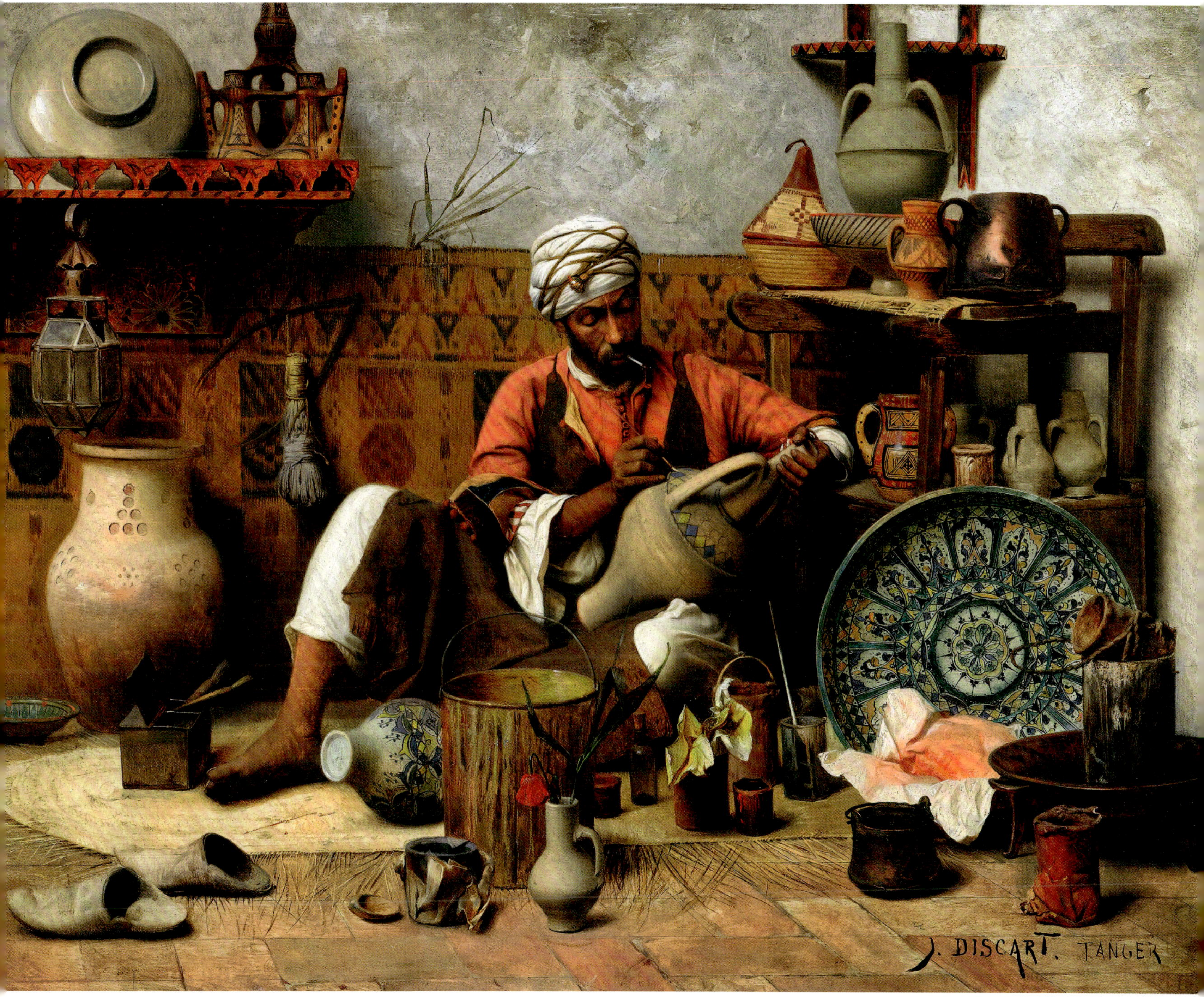
J. DISCART. TANGER

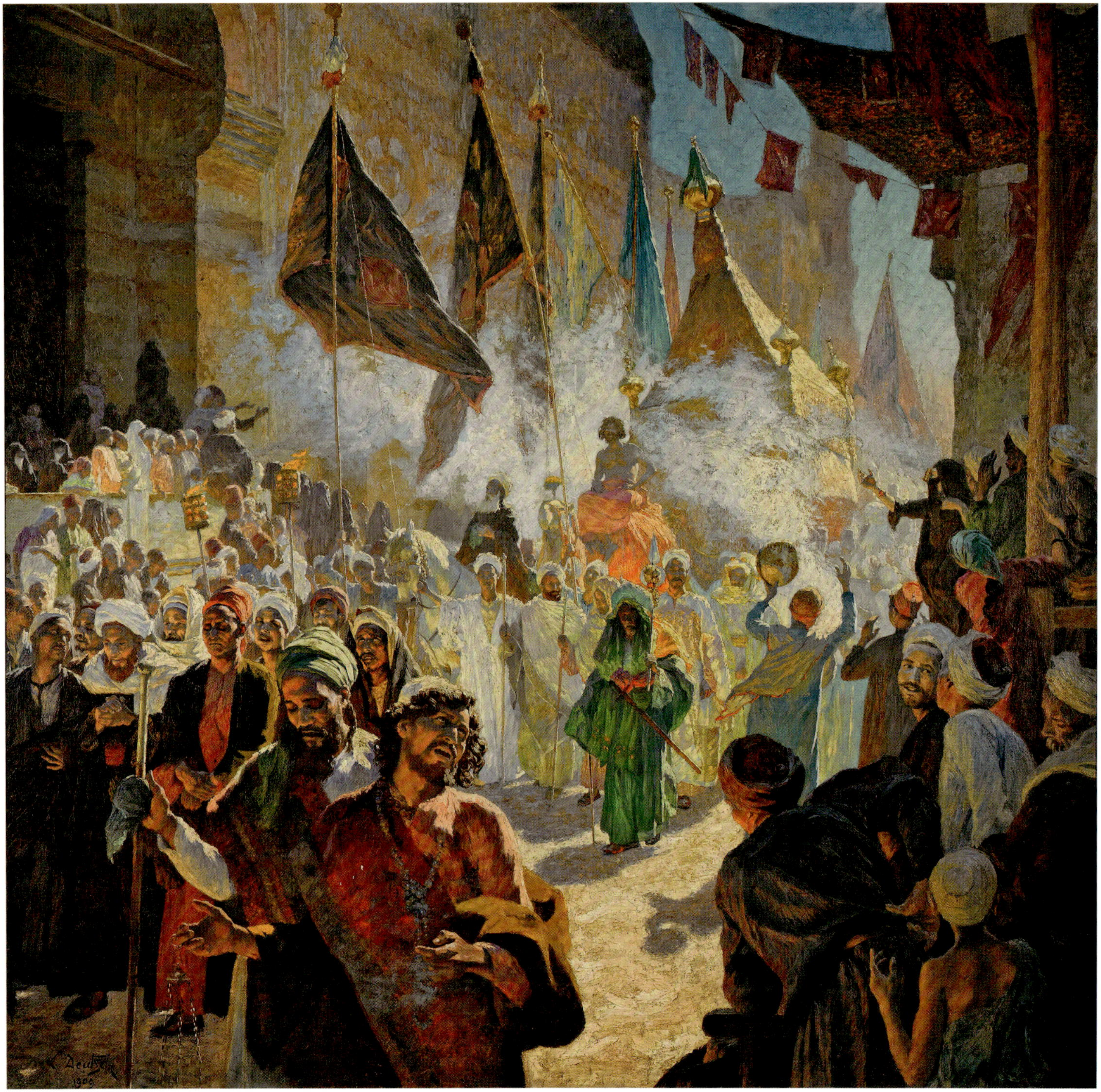

matter at this time, focusing his attention, for example, on scenes of everyday life along the Nile. However, for his most dazzling work in the new technique he returned to Cairo for a portrayal of the *mahmal*, captured in the most exuberant and expansive fashion by Deutsch as it processed through the city.* It was as bold a statement as any that Orientalism was far from finished.

Deutsch's dramatic foray into new territory also defied the prevailing view that as a group the Orientalists were incapable or unwilling to evolve. Artists such as Étienne Dinet were also demonstrating a shift away from stilted genre scenes in favor of "stills of life," photographic-style visual snapshots that showed movement and vitality in a way that earlier generations of Orientalists had either struggled to achieve or considered less important. Meanwhile, the watercolorist Arthur Melville (1855–1904)—who had trained in France and has often been dubbed "the Scottish Impressionist"—presented his views of Egypt (where he spent two years), Tangier, and Constantinople in a loose and often idiosyncratic manner that signaled how Orientalist subject matter and more contemporary forms of interpretation and practice were by no means mutually exclusive.

Yet none of this was enough to stem the tide. Tastes had changed, but so too had definitions. Even the meaning of the word "Orient" was under revision, as attention—political, economic, and cultural—looked ever further east and toward Japan in particular. The opening of that country to the West during the second half of the nineteenth century was to affect some of the leading artists of the day, with Manet, Monet, Van Gogh, and Rodin all enthusiastic about the core principles of Japanese art and how these might inform their own artistic outlook.** Such attention meant renewed interest in a sense of the exotic, although with a few exceptions, such as Paul Klee (1879–1940) and Wassily Kandinsky (1866–1944) (see page 241), it was not to the Middle East that artists turned but to the Far East and—as notably with Paul Gauguin—even further afield. The Orient of the Orientalists, of noble ruins, palace guards, bazaar scenes, and skirmishes in the desert, seemed to have lost its center of gravity.

In May 1906 Henri Matisse (1869–1954) arrived in Algeria on his first trip to North Africa. He was not immediately impressed, declaring Algiers to be "even more repellent than Paris" and taking a dim view of the country's cultural offerings: "As for the belly-dancing side of things . . . it was only quite by chance that I saw a quarter of an hour of it in Biskra. And as for the famous Ouled Naïl, who are they kidding? It was ten times better at the Exhibition."[89] It was not an auspicious introduction to the Orient, yet the influence of North Africa on Matisse proved to be profound. He was inspired by an avid interest in Islamic art to use aspects of Islamic

101. Ludwig Deutsch, *The Procession of the Mahmal through the Streets of Cairo* (1909). Oil on canvas, 284 x 294 cm. Impressionistic in style, this painting marked a departure for Deutsch from the painstakingly accurate detail of his earlier works.

* See page 159 for more information on the *mahmal*.

** There is little evidence of the Orientalists physically extending their horizons as far as Japan. The chief exception was Frank Dillon, who traveled there in 1875 and spent a year in Osaka with his son. He was one of the first Western artists to visit the country and retained a lifelong affection for it.

decorative motifs and geometry in his work. Especially fascinated by Oriental rugs and the ways in which vibrant colors were used mosaic-like to create surfaces rather than simply cover them, he sought to apply this approach to his own paintings. It was an aspect of the old Orient that the traditional Orientalists had valued as context, but had been unable to take further.

Visits to Andalusia in 1910 and to Morocco in 1912 and 1913 confirmed Matisse in his conviction that the Orient offered a "new depth of sensation" and proclaimed the validity of North Africa in particular as a source of contemporary artistic influence. A new traffic of ideas began to flow, via Matisse, in which principles derived from traditional Oriental art and architecture began to infiltrate modern Western art. The Orient was heading north again. This latest chapter in the history of artistic exchange between North and South, East and West, did however mark the close of the Orientalism that had held the West in thrall fifty years earlier. Deutsch's flurry of Post-Impressionism at about the same time as Matisse was reveling in the Maghreb did not prevent him dying in relative obscurity in 1935, a decade that saw the passing also of several of the last great names in the nineteenth-century Orientalist cadre. It was nearly another half a century before their paintings were brought out of basements, dusted off, and marveled at afresh.

Epilogue

In April 2013 a Ludwig Deutsch masterpiece, *The Offering*, was brought to auction by Sotheby's in London (Figure 102). Painted in 1897, it was the first time in over a century that the painting had been put up for sale. Bought from an Edinburgh dealer in 1900, it had resided in a private collection ever since, during which time it appears never to have been exhibited. A classic Deutsch composition, it depicts a delegation of lavishly appareled men bearing tributes and approaching a ceremonial portal guarded by a Nubian sentinel. The painstakingly precise portrayal of the clothing, artifacts, and figures all exemplify the strengths of Deutsch as an unerringly accurate recorder of his version of the Orient. An additional dimension is provided by the theatrical architectural context, features of which can be attributed to Cairo's Sultan Hassan Mosque, a fourteenth-century building that Deutsch almost certainly knew personally from his visits to Egypt and which had also been depicted by David Roberts and John Frederick Lewis. With so many keynote elements of Deutsch's oeuvre in place, it was clear that this was one of his most important works. Yet few of those watching the sale were prepared for the conclusion of the bidding, which saw the hammer coming down at £1.85 million—a new world record for the artist.

It was a remarkable outcome for a painting that had sat quietly unnoticed by the art world for 113 years. Yet its dramatic changes in fortune are symbolic of the rollercoaster ride that Orientalism has undergone since its heyday during the mid- to late nineteenth century. The opening years of the 1900s confirmed the style's waning popularity with collectors and the public alike, with little prospect of relief on the horizon as Europe lurched toward war in 1914. With travel routes disrupted, populations displaced, and once friendly nations locked in conflict, the specifically international dimension of Orientalism seemed even more anachronistic and outmoded. The rearrangement of the political landscape following the 1919 Treaty of Versailles and the ensuing demise and dismantling of the Ottoman Empire helped confirm that many of the old Oriental certainties were shattered beyond repair.

A new world order emerged, one still governed by colonialism but in which the Western artistic love affair with

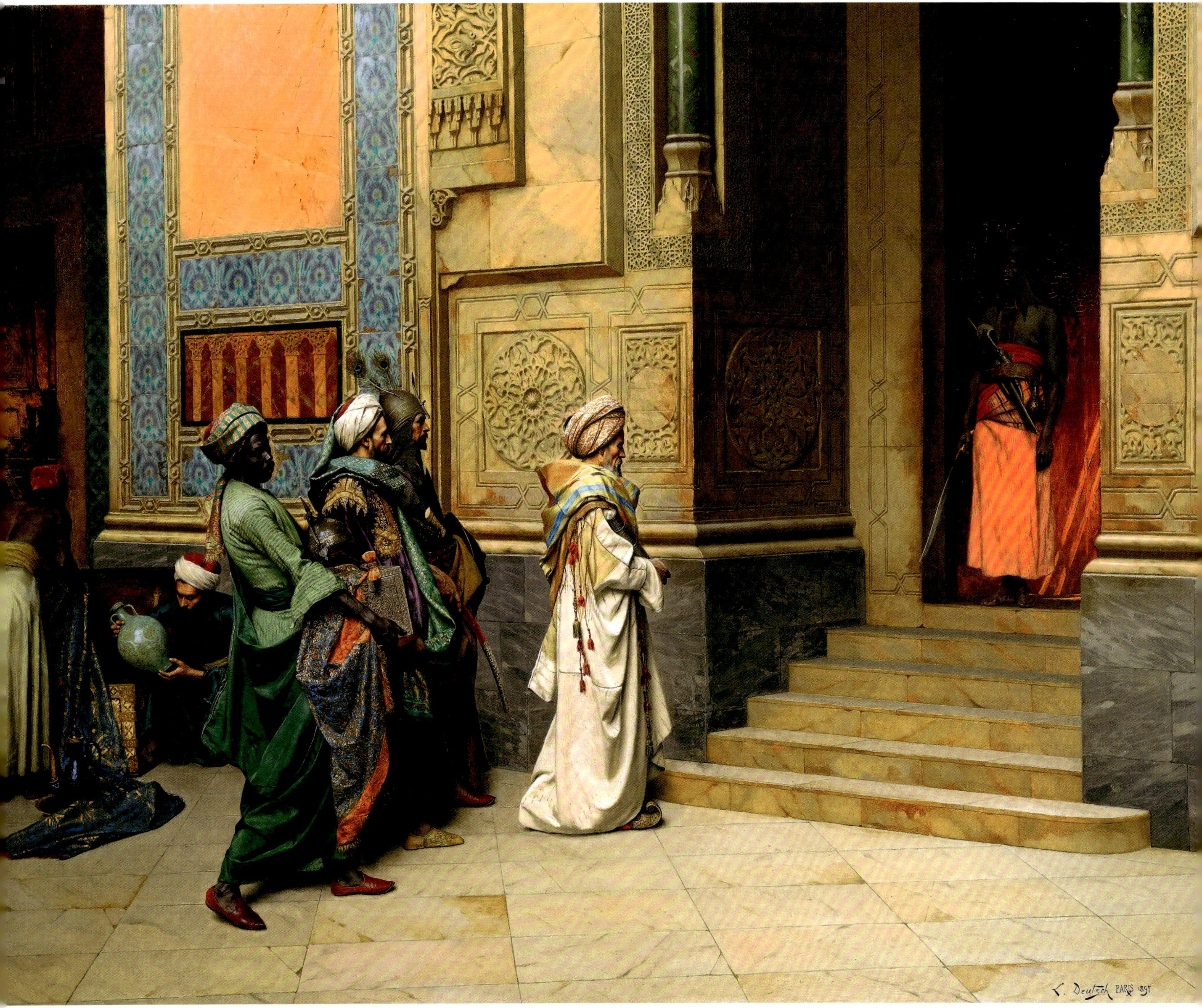
L. Deutsch PARIS 1897

the Orient showed signs of lapsing. The sense of change was confirmed by the economic disorder and instability of the 1920s and 1930s, characterized by financial crises and political strife both at home and abroad, not least in the colonial possessions and post-Versailles mandates in what was now usually referred to as the Near East. For the British in Palestine and the French in Syria, the post-1919 increase in the number of colonial administrators helped ensure that the new relationship was one shaped more overtly by politics than by considerations such as art and culture, with definitions changing accordingly. The "Orientalists" were now confirmed as (often Arabic-speaking) colonial administrators charged with enforcing imperial rule, rather than peripatetic artists wandering the landscape in search of subjects for their paintings.

Some have argued that Western artistic interest in the region remained as keen as ever during this period. "What had fallen from favour was not the Orient," observed one commentator, "it was the old manner of painting it."[1] Certainly, artists such as Kandinsky and Klee were drawn to the region, interpreting it through innovative works that reflected wider changes in artistic perception and practice and seemingly positioned the Orient as a catalyst for new directions in art.

Hugely influenced by the Persian miniatures he had seen in the Kaiser Friedrich Museum in Berlin and by a major exhibition of Islamic art held in Munich in 1903, Kandinsky traveled to Tunisia for the first time toward the end of the following year and stayed until April 1905. It was a visit that was to prove seminal in the careers of both him and his traveling companion, fellow artist and soulmate Gabriele Münter. For Kandinsky, their time in Tunisia inspired a shift away from figurative conventions toward abstraction based on the use of color to denote form.

102. Ludwig Deutsch, *The Offering* (1897). Oil on panel, 61.5 x 80 cm. Three years after painting this classic example of his trademark style, Deutsch received a gold medal at the *Exposition Universelle* in Paris, and later the *Chevalier de la Légion d'honneur*.

It was a theme that resonated also with Paul Klee, who visited Tunisia with fellow artists August Macke and Louis Moilliet in April 1914. For Klee, the intensity of the colors he encountered there helped forge new directions in his creativity. "Colour possesses me," he wrote in his diary. "It will possess me always, I know that now. . . . Colour and I are one."[2] Klee's Tunisian paintings reflect both this love of color sensations and his interest in Cubism, with works such as *Two Oriental Watercolours* (1914) (Figure 103) characterized by a grid-like structure and the juxtaposition of vibrant reds with subdued grays and purples. The precise documentary-style way in which artists such as Roberts, Gérôme, Deutsch, and Ernst had presented Islamic architecture—and its sense of fixed perspective—in their paintings was swept away by Klee's abstract portrayals of seemingly mobile crenellations, cupolas, and arches.

The realist materialism of Orientalist art half a century earlier was thereby replaced by an altogether more conceptual approach, one that was concerned not so much with the visual enactment of different aspects of the Orient but with the use of the region's elemental qualities as a catalyst for the creation of a form of art that was repositioned beyond that of pure representation. The Orient was no longer an artistic end in itself but a vehicle for the attainment of more conceptual expression, to the extent that the art associated

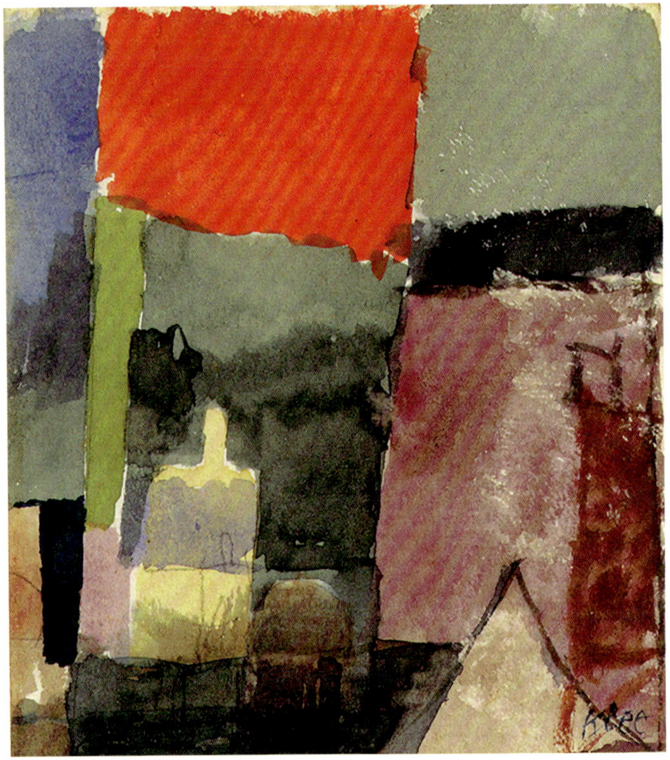

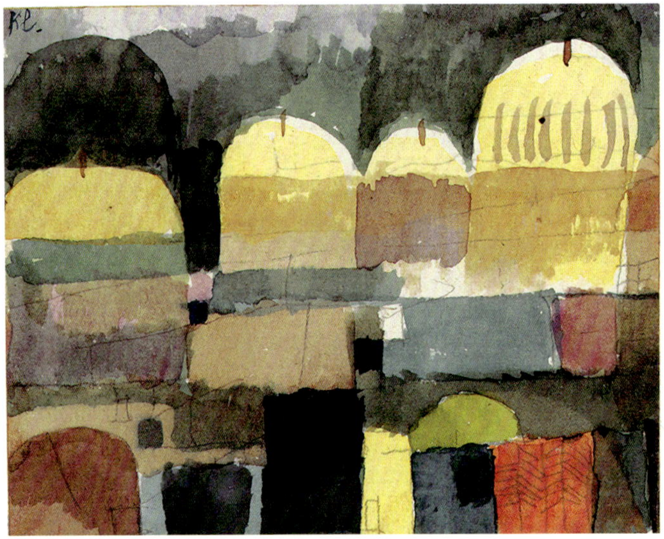

103. Paul Klee, *Two Oriental Watercolours* (1914). Watercolor, 8 x 7.3 cm and 7 x 8.7 cm. Klee was deeply inspired by his 1914 visit to Tunisia, writing how he had left the country "so full it keeps bubbling out."

with it was arguably no longer specific or discrete enough to qualify as "Orientalist." The centuries-old link between artists and their audiences—in terms of the latter receiving from the former direct information on the appearance of the landscapes, architecture, people, and customs of the Orient—had become increasingly incoherent.

Regardless of whether or not artists in the first decades of the twentieth century still found the Orient an appealing subject, attitudes and tastes were changing dramatically around them. The art-collecting business tycoons and wealthy artistic elite that had sustained the Orientalist market during the second half of the nineteenth century had been lured elsewhere, their attention no longer sustained by opulent images of harems, bazaars, and Bedouin encampments. Instead, it was the budding generation of advertising executives and future media moguls who alighted on the Orient. They saw it as an exotic marketing device through which they could reach new audiences and sell their products. In this way the Orient remained a commercial proposition for the West, much as it had been for artists decades earlier, except that now it was being pitched at the mass consumer market rather than the artistic elite.

The marketing of two bestselling commodities epitomized this shift. First, the launch in 1913 by the R.J. Reynolds Tobacco Company of Camel cigarettes, with what was to become an iconic packet design featuring a dromedary against a backdrop of date palms and the Pyramids. It was to prove a powerful and enduring image and one that by the time of the brand's centenary in 2013 had helped propel it to sales of over four trillion cigarettes. The value of the exotic Orient as a marketing device was also picked up on by Palmolive, which by 1900 was already the world's bestselling soap. An advert in a 1918 edition of the popular American magazine *Ladies' Home Journal* extolled the virtues of (a somewhat demoted) Cleopatra as a purveyor of beauty tips: "Just as the Egyptian Princess of 3000 years ago bequeathed a heritage of beauty to the modern girl, so did she also hand down knowledge of the surest way to keep it. She knew that Palm and Olive oils were mild, beneficial, natural cleansers, as soothing in their action as a lotion. A crude combination is all she could command—today she would use Palmolive."

The new position of the Orient as a factor in popular consumer culture rather than art was confirmed by the runaway success of the 1921 silent film *The Sheik*. Starring Rudolph Valentino as the eponymous hero, the film (based on a book of the same name) tells the story of an English aristocrat who sets off into the desert accompanied only by her Arab guides. The starting point of her expedition was ironically the real-life Algerian town of Biskra, once the haunt of Orientalists such as Bridgman, Dinet, Fromentin, and Guillaumet. In a contemporary twist on the hackneyed Western fantasy of the Orient, the film's heroine is variously kidnapped by the local sheikh, tries to escape several times, is rescued from bandits, and eventually declares her love for her kidnapper, who is revealed to be a European brought up by Arabs. The storyline, however muddled and incredible, can be read as a curious but telling parody of the West's enduring preoccupation with the East.

So it was that the Orient remained in Western eyes, not through glittering masterpieces on the walls of the major museums or in the private galleries and apartments of the

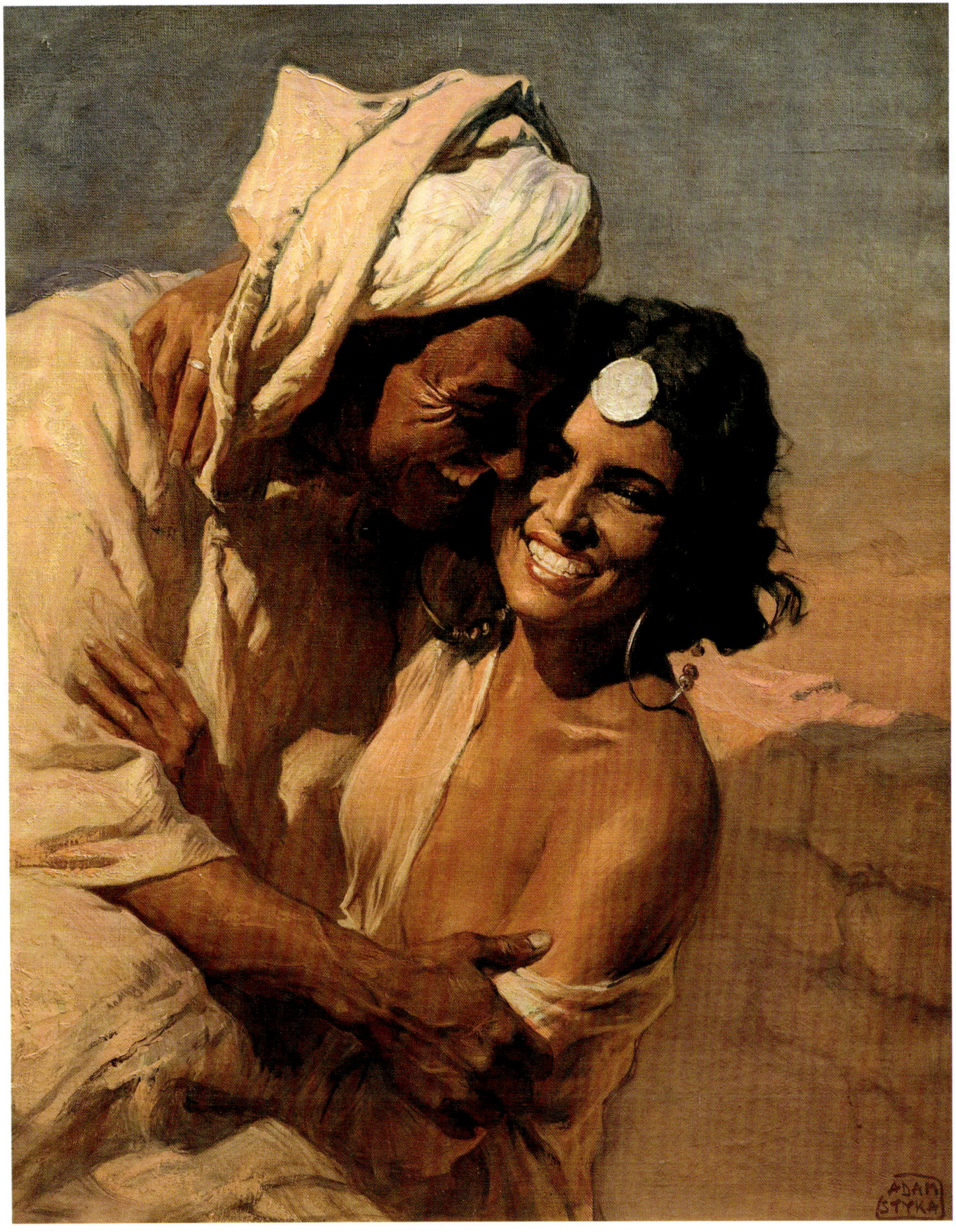
ADAM
STYKA

good and the great in Baltimore, Manchester, or Nice but through soap advertisements in ladies' magazines and a blatantly commercial film playing to packed picture houses across Europe and North America. Gone were the days when the paintings of the Orientalists provided Western audiences with their only visual images of the East, the works of Deutsch, Ernst, Gérôme, and others serving as precursors to the newsreels and films of the 1920s onward.

The next half-century were the wilderness years for Orientalist art, its style and content having fallen from grace and with the Orient itself reduced largely to a marketing and entertainment vehicle, at least as far as Western audiences were concerned. Paintings by even the best-regarded artists failed to reach their reserves in the salerooms and Orientalist works in public collections were relegated to basements and storerooms (as happened with many of Gérôme's works in France, for example). This decline in the value and status accorded to Orientalist art was mirrored by increasingly unfavorable academic analysis of Orientalism as a concept, a critique exemplified by Edward Said's 1978 book, *Orientalism.*

While Said did not specifically mention Orientalist art in his attack on the scholarly field of Oriental studies, others were happy to extrapolate his arguments more broadly and do the job for him. Orientalist paintings were branded accordingly as crass reflections of the Eurocentric prejudice against which Said had railed, vulgar emblems of Western arrogance toward the Arab and Islamic worlds, and no more than the tawdry flags of an unremitting imperialist agenda. En route, the quality (or not) of the art itself was lost sight of and, in most cases, its creators simply dismissed as colonial stooges bent on exploitation and oppression.

Then as now, the evidence in support of such a contention is less than compelling. Renewed appreciation of leading Orientalist artists such as Gérôme, Deutsch, and Ernst was already underway by the time that Said launched his critique. Foremost among the handful of galleries who were effectively challenging the prevailing ethos of the time was the Mathaf Gallery, established in London by Brian MacDermot in 1975—three years before publication of Said's *Orientalism.* The gallery soon became a leading hub for the initially very modest group of collectors and scholars interested in Orientalist works and, as a result of the efforts of MacDermot and others, the market began to change as greater levels of interest in the quality and content of these paintings were reflected in rapidly increasing prices. The Mathaf Gallery in particular played a key role in the development of interest in Orientalist art among collectors based within the Middle East.

Signs of a more measured assessment, if not quite yet a turning tide, appeared a few years after the publication of Said's tome with exhibitions of Orientalist paintings at the Fine Art Society in London. These were followed in 1984 by a landmark exhibition at the Royal Academy. *The Orientalists: Delacroix to Matisse* brought many Orientalist showpieces back into public view for the first time in decades, including works from American collections that had not been seen in Europe since their creation and dispatch to the other side of

104. Adam Styka, *Secrets* (date unknown). Oil on canvas, 81.4 x 64.7 cm. Polish-born Styka (1890–1959) studied in Paris and traveled regularly to North Africa. Love and romance featured prominently in his works, which are reminiscent of contemporary cinematic film posters in their style and content.

the Atlantic over a century earlier. The following year saw the acquisition by the Victoria and Albert Museum of the Rodney Searight Collection of watercolors, prints, drawings, and books about the Middle East. Although Searight maintained that his "was not an orientalist collection,"[3] the two thousand-plus works he amassed served to illustrate the various chapters in the development of Western artistic engagement with the region. Searight spent over three decades living and working in the Middle East and the significance of his collection—the foundation of which had been a David Roberts watercolor view of Cairo, bought in 1960—had become increasingly valued following his first exhibition at London's Leighton House in 1969.

More broadly, the last quarter of the twentieth century saw a political revisionism that prompted—in some quarters, at least—a reassessment of colonial relationships and specifically the nature of the artistic and cultural expressions that underpinned colonialism. These included, notably in North Africa, the establishment of arts institutions and cultural infrastructure which have stood the test of time and remain valued by local people. While this reevaluation did not always leave Orientalism in the best of lights, it did at least encourage renewed debate about cultural identity, a subject on which Orientalist art has much to say.

Most importantly, the artists themselves started to reemerge. Increased research into the lives and works of some of the leading Orientalists began to reveal figures who were not so much cultural apparatchiks acting at the premeditated behest of their authoritarian governments but insightful free spirits who reveled in their travels, made the most of the opportunities that came their way, and enjoyed being ambassadors for the Orient once back in their home countries. It is difficult to see a figure such as David Roberts as anything other than a professional artist seeking to make his living, but—his artistic ambition aside—he clearly relished what he saw and experienced as he traveled through Egypt and the Levant, and was later able to speak coherently, convincingly, and with understanding about what he had found there.

As the accounts, diaries, and letters of other artists featured in this book reveal, their responses to the Orient were similarly finessed. It is always easy to find negative off-the-cuff responses from foreign travelers when on the road in testing and unfamiliar surroundings. More difficult has been tracing their more profound responses to what they encountered, and identifying how and where artists were able to achieve something greater than a superficial connection with people and place. Nineteenth-century Orientalist artists were as much the products of their time as any of us, and there is little point in retrospectively attributing agendas and motivations to them for which there is no historical evidence. Much more valid and useful is an assessment of what they actually said and did, and how their experiences abroad—both individually and collectively—helped change their view of society, whether Oriental or their own.

There is a demonstrable warmth, humor, and humanity in the writing of artists such as Frederick Arthur Bridgman, Elisabeth Jerichau-Baumann, and Thomas Seddon, for example. Their comments and conclusions on subjects such as the role of women, attitudes to people of different religions, and cross-cultural language differences fly in the face of many prejudices, both contemporary and more latter-day, and stand out as a vindication of the mind-broadening benefits of travel generally and as one of the most positive milestones along the Orientalist road specifically. Individual artists' levels of engagement with the Orient and its people and cultures varied greatly and there was always going to be an element of cultural distance between visitor and visited, not least because even those artists who traveled extensively did so with the accumulated baggage of their backgrounds. Nonetheless, there is ample evidence of a genuine willingness on the part of many to try and "know" their subject, ranging from attempts to master Arabic and forge friendships with local guides to, on a more esoteric level, cultural cross-dressing and embedded self-portraiture. Gestures, perhaps, but also evidence of a desire to learn more and appreciate better.

Most of the artists who visited the Orient were deeply inspired and affected by what they found there. For many it was a life-changing experience, both professionally and personally, and they returned home full of inspirational memories, mental snapshots, and, in many instances, laden with the physical accoutrements of their travels and sojourns abroad. The fact that some went so far as to recreate the East in the West, decorating their studios and homes in Oriental style, is evidence of their sense of attachment to, pride in, and affection for a part of the world that had played such a defining role in their careers and lives.

What, though, do the Orientalists have to say to us today? Resurrected and revalued over the last three decades, they now stand proud again, the subject of increased commercial and academic interest and with paintings by the likes of Bridgman, Gérôme, and Lewis—members of the high command of the Orientalist canon—achieving stratospherically high prices. They have been joined by others, such as Bauernfeind and Deutsch who never achieved such acclaim in their lifetimes but whose paintings are now as eagerly sought after. Year for year, the prices currently reached by Orientalist works are often (in today's terms) in excess of those commanded when the paintings were created during the Orientalist frenzy of the mid- to late nineteenth century—a remarkable turnaround from the doldrums of a few decades ago. International collector interest is more intense than ever, with particularly keen attention coming from the oil-rich states of the Arabian Peninsula, where private collectors have vied with government buyers eager to fill the gallery spaces of the region's rapidly proliferating network of museums.

Much has changed, therefore, in the post-Saidian world. Far from being viewed generically as a colonial expression that belittles or caricatures Arab culture, individual Orientalist works are now respected and in demand across the Gulf and elsewhere as an important element in the region's heritage and history. Not only can they fulfill an important documentary value as records of cultural traditions now lost, of buildings long since demolished, and of landscapes transformed out of recognition by the white heat of modernization but they can also serve as symbols of connection and reciprocity rather than cultural imperialism—an approach that has turned much of the agenda-laden rhetoric of the 1970s and early 1980s on its head. In a time of such profound reflection and reappraisal, it is appropriate that it is *A Young Emir Studying*, a 1905 painting by the Turkish Orientalist Osman Hamdi, which has become one of the publicity icons of the Louvre Abu Dhabi.

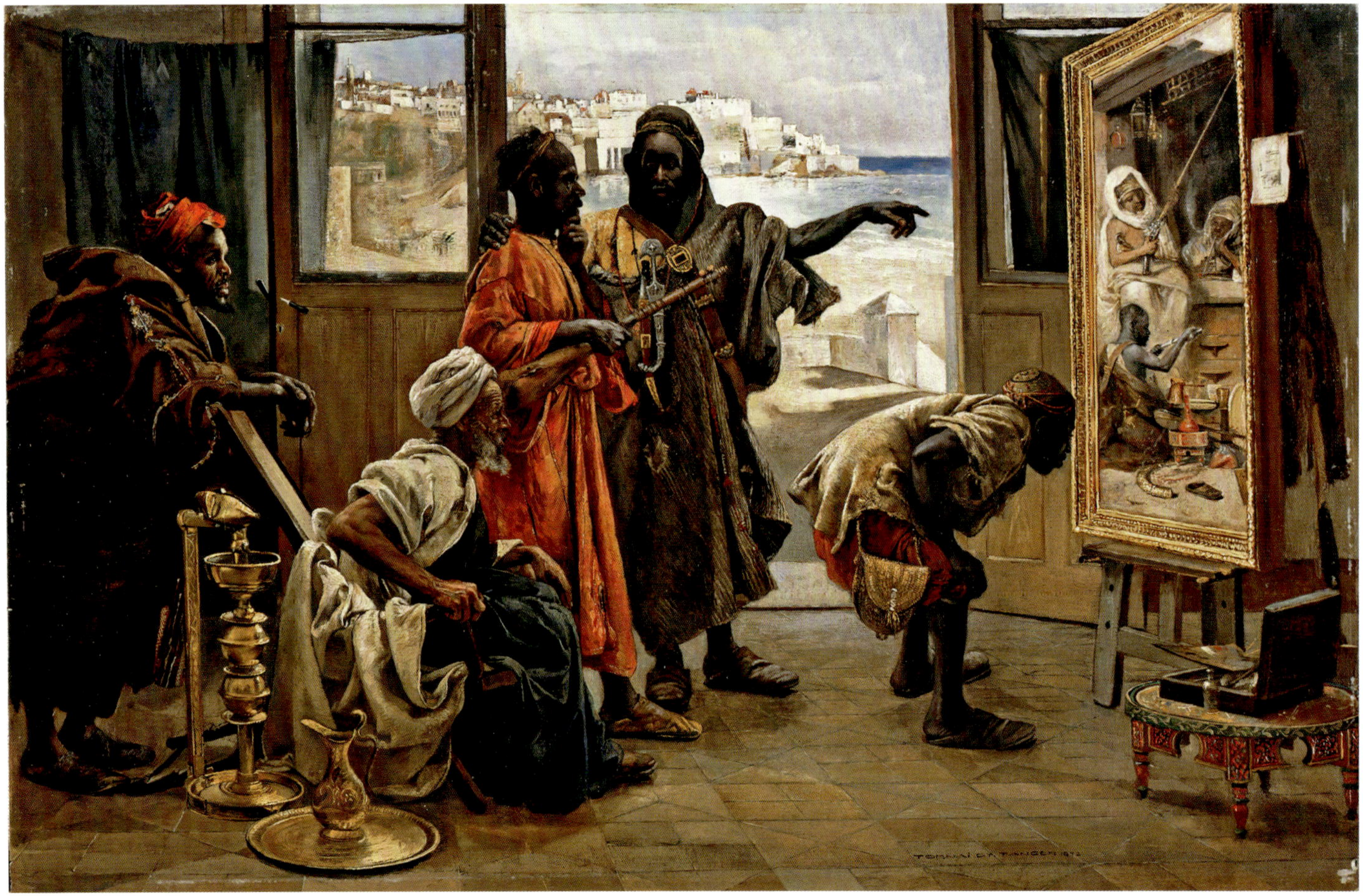

105. Gyula Tornai, *The Connoisseurs* (1892). Oil on panel, 45.7 x 71.1 cm. Tornai (1861–1928) was born in Hungary, studied in Vienna, and moved to Tangier during the winter of 1890–91. This work exemplifies the humor and irony he wove into his work, with a group of seemingly perplexed and bemused Arabs contemplating an Orientalist painting.

More broadly, one of the great strengths and successes of Orientalism was the way in which it cut across different artistic media and was expressed equally distinctly in art, architecture, music, and design. In an age characterized by globalism and the increased movement of peoples, cultures, and ideas, these principles continue to hold good, above all in their affirmation that cultural interaction and exchange are intrinsically productive and beneficial, both on an individual level and for society as a whole. This idea of geographical dialogue has taken on a significant new dimension with the enormous growth over the last decade in the market for contemporary Middle Eastern art, a phenomenon that has mirrored—perhaps not entirely coincidentally—the revival of interest in the Orientalist masters. Middle Eastern artists, often educated and trained in Europe or North America, and working in a wide range of media, are now creating images of their "Orient." While it is a place characterized by very different concerns from those that preoccupied the Orientalists, it nonetheless constitutes the latest chapter in the dynamic and ongoing history of cultural traffic between East and West.

Meanwhile, our understanding of the Orientalists continues to improve and evolve, as we become more effective at identifying the connections between the individuals concerned and exploring the themes that variously unite, divide, and complement them. This book has sought to identify and explain what characterized them as a group and as individuals, exploring their motivations and responses to the Orient and highlighting their significance in the history of cultural dialogue between East and West and in explaining the Orient to a Western audience. Stripped of the heavy hand of politics and of an art historical analysis confounded by its addiction to jargon, the artists have been allowed to speak. Even so, some of them remain enigmatic and almost impenetrable figures, awaiting greater research or the discovery of hitherto undetected archival material. There will undoubtedly be further conclusions to draw and lessons to learn, but if the Orientalists teach us only one thing it must surely be that from dialogue and knowledge come understanding and appreciation. If great art also ensues, then we are all much the richer.

Appendix One

Biographies of the principal artists and photographers featured in the text and who produced Orientalist works.

WILLIAM ALLEN, BRITISH (1782–1850)
Born in Edinburgh, Scotland, Allen trained there before moving to London. From 1805 he spent several years in Russia, Ukraine, and the Crimea, developing a deep interest in the culture of the Circassians, Cossacks, and Tartars, subjects that were to feature prominently in his work. In 1829–30 he visited Turkey, which provided the inspiration for his melodramatic painting *The Slave Market, Constantinople* (1838).

WILLIAM HENRY BARTLETT, BRITISH (1809–54)
One of the pre-eminent travel illustrators of his day, London-born Bartlett traveled extensively in the Balkans and Middle East, as well as to North America. His collaboration with writer Julia Pardoe on *The Beauties of the Bosphorus* (1838) proved to be one of his most successful ventures.

GUSTAV BAUERNFEIND, GERMAN (1848–1904)
After training as an architect in his native Stuttgart, Bauernfeind concentrated on architectural and topographical studies designed for engraving before securing a commission from King Ludwig of Bavaria for a watercolor painting of the Bayreuth opera house. He subsequently traveled to the Middle East, where he began producing the large-scale works, often set at key sites in Palestine and Syria, which were to become his hallmark. He finally settled in Jerusalem, where he died in poverty.

LÉON BELLY, FRENCH (1827–77)
Contact with the Barbizon painters saw Belly, from St. Omer in northern France, influenced by the works of Millet, Corot, and Rousseau. He made three trips to the Middle East, his depictions of the Levant, Palestine, and Egypt (particularly of the fellaheen and of desert settings) marking him out as an Orientalist of skill and with firsthand experience of the region. One of his most acclaimed works was *Pilgrims Going to Mecca* (1861).

Jean-Joseph Benjamin-Constant, French (1845–1902)

Trained at the École des Beaux-Arts in his native Paris, Benjamin-Constant was heavily influenced by a subsequent expedition to Spain and Morocco. Returning with an extensive collection of artifacts with which to populate his paintings, he became renowned for his sumptuous, stylized interiors. He later focused on portraiture, with Queen Victoria among his high profile sitters.

Léon Bonnat, French (1833–1922)

Although not regarded primarily as an Orientalist artist, Bonnat traveled to the Middle East in 1868 with a party that included Jean-Léon Gérôme. Although continuing to focus mainly on European (often Italian) religious and historical scenes, he also produced several works inspired by his travels to the region, including *An Egyptian Peasant Woman and Her Child* (1870), exemplifying the way in which Oriental subjects were adapted to suit traditional Western themes (in this case the Madonna and Child).

Gustave Boulanger, French (1824–88)

After studying in the atelier of Paul Delaroche, Boulanger traveled to Algeria to help alleviate a chronic chest condition and stayed there for eight months before returning to Paris. He exhibited regularly at the Salon, including works based on his Algerian travels, was a professor at the École des Beaux-Arts, and was good friends with Jean-Léon Gérôme, whose precise academic style of work he shared.

Frederick Arthur Bridgman, American (1846–1928)

Arriving in France after the American Civil War, Bridgman studied with Jean-Léon Gérôme before undertaking the first of several visits to the Maghreb and Egypt. From his base in Paris, he traveled to Algiers regularly, forming a friendship with a local family and thereby gaining privileged access to the domestic interiors and genre scenes that were to form the basis of many of his most successful works (and his 1890 book, *Winters in Algeria*). He also traveled extensively within Algeria, including to the oasis towns of the interior, and became one of the most renowned Orientalist artists of his day.

Henriette Browne, French (1829–1901)

Born in Paris and linked by marriage to the diplomatic world, Browne traveled extensively and is best known for her harem paintings, which were exhibited at the Salon in 1861. They gave a rare and privileged insight into a world that male artists could only imagine and fantasize about, but which Browne had seen with her own eyes. As with other women artists tackling Orientalist subjects, Browne faced criticism and cynicism over her work but nonetheless showed regularly at the Salon for a quarter of a century.

Stanisław Chlebowski, Polish (1835–84)

After studies in Odessa, St. Petersburg, and Munich, Chlebowski traveled to Paris, where he attended the studio of Jean-Léon Gérôme. His work—then centered around Polish, Russian, and French historical themes—attracted the attention of the Ottoman sultan, Abdülaziz, and in 1864 Chlebowski was invited to Constantinople as court painter, remaining there for thirteen years. He traveled extensively elsewhere in the Middle East, particularly to Egypt, and his work comprised genre scenes, portraits of the sultan, and battle paintings inspired by key episodes in Ottoman history.

Herman Corrodi, Italian (1844–1905)
The son of a successful watercolor artist, Corrodi studied in Geneva, Rome, and Paris. Specializing in landscape and genre scenes, he became very well connected and attracted the patronage of the British and German royal families, the Ottoman emperor, and other senior collectors. Travels to the Balkans and the Middle East in 1876–77 provided him with a wealth of material and subjects for his paintings, but tragically Corrodi was to lose many works and most of his collection of Oriental artifacts in a fire at his studio in Rome in 1892.

Richard Dadd, British (1817–86)
Trained at the Royal Academy Schools in London, Dadd painted scenes from history and literature, notably fairy subjects. In 1842 he was commissioned to join Sir Thomas Phillips on what became one of the most infamous tours in Orientalist history. After ten exhausting months traveling through Europe and the Middle East, Dadd returned to England with psychotic delusions, which caused him to murder his father. Sentenced to an asylum for the rest of his life, he nonetheless continued to produce exceptional watercolors, including several inspired by his Oriental travels.

Émile Deckers, Belgian (1885–1968)
After studies in Liège and Paris, in 1920 Deckers traveled to Algeria, a country for which he was to have an enduring fascination. He spent most of the next half-century there, only returning permanently to Belgium in 1966. His main specialism was portraiture, and particularly the depiction of the local Algerians among whom he lived. His ability to express their individual personalities through his work marks him out in the Orientalist canon.

Eugène Delacroix, French (1798–1863)
Although he only made one expedition to the Orient, to North Africa in 1832, Delacroix's interest in the region proved seminal. He produced a series of Orientalist works based on his experiences there, such as *Women of Algiers in Their Apartment* (1847–49), which helped cement his position as one of the most influential artists of his day. He was particularly taken by the notion of the Orient as a reincarnation of classical Greece and Rome, remarking on one scene that he witnessed, "It is beautiful, like the age of Homer!"

Ludwig Deutsch, Austrian (1855–1935)
Little appreciated during his lifetime, Deutsch now stands as one of the masters of Orientalist art. After studying in Vienna, he moved to France and chose to base himself there for the rest of his life. His highly detailed works, mostly studies of individual men and often in complex settings, are the result of a carefully constructed artistic process. In addition to using his on-the-spot sketches and (probably) photographs, Deutsch conducted extensive studio work involving his diverse collection of Oriental artifacts and Paris-based models to achieve the required final effect in his paintings. Toward the end of his career he experimented with a new style influenced by Post-Impressionism, thereby marking a transition in the path of Orientalist art.

Frank Dillon, British (1823–1909)
The son of a silk merchant and collector of watercolors, Dillon studied at the Royal Academy Schools and later with landscape artist James Holland. His first trip to the Orient was to Egypt, in 1854–55, and he became fascinated by the country's traditional architecture and decorative styles. He returned on three more occasions, specializing in architectural scenes and compositions, of both interiors and exteriors, of landmark buildings under threat from the modernization of Cairo. In 1875–76 he visited Japan, one of the first Western artists to do so.

Étienne Dinet, French (1861–1929)
Having already exhibited at the Salon, Dinet's first foray to the Orient came in 1884 when he accompanied a friend to Algeria. Their trip marked the start of Dinet's lifelong love affair with the country, which saw him spend every summer there among the people of the desert edge (mostly in Bou-Saâda), before returning to Paris in the winter to work up his paintings. He is most renowned for his depictions of everyday life among the Ouled Naïl tribe, often intimate scenes which reveal the unusually privileged degree of access that Dinet, a fluent Arabic speaker, was able to achieve. His close friendship with the Algerian Sliman ben Ibrahim, with whom he produced a series of books, also gave him a profound insight into local life.

Johann (Jean) Discart, Austrian (1856–??)
Born in Italy to an officer in the Austrian army, Discart later moved with his family to Vienna and studied art there. In 1877 he relocated to Paris, along with other notable Austrian émigrés including Ludwig Deutsch, with whom Discart was friends. His paintings, often similar in style and content to those of Deutsch, appear regularly in exhibitions from 1884 until the 1920s, but next to nothing is known of his life during this period. Many of his works have Moroccan themes or titles, so it is almost certain that he traveled there.

Amelia Edwards, British (1831–92)
Already a successful novelist when she visited Egypt for the first time in 1873–74, Edwards became fascinated by the country's history and culture. Her book about that trip, *A Thousand Miles up the Nile* (1877), was illustrated by her own sketches and provided a lyrical and personal account of a heritage that Edwards perceived as under increasing threat. She became an avid advocate for the greater protection of Egypt's monuments, and largely abandoned her painting and literary work in favor of campaigning and fundraising.

Rudolf Ernst, Austria (1854–1932)
The son of an architectural painter, Ernst studied first in Vienna at the Academy of Fine Art but relocated to Paris following a disagreement over his academic fees. It was here that he was later to meet Ludwig Deutsch, with whom he became good friends, and to develop his career as an Orientalist. He is known to have traveled to North Africa and Turkey and to have used on-the-spot sketches and photographs to create his paintings, which show similar subjects to those favored by Deutsch. Very interested in Oriental crafts, Ernst was also an expert in the decoration of faience tiles.

Roger Fenton, British (1819–69)
After initially studying painting and law, Fenton traveled to Paris, where he became inspired to take up photography. In 1853 he helped found the Royal Photographic Society and two years later was appointed by the British government as official photographer of the Crimean War, the success of his images confirming his role as one of his country's pre-eminent photographers. His later Eastern-inspired image *Pasha and Bayadère* (1858) became a potent symbol of the increasing interface between Orientalist art and photography, although Fenton was ultimately to abandon the new medium and return to law.

Arthur von Ferraris, Hungarian (1856–1936)
Born in rural Hungary, von Ferraris studied with the celebrated portraitist Joseph Matthaus in Vienna before leaving for Paris, where he was taught by both Gérôme and Jules Lefebre. He exhibited regularly at the Salon, both portraits and Orientalist scenes, the latter somewhat similar in style to the work of Ludwig Deutsch, with whom von Ferraris was good friends and traveled to Egypt on at least one occasion.

Théodore Frère, French (1814–88)
Unusual among French Orientalists in that his works were inspired not only by North Africa but also by the Holy Land and Syria, Frère became one of the most commercially successful Orientalists of his day. He traveled extensively to various parts of the region for over three decades, including his final trip to Egypt, with Empress Eugénie, for the opening of the Suez Canal in 1869. Frère specialized particularly in the depiction of markets, desert encampments, and landscape views, often shown at dusk.

Francis Frith, British (1822–98)
Success with a grocery, and subsequently a printing business, enabled Frith to develop his interest in photography. He was one of the first practitioners of the still-new medium to understand the potential appeal to armchair travelers of camera images of overseas destinations, not least the Orient. Also a skilled amateur painter, he made three trips to the region, describing and illustrating his travels in his 1859 publication *Egypt and Palestine* and opening a specialist photographic publishing company on his return to England.

Eugène Fromentin, French (1820–76)
Originally set to follow in his father's profession as a lawyer, Fromentin decided later to pursue an artistic career instead. In 1846 he traveled to Algeria, the first of three visits during which he became fascinated by the life and culture of the tribes living on the fringes of the Sahara. Local traditions such as falconry and horsemanship feature prominently in his paintings, and his two books, *Un Été dans le Sahara* (1857) and *Une Année dans le Sahel* (1859), stand as two of the most lyrical yet perceptive European responses to the appeal and challenge of the Orient.

Jean-Léon Gérôme, French (1824–1904)
Arguably the most famous and influential Orientalist artist of his day, Gérôme trained in the École des Beaux-Arts in Paris, in the atelier of Paul Delaroche (and, later, Charles Gleyre), and initially specialized in scenes inspired by ancient Greece and Rome. Following his first trip to the Orient, in 1856, he began producing paintings of a wide range of Orientalist subjects, in the highly detailed and accurate style for which

he became renowned. His fascination for the visual documentation of costume and ethnic diversity set the standard for other artists to follow, with many younger Orientalists learning their craft in his teaching studio. Thanks largely to the entrepreneurial efforts of his father-in-law, dealer Adolphe Goupil, Gérôme's works were much in demand among European and American collectors.

EUGÈNE GIRARDET, FRENCH (1853–1907)
Born to a family of professional artists, some of whom had visited Algeria, Girardet was already selling works at the age of seventeen. He then studied with Gérôme, taking up his teacher's advice to travel to the Orient and ultimately visiting North Africa many times, as well as Egypt and Palestine. Girardet reveled in traveling off the beaten track and immersing himself in local culture, gathering material for the everyday scenes in which he specialized. Many of these were inspired by his time in Bou-Saâda, where he met Étienne Dinet.

CHARLES GLEYRE, FRENCH (1806–74)
A graduate of the École des Beaux-Arts in Paris, Gleyre's first encounter with the Orient came in 1834. He was commissioned by the American John Lowell, Jr., to accompany him as his personal artist on a trip to Greece, Turkey, and Egypt, where the two men parted. Lowell sent the works produced by Gleyre back home to Boston and the artist continued traveling alone through Egypt and Syria, not returning to Paris until 1838. He later took over Paul Delaroche's atelier and taught Gérôme, among others, but by this time Gleyre's oeuvre was dominated by historical and classical subjects rather than Orientalist themes.

FREDERICK GOODALL, BRITISH (1822–1904)
The son of an engraver, Goodall demonstrated a precocious talent for painting, and four of his watercolors were exhibited at the Royal Academy when he was only sixteen. He first specialized in rustic genre scenes and history subjects, showing the influence of David Wilkie, but began to travel in search of new material. A visit to the Crimea in 1854 was followed by trips to Morocco, Spain, Portugal, and Italy and then, in 1858, to Egypt for the first time. Goodall stayed there for several months, sharing a house in Cairo with Carl Haag and traveling with him to Giza and Suez. Goodall's first Orientalist works were exhibited at the Royal Academy in 1860 and in the years that followed he became a prolific and, for a time, hugely successful artist of often Bible-themed paintings.

GUSTAVE GUILLAUMET, FRENCH (1840–87)
Trained at the École des Beaux-Arts in Paris, Guillaumet was on his way to Rome in 1867 but had a sudden change of mind and decided to go to Algeria instead. It was a decision that redefined the trajectory of his artistic career, marking the first of nine such visits to that country. He developed a close artistic relationship with oasis towns such as Biskra and Bou-Saâda, initially excelling in melodramatic depictions of famine, drought, and death, as in his 1867 work, *Le Sahara* (The Desert). His style and content later evolved in favor of more nuanced and positive depictions of rural life, labor, customs, and domestic situations, scenes which he also described in his book, *Tableaux algériens* (1888).

Carl Haag, GERMAN (1820–1915)
Born in Bavaria, Haag initially specialized in portrait miniatures before traveling to London to study watercolor painting. He was introduced to Queen Victoria and Prince Albert, who invited him to Balmoral and commissioned two paintings which the couple exchanged as Christmas gifts. In 1858 Haag journeyed to Egypt, living and traveling with Frederick Goodall for several months and then proceeding to Jerusalem to paint the Dome of the Rock for Queen Victoria. He also spent time traveling with Bedouin tribes and returned to London to specialize in Orientalist works based on his experiences. He later became a naturalized British citizen, and his Oriental-themed house and studio in Hampstead was one of the best examples of its type.

Osman Hamdi Bey, TURKISH (1842–1910)
A true polymath, Hamdi was born to a leading Constantinople family and originally sent to Paris to study law. He chose instead to pursue art under the tutelage of Gustave Boulanger and Jean-Léon Gérôme, learning the highly finished and academic style which was to become a hallmark of his paintings. Upon his return to Turkey he joined the Ottoman civil service, later becoming director of the Imperial Ottoman Museum and playing an instrumental role in the founding of the Imperial School of Fine Arts, where he taught painting. Passionate about the art, architecture, crafts, and traditions of his native country, he used a Westernized and Orientalist style of painting to convey what he saw as the continuing importance and relevance of this heritage.

Gavin Hamilton, BRITISH (1723–98)
A specialist in classical Greek and Roman subjects, Hamilton studied classics at the University of Glasgow before traveling to Italy to visit Rome, Naples, and Venice. On his return to London he worked as a portrait painter before deciding to base himself in Italy, taking up residence in Rome and remaining there until his death over forty years later. His main contribution to the Orientalist canon was *James Dawkins and Robert Wood Discovering the Ruins of Palmyra* (1758), commissioned by Dawkins's brother, Henry, and exemplifying European interest in the Orient as the focus of a "new antiquity."

William Holman Hunt, BRITISH (1827–1910)
One of the founders of the Pre-Raphaelite Brotherhood, Hunt was inspired by his Christian faith to travel to the Holy Land to document the "reality" of the Bible more accurately in his works. He set off in 1854 on the first of his four expeditions to the Middle East, traveling for some of the time with Thomas Seddon, to Cairo and Jerusalem, and from there visiting Constantinople, Damascus, and Beirut. Following the success of *The Scapegoat* in 1856, Hunt was hugely successful as the leading exponent of a new style of religious painting based on symbolic content, attention to authentic detail, and direct personal experience of the Holy Land. He returned there on further extended trips, including with his family. Hunt rejected traditional academic approaches to art and was never elected to the Royal Academy.

Elisabeth Jerichau-Baumann, DANISH (1819–81)
Polish-born and trained in art in Germany, Jerichau-Baumann later married the Danish sculptor Jens Jerichau and settled in his homeland. She enjoyed success as a portrait painter and, through the patronage of the royal families in both Denmark and Britain, was able to secure commissions and high level contacts in preparation for traveling to the Orient for the first time in 1869. As a woman, during her visits to the region she was able to gain access to spheres of life denied to her male peers, and she excelled particularly at the portrayal of Egyptian women fellaheen engaged in their daily activities.

Paul Klee, SWISS–GERMAN (1879–1940)
Painter, printmaker, and draftsman Klee trained in Munich and was part of the German Expressionist group *Der Blaue Reiter*. Also influenced by Surrealism and Cubism, he concentrated mainly on graphic art, but his 1914 visit to Tunisia prompted a dramatic change in his oeuvre. Deeply impressed by the color and light that he encountered in North Africa, he became fascinated by further exploration of both aspects while teaching at the Bauhaus in Weimar. A second visit to the Orient, to Egypt in 1928, proved equally inspirational.

Ernst Körner, GERMAN (1846–1927)
An inveterate traveler, Körner undertook expeditions to many parts of Europe, as well as to the Middle East. He studied in Berlin as a landscape painter, and used his classical training to rekindle notions of the great seventeenth-century European masters in the landscapes of Egypt particularly, one of his favorite subjects. A keen amateur archaeologist, he was fascinated by the country's pharaonic heritage and incorporated many of the main monuments into his works.

Edward Lear, BRITISH (1812–88)
Although not primarily regarded as an Orientalist artist—his fame rests more on his literary work, in both prose and poetry, and on his book illustrations—Lear traveled extensively in the region and looms larger than life in the Orientalist suite. A self-taught polymath, he began his career drawing birds but switched to landscapes when his eyesight started to fail. Much taken by the light and colors of the Orient, he described himself as a "Painter of Poetical Topography" and excelled in on-the-spot sketches, some of which he later worked up into paintings. His written accounts of expeditions to Greece, Egypt, and Palestine stand as some of the most amusing and insightful of any traveling artist.

Frederic Leighton, BRITISH (1830–96)
Trained in Frankfurt, Leighton spent several years in Rome and Paris before settling in London, where he specialized in works inspired by classical themes. He traveled extensively in the Middle East, making sketches of buildings and street scenes in cities such as Damascus, which he then used to inform his later paintings. These observations were also seminal in the design and execution of the magnificent Arab Hall that Leighton had installed in his London home in 1877–79.

John Frederick Lewis, BRITISH (1804–76)
The son of an engraver, Lewis as a young man was a gifted painter of animals and developed a particular skill for watercolor. From 1832 onward, he spent seventeen of the next

twenty years outside England, first in Spain and Morocco, and later in Istanbul and then Egypt, where he lived for a decade. His time there, during which he was famously visited by William Thackeray, came to define his career as one of Britain's leading Orientalists, with his first exhibit in this genre, *The Hhareem*, dramatically well received in 1850, shortly before his return to England. In the years that followed, Lewis continued to produce a range of highly acclaimed works in both oils and watercolors, based on his experiences abroad. He often incorporated figures in his works that are now read as being Orientalized representations of the artist himself.

Marie Aimée Lucas-Robiquet, FRENCH (1858–1959)
Born in Normandy, Lucas-Robiquet was taught art privately, the École des Beaux-Arts in Paris being for men only at the time. She became a highly acclaimed and successful artist, exhibiting regularly at the Salon before moving to Algeria in 1891 with her husband, a captain in the French army. She lived there for the next fourteen years, sending her paintings back to Paris regularly for exhibition. Although her oeuvre spanned a range of subjects, it was Lucas-Robiquet's Orientalist works that attracted most favorable attention, especially her scenes of everyday activities such as date harvesting and weaving.

Konstantin Makovsky, RUSSIAN (1839–1915)
From an artistic family, Makovsky trained in Moscow and St. Petersburg before embarking on a career as a socio-realist painter specializing in scenes drawn from Russian history and everyday life. His work changed noticeably following a trip he made in 1873 to the Balkans and Egypt, where he was deeply affected by the colorful culture and dramatic light he encountered. Works such as *The Handing Over of the Sacred Carpet in Cairo* (1876) confirmed his position as one of the leading Russian painters of the time.

Henri Matisse, FRENCH (1869–1954)
Three visits to the Orient had a profound impact on Matisse, who used his experiences there to move his art in new and influential directions. He produced twenty works while in Morocco, now seen as significant for marking an important interaction between experimental abstraction and traditional Orientalist ideas associated with Islamic architecture, geometric designs, and ethnography. Matisse talked of the Orient as a "revelation" that sparked new sensations in him, and later was to paint a series of odalisques as a homage to Ingres and Delacroix, among others.

Leopold Carl Müller, AUSTRIAN (1835–92)
Born in Germany, Müller was the son of a lithographer and trained at the Vienna Academy before working as an illustrator for a satirical newspaper. A visit to Paris in 1867 brought him into contact with the work of Orientalists such as Eugène Fromentin, and from 1873 onward Müller traveled frequently to the Orient. Fascinated particularly by Egypt, to which he made a total of nine visits, often spending months at a time, he specialized in genre scenes and portraits. Müller also taught art, with younger Orientalist artists such as Rudolf Swoboda (who was his nephew) and Franz Kosler among his pupils. After befriending the Prince of Wales, he was particularly successful in selling his works to British collectors.

William James Müller, British (1812–45)
Born in Bristol and the pupil of a local landscape artist, James Baker Pyne, Müller was one of the first British artists to create realistic depictions of the Orient. He first ventured abroad, through Europe to Italy, in 1834–35, and three years later set off for Egypt via Greece. He traveled as far as Luxor, his journey on the Nile taking place at the same time as that of David Roberts, although the two men did not meet. Adept at sketching in situ, capturing the light and color of the Eastern landscapes, on his return to London Müller exhibited oils of Egyptian genre subjects. After his early death at the age of thirty-two, his oils brought him a considerable posthumous reputation, but it is for the considerable vigor and spontaneity of his watercolors that he is valued today.

Amadeo Preziosi, Maltese (1816–82)
Born to an aristocratic Maltese family, Preziosi studied art in Paris before settling in Constantinople about 1842. He lived there until his death forty years later, making a highly lucrative living from selling views of the city and its diverse inhabitants to European residents and visitors. He sold many of his works as lithographs, taking advantage of changes in reproduction techniques that helped expand the market and audience for such images.

Pierre-Auguste Renoir, French (1841–1919)
After initial training as a porcelain painter, in 1862 Renoir entered the atelier of Charles Gleyre. There he met future fellow exponents of Impressionism, including Claude Monet and Alfred Sisley, and painted contemporary subjects. Renoir was a great admirer of Eugène Delacroix and was inspired to express aspects of the Orient in his own art. He painted his earliest Orientalist works, notably *Femme d'Alger ou Odalisque* (1870), over a decade before his first visit to the region, to Algeria in 1881. Deeply affected by the visual drama of the Maghreb, he painted landscapes and crowd scenes during this trip and returned the following year to create a series of portraits.

David Roberts, British (1796–1864)
With no formal art education, Roberts trained initially as a painter and designer of theater scenery in his native Scotland and it was in this capacity that he moved to London in 1822. He exhibited his first painting two years later, and success as an artist enabled him to give up his previous career and specialize in architectural views. In 1832 he traveled to Spain and (briefly) Morocco, a precursor to his iconic trip to Egypt and the Holy Land in 1838–39. On his return, the exhibition of his oil paintings of the historic monuments and biblical landscapes of the Levant brought him considerable renown, as well as election as a Royal Academician in 1841. The ensuing success of Roberts's series of lithographs (with Louis Haghe), published in *The Holy Land, Syria, Idumea, Arabia, Egypt and Nubia* (1842–49), secured his reputation as one of the most influential Orientalists, even though he never traveled to the region again.

Charles Robertson, British (1844–91)
Following his first visit to North Africa at the young age of eighteen, Robertson traveled extensively to many parts of the Middle East over the next quarter of a century. He produced highly detailed works, mainly of street scenes and interiors,

and worked exclusively in oils until 1880. He then switched entirely to watercolor, in which medium he became one of the most accomplished Orientalist practitioners.

Henri Rousseau, French (1875–1933)
The son of an engineer who worked on the Suez Canal, and unusual among Orientalists in that he was born in the region (in Cairo), Rousseau spent his early life in Egypt before moving to study art in Paris. He subsequently made regular visits to North Africa and became renowned for his skilled depictions of horses and falconry hunts.

John Singer Sargent, American (1856–1925)
Renowned as one of his day's most accomplished and acclaimed society portrait painters, Sargent visited the Middle East several times. His most significant project inspired by the region was the commission to paint a set of biblical murals at the Boston Public Library, which saw him set up a temporary studio in Cairo and use local people and scenes to help create the appropriate content and style for the murals.

Antonio (Anton) Schranz, German (1801–65)
A member of a German family that settled in Malta in 1818, Schranz followed in the footsteps of his father (also Antonio) and elder brother Giovanni in becoming an artist. He specialized in the depiction of landscapes and seascapes, and traveled extensively across the eastern Mediterranean, Egypt and the Holy Land as a draughtsman for wealthy patrons. These included Viscount Castlereagh, with whom Schranz journeyed in 1842. He later turned to photography, opening what was almost certainly the first studio dedicated to that medium in Cairo.

Thomas Seddon, British (1821–56)
The son of a London cabinet-maker, Seddon trained as a designer and studied ornamental art. He later took drawing lessons and set up his own art school for working men, the North London School of Design. A leading light among the Pre-Raphaelites, he was a friend of Ford Madox Brown, the Rossettis, and William Holman Hunt. After a near-fatal attack of rheumatic fever in 1850–51, Seddon enthusiastically embraced Christianity and traveled to Egypt and the Holy Land (with Hunt) in 1853–54. He returned to Egypt in 1856, but died in Cairo of dysentery in November that year. Among his most renowned works are *Jerusalem and the Valley of Jehoshaphat from the Hill of Evil Counsel* (1854–55) and his 1854 portrait of the great Arabist, Richard Burton.

William Simpson, British (1823–99)
Initially trained as a lithographic printer and draftsman, Simpson was commissioned to produce views of the Great Exhibition in London in 1851 and later to capture the events of the Crimean War in watercolor and for production as lithographs, in *The Seat of War in the East* (1855–56). His very successful career as a war artist, working primarily for the *Illustrated London News*, saw him travel to India, Abyssinia, and to the battlefields of the 1870 Franco-Prussian War, as well as to Egypt in 1869 (for the opening of the Suez Canal), Palestine, Syria, and Turkey. He was a prolific watercolorist, producing numerous works based on his Oriental travels.

RUDOLF SWOBODA, AUSTRIAN (1859–1914)
The nephew of Leopold Carl Müller, Swoboda was taught by his uncle from 1878 to 1884 and visited him in Cairo in 1879, the first of six visits made by Swoboda to Egypt. He produced a number of Orientalist works, including genre scenes, but is perhaps best known for his acutely observed portraits. His skill in that area was noticed by Queen Victoria, who appointed him as official court painter and sent him to India to produce a series of portraits of the Indian people.

HORACE VERNET, FRENCH (1789–1863)
From a family of celebrated artists, Vernet specialized in historical scenes and was well established as an artist before he first visited the Orient in 1833. His trip to Algeria with the French army was the first of several to North Africa, and in 1839 he traveled to Egypt with his nephew Frédéric Goupil-Fesquet to make the first known daguerreotype images of the region. Vernet's Orientalist paintings are primarily biblical or battle scenes, the participants dramatically cast in Oriental costumes, and he became one of the most lauded artists of his day.

ÉDOUARD VERSCHAFFELT, BELGIAN (1874–1955)
A graduate of the Royal Academy of Fine Arts in Antwerp, Verschaffelt was later to leave Belgium for Algeria, where he was to spend much of the rest of his life. He became very integrated with the tribes of the desert edge, working on carefully produced portraits that marked a new departure in terms of the way in which Orientalist artists presented local people, their customs, and culture.

EDWIN LORD WEEKS, AMERICAN (1849–1903)
Born to an affluent family in Boston, as a young man Weeks traveled extensively, including his first expedition to the Orient in 1872. Two years later, with his works based on that visit much lauded by the American public, Weeks left for Paris in order to study with Léon Bonnat and Jean-Léon Gérôme. Further travels followed, including to Persia and India, and Weeks proved to be a prolific artist, specializing in landscapes and commanding prices at the very top of the market.

RUDOLF WEISS, AUSTRIAN (1859–1930)
Another of the Austrian artist émigrés who made their way from Vienna to Paris, Weiss may never have visited the Middle East or North Africa. His Orientalist works were therefore probably created from his extensive collection of artifacts, photographs, and other source material in his studio, used to assemble the highly detailed capriccio-style paintings that were to become his hallmark.

DAVID WILKIE, BRITISH (1785–1841)
Drawn to the Orient in search of inspiration and material that he could use to depict biblical subjects, Wilkie studied in Edinburgh and London and was an established and highly regarded history and genre painter before he left England in 1840. He visited Turkey, Palestine, and Egypt, painting portraits of notable people that he encountered, as well as scenes of contemporary life, only to die at sea off Gibraltar on his way home.

Appendix Two

Middle Eastern and North African countries visited by the principal artists and photographers featured in the text. Dates given are for main visits (rather than simple transit stops, for example at Alexandria for Jaffa) and in some cases are approximate.

Algeria and Tunisia

Gustave Boulanger, 1845
Frederick Arthur Bridgman, 1872–73, 1879, 1885–86
Émile Deckers, semi-resident, 1920–66
Eugène Delacroix, 1832
Étienne Dinet, numerous visits from 1884 and semi-resident from 1904–29
Rudolf Ernst, late 1880s (possibly Tunisia only)
Théodore Frère, 1836–39
Eugène Fromentin, 1846, 1847–48, 1852–53
Jean-Léon Gérôme, 1873, 1883
Eugène Girardet, 1874 (Tunisia only), several visits between 1879 and the 1890s
Gustave Guillaumet, ten visits between 1862 and 1884 (including some also to Morocco)
Wassily Kandinsky, 1904–05 (Tunisia only)
Paul Klee, 1914 (Tunisia only)
Frederic Leighton, 1857
Marie-Aimée Lucas-Robiquet, resident 1891–1905
Henri Matisse, 1906, 1912–13
Arthur Melville, several visits during the 1890s
Pierre-Auguste Renoir, 1881, 1882
Charles Robertson, 1862
Henri Rousseau, several visits, first in 1901
John Singer Sargent, 1880
William Sartain, 1876
Horace Vernet, five visits between 1833 and 1853
Édouard Verschaffelt, semi-resident, 1919–55

Egypt

William Henry Bartlett, 1834, 1845
Gustav Bauernfeind, 1880
Léon Belly, 1851, 1855–56, 1857

Léon Bonnat, 1868, 1869
Frederick Arthur Bridgman, 1873–74
Henriette Browne, 1868–69
Stanisław Chlebowski, several visits, 1865–mid-70s
Hermann Corrodi, 1876–77
Richard Dadd, 1842–43
Ludwig Deutsch, several visits during the 1880s and 90s
Frank Dillon, 1854–55, 1861–62, 1869–70, 1873–74
Étienne Dinet, 1897
Rudolf Ernst, late 1880s
Arthur von Ferraris, 1885
Théodore Frère, *c.*1853, 1869
Eugène Fromentin, 1869
Jean-Léon Gérôme, at least seven visits between 1856 and 1881
Eugène Girardet, 1898
Charles Gleyre, 1834–35, 1837
Frederick Goodall, 1858–59, 1870–71
Carl Haag, 1858–60, 1873–74
William Holman Hunt, 1854, 1892
Elisabeth Jerichau-Baumann, 1870, 1876
Paul Klee, 1928
Ernst Körner, 1873–74, 1878, 1887, 1905
Edward Lear, 1849, 1854, 1866–67, 1872
Frederic Leighton, 1868, 1882
John Frederick Lewis, 1841–51
Konstantin Makovsky, 1873–74
Arthur Melville, 1880–82
Leopold Carl Müller, nine visits between 1873 and 1886
William Müller, 1838–39
Amadeo Preziosi, 1862
David Roberts, 1838–39
Charles Robertson, 1876, 1889
Henri Rousseau, 1875–80s?
John Singer Sargent, 1890–91
Thomas Seddon, 1853–54, 1856
William Simpson, 1869
Rudolf Swoboda, six visits between 1879 and 1891
Horace Vernet, 1839–40
Edwin Lord Weeks, 1872, 1875
David Wilkie, 1841

Lebanon/Syria

William Henry Bartlett, 1834
Gustav Bauernfeind, 1880–81, 1884–87, 1888–89, 1896–1904
Léon Belly, 1851
Léon Bonnat, 1868
Frederick Arthur Bridgman, dates unknown
Henriette Browne, 1868–69
Hermann Corrodi, 1877
Richard Dadd, 1842
Théodore Frère, *c.*1853
Jean-Léon Gérôme, 1862
Charles Gleyre, *c.*1836–37
Carl Haag, 1859
William Holman Hunt, 1855–56
Ernst Körner, 1874
Edward Lear, 1858
Frederic Leighton, 1873
Amadeo Preziosi, 1862
David Roberts, 1839

Charles Robertson, 1889
John Singer Sargent, 1905–06
William Simpson, 1870
Horace Vernet, 1840
Edwin Lord Weeks, 1872

Morocco

William Allen, 1834
Jean-Joseph Benjamin-Constant, 1872–73
Frederick Arthur Bridgman, 1872–73
Henriette Browne, 1865
Eugène Delacroix, 1832
Frank Dillon, 1881–82
Johann Discart, probably but dates uncertain
Rudolf Ernst, late 1880s
Eugène Girardet, 1874
Gustave Guillaumet (see **Algeria** and **Tunisia**, above)
John Frederick Lewis, 1833
Henri Matisse, 1912, 1913
David Roberts, 1833
Charles Robertson, 1876
Henri Rousseau, several visits, first in 1920
John Singer Sargent, 1880
Edwin Lord Weeks, 1872, 1875–76, 1877–78

Palestine

William Henry Bartlett, 1834, 1842, 1845
Gustav Bauernfeind, 1880–81, 1884–87, 1888–89, 1896–1904
Léon Belly, 1850
Léon Bonnat, 1868
Hermann Corrodi, 1877
Richard Dadd, 1842
Théodore Frère, *c.*1853
Jean-Léon Gérôme, 1862, 1868
Eugène Girardet, 1898
Carl Haag, 1859
William Holman Hunt, 1854–55, 1869–72, 1875–78, 1892
Ernst Körner, 1874
Edward Lear, 1858, 1867
David Roberts, 1839
Charles Robertson, 1872, 1889
John Singer Sargent, 1891, 1905–06
Thomas Seddon, 1854
William Simpson, 1869
Horace Vernet, 1839–40
Edwin Lord Weeks, 1872
David Wilkie, 1841

Turkey

William Allen, 1829–30
William Henry Bartlett, 1834, 1837–38, 1842, 1854
Léon Bonnat, 1868
Frederick Arthur Bridgman, *c.*1880
Henriette Browne, 1860
Stanisław Chlebowski, resident 1864–76
Hermann Corrodi, 1870s
Richard Dadd, 1842
Rudolf Ernst, late 1880s–1890
Théodore Frère, 1851–52
Jean-Léon Gérôme, 1853, 1854, 1871, 1875, 1879, ?1881
Charles Gleyre, 1834

Osman Hamdi, largely resident other than when studying in Paris 1860–68
William Holman Hunt, 1856
Elisabeth Jerichau-Baumann, 1869, 1874–75
Ernst Körner, 1874
Edward Lear, 1848, 1856
Frederic Leighton, 1867
John Frederick Lewis, 1840–41
Arthur Melville, 1882
Leopold Carl Müller, 1873–74
William Müller, 1843–44
Amadeo Preziosi, 1842–82
Charles Robertson, 1872, 1889
John Singer Sargent, 1891
William Simpson, 1855, 1870
Horace Vernet, 1840s
Edwin Lord Weeks, 1892
David Wilkie, 1840–41

Notes

Prologue

1. Ballantine, *The Life of David Roberts*, 138.
2. Peltre, *Orientalism in Art*, 17.
3. Lemaire, *The Orient in Western Art*, 43.
4. Rifat, *Portraits from the Empire*, 96–97.

Chapter 1: Departure

1. Boswell, *The Life of Samuel Johnson*, 1824 edition, vol. III, 201.
2. Issawi, *An Economic History of the Middle East*, 46.
3. Green, *The Lost World of the London Coffeehouse.*
4. Montagu, *The Turkish Embassy Letters*, 104.
5. Montagu, *The Turkish Embassy Letters*, 58–59.
6. Montagu, *The Turkish Embassy Letters*, 59.
7. Denon, *Voyage dans la Basse et la Haute Égypte*, 51.
8. Cited in Thompson, "An Account of the Journeys and Writings of The Indefatigable Mr. Lane," 30. See also Thompson, *Edward William Lane: The Life of the Pioneering Egyptologist and Orientalist.*
9. Leila Ahmed, cited in Thompson, "An Account of the Journeys and Writings of The Indefatigable Mr Lane," 33.
10. Lear to the 13th Earl of Derby, 12 January 1849, in Noakes, *Edward Lear: Selected Letters*, 97.
11. See Llewellyn, "Friend and Foe," 47–74.
12. For more detail on Prisse's fascination with Egypt, see Volait, "Avec le double empressement d'un artiste et d'un antiquaire."
13. Pardoe, *The Beauties of the Bosphorus*, 4.
14. Pardoe, *The City of the Sultan*, ix.
15. Lane, *An Account of the Manners and Customs of the Modern Egyptians*, xiv.
16. Russell, *The Natural History of Aleppo and Parts Adjacent*, 83–84.
17. Lister, *Murray's Handbooks for Travellers*, x.
18. Hunt to Rossetti, letter dated 12 August 1855 (MS, Huntington Library).
19. Wilkinson, *Hand-book for Travellers in Egypt*, 7.
20. Murray, *A Hand-Book for Travellers in the Ionian Islands, Greece, Turkey, Asia Minor and Constantinople*, iv.
21. Budge, *Cook's Handbook for Egypt and the Sudan*, 20.
22. From the notice that prefaced Roberts's *The Holy Land, Syria, Idumea, Arabia, Egypt and Nubia* of 1842–49.
23. Cook, *Art and Artists of Our Time*, vol. 1, 261.
24. Tromans, *The Lure of the East*, 14.
25. Peltre, *Orientalism in Art*, 106.
26. Thackeray, *Notes of a Journey from Cornhill to Grand Cairo*, 278–79.
27. *A Journey to Damascus Through Egypt, Nubia, Arabia Petraea, Palestine, and Syria* (Henry Colburn, 1847).
28. Ballantine, *The Life of David Roberts*, 40.
29. Ballantine, *The Life of David Roberts*, 41.

30. Letter dated 28 January 1833 from David Wilkie to David Roberts, in Ballantine, *The Life of David Roberts*, 46.
31. See Llewellyn, "David Wilkie and John Frederick Lewis in Constantinople, 1840: An Artistic Dialogue," 629 and fn 37. Also letter from Roberts to David Ramsay Hay, 6 January 1831 (National Library of Scotland, MS 3521, fol.27v); I am grateful to Briony Llewellyn for drawing this to my attention. Also letter from Cotman to Dawson Turner, 25 February 1834, quoted in Kitson, *The Life of John Sell Cotman*, 310–11. For later evidence of the friendship, see Lewis, *John Frederick Lewis*, 37–38.
32. In a letter to David Ramsay Hay; see Ballantine, *The Life of David Roberts*, 47.
33. Richard Ford to Henry Unwin Addington, Madrid, 17 July 1832, see Prothero, *The Letters of Richard Ford*, 95. Also cited in Robertson, *Richard Ford*, 117.
34. Ackerman, *The Life and Work of Jean-Léon Gérôme*, 30.
35. Hunt, *Pre-Raphaelitism and the Pre-Raphaelite Brotherhood*, vol. 1, 348.
36. Hunt, *Pre-Raphaelitism and the Pre-Raphaelite Brotherhood*, vol. 1, 349–50.
37. Hunt, *Pre-Raphaelitism and the Pre-Raphaelite Brotherhood*, vol. 1, 348–49.
38. Llewellyn, "David Wilkie and John Frederick Lewis in Constantinople, 1840: An Artistic Dialogue," 627.
39. Carmel and Schmid, *The Life and Work of Gustav Bauernfeind*, 91.
40. Kuehn, "Elisabeth Jerichau-Baumann 'Egypt 1870,'" 258.
41. I am grateful to Max Bendixen for sharing this information with me.
42. Hunt, *Pre-Raphaelitism and the Pre-Raphaelite Brotherhood*, vol. 1, 346.
43. Ballantine, *The Life of David Roberts*, 79.

Chapter 2: Arrival

1. Fromentin, *Between Sea and Sahara*, 1.
2. Steegmuller, *Flaubert in Egypt*, 29.
3. Ballantine, *The Life of David Roberts*, 81.
4. Cited in Frith, *My Autobiography and Reminiscences*, vol. II, 138–139.
5. Cited in Cunningham, *The Life of Sir David Wilkie*, 319–320.
6. Ackerman, *The Life and Work of Jean-Léon Gérôme*, 45.
7. Bridgman, *Winters in Algeria*, 4.
8. Ackerman, *American Orientalists*, 234.
9. Weeks, *From the Black Sea through Persia and India*, 7.
10. Goodall, *Reminiscences*, 66.
11. Ballantine, *The Life of David Roberts*, 82.
12. Weeks, "Two Centres of Moorish Art," 441.
13. Taylor, "Hermann Corrodi," 217.
14. Majda, *Orientalism in Polish Art*, 331.
15. Seddon, *Memoir and Letters of the Late Thomas Seddon*, 88.
16. Cited in Oelwein, "Carl Haag 1820–1915: Fact or Fantasy?," 26.
17. Simpson, *Autobiography*, 213–14.
18. Cited in Sattin, *Lifting the Veil: British Society in Egypt*, 20.
19. Cited in Mansel, *Levant: Splendour and Catastrophe on the Mediterranean*, 72.
20. Ballantine, *The Life of David Roberts*, 106.
21. Thackeray, *Notes of a Journey from Cornhill to Grand Cairo*, 257.
22. Stephens, *Incidents of Travel in the Russian and Turkish Empires*, 229.
23. Hodgson, *Dreaming of East: Western Women and the Exotic Allure of the Orient*, 44.
24. See Brahimi, *La Vie et l'oeuvre d'Étienne Dinet*, 12–22.
25. Cited in Thornton, *The Orientalists: Painter-Travellers*, 206.
26. Goodall, *Reminiscences*, 66–67.
27. Ackerman, *American Orientalists*, 8.
28. Hering, *Gérôme: The Life and Works of of Jean Léon Gérôme*, 118.
29. Seddon, *Memoir and Letters of the Late Thomas Seddon*, 29.

30. Ballantine, *The Life of David Roberts*, 82. Roberts included a portrayal of the slave market in Cairo in his *Egypt and Nubia* volume.
31. Cited in Roget, *A History of The 'Old Water-Colour' Society*, vol. II, 349.
32. Cited in Bronkhurst, "William Holman Hunt's Visits to Egypt: Passion, Prejudice and Truth to Nature."
33. Hunt, *Pre-Raphaelitism and the Pre-Raphaelite Brotherhood*, vol. I, 373.
34. See Gurcaglar, "The Dragoman Who Commissioned His Own Portrait," 211–219.
35. Cited in Starkey, *Travellers in Egypt*, 100.
36. Cited in Ballantine, *The Life of David Roberts*, 107.
37. Seddon, *Memoir and Letters of the Late Thomas Seddon*, 38–39.
38. Seddon, *Memoir and Letters of the Late Thomas Seddon*, 63–64.
39. Bronkhurst, *William Holman Hunt, A Catalogue Raisonné*, vol. II, 263–264.
40. Carmel and Schmid, *The Life and Works of Gustav Bauernfeind*, 98.
41. Seddon, *Memoir and Letters of the Late Thomas Seddon*, 60.
42. Goodall, *Reminiscences*, 69–70.
43. Goodall, *Reminiscences*, 83–84.
44. I am grateful to Nicholas Warner for sharing with me his knowledge and analysis of the material that describes and depicts Lewis's house in Cairo.
45. Seddon, *Memoir and Letters of the Late Thomas Seddon*, 164–65.
46. Jerningham, *To and From Constantinople*, 329–30.
47. Hunt, *Pre-Raphaelitism and the Pre-Raphaelite Brotherhood*, vol. II, 287.
48. Hunt, *Pre-Raphaelitism and the Pre-Raphaelite Brotherhood*, vol. II, 317.
49. Carmel and Schmid, *The Life and Works of Gustav Bauernfeind*, 111.
50. Goodall, *Reminiscences*, 267.
51. Masson, "J.L. Gérôme," 30.
52. Hunt, *Pre-Raphaelitism and the Pre-Raphaelite Brotherhood*, vol. 1, 380.
53. Egerton, *Journal of a Tour in The Holy Land*, 137–38.
54. Edwards, *A Thousand Miles up the Nile*, 9.
55. Ballantine, *The Life of David Roberts*, 104.
56. Bartlett, *The Nile boat*, 109–110.
57. Edwards, *A Thousand Miles up the Nile*, 65.
58. Thackeray, *Notes of a Journey from Cornhill to Grand Cairo*, 291.
59. Goodall, *Reminiscences*, 75–76 and 387.
60. Hering, *Gérôme: The Life and Works of Jean Léon Gérôme*, 96.
61. Cited in Oelwein, "Carl Haag 1820–1915: Fact or Fantasy?"
62. Lear, "A Leaf from the Journals of a Landscape Painter," 413.
63. Ballantine, *The Life of David Roberts*, 116.
64. Seddon, *Memoir and Letters of the Late Thomas Seddon*, 100.
65. Strachey, *Letters of Edward Lear*, 98.
66. From a three-page untitled typescript account in the Edwin Lord Weeks Papers [*c.*1885–1976], Archives of American Art, Smithsonian Institution, Washington DC, US.
67. Cited in Ackerman, *American Orientalists*, 238.
68. Goodall, *Reminiscences*, 127–28.
69. Cited in Peltre, *Orientalism*, 80.
70. Edwards, *A Thousand Miles up the Nile*, 281–82.
71. Letter from Edward Lane to Robert Hay, 27 April 1831, Bodleian Library, Department of Western Manuscripts, Ms Eng. lett d 165, f. 44.
72. Jason Thompson, personal communication.
73. Carmel and Schmid, *The Life and Works of Gustav Bauernfeind*, 118.
74. Hunt, *Pre-Raphaelitism and the Pre-Raphaelite Brotherhood*, vol. II, 321.
75. Goodall, *Reminiscences*, 90.
76. Hunt, *Pre-Raphaelitism and the Pre-Raphaelite Brotherhood*, vol. 1, 378.
77. See Bronkhurst, *William Holman Hunt, A Catalogue Raisonné*, vol. II, 264.
78. Letter dated 4 January 1839, National Library of Scotland (MS 2255, f.88).

79. Letter from Delacroix to J.-B. Pierret, 2 April 1832, cited in Stewart, *Eugène Delacroix: Selected Letters*, 191.
80. Letter of 31 January 1839, cited in Ballantine *The Life of David Roberts*, 113.
81. Strachey, *Letters of Edward Lear*, 102.
82. Strachey, *Letters of Edward Lear*, 103.
83. Ballantine, *The Life of David Roberts*, 109.
84. Carmel and Schmid, *The Life and Works of Gustav Bauernfeind*, 145.
85. Carmel and Schmid, *The Life and Works of Gustav Bauernfeind*, 98.
86. Carmel and Schmid, *The Life and Works of Gustav Bauernfeind*, 107.
87. Cited in Sim, *David Roberts*, 154.
88. Bridgman, *Winters in Algeria*, 69.
89. See Williams, 'John Frederick Lewis: "Reflections of Reality," 227–43.
90. Ackerman, "Why Some Orientalists Traveled to the East."
91. Seddon, *Memoir and Letters of the Late Thomas Seddon*, 126.
92. Carmel and Schmid, *The Life and Works of Gustav Bauernfeind*, 123.

Chapter 3: People

1. From a letter from Renoir to Duran-Ruel, March 1882, cited in Benjamin, *Orientalism: Delacroix to Klee*, 134.
2. Cited in Hering, *Gérôme: The Life and Works of Jean Léon Gérôme*, 118.
3. Thompson, "Osman Effendi: A Scottish Convert to Islam," 81.
4. Steegmuller, *Flaubert in Egypt*, 29.
5. Hunt to Rossetti, 12–13 March 1854, MS, Huntington Library, Piggott Coll., HM 12961; cited in Bronkhurst, *William Holman Hunt, A Catalogue Raisonné*, vol. I, 170.
6. Bronkhurst, 'William Holman Hunt's Visits to Egypt," 51.
7. Seddon, *Memoir and Letters of the Late Thomas Seddon*, 32.
8. Seddon, *Memoir and Letters of the Late Thomas Seddon*, 30.
9. Seddon, *Memoir and Letters of the Late Thomas Seddon*, 45.
10. See Weeks, *19th Century Orientalist Paintings from the Collection of Terence Garnett*, 48.
11. Bridgman, *Winters in Algeria*, 25.
12. Weeks, 'Two Centres of Moorish Art," 441–42.
13. Seddon, *Memoir and Letters of the Late Thomas Seddon*, 29.
14. Castlereagh, *A Journey to Damascus*, 89–90.
15. Goodall, *Reminiscences*, 70–71.
16. Bridgman, *Winters in Algeria*, 141–42.
17. Thompson, "Osman Effendi: A Scottish Convert to Islam," 86.
18. Griffith Institute, Oxford, Lane collection, typescript of Robert Hay's diary; cited in Thompson, "Osman Effendi: A Scottish Convert to Islam," 87.
19. National Library of Scotland, Department of Manuscripts, Box II, Acc 7967/1, David Roberts Eastern Journals, vol. 1, 154–155, cited in Thompson, "Osman Effendi: A Scottish Convert to Islam," 97.
20. I am grateful to Briony Llewellyn for sharing with me her research into Hanafi Ismael.
21. Hering, *Gérôme: The Life and Works of Jean Léon Gérôme*, 128.
22. Jerichau-Baumann, "Motley Images of Travel," 270–71.
23. Cook and Wedderburn, *The Works of John Ruskin*, vol. 14, 74.
24. Warburton, "Episodes of Eastern Travel," 433.
25. Castlereagh, *A Journey to Damascus*, 259.
26. Cited in Ballantine in *The Life of David Roberts*, 104–105.
27. Seddon, *Memoir and Letters of the Late Thomas Seddon*, 52.
28. Edwards, *A Thousand Miles up the Nile*, 147.
29. Ballantine, *The Life of David Roberts*, 104.
30. For further discussion on Roberts's use of figures in his works, see Guiterman and Llewellyn, *David Roberts*, 81–85.
31. Goodall, *Reminiscences*, 80.
32. Goodall, *Reminiscences*, 101.
33. Wedmore, "Carl Haag, R.W.S," 52–61.
34. Llewellyn and Newton, *The People and Places of Constantinople*, 15–16. See also Inankur, "Painter of Istanbul and his story."
35. Morton, "Étienne Dinet, Painter of the Orient," 251, 255.
36. Morton, "Étienne Dinet, Painter of the Orient," 259–60.

37. Castlereagh, *A Journey to Damascus*, vol. 1, 195–96.
38. Peltre, *Orientalism*, 32.
39. Hunt, *Pre-Raphaelitism and the Pre-Raphaelite Brotherhood*, vol. I, 380.
40. Noakes, *Edward Lear, Selected Letters*, 209.
41. Untitled typescript from the Edwin Lord Weeks Papers, Smithsonian Institution.
42. Steegmuller, *Flaubert in Egypt*, 35.
43. Cited in Sattin, *A Winter on the Nile*, 183.
44. Cited in Sattin, *A Winter on the Nile*, 182.
45. Cited in Sattin, *A Winter on the Nile*, 183.
46. Strachey, *Letters of Edward Lear*, 103.
47. Jerichau-Baumann, "Motley Images of Travel, 'Egypt 1870,'" 268–69.
48. Carmel and Schmid, *The Life and Works of Gustav Bauernfeind*, 107, 118.
49. Letter from Castlereagh to Lewis, dated 10 May 1842 and cited in Weeks, *Cultures Crossed*, 129.
50. Castlereagh, *A Journey to Damascus*, vol. I, 260.
51. Bridgman, *Winters in Algeria*, 221–22.
52. From "Cairo Notes" in the Edwin Lord Weeks Papers, Smithsonian.
53. Jerichau-Baumann, "Motley Images of Travel, 'Egypt 1870,'" 274.
54. Carmel and Schmid, *The Life and Works of Gustav Bauernfeind*, 118.
55. Jerichau-Baumann, "Motley Images of Travel, 'Egypt 1870,'" 274.
56. Llewellyn, "Friend and Foe," 60 fn 44.
57. Llewellyn, "The Woman in Blue," 93.
58. Jerichau-Baumann, "Motley Images of Travel," 274–75.
59. Letter from Seddon to his future wife, 13 August 1854. See Landow, "William Holman Hunt's Letters to Thomas Seddon," 160 fn 35.
60. Hunt, *Pre-Raphaelitism and the Pre-Raphaelite Brotherhood*, vol. I, 382–83.
61. Ackerman, *American Orientalists*, 238.
62. Llewellyn, "Friend and Foe," 56
63. For a full account see Llewellyn, "Friend and Foe," 47–74.
64. Ackerman, *American Orientalists*, 189.
65. Bridgman, *Winters in Algeria*, 145.
66. Zemen, *Leopold Carl Müller*, letter no. 309, 400.
67. Jerichau-Baumann, "Motley Images of Travel," 277.
68. Cited in Thornton, *Women as Portrayed in Orientalist Painting*, 154
69. Jerichau-Baumann, "Motley Images of Travel," 275.
70. Edwards, *A Thousand Miles up the Nile*, 435.
71. Fromentin, *Un Été dans le Sahara*, 151, 1877 edition, text translated from the original; see comments on this in bibliography.
72. Cited in Fetvaci, *The Art of Osman Hamdi*, 4. See also Eldem, "An Ottoman Traveler to the Orient," 168–81.
73. See Tromans, "Harem and Home," 128.
74. For a full account, see Roberts, *Intimate Outsiders*, 109–117.
75. Gautier, *Abécédaire du Salon de 1861*, 72–77.
76. Bridgman, *Winters in Algeria*, 25–26.
77. Tromans, "Harem and Home," 132.
78. Gautier, "Gérôme: Tableaux, études, et croquis de voyage," 23.
79. Cited in Gautier, "MM. Gérôme, Mottez," 245–49.
80. Weeks, *19th Century Orientalist Paintings from the Collection of Terence Garnett*, 24.
81. Cited in Weeks, *19th Century Orientalist Paintings from the Collection of Terence Garnett*, 20.
82. Hunt, *Pre-Raphaelitism and the Pre-Raphaelite Brotherhood*, vol. 1, 349.
83. Hunt, *Pre-Raphaelitism and the Pre-Raphaelite Brotherhood*, vol. 1. 377.
84. Cited in Mathur, *India by Design*, 87.

Chapter 4: Image

1. Phipps-Jackson, "Cairo in London," 71.
2. Day, "The Artist's Eye," 97, 100.
3. Phipps-Jackson, "Cairo in London," 72.
4. Sweetman, *The Oriental Obsession*, 225.
5. Goodall, *Reminiscences*, 293.
6. Goodall, *Reminiscences*, 294.
7. Phipps-Jackson, "Cairo in London," 71.

8. I am grateful to Professor Herbert Zemen for this information.
9. Cited in Noon, "Colour and Effect," 27.
10. Cited in Millar, *Queen Victoria's Life in the Scottish Highlands*, 143–44.
11. Cited in Lewis, *John Frederick Lewis*, 28.
12. Letter from John Frederick Lewis to Thomas Griffith, 3 February 1858, private collection, cited in Lewis, *John Frederick Lewis*, 30.
13. See Emily M. Weeks, http://www.19thc-artworldwide.org/autumn13/new-discoveries-re-discovering-john-frederick-lewis-1804-76
14. Carmel and Schmid, *The Life and Works of Gustav Bauernfeind*, 103–104.
15. Carmel and Schmid, *The Life and Works of Gustav Bauernfeind*, 99.
16. Carmel and Schmid, *The Life and Works of Gustav Bauernfeind*, 106.
17. Peltre, *Orientalism*, 132.
18. Jacobson, *Odalisques & Arabesques*, 20.
19. Cited in Peltre, *Orientalism*, 134–35.
20. Steegmuller, *Flaubert in Egypt*, 102.
21. Baudelaire, *Selected Writings on Art and Artists*, 296–97.
22. Peltre, *Orientalism in Art*, 167.
23. I am grateful to Ken Jacobson for this reference, from Wheelhouse and El-Hage, *Narrative of a Yacht Voyage*, 114. See also Jacobson, *Odalisques & Arabesques*, 69.
24. Seddon, *Memoir and Letters of the Late Thomas Seddon*, 111.
25. Hannavy, *Encyclopedia of Nineteenth-Century Photography*, 606.
26. Seddon, *Memoir and Letters of the Late Thomas Seddon*, 119.
27. Hunt, *Pre-Raphaelitism and the Pre-Raphaelite Brotherhood*, vol. 2, 50.
28. Hunt, *Pre-Raphaelitism and the Pre-Raphaelite Brotherhood*, vol. 1, 426.
29. Jacobson, *Odalisques & Arabesques*, 269; see also Sattin, *Florence Nightingale*, 201.
30. Jacobson, *Odalisques & Arabesques*, 268–69.
31. Jacobson, *Odalisques & Arabesques*, 34.
32. Jacobson, *Odalisques & Arabesques*, 36.
33. Gordon, *Cairo to Constantinople*, 15.
34. Gordon, *Cairo to Constantinople*, 41.
35. Jacobson, *Odalisques & Arabesques*, 71.
36. Jacobson, *Odalisques & Arabesques*, 70.
37. Carmel and Schmid, *The Life and Works of Gustav Bauernfeind*, 101–102.
38. Carmel and Schmid, *The Life and Works of Gustav Bauernfeind*, 96, fn 49.
39. Bridgman, *Winters in Algeria*, 84.
40. Carmel and Schmid, *The Life and Works of Gustav Bauernfeind*, 116.
41. I am grateful to Ken Jacobson for this information.
42. Bridgman, *Winters in Algeria*, 84.
43. Tyssen-Amherst, *A Few Egyptian Memories*.
44. Haja and Wimmer, *Les Orientalistes des Écoles allemande et autrichienne*, 198.
45. Sotheby's *Orientalist Sale 12 November 2008* catalogue, 30.
46. Sotheby's *Orientalist Sale 12 November 2008* catalogue, 22.
47. Seddon, *Memoir and Letters of the Late Thomas Seddon*, 131–32.
48. Carmel and Schmid, *The Life and Works of Gustav Bauernfeind*, 125.
49. Goodall, *Reminiscences*, 268–69.
50. Phipps-Jackson, "Cairo in London," 72.
51. Rosenthal, *Orientalism, the Near East in French painting*, 125.
52. Cited in Rosenthal, *Orientalism, the Near East in French painting*, 122.
53. Jacobson, *Odalisques & Arabesques*, 69.
54. Jacobson, *Odalisques & Arabesques*, 72.
55. See De Font Réaulx, "Gérôme and Photography."
56. Peltre, *Orientalism in Art*, 168.
57. De Font Réaulx, "Gérôme and Photography," 226–27.
58. Jacobson, *Odalisques & Arabesques*, 69–70.
59. Denny, "Quotations in and out of Context," 220–21.
60. See, www.sothebys.com/es/auctions/ecatalogue/lot.pdf.N08431.html/f/186/N08431-186.pdf
61. Fetvaci, *The Art of Osman Hamdi*.

62. Baldwin, *Roger Fenton: Pasha and Bayadère*, 10.
63. Baldwin *et al.*, *All The Mighty World: The Photographs of Roger Fenton*, 87.
64. Baldwin *et al.*, *All The Mighty World: The Photographs of Roger Fenton*, 84.
65. Baldwin, *Roger Fenton: Pasha and Bayadère*, 43. Another possible source of inspiration for *The Song of the Nubian Slave* was Prisse d'Avennes; see Llewellyn, "Friend and Foe," 65–70.
66. For a full account of the Fenton and Haag commission, see Baldwin *et al.*, *All The Mighty World: The Photographs of Roger Fenton*, 76–78.
67. Baldwin, *Roger Fenton: Pasha and Bayadère*, 46.
68. Jacobson, *Odalisques & Arabesques*, 240.
69. Bartram, *The Pre-Raphaelite Camera*, 118.
70. Cited in Baldwin, *Roger Fenton: Pasha and Bayadère*, 54.
71. Cited in Baldwin, *Roger Fenton: Pasha and Bayadère*, 54.
72. *Littell's Living Age* (no. 31, 4 October 1851), 17.
73. Gartlan, "Dandies on the Pyramids," 134.
74. Gartlan, "Dandies on the Pyramids," 136.
75. Jacobson, *Odalisques & Arabesques*, 244.
76. *Egypt: Descriptive, Historical, and Picturesque* (Cassell, 1885).
77. Hunt, *Pre-Raphaelitism and the Pre-Raphaelite Brotherhood*, vol. 2, 95–96.
78. Miller, "The Reception of John Frederick Miller at the Exposition Universelle in 1855," 260.
79. Hering, *Gérôme: The Life and Works of Jean Léon Gérôme*, vii.
80. Denny, "Quotations in and out of Context," 220.
81. I am grateful to Caroline Williams for this information.
82. Williams in Rafif, *Masterpieces of Orientalist Art: The Shafik Gabr Collection*, 168–69.
83. Williams in Rafif, *Masterpieces of Orientalist Art: The Shafik Gabr Collection*, 156–57.
84. I am grateful to Caroline Williams for sharing with me the results of her research into this aspect of Deutsch's work.
85. I am grateful to Caroline Williams for sharing with me the results of her research into this aspect of Deutsch's work.
86. I am grateful for the help of Caroline Williams in analyzing and comparing the different features of the mosque.
87. Ackerman in Rafif, *Masterpieces of Orientalist Art: The Shafik Gabr Collection*, 257.
88. Denny, "Quotations in and out of Context," 221.
89. Cited by Sarah Anderson, preface to Fromentin, *Between Sea and Sahara*, x.
90. Cook, *Art and Artists of Our Time*, 262.

Chapter 5: Influence

1. Letter from Roberts to Hay, 13 February 1840, National Library of Scotland (MS 3521, f.107).
2. Cited in Sim, *David Roberts*, 211.
3. Cited in Llewellyn, "'Solitary Eagle?' The Public and Private Personas of John Frederick Lewis," 171.
4. *Art-Union: Monthly Journal of the Fine Arts*, vol. 3, 1841, 29.
5. For more on promotional portraiture, see Riding, "Travellers and Sitters: The Orientalist Portrait," 48–75.
6. Peltre, *Orientalism*, 114.
7. Thornton, *The Orientalists: Painter-Travellers*, 152.
8. Thompson, *The East: Imagined, Experienced, Remembered*, 79.
9. Seddon, *Memoir and Letters of the Late Thomas Seddon*, 39, 63.
10. Van Druten, "La naissance d'un orientaliste nordique," 153.
11. Bronkhurst, *William Holman Hunt, A Catalogue Raisonné*, vol. 1, 212.
12. *Illustrated London News*, Supplement, 25 March 1865, 285.
13. Cook and Wedderburn, *The Works of John Ruskin*, vol. 35, 406.
14. Weeks, *Cultures Crossed: John Frederick Lewis and the Art of Orientalism*, 36.
15. Llewellyn, "'Solitary Eagle?' The Public and Private Personas of John Frederick Lewis," 170
16. Llewellyn, "'Solitary Eagle?' The Public and Private Personas of John Frederick Lewis," 173.
17. Weeks, *Cultures Crossed: John Frederick Lewis and The Art of Orientalism*, 23.
18. Llewellyn, "'Solitary Eagle?' The Public and Private Personas of John Frederick Lewis," 167.

19. See Fetvaci, *The Art of Osman Hamdi.*
20. Roget, *A History of The 'Old Water-Colour' Society*, vol. II, 140.
21. Letter from Daniel Maclise to David Roberts, 25 January 1850, Album of letters to David Roberts, compiled by Henry Sanford Bicknell, MSS 34, Yale Center for British Art.
22. See Llewellyn, "'Solitary Eagle?' The Public and Private Personas of John Frederick Lewis," 170, and Weeks, *Cultures Crossed: John Frederick Lewis and the Art of Orientalism*, 21. As both authors affirm, the evidence to support a deal is far from conclusive and the idea of any such agreement between Lewis and Thackeray remains purely speculative.
23. Cited in Sim, *David Roberts*, 101.
24. Ballantine, *The Life of David Roberts*, 140. In the event, a total of six volumes were published.
25. Ballantine, *The Life of David Roberts*, 141.
26. Ballantine, *The Life of David Roberts*, 146.
27. Cook and Wedderburn, *The Works of John Ruskin*, vol. 3, 598.
28. Cited in Sim, *David Roberts*, 212.
29. Thornton, *The Orientalists: Painter Travellers*, 24–25, 116.
30. Cited in Lafont-Couturier, "Mr. Gérôme works for Goupil," 13.
31. Zola, "Our artists on the Champs de Mars," 184.
32. Lafont-Couturier, "Mr. Gérôme works for Goupil," 19.
33. Cited in Lafont-Couturier, "Mr. Gérôme works for Goupil," 21.
34. Letter to Knoedler, 8 June 1903, Custodia Foundation, Fritz Lugt Collection, Netherlands Institute, Paris, cited in Lafont-Couturier, "Mr. Gérôme works for Goupil," 21.
35. Lafont-Couturier, "Mr. Gérôme works for Goupil," 27.
36. Sim, *David Roberts*, 297.
37. Cited in Macleod, *Art and the Victorian middle class*, 5.
38. Goodall, *Reminiscences*, 194.
39. See Chagnon-Burke, "Rue Laffitte: Looking at and Buying Contemporary Art in Mid-Nineteenth-Century Paris."
40. Peltre, *Orientalism in Art*, 253.
41. Maas, *Gambart: Prince of the Victorian Art World* , 195.
42. Goodall, *Reminiscences*, 176.
43. Goodall, *Reminiscences*, 93.
44. Cited in Macleod, *Art and the Victorian middle class*, 209.
45. Cited in Macleod, *Art and the Victorian middle class*, 235.
46. Ackerman, *American Orientalists*, 32.
47. Roget, *A History of The 'Old Water-Colour' Society*, vol. II, 351.
48. Phipps-Jackson, "Cairo in London," 74.
49. Bronkhurst, *William Holman Hunt, A Catalogue Raisonné*, vol. 1, 173.
50. Hunt, *Pre-Raphaelitism and the Pre-Raphaelite Brotherhood*, vol. 2, 106.
51. Hunt, *Pre-Raphaelitism and the Pre-Raphaelite Brotherhood*, vol. 2, 108.
52. Macleod, *Art and the Victorian middle class*, 194.
53. Cited in Weeks, "For Love or For Money: Collecting the Orientalist Pictures of John Frederick Lewis," 42.
54. Ackerman, *The life and work of Jean-Léon Gérôme*, 59.
55. Maas, *Gambart: Prince of the Victorian Art World*, 28.
56. Seddon, *Memoir and Letters of the Late Thomas Seddon*, 111.
57. Maas, *Gambart: Prince of the Victorian Art World*, 45.
58. Carmel and Schmid, *The Life and Works of Gustav Bauernfeind, Orientalist Painter*, 125.
59. Carmel and Schmid, *The Life and Works of Gustav Bauernfeind, Orientalist Painter*, 106.
60. Carmel and Schmid, *The Life and Works of Gustav Bauernfeind, Orientalist Painter*, 94.
61. Carmel and Schmid, *The Life and Works of Gustav Bauernfeind, Orientalist Painter*, 125.
62. Carmel and Schmid, *The Life and Works of Gustav Bauernfeind, Orientalist Painter*, 131.
63. Carmel and Schmid, *The Life and Works of Gustav Bauernfeind, Orientalist Painter*, 79.
64. Benjamin, *Orientalist Aesthetics*, 25–27.
65. Benjamin, *Orientalist Aesthetics*, 59.
66. Benjamin, *Orientalist Aesthetics*, 59.
67. Guillaumet, *Tableaux algériens*, 269–72.
68. Zemen, *Leopold Carl Müller*, 193. Excerpt translated by Waltraud Chapman.
69. De Nerval in *Œuvres*, 1:933.

70. De Nerval to Théophile Gautier, cited in Said, *Orientalism*, 101.
71. Weeks, "Two Centres of Moorish Art," 434.
72. From Bénédite's preface to Étienne Dinet and Sliman Ben Ibrahim, *Tableaux de la vie arabe*, cited in Benjamin, *Orientalist Aesthetics*, 59.
73. Letter from Müller to J. Satterfield dated 22 September 1844, cited in Solly, *Memoir of the Life of William James Müller*, 226. Müller was referring to the excavations of Charles Fellows, who removed Lycian antiquities and shipped them to England for the British Museum.
74. Cited in Ziter, *The Orient on the Victorian Stage*, 49.
75. Ruskin, *Academy Notes* 1855–1888, 218.
76. Cited in Peltre, *Orientalism*, 217.
77. Cited in Peltre, *Orientalism*, 222.
78. Weeks, *Cultures Crossed: John Frederick Lewis and The Art of Orientalism*, 140–41.
79. 'John Frederick Lewis, R.A.,' *The Portfolio*, vol. XXIII (1892), 96.
80. Stephens, "The Collection of Mr. W. Cuthbert Quilter, M.P.," 260.
81. Ganley and Paddock, *The Art of Edwin Lord Weeks*, 11.
82. Ackerman, *American Orientalists*, 32.
83. Cited in Slarke, *F. Goodall*, 71.
84. Slarke, *F. Goodall*, 74.
85. *The Times*, 1 August 1904, cited in Slarke, *F. Goodall*, 72.
86. Bronkhurst, *William Holman Hunt, A Catalogue Raisonné*, vol. 1, 22.
87. *Nation*, LXXXIII, 25 October 1906, cited in Bronkhurst, *William Holman Hunt, A Catalogue Raisonné*, vol. 1, 35.
88. Ackerman, *The Life and Works of Jean-Léon Gérôme*, 144.
89. Cited in Lemaire, *The Orient in Western Art*, 295.

Epilogue

1. Thornton, *The Orientalists: Painter-Travellers*, 13.
2. Klee, *The Diaries of Paul Klee*, 297; see also Benjamin, *Orientalism: from Delacroix to Klee*, 180–81.
3. Searight, "Vision of the Middle East," 32–39.

Bibliography

Ackerman, Gerald M. *American Orientalists*. ACR Édition, 1994.

Ackerman, Gerald M. *The Life and Work of Jean-Léon Gérôme*. London: Sotheby's, 1986.

Ackerman, Gerald M. "Why Some Orientalists Traveled to the East: Some Sobering Statistics," *Picturing the Middle East: A Hundred Years of European Orientalism. A Symposium*. Dahesh Museum of Art, 1996. 1–13.

Aldrich, Robert. *Colonialism and Homosexuality*. Routledge, 2002.

Allan, Scott Christopher and Mary G. Morton (eds). *Reconsidering Gérôme*. Getty Trust Publications, 2010.

The Art Institute of Chicago. *Catalogue of Pictures and Studies by F. A. Bridgman*. Knight & Leonard Co, 1890.

Baldwin, Gordon. *Roger Fenton: Pasha and Bayadère*. Getty Museum Studies on Art, 1996.

Baldwin, Gordon, Malcolm Daniel, and Sarah Greenough. *All The Mighty World: The Photographs of Roger Fenton, 1852–1860*. Yale University Press, 2004.

Ballantine, James. *The Life of David Roberts, R.A.* Adam and Charles Black, 1866.

Bartlett, William Henry. *The Nile boat; or, glimpses of the land of Egypt*. Arthur Hall, 1849.

Bartram, Michael. *The Pre-Raphaelite Camera: Aspects of Victorian Photography*. Weidenfeld & Nicolson, 1989.

Baudelaire, Charles. *Selected Writings on Art and Artists*. Cambridge University Press, 1981.

Behdad, Ali. *Belated Travelers: Orientalism in the Age of Colonial Dissolution*. Duke University Press, 1994.

Béguin, Albert and Jean Richet (eds), *Gérard de Nerval, Œuvres*. Gallimard, 1960.

Benjamin, Roger. *Kandinsky and Klee in Tunisia*. University of California Press, 2015.

Benjamin, Roger. *Orientalism: Delacroix to Klee*. The Art Gallery of New South Wales, 1997.

Benjamin, Roger. *Orientalist Aesthetics: Art, Colonialism, and French North Africa, 1880–1930*. University of California Press, 2003.

Boswell, James. *The Life of Samuel Johnson, LL.D.* Ewer and Bedlington, originally published 1791, 1824 edition.

Brahimi, Denise. *La Vie et l'oeuvre d'Étienne Dinet*. ACR Éditions, 1991.

Bridgman, Frederick Arthur. *Winters in Algeria*. Harper & Bros, 1890.

Bronkhurst, Judith. *William Holman Hunt, A Catalogue Raisonné*. Paul Mellon Centre for Studies in British Art/Yale University Press, 2006.

Bronkhurst, Judith. "William Holman Hunt's Visits to Egypt: Passion, Prejudice and Truth to Nature." In *Interpreting the Orient*, edited by Paul and Janet Starkey. Ithaca Press, 2001.

Brotton, Jerry. *This Orient Isle: Elizabethan England and the Islamic World*. Allen Lane, 2016.

Budge, E.A. Wallis. *Cook's Handbook for Egypt and the Sudan*. London, 1906.
Cannadine, David. *Ornamentalism: How the British Saw Their Empire*. Oxford University Press, 2001.
Carmel, Alex and Hugo Schmid. *The Life and Works of Gustav Bauernfeind, Orientalist Painter, 1848–1904*. Hauswedell & Co, 1990.
Carne, John. *Syria, The Holy Land, Asia Minor, &c*. Fisher, Son, & Co, 1836.
Castlereagh, Viscount. *A Journey to Damascus Through Egypt, Nubia, Arabia Petraea, Palestine, and Syria*. Henry Colburn, 1847.
Çelik, Zeynep. *Displaying the Orient: Architecture of Islam at Nineteenth-Century World's Fairs*. University of California Press, 1992.
Chagnon-Burke, Véronique. "Rue Laffitte: Looking at and Buying Contemporary Art in Mid-Nineteenth-Century Paris," on www.19thc-artworldwide.org/summer12/veronique-chagnon-burke-looking-at-and-buying-contemporary-art-in-mid-nineteenth-century-paris
Clancy-Smith, Julia Ann. *Mediterraneans: North Africa and Europe in an Age of Migration, c.1800–1900*. University of California Press, 2011.
Cook, Clarence. *Art and Artists of Our Time*. Selmar Hess, 1888.
Cook, E.T. and Alexander Wedderburn (eds). *The Works of John Ruskin*. George Allen, 1903–12.
Cunningham, Allan. *The Life of Sir David Wilkie*. John Murray, 1843.
Davies, Kristian. *The Orientalists: Western Artists in Arabia, The Sahara, Persia and India*. Laynfaroh, 1999.
Day, Susan. "The Artist's Eye: Carpet and Textile Collections of the Orientalists," *Hali*, issue 126 (2003), 92–104.
De Font Réaulx, Dominique. "Gérôme and Photography." In *Jean-Léon Gérôme (1824–1904)*. Musée d'Orsay/Getty Museum/Skira, 2010.
De Nerval, Gérard. *Œuvres*, edited by Albert Béguin and Jean Richet. Gallimard, 1960.
Delacroix, Eugène. *Correspondance générale d'Eugène Delacroix*, edited by André Joubin. Paris, 1935–38.
Denny, Walter B. "Quotations in and out of Context: Ottoman Turkish Art and European Orientalist Painting," *Muqarnas*, vol. 10 (1993).
Denon, Dominique Vivant. *Voyage dans la Basse et la Haute Égypte*. Introduction by Jean-Claude Vatin. Cairo: Institut Français d'Archéologie Orientale, Cairo, 1989.
Dinet, Étienne and Sliman Ben Ibrahim. *Tableaux de la vie arabe*. Paris: Piazza, 1908.
Drewett Neate. *Watercolours by Carl Haag*. Sale catalogue, 6 June 2000.
Ebers, Georg. *Egypt: Descriptive, Historical, and Picturesque*. Cassell, 1885.
Edhem Eldem, "An Ottoman Traveler to the Orient: Osman Hamdi." In *The Poetics and Politics of Place: Ottoman Istanbul and British Orientalism*, edied by Inankur, Lewis and Roberts. Suna and Inan Kiraç Foundation/Pera Museum, 2011. 168–81.
Edidin, Stephen. "*Gérôme's Orientalisms*." In *Gérôme & Goupil: Art and Enterprise*. Réunion des Musées Nationaux; Dahesh Museum of Art; Frick Art and Historical Center, 2000. 109–138.
Edwards, Amelia. *A Thousand Miles up the Nile*. A.L. Burt, 1877.
Egerton, Lady Francis. *Journal of a Tour in the Holy Land, in May and June, 1840*. Harrison and Co., 1841.
Fetvaci, Emine. *The Art of Osman Hamdi*. www.ottomanlands.com
Frith, W.P. *My Autobiography and Reminiscences*. Harper & Bros, 1888.
Fromentin, Eugène. *Between Sea and Sahara*. London: I.B.Tauris, 2004. From *Une Année dans le Sahel*, 1859.
Fromentin, Eugène. *Un Été dans le Sahara*. Michel Lévy, 1857
Ganley, Kathleen Duff and Leslie K. Paddock. *The Art of Edwin Lord Weeks (1849–1903)*. University of New Hampshire Art Galleries, 1976.
Gartlan, Luke. "Dandies on the Pyramids: Photography and German-Speaking Artists in Cairo." In *Photography's Orientalism: New Essays on Colonial Representation*, edited by Ali Behdad and Luke Gartlan. Getty Research Institute, 2013.
Gautier, Théophile. *Abécédaire du Salon de 1861*. Libraire de la Société des gens de lettres, 1861.

Gautier, Théophile. "Gérôme: Tableaux, études, et croquis de voyage," *L'Artiste*, vol. 3, 28 December 1856.

Gautier, Théophile. "MM. Gérôme, Mottez," *L'Artiste* vol. 4, 5 July 1857.

Goodall, Frederick. *The Reminiscences of Frederick Goodall, R.A.* Walter Scott, 1902.

Gordon, Sophie. *Cairo to Constantinople: Francis Bedford's Photographs of the Middle East*. London: Royal Collection, 2014.

Green, Matthew. *The Lost World of the London Coffeehouse*. London: Idler Books, 2013.

Guillaumet, Gustave. *Tableaux algériens*. Librairie Plon, 1888.

Guiterman, Helen and Briony Llewellyn. *David Roberts*: Phaidon Press and Barbican Art Gallery, 1986.

Gurcaglar, Aygut. "The Dragoman Who Commissioned His Own Portrait." In *The Poetics and Politics of Place: Ottoman Istanbul and British Orientalism,* edited by Zeynep Inankur, Reina Lewis, and Mary Roberts. Sunan and Inan Kiraç Foundation, 2011.

Haja, Martina and Günther Wimmer. *Les Orientalistes des Écoles allemande et autrichienne*. ACR Édition, 2000.

Hannavy John (ed.), *Encyclopedia of Nineteenth-Century Photography*. Routledge, 2007.

Healy, Mary. "Uncovering French Women Orientalist Artists: Marie Elisabeth Aimée Lucas–Robiquet (1858–1959)," *Women's Studies*, vol. 44, issue 8 (2015), 1178–99.

Hering, Fanny Field. *Gérôme: The Life and Works of Jean Léon Gérôme*. Cassell, 1889.

Hodgson, Barbara. *Dreaming of East: Western Women and the Exotic Allure of the Orient*. Greystone Books, 2005.

Hunt, William Holman. *Pre-Raphaelitism and the Pre-Raphaelite Brotherhood*. London: Macmillan, 1905.

Inankur, Zeynep. "Painter of Istanbul and his story." In *Amadeo Preziosi*, edited by Begum Kovulmaz. Yapi Kredi Yayinlari, 2007.

Irving, Washington. *The Alhambra: a series of tales and sketches of the Moors and Spaniards*. Lea & Cary and Henry Colburn, 1832.

Issawi, Charles. *An Economic History of the Middle East and North Africa*. Columbia University Press, 1982.

Jacobson, Ken. *Odalisques & Arabesques: Orientalist Photography 1839–1925*. Quaritch, 2007.

Jánosi, Peter. "Leopold Carl Müller's Travels to Egypt with a Special Remark on his Eighth Trip, on which he was accompanied by his sister Maria, 1883/84." In *Egypt and Austria I: Proceedings of a Symposium*, edited by Johanna Holaubek and Hana Navrátilova. 2005.

Jerichau-Baumann, Elisabeth. "Motley Images of Travel, 'Egypt 1870.'" Translated by Ragnheidur Olafsdottir. In *Victorian Literature and Culture* 38. Cambridge: Cambridge University Press, 2010. 267–84.

Jerningham, Hubert E.H. *To and From Constantinople*. Hurst and Blackett, 1873.

Juler, Caroline. *Les Orientalistes de'École Italienne*. ACR Édition, 1994.

Juler Caroline. *Najd: Collection of Orientalist Paintings*. London: Mathaf Gallery, 1989.

Kinglake, Alexander William. *Eothen; or Traces of travel brought home from the East*. J. Ollivier, 1844.

Kitson, Sydney D. *The Life of John Sell Cotman*. London: Faber and Faber, 1937.

Klee, Felix (ed.). *The Diaries of Paul Klee*. University of California Press, 1964.

Kuehn, Julia. "Elisabeth Jerichau-Baumann 'Egypt 1870.'" In *Victorian Literature and Culture* 38. Cambridge: Cambridge University Press, 2010. 257–66.

Lafont-Couturier, Hélène. "Mr Gérôme works for Goupil," *Gérôme & Goupil: Art and Enterprise*. Réunion des Musées Nationaux; Dahesh Museum of Art; Frick Art and Historical Center, 2000. 13–29.

Landow, George P. "William Holman Hunt's Letters to Thomas Seddon," in Bulletin of the John Rylands University Library of Manchester, 66 (1983).

Lane, Edward William. *An Account of the Manners and Customs of the Modern Egyptians*. John Murray, 1860 edition.

Lane, Edward William. *Description of Egypt*. Edited by Jason Thompson. Cairo: American University in Cairo Press, 2000.

Lear, Edward. "A Leaf from the Journals of a Landscape Painter," *Macmillan's Magazine* vol. LXXV (1897).

Lemaire, Gérard-Georges. *The Orient in Western Art*. H.F. Ullmann, 2008.

Levallois, Nicole. *Les déserts d'Égypte*. ACR Édition, 1996.

Lewis, Michael. *John Frederick Lewis R.A. 1805–1876*. F. Lewis, 1978.

Lewis, Reina. *Gendering Orientalism: Race, Femininity and Representation*. Routledge, 1996.

Lister, W.B.C. *Murray's Handbooks for Travellers*. University Publications of America, 1993.

Llewellyn, Briony. "David Wilkie and John Frederick Lewis in Constantinople, 1840: An Artistic Dialogue," *The Burlington Magazine*, Vol. 145, No. 1206 (September 2003), 624–31.

Llewellyn, Briony. "Friend and Foe: Émile Prisse d'Avennes, George Lloyd, John Frederick Lewis and the Interconnecting Circles of the British in Egypt." In Mercedes Volait (ed.), *Émile Prisse d'Avennes—Un artiste-antiquaire en Égypte au XIXe siècle*. Institut Français d'Archéologie Orientale, 2013. 47–74.

Llewellyn, Briony. "A 'Masquerade' Unmasked: An Aspect of John Frederick Lewis's Encounter with Egypt." In Jason Thompson (ed.), *Egyptian Encounters*, vol. 23, no. 3 of *Cairo Papers in Social Science* (2002), 133–51.

Llewellyn, Briony. *The Orient Observed: Images of the Middle East from the Searight Collection*. London: Victoria and Albert Museum, 1989.

Llewellyn, Briony. "Point counter-point: John Frederick Lewis and the Khan al-Khalili, Cairo," *The Burlington Magazine*, Vol. 156, No. 1336 (July 2014), 454–59.

Llewellyn, Briony. "'Solitary Eagle?' The Public and Private Personas of John Frederick Lewis (1804–1876)." In *The Poetics and Politics of Place: Ottoman Istanbul and British Orientalism*, edited by Inankur, Lewis and Roberts. Suna and Inan Kiraç Foundation/Pera Museum, 2011. 167–81.

Llewellyn, Briony. "The Woman in Blue: John Frederick Lewis's Cairo figure studies," *British Paintings Watercolours and Drawings*. Lowell Libson Ltd, 2010.

Llewellyn, Briony and Charles Newton. *The People and Places of Constantinople: Watercolours by Amadeo Count Preziosi*. London: The Victoria and Albert Museum, 1985.

Maas, Jeremy. *Gambart: Prince of the Victorian Art World*. Barrie & Jenkins, 1975.

Macleod, Dianne Sachko. *Art and the Victorian middle class: Money and the making of cultural identity*. Cambridge: Cambridge University Press, 1996.

Macmillan's *Guide to Egypt and the Sûdân* (1916 edition).

Majda, Tadeusz, R Bariş Kibris, Begüm Akkonunlu Ersöz and Tania Bahar (eds). *Orientalism in Polish Art* (*Polonya Sanatinda Oryantalizm*). Pera Museum, 2014.

Mansel, Philip. *Levant: Splendour and Catastrophe on the Mediterranean*. John Murray, 2010.

Masson, Frédéric. "J.L. Gérôme. Notes et fragments des souvenirs inédits du maître," *Les Arts*, 1902.

Mathur, Saloni. *India by Design: Colonial History and Cultural Display*. University of California Press, 2007.

McIntosh, DeCourcy E. "Goupil and the American Triumph of Jean-Léon Gérôme," *Gérôme & Goupil: Art and Enterprise*. Réunion des Musées Nationaux; Dahesh Museum of Art; Frick Art and Historical Center, 2000. 31–43.

Millar, Delia. *Queen Victoria's Life in the Scottish Highlands: Depicted by Her Watercolour Artists*. London: Philip Wilson Publishers, 1985.

Miller, Peter Benson. "The Reception of John Frederick Miller at the Exposition Universelle in 1855." In *The Poetics and Politics of Place, Ottoman Istanbul and British Orientalism*, edited by Zeynep Inankur, Reina Lewis, and Mary Roberts. Sunan and Inan Kiraç Foundation/Pera Museum, 2011.

Montagu, Lady Mary Wortley. *The Turkish Embassy Letters*, edited by Malcolm Jack. Virago Press, 1994.

Morton, Frederick W. "Étienne Dinet, Painter of the Orient," in *Brush and Pencil*, vol. 13, no. 4 (Jan. 1904).

Murray, John. *A Hand-book for Travellers in the Ionian Islands, Greece, Turkey, Asia Minor, and Constantinople: Being a Guide to the Principal Routes in Those Countries, Including a Description of Malta, with Maxims and Hints for Travellers in the East*. John Murray, 1840.

Nefedova, Olga. *A Journey into the World of the Ottmans: The Art of Jean-Baptiste Vanmour*. Skira, 2009.

Netton, Ian Richard (ed.). *Orientalism Revisited: Art, Land and Voyage*. Routledge, 2013.
Noakes, Vivien. *Edward Lear: The Life of a Wanderer*. Collins, 1968.
Noakes, Vivien. *Edward Lear: Selected Letters*. Oxford: Clarendon Press/Oxford University Press, 1988.
Noon, Patrick. "Colour and Effect: Anglo-French Painting in London and Paris," *Constable to Delacroix: British Art and the French Romantics*. London: Tate, 2003.
Noon, Patrick and Christopher Riopelle. *Delacroix: And the Rise of Modern Art*. The National Gallery in association with Minneapolis Institute of Art, 2015.
Oelwein, Cornelia. "Carl Haag 1820–1915: Fact or Fantasy?" In *Interpreting the Orient: Travellers in Egypt and the Near East*, edited by Paul and Janet Starkey. Ithaca Press, 2001.
Ousterhout, Robert G. *John Henry Haynes: A Photographer and Archaeologist in the Ottoman Empire 1881–1900*. Cornucopia, 2011.
Pardoe, Julia. *The Beauties of the Bosphorus*. George Virtue, 1838.
Pardoe, Julia. *The City of the Sultan; and the Domestic Manners of the Turks, in 1836*. Henry Colburn, 1837.
Peltre, Christine. *Orientalism*. Terrail, 2004.
Peltre, Christine. *Orientalism in Art*. Abbeville Press, 1998.
Phipps-Jackson, M. "Cairo in London: Carl Haag's Studio," *The Art Journal* (1883).
Poole, Sophia Lane. *The Englishwoman in Egypt: Letters from Cairo*. Charles Knight & Co, 1844.
Prisse d'Avennes, Achille-Constant-Théodore-Émile (with James Augustus St John). *Oriental Album—Characters, Costumes, and Modes of Life, in the Valley of the Nile*. London: James Madden, 1848.
Prisse d'Avennes, Achille-Constant-Théodore-Émile. *L'Art arabe d'après les monuments du Kaire depuis le VIIe siècle jusqu'à la fin du XVIIIe*. Paris, V. A. Morel, 1869–77.
Prothero, R.E. *The Letters of Richard Ford, 1796–1858*. John Murray, 1905.
Rafif, Ahmed Chaouki (ed.). *Masterpieces of Orientalist Art: The Shafik Gabr Collection*. ACR Édition, 2012 edition.
Riding, Christine. "Travellers and Sitters: The Orientalist Portrait." In *The Lure of the East: British Orientalist Painting*, edited by Nicholas Tromans. London: Tate, 2008.
Rifat, Samih, Bariş Kibris and Begüm Akkoyunlu (eds.). *Portraits from the Empire: The Ottoman World and the Ottomans from the 18th to the 20th Century with Selected Works from the Suna and İnan Kıraç Foundation Collection*. Suna and Inan Kiraç Foundation/Pera Museum, 2005.
Roberts, David. *The Holy Land, Syria, Idumea, Arabia, Egypt and Nubia*. 6 vols, 1842–49.
Roberts, Mary. *Intimate Outsiders: The Harem in Ottoman and Orientalist Art and Travel Literature*. Duke University Press, 2007.
Robertson, Ian. *Richard Ford 1796–1858: Hispanophile, Connoisseur and Critic*. Michael Russell Publishing, 2004.
Rodenbeck, John. "Dressing Native." In *Unfolding the Orient—Travellers in Egypt and the Near East*, edited by Paul and Janet Starkey. Ithaca Press, 2001. 65–100.
Roget, John Lewis. *A History of The 'Old Water-Colour' Society now The Royal Society of Painters in Water Colours*. Longmans, Green, and Co, 1891.
Rosenthal, Donald A. *Orientalism, the Near East in French painting 1800–1880*. Memorial Art Gallery of the University of Rochester, 1982.
Ruskin, John. *Academy Notes 1855–1888*. George Allen, 1904.
Russell, Alexander. *The Natural History of Aleppo and Parts Adjacent*. A. Millar, 1756.
Said, Edward. *Orientalism*. London: Vintage Books Edition, 1979.
Sattin, Anthony. *Florence Nightingale, Letters from Egypt, A Journey on the Nile 1849–1850*. Barrie & Jenkins, 1987.
Sattin, Anthony. *Lifting The Veil: British Society in Egypt 1768–1956*. J.M. Dent & Sons, 1988.
Sattin, Anthony. *A Winter on the Nile*. Hutchinson, 2010.
Searight, Sarah. "Vision of the Middle East," *Saudi Aramco World* (May/June 1984), 32–39.
Secor, Anna. "Orientalism, gender and class in Lady Mary Wortley Montagu's Turkish Embassy Letters: to persons of distinction, men of letters and c," *Cultural Geographies* (formerly *Ecumene*), Volume 6, Issue 4, 375–98. Arnold Publishers, 1999.

Seddon, John Pollard. *Memoir and Letters of the Late Thomas Seddon*. James Nisbet & Co, 1858.
Sim, Katharine. *David Roberts R.A., 1796-1864: A Biography*. Quartet Books, 1984.
Simpson, William. *The Autobiography of William Simpson, R.I.* T. Fisher Unwin, 1903.
Slarke, N.G. *F. Goodall, R.A.* Oundle, 1981.
Solly, N. Neal. *Memoir of the Life of William James Müller*. Chapman and Hall, 1875.
Sotheby's London. *The Orientalist Sale* (catalogues, 12 November 2008, 2 June 2010, 23 April 2013, 8 April 2014, 19 April 2016).
Starkey, Paul and Janet Starkey (eds). *Interpreting the Orient: Travellers in Egypt and the Near East*. Ithaca Press, 2001.
Starkey, Paul and Janet Starkey (eds). *Travellers in Egypt*. London: I.B.Tauris, 1998.
Starkey, Paul and Janet Starkey (eds). *Unfolding the Orient: Travellers in Egypt and the Near East*. Ithaca Press, 2001.
Steegmuller, Francis (ed.). *Flaubert in Egypt: A Sensibility on Tour*. Academy Chicago, 1979.
Stephens, F.G. "The Collection of Mr. W. Cuthbert Quilter, M.P.," *The Magazine of Art*, vol. 20, November 1896–April 1897, 260.
Stephens, F.G. *William Holman Hunt and His Works: A Memoir of the Artist's Life, with Description of His Pictures*. Nisbet, 1861.
Stephens, J.L. *Incidents of Travel in the Russian and Turkish Empires*. Richard Bentley, 1839.
Stewart, Jean (ed.), *Eugène Delacroix: Selected Letters, 1813–1863*. Eyre & Spottiswoode, 1971.
Sweetman, John. *The Oriental Obsession: Islamic Inspiration in British and American Art and Architecture 1500–1920*. Cambridge: Cambridge University Press, 1988.
Taylor, M. S. "Hermann Corrodi," *The Magazine of Art*, vol. 12 (Cassell & Co, 1889), 217–33.
Thackeray, William Makepeace. *Notes of a Journey from Cornhill to Grand Cairo*. Chapman and Hall, 1846.
Thompson, James. *The East: Imagined, Experienced, Remembered*. National Gallery of Ireland/National Museums and Galleries on Merseyside, 1988.
Thompson, James and Barbara Wright. *La Vie et l'oeuvre d'Eugène Fromentin*. ACR Édition, 1987.
Thompson, Jason. "An Account of the Journeys and Writings of The Indefatigable Mr. Lane." *Saudi Aramco World* (March/April 2008), 30–39.
Thompson, Jason. *Edward William Lane: The Life of the Pioneering Egyptologist and Orientalist*. Haus Publishing, 2010.
Thompson, Jason (ed.). *Egyptian Encounters*, vol. 23, no. 3 of *Cairo Papers in Social Science* (2000).
Thompson, Jason. "Osman Effendi: A Scottish Convert to Islam in Early Nineteenth-Century Egypt." In *Historians in Cairo: Essays in Honor of George Scanlon*, edited by Jill Edwards. Cairo: American University in Cairo Press, 2002. 81–106.
Thompson, Jason. *Sir Gardner Wilkinson and His Circle*. University of Texas Press, 1992.
Thornton, Lynne. *The Orientalists: Painter-Travellers*. ACR Édition, 1983.
Thornton, Lynne. *Women as Portrayed in Orientalist Painting*. ACR Édition, 1985.
Tromans, Nicholas. "British Orientalist Painting." In *The Lure of The East: British Orientalist Painting*. London: Tate, 2008. 10–21.
Tromans, Nicholas. "Harem and Home." In *The Lure of the East: British Orientalist Painting*. London: Tate, 2008. 128–137.
Tromans, Nicholas. *Richard Dadd: The Artist and the Asylum*. London: Tate, 2011.
Tyssen-Amherst, Mary. *A Few Egyptian Memories*. Unpublished, Amherst Family Archives.
Van Druten, Terry. "La naissance d'un orientaliste nordique: l'influence de l'expédition d'Émile Prisse d'Avennes sur l'oeuvre de Willem de Famars Testas." In *Émile Prisse d'Avennes—Un artiste-antiquaire en Égypte au XIXe siècle*, edited by Mercedes Volait. Institut Français d'Archéologie Orientale, 2013.
Volait, Mercedes. "Avec le double empressement d'un artiste et d'un antiquaire: Les arts de l'Égypte médiévale vus par Émile Prisse d'Avennes," *Visions d'Égypte, Émile Prisse d'Avennes (1807–1879)*. Paris: Bibliothèque nationale de France, 2011. 93–117.

Warburton, Eliot. "Episodes of Eastern Travel," *The Dublin University Magazine*, vol. XXII (1843).
Wedmore, Frederick. "Carl Haag, R.W.S," *The Magazine of Art* (1890), 52–61.
Weeks, Edwin Lord. "Cairo Notes," Edwin Lord Weeks Papers [*c.*1885–1976] (box 1), Archives of American Art, Smithsonian Institution, Washington DC .
Weeks, Edwin Lord. *From the Black Sea through Persia and India*. Harper & Brothers, 1896.
Weeks, Edwin Lord. 'Two Centres of Moorish Art," *Scribner's Magazine* (vol. 29, 1901), 433–52.
Weeks, Edwin Lord. Untitled typescript of visit to Beirut, Edwin Lord Weeks Papers [*c.*1885–1976] (box 1), Archives of American Art, Smithsonian Institution, Washington DC, US.
Weeks, Emily M. *19th Century Orientalist Paintings from the Collection of Terence Garnett*. London: Sotheby's, 2007.
Weeks, Emily M. *Cultures Crossed: John Frederick Lewis and the Art of Orientalism*. New Haven, CT: Yale University Press for the Paul Mellon Centre for Studies in British Art, 2014.
Weeks, Emily M. "For Love or For Money: Collecting the Orientalist Pictures of John Frederick Lewis," *Fine Art Connoisseur* (4.1, 2007), 40–47.
Weeks, Emily M. "John Frederick Lewis (1805–1876): Mythology as Biography, or Disorienting the 'languid Lotus-eater.'" In *Travellers in the Levant: Voyages and Visionaries*, edited by Sarah Searight and Malcolm Wagstaff. ASTENE, 2001.
Wheelhouse, Claudius Galen and Badr El-Hage. *Narrative of a Yacht Voyage in the Mediterranean 1849–1850*. Folios Ltd. & National Museum of Photography, Film and Television, 2006.
Wilkie, Sir David. *Oriental Sketches* [Sketches in Turkey, Syria and Egypt, 1840 & 1841]. Graves and Warmly, 1843.
Wilkinson, John Gardner. *Hand-book for Travellers in Egypt*. John Murray, 1847.
Wilkinson, John Gardner. *The Manners and Customs of the Ancient Egyptians*. John Murray, 1837.
Williams, Caroline. *Islamic Monuments in Cairo: The Practical Guide*. Cairo: American University in Cairo Press, 2008.
Williams, Caroline. "John Frederick Lewis: Reflections of Reality." In *Muqarnas: An Annual on the Visual Culture of the Islamic World*, 18 (2001), 227–43.
Williams, Caroline. "Orientalist Images Inspired by Egypt: A Nineteenth-Century Overview." In *Masterpieces of Orientalist Art: The Shafik Gabr Collection*, edited by Ahmed Chaouki Rafif. ACR Édition, 2012 edition.
Wójcik, Agata. "Jean-Léon Gérôme and Stanisław Chlebowski: The Story of a Friendship," *RIHA Journal* 0014 (27 December 2010), www.riha-journal.org/articles/2010/wojcik-gerome-chlebowski-en.
Yeazell, Ruth Bernard. *Harems of the Mind*. New Haven, CT: Yale University Press, 2000.
Zemen, Herbert. *Leopold Carl Müller 1834–1892: ein Künstlerbildnis nach Briefen und Dokumenten*. Vienna, 2001.
Ziter, Edward. *The Orient on the Victorian Stage*. Cambridge: Cambridge University Press, 2007.
Zola, Émile. "Our artists on the Champs de Mars," *Écrits sur l'art*. Gallimard, 1867.

Sources of Illustrations

1. Walker Art Gallery, National Museums Liverpool/Bridgeman Images
2. The Shafik Gabr Collection
3. Pinacoteca Di Brera, Milan, De Agostini Picture Library/Bridgeman Images
4. Berlin, SMB, Nationalgalerie/AKG Images
5. The University of Birmingham Research and Cultural Collections
6. Suna and İnan Kıraç Foundation Orientalist Paintings Collection, Istanbul/© Uğur Ataç
7. The Trustees of the British Museum
8. Scottish National Gallery, Edinburgh
9. National Portrait Gallery, London
10. National Portrait Gallery, London
11. The British Library
12. University of St Andrews Library
13. Victoria and Albert Museum
14. Alinari Archives, Florence
15. Tate Images
16. Private collection/Photo © Agnew's, London/Bridgeman Images
17. Laing Art Gallery, Newcastle-upon-Tyne, UK/© Tyne & Wear Archives & Museums/Bridgeman Images
18. National Museum of Antiquities, Leiden
19. The Royal Library, National Library of Denmark and Copenhagen University Library
20. Bethlem Museum of the Mind
21. Photograph courtesy of Sotheby's
22. Dahesh Museum of Art, New York, USA/Bridgeman Images
23. The Shafik Gabr Collection
24. Victoria and Albert Museum
25. The Trustees of the British Museum
26. The Shafik Gabr Collection
27. The Huntington Library, San Marino, California
28. Private collection
29. © 1996 Christie's Images Ltd
30. Tate Images
31. The Shafik Gabr Collection
32. The Shafik Gabr Collection
33. The Shafik Gabr Collection
34. Pictures from History/Bridgeman Images
35. The Shafik Gabr Collection
36. The Shafik Gabr Collection
37. Manchester Art Gallery/Bridgeman Images
38. The Shafik Gabr Collection
39. Lyme Park © National Trust/Robert Thrift
40. The Royal Castle, Warsaw-Museum
41. Yale Center for British Art, Paul Mellon Collection, USA/Bridgeman Images
42. The Shafik Gabr Collection

43. Private collection/© Dreweatt Neate Fine Art Auctioneers/ Bridgeman Images
44. Reproduced from copy of *Tableaux de la vie arabe* by Étienne Dinet and Sliman Ben Ibrahim (1908).
45. Private collection, The Fine Art Society, London/ Bridgeman Images
46. The Shafik Gabr Collection
47. The Shafik Gabr Collection
48. Photograph courtesy of Sotheby's
49. The Shafik Gabr Collection
50. The Shafik Gabr Collection
51. Photograph courtesy of Sotheby's
52. Roy Miles Fine Paintings/Bridgeman Images
53. Private collection/© Christie's Images/Bridgeman Images
54. The Shafik Gabr Collection
55. Yapı Kredi Kültür Sanat Yayıncılık, Istanbul
56. Private collection
57. The Shafik Gabr Collection
58. The Shafik Gabr Collection
59. The Shafik Gabr Collection
60. © 2002 Christie's Images Limited
61. The Shafik Gabr Collection
62. The Shafik Gabr Collection
63. Musée Bartholdi, Colmar/reproduction by Christian Kempf
64. Kodak Collection/National Media Museum/Science & Society Picture Library
65. State Russian Museum, St Petersburg/Bridgeman Images
66. The Shafik Gabr Collection
67. Musée Bartholdi, Colmar/reproduction by Christian Kempf
68. The Haggin Museum, Stockton, California
69. Photograph courtesy of Sotheby's
70. Courtesy of Penn Museum, Philadelphia
71. © National Media Museum/Science & Society Picture Library
72. Photoinstitut Bonartes, Vienna
73. The Shafik Gabr Collection
74. The Shafik Gabr Collection
75. The Shafik Gabr Collection
76. Photograph courtesy of Sotheby's
77. The Shafik Gabr Collection
78. Najd Collection, Mathaf Gallery
79. Scottish National Portrait Gallery, Edinburgh
80. 80a and 80b. Private collection
81. Reproduced from *The Holy Land, Syria, Idumea, Arabia, Egypt and Nubia*, 6 vols, 1842–49, by David Roberts.
82. National Portrait Gallery, London
83. Reproduced from Seddon, *Memoir and Letters of the Late Thomas Seddon*, 39
84. Special Collections, Arizona State University
85. National Media Museum/Science & Society Picture Library
86. The Shafik Gabr Collection
87. Yale Center for British Art, Paul Mellon Collection, USA/ Bridgeman Images
88. The Shafik Gabr Collection
89. Private collection/Bridgeman Images
90. Tate Images
91. Walters Art Gallery, Baltimore
92. The Maas Gallery, London
93. National Portrait Gallery, London
94. From *The Art Journal*, 1883.
95. Birmingham Museums and Art Gallery/Bridgeman Images
96. Private collection/Photograph © Christie's Images/ Bridgeman Images
97. Victoria and Albert Museum
98. The Shafik Gabr Collection
99. Pictures from History/Bridgeman Images
100. The Shafik Gabr Collection
101. Photograph courtesy of Sotheby's
102. The Shafik Gabr Collection
103. Rosengart Collection Museum, Lucerne
104. The Shafik Gabr Collection
105. The Shafik Gabr Collection

Index

Page references to illustrations are in italics